Eighteenth-Century Poetry

and the

Rise of the Novel Reconsidered

T R A N S I T S :
LITERATURE, THOUGHT & CULTURE

Series Editor
Greg Clingham
Bucknell University

Transits is the next horizon. The series of books, essays, and monographs aims to extend recent achievements in eighteenth-century studies and to publish work on any aspects of the literature, thought, and culture of the years 1650–1850. Without ideological or methodological restrictions, *Transits* seeks to provide transformative readings of the literary, cultural, and historical interconnections between Britain, Europe, the Far East, Oceania, and the Americas in the long eighteenth century, and as they extend down to present time. In addition to literature and history, such "global" perspectives might entail considerations of time, space, nature, economics, politics, environment, and material culture, and might necessitate the development of new modes of critical imagination, which we welcome. But the series does not thereby repudiate the local and the national for original new work on particular writers and readers in particular places in time continues to be the bedrock of the discipline.

Titles in the Series

For a complete list of titles in this series, please visit http://www.bucknell
.edu/universitypress

TRANSITS

Eighteenth-Century Poetry and the Rise of the Novel Reconsidered

EDITED BY KATE PARKER
AND COURTNEY WEISS SMITH

LEWISBURG
BUCKNELL UNIVERSITY PRESS

Published by Bucknell University Press
Copublished with Rowman & Littlefield
4501 Forbes Boulevard, Suite 200, Lanham, Maryland 20706
www.rowman.com

10 Thornbury Road, Plymouth PL6 7PP, United Kingdom

British Library Cataloguing in Publication Information Available

Library of Congress Cataloging-in-Publication Data
Eighteenth-Century Poetry and the Rise of the Novel Reconsidered / edited by
Kate Parker and Courtney Weiss Smith.
    pages cm. — (Transits: Literature, Thought & Culture)
  Includes bibliographical references and index.
  ISBN 978-1-61148-483-0 (cloth : alk. paper) — ISBN 978-1-61148-484-7
(electronic) 1. English poetry—18th century—History and criticism. 2. English
fiction—18th century—History and criticism. 3. Poetics. 4. Literature and
society—England—History—18th century. I. Parker, Kate, 1980- editor of
compilation. II. Smith, Courtney Weiss, editor of compilation.
  PR551.E39 2014
  821'.509—dc23
  ISBN: 978-1-6114-8702-2 (pbk:alk, paper)   2013037417

CONTENTS

CONTENTS

T HE EDITORS WOULD LIKE TO THANK the countless colleagues and students whose varied insights have helped to foster our shared fascination with the relationships between eighteenth-century poetry and prose. Above all, we are grateful to our contributors, who graciously shared their ideas and their work with us, and whose voices have shaped and enriched this volume immeasurably. We feel extremely privileged to have worked with such a smart and generous group and hope they are as pleased with the final product as we are. Special mention must go to our mentor, Wolfram Schmidgen, who helped spark the interests motivating this volume and who continues to engage us in conversations that make our thinking sharper and richer. This book would also not exist without Greg Clingham's early, unflagging enthusiasm and support. We are indebted to the Press' anonymous reader for an illuminating and thorough commentary, and we deeply appreciate all of the staff at Bucknell University Press who helped to make this publication such a smooth and intellectually rewarding process. The volume also benefited from the intelligence and kindness of friends and colleagues at our respective institutions: first, at Washington University in St. Louis and more recently at Wesleyan University and the University of Wisconsin-La Crosse. Courtney wishes to thank her wonderful colleagues at Wesleyan for their insight and support, and Kate wants to thanks hers at UW-L, especially those who offered inspiration and good cheer during the English Department's William J. and Yvonne Hyde Colloquium Series.

Finally, we each would like to thank our families and friends for their love and support, and particularly for their patience during our endless Skype sessions. Nothing we do would be possible without you.

*E*IGHTEENTH-CENTURY POETRY *and the Rise of the Novel Reconsidered* begins from the brute fact that, in eighteenth-century England, poetry jostled up alongside novels in bookstalls and private closets, in the pages of critical monthlies and in the minds of readers. Many authors wrote both poetry and novels, and some texts in themselves challenged the stability of these categories, such as Henry Fielding's "comic Epic-Poem in Prose" and Ossian's prosaic poems. That these literary forms existed together, in constant contact and conversation, seems an obvious truth, but it is one that can be overlooked. We too often let generic divisions organize our teaching and guide our research. Indeed, this volume proceeds from a concern that our working assumptions in teaching and research—and the critical narratives about the eighteenth century that motivate these assumptions—can somewhat obfuscate the realities of eighteenth-century bookstalls and the habits of eighteenth-century readers.

In recent decades, the stories we tell about the period have been dominated by the novel. Graceful and influential work on the "rise of the novel" contends that the novel emblematizes (and even, in its moment, encouraged) the incipient forces of modernity it emerged alongside: consumer culture, new science, journalism, secularism, domesticity, the public sphere, and the liberal subject. This scholarship revitalized eighteenth-century studies and—illuminating links between literary form and cultural history—continues to shape its future in important ways. Yet, the novel's aptness to its quickly changing cultural moment both illuminates and overshadows: it can lead us to overlook the novel's relationships to other literary genres, as well as these genres' engagements with the cultural moment.

It can lead us to overlook, for instance, the stubborn truth that poetry remained the most influential literary genre in eighteenth-century England. While the novel was new and fledging—like one of its own heroines, on a journey from obscure beginnings towards respectability and stability—poetry's importance was never questioned. Sanctioned as it was by both the classical and the English canon, poetry was *the* form for high literature, but it also was popular in its lower and more ephemeral forms, as a vehicle for scandal, gossip, politics and news. The facts of the eighteenth-century English print market confirm poetry's centrality: John Brewer notes that poetry was "the most frequently published type of literature, accounting for 47 percent of all titles" and "far exceed[ing] any new literary forms of prose." Novels, by contrast, represented less than 11 percent—much, much less by some estimates.[1] The novelists themselves also confirm this: it seems Daniel Defoe spent more time perfecting what he hoped would be his masterpiece—the twelve-book epic poem *Jure Divino* (1706)—than he did on *Robinson Crusoe* (1721), *Moll Flanders* (1722), and *Roxana* (1724) combined, and, even by the end of the century that saw the novel's rise, Jane Austen could complain that "the man who collects and publishes in a volume some dozen lines of Milton, Pope, and Prior" with some miscellaneous moralizing prose got more respect than the best novelist.[2] These facts fit oddly into our narratives about the novel and about the period generally.

In her 1985 book *The Daring Muse*, Margaret Doody lamented the way that generic separations structure the study of eighteenth-century literature, and she issued an important call: "Our understanding of both" eighteenth-century "novels and poetry would be improved by studying both together."[3] Doody went beyond the traditional kinds of trans-generic couplings that are licensed by historical friendship or explicit mention in texts (Bluestocking poetry and prose, or Fielding in light of Homeric epic) to make unusual, telling connections: "Thomson and Cowper and Crabbe—and also Defoe and Richardson and Smollett and Sterne."[4] In fact, Doody's book worked to redress our field's novel-centrism by proposing a literary history that featured eighteenth-century poetry coming to terms with the cultural forces more usually associated with the novel.

Over twenty-five years after *The Daring Muse*, however, Doody's point about generic divisions in our field still rings profoundly true, and phenomena like Defoe's poetry and the novel's paltry percentage share of literature still seem hard to reconcile with the stories we tell about the period. *Eighteenth-Century Poetry and the Rise of the Novel Reconsidered* seeks to change this. Capitalizing on a recent resurgence in critical attention to poetry and on important new questions about the novel's rise, this volume's contributors grapple with unexpected collisions and collusions between poetry and novels.[5] They use these relationships to reconsider our most fundamental assumptions about both literary and cultural history.

The essays in part I situate eighteenth-century poetry alongside novels on those bookstalls, thereby exploring some central questions of literary history. These essays take their cue from John Gay's depictions of London bookstalls in *Trivia* (1716), where we are invited to imagine William Congreve's prose fiction or plays jammed in between mock-heroic poems, literary criticism, and volumes of Plutarch or Francis Bacon and where these varying "Volumes, on shelter'd stalls" actually "lure" people, like little bees, to gather up pollen from "learning's flow'rs."[6] Our contributors demonstrate that poetry, novels, plays, and even science all influenced one another; that older texts co-existed with and anticipated new literary experiments; and that "rising" could involve taking "spoil" from other genres, or (stretching Gay's metaphor toward that of his Scriblerian friend, Jonathan Swift, in a piece of fiction) using their pollen to produce different kinds of "Honey *and* Wax" or "Sweetness *and* Light."[7] The essays in part II, then, turn from literary to cultural history, placing both poetry and novels right in the midst of the world bustling and metamorphosing around those bookstalls. Troubling the influential association of the novel's rise with the emergence of the autonomous subject and the inert object, our contributors propose that eighteenth-century readers thought of those "Volumes" as objects that could shoot electricity along their veins or help guard *against* the worrying prospect of unfettered autonomy and interiority. In fact, the essays in this volume recover understandings of the world that echo the multiplicity and "copious" abundance of *Trivia*'s stalls and markets more generally (bursting with not only different kinds of books but also "veal," "cheeses," "fruits," "old suits," and "bills" boasting of physicians' skills).[8] Our contributors suggest that in eighteenth-century England both minds and things were "copious," collective and mixed, and that the boundaries between them were unstable—insights that raise questions about the very category of "the modern."

Mikhail Bakhtin once said "that the novel gets on poorly with other genres," "squeez[ing] out some genres and incorporat[ing] others into its own peculiar structure."[9] We might extend this to say that the history and criticism of the novel sometimes "gets on poorly" in a similar way with the history and criticism of eighteenth-century poetry. Novel narratives can "squeeze" poetry such that it can seem out of place, conservatively backwards-looking or presciently "pre-Romantic."[10] Other work seeks to "incorporate" poetry into our narratives about the novel, as Bakhtin says, "re-formulating and re-accenting."

Amid the boom of interest in "rise of the novel" narratives in the 1980s and 1990s, the best scholarship to consider the relationship between poetry and novels showed the possibilities and payoffs of this latter, "incorporating" or accommodating approach. For example, Anthony Low has narrated a parallel to the novel's rise, whereby similar cultural forces (the New Science, changes in the economic system, and a brand of Protestantism that values the individual's labor) reach their climax not with the novel but with georgic poetry.[11] Brean Hammond also shows how modernizing forces shaped poetry—in his case, the poetry of a late seventeenth-century "mock-heroic moment," including English translations of Nicolas Boileau, Samuel Garth's *The Dispensary* (1699) and John Dryden's ambitious Virgil project. Hammond continues to suggest that these texts were part of a thorough-going cultural tendency towards "novelization" that actually influenced the emerging prose form.[12] Even further underscoring the similar trajectories of the two forms, Blanford Parker's *The Triumph of Augustan Poetics* (1998) registers its debt to Ian Watt's canonical *Rise of the Novel* in its very title, and Parker's argument for the invention of "a novel literalism" in eighteenth-century poetry intriguingly echoes Watt's, for the emergence of "formal realism": "The natural world and the world of incidental appearances, stripped for the first time of their iconic burden, burst forth and flooded the scene of eighteenth-century writing."[13] These works suggest that poetry paralleled the novel's rise: it evinced a "novel" interest in particularity and contemporaneity, the literal and the real.

Other work in the 1980s and 1990s accommodates poetry to the novel rather differently, finding in eighteenth-century poetry a parallel to the new understanding of the individual that underpins the novel's rise. Scholars trace in the period's poetry the emergence of a disembedded expressive subject—what Watt and his heirs trace under the sign of "individualism" or "private experience."[14] For instance, John Sitter argues that mid-century poets and novelists develop different techniques to address intensifying concern about the solitary individual. Sitter suggests that, where novelists firmly situate the individual's private experience in the context of social relationships and circumstances, poets like Mark Akenside, Edward Young, and Thomas Gray dramatize an intense solitude: not only do their personas speak from lonely haunts, but the poems take seriously the possibility of "inescapable egocentricity" and aim "to enact a radical break from the temporal, mundane order."[15] More recently, G. Gabrielle Starr's 2004 *Lyric Generations* has extended this insight about private experience and genre. She argues that the novel, "the most extensive ground for the literary exploration of individual experience in the century," helped shape the Romantic lyric into "a mode deeply implicated by subjective relations." Domestic novels and Romantic lyrics share not only a new understanding of subjectivity but also particular "fictions of consciousness" and "representational practices" that helped "focus readers' movements" from their own world into the texts'.[16] If novels helped forge a new kind of individual, poetry participated in or partook of the invention.

These accounts enrich our understanding of the literary and cultural landscape of eighteenth-century England, but there is yet more to be said on the relationship between poetry and novels. Starr thought so, and her book ends by advocating for yet more work that mixes genres and "historiciz[es] forms."[17] Starr's point is even more timely today, for in the years since *Lyric Generations* the "rise of the novel" trajectory to which scholars accommodate their readings of poetry has been questioned in pressing new ways. Of course, this critical teleology was never uncontested; we have long asked about the persistence of romance and the importance of women writers, for example. More recent revisionary work, however, has begun to trouble the critical narrative's most fundamental logics and cultural-historical commonplaces. For example, Julie Park has proposed a reorientation from "the rise of the novel" to the "drift of fiction," and Clifford Siskin has suggested that we pay attention to the more fundamental categories of "writing" (his "shorthand for" an influential "configuration of writing, print, and silent reading") and "Literature," almost tamed by the end of the eighteenth century into modern configurations.[18] Park explains that such reorientations "seek[ ] to loosen and uncover fiction from the confines of a dominating term that has tended overly to determine the direction of its critique."[19] (It seems that even the novel itself has been "squeezed" or "re-accented" by the stories we tell about it).

A related reorientation or "loosening" has scholars rethinking the cultural-historical assumptions about eighteenth-century people and things that figure so importantly in "rise of the novel" narratives. Adela Pinch, Deidre Lynch, Dror Wahrman, Nancy Yousef, Helen Thompson, Sandra Macpherson and others have reimagined the eighteenth-century self by deflating its pretensions to autonomy, subsuming it in collectives, questioning its self-enclosedness, and making its boundaries more permeable.[20] And scholars like Wolfram Schmidgen, Cynthia Wall, Lynn Festa, Mark Blackwell, Joanna Picciotto, and Jonathan Lamb have demonstrated that eighteenth-century things could be active, meaningful, stubborn and strange—even somehow alive.[21] These critics help us see that the expressive subject and the inert literal particular traced by Starr and Parker are only part of the cultural realities that shaped the period's literature.

It is no accident, we would suggest, that some of the most exciting revisionary work on the "rise" narrative manages such insight by reading novels alongside poetry.

For example, Jonathan Kramnick's 2010 book, *Actions and Objects from Hobbes to Richardson,* raises questions about what he calls "the novel + empiricism = interiority or 'modern subject' thesis" by reading Eliza Haywood and Samuel Richardson in the same literary genealogy as John Wilmot, Earl of Rochester and seventeenth-century translators of Lucretius.[22] Sophie Gee's 2010 *Making Waste* explores our period's material culture and its relationship to enlightenment by weaving between such disparate texts as *Paradise Lost* (1667), *Journal of a Plague Year* (1722), *The Dunciad* (1729) and *Tom Jones* (1749).[23] No accident, we say, not to suggest that the insights of these books are somehow familiar; Kramnick and Gee provide glitteringly original, nuanced readings and ask questions that are resonating far beyond revisionary work on the novel. Rather, these critics—like Doody in the *Daring Muse*—bring together different texts and genres in ways that trouble our usual assumptions about the histories and cultural implications of specific forms.

Our volume embraces such decentering. In fact, it proposes—and seeks to demonstrate—that reading across forms and genres helpfully disrupts the hold of the assumptions, logics, and cultural-historical commonplaces that have attached so powerfully to forms like the novel and the lyric.[24] We thus bring together a broad range of texts, including satires, epistles, lyrics, theodicies, adventure fictions, sentimental novels, it-narratives, and even plays, rhetorical treatises, scientific reports, and devotional books. And we consider the relationships between these forms *in, through,* and *against* narratives of "rise" or modernization forged around the novel, rather than simply alongside them.

In keeping with the aim of encouraging new juxtapositions and examining entrenched assumptions, this volume is also methodologically diverse. Much work on the relationship between poetry and the novel is essentially formalist, and, certainly, essays in this collection draw energy from the resurgent recent interest in forms and formalisms.[25] Our contributors, however, supplement close readings with other timely methods and theoretical trends: actor-network theory (Christina Lupton and Aran Ruth), the history of books and reading (Joshua Swidzinski), the history of science (Wolfram Schmidgen and David Fairer), and contemporary neuroscience (Natalie Phillips). Putting very different kinds of poetry and novels in significant conversation with one another and approaching these combinations in innovative ways, our contributors let the texts themselves take the lead—telling us how they relate to one another, what kind of individuals they feature, and how they engage the material world.

Eighteenth-Century Poetry and the Rise of the Novel Reconsidered brings this open-ended, searching spirit to our most basic assumptions about poetry, novels, people, and things in the period. Foregrounding questions of literary history, part I, "Reconsidering Genres: Rising, Borrowing, Circulating" asks: how did novels "squeeze" or push poetry, and in what ways did poetry's own progresses impact fiction's "drift"? The answers, here, are many, as contributors trace lines of influence running both directions and investigate inclusions, parallels and divergences. Pope's *Rape of the Lock* (1714) is a touchstone in the first pair of essays. Sophie Gee situates Pope's Belinda in a history of character spanning from Milton's Eve to Austen's Anne Elliot. In Gee's reading, Pope experiments with characters that work like Anne Elliot's but his engagement with this emerging model of character and selfhood is richly ambivalent. Even as his mock-heroic tempts us to laugh at Belinda's superficiality, it gives us suggestive glimpses of her inner life; and, though (like the reader) Belinda is unable truly to access these depths, she is punished for them. While Austen might have learned from Pope's possibilities, Kate Parker's essay explores a more contested novelistic appropriation of Belinda. Parker argues that Eliza Haywood's *The History of Miss Betsy Thoughtless* (1751) simultaneously enacts and critiques the mock-heroic "battle without killing." In reworking Belinda's "rape" as incessantly repeated violent assaults on Betsy, Haywood highlights the trope's problematic way of trivializing women and inviting laughter at the possibility of sexual violence. Parker further suggests that Haywood's self-conscious crafting of her authorial identity involves a related "instantiation and critique" of Pope's *Dunciad* depiction of her (a depiction that casts her as a sort of Belinda or Betsy).[26] The next pair of essays charts the novel's shifting relationships with different kinds of poetry still, and especially with the roles poetry could play in everyday life. Christina Lupton and Aran Ruth propose that mid-century novels, including *Polly Honeycombe* (1760) and *The Man of Feeling* (1771), had "poem envy." This envy is not related (as we might expect) to poetry's prestige or technical virtuosity but is instead motivated by its most mobile and material forms: poems spoken by pieces of paper, scratched into windows, or found under foodstuffs. Lupton and Ruth show that this poetry, with its distinctive way of retaining material traces of its writing and circulation, got significant social agency, and that these traits continued to exert influence on both sentimental novels and Romantic poetry even as they were challenged by "transcendent" notions of literature emerging towards the century's end. Shelley King then focuses on such transcendence itself—on lyric's seductive (if impossible) promises of spontaneity, immediacy, and immateriality. King argues that, in the tales of Amelia Opie, lyric utterance does not exist in tension with domestic fiction but is, instead, "integral" to the project of psychological realism, playing a crucial role in the development of novelistic character, plot and theme. King further contends that poetry's inclusion in novels as a powerful affective medium actually modeled certain real-life emotional practices for readers. Throughout this section, poetry precedes novels or mocks them; it prefigures the novel's techniques, poses problems for it to deal with, and suggests possibilities for the authorial identities of novelists. Novels envy or condemn poetry. They dissolve into poetry while insisting that they are still novels; they subsume poetry into their larger structures in an attempt to belittle or control poetry, or they turn to poetry for access to things that prose cannot offer.

Part II, "Reconsidering Subjects and Objects," in turn, takes on the most basic cultural-historical categories of the "rise of the novel" tradition and its recent revisions. The first two essays challenge Ian Watt's influential arguments about subjects and objects by attending to the profound instability of the boundaries between the two. Wolfram Schmidgen provocatively critiques the degree to which our literary and cultural histories privilege myths about "the modern": they are structured around important differentiations (subject/object, inside/outside, individual/society) and stress modern values like "identity, continuity, interiority, development, and boundedness."[27] Schmidgen counters these emphases by demonstrating their inadequacy to the work of even Whiggish, progressive figures in the moment. James Thomson's poetry, Daniel Defoe's novels, and early eighteenth-century theories of the sublime feature an aesthetic of "variety" that serves to muddy distinction and dramatize an incoherence in the human subject. Similarly objecting to strict differentiation between subject and object, Heather Keenleyside investigates how eighteenth-century personifications work. Indeed, reading eighteenth-century theories of personification by Lord Kames and Hugh Blair alongside examples of their logic—an apostrophe to an arm in *All for Love* (1678), *Pamela*'s conversations with her "lumpish" heart, John Locke's analogy between a human being and "a Tennisball"—Keenleyside shows that personifications illuminate how eighteenth-century *personhood* works. They highlight something fundamental to human experience in the period: "the feeling of being an object among others, of acting and being acted upon in turn."[28] In the next essay, David Fairer focuses on the in-between itself, on the spaces and gaps that mediate between things and minds and amongst bodies in a room. Fairer recovers a tradition of "empirical erotics" in the work of experimenters like Francis Hauksbee, poets like Aaron Hill, and novelists like Laurence Sterne. This tradition celebrates how language can concretize—and contribute to—electric atmospheres that invite emotions to circulate around and through souls, veins, objects, abstractions, and spirits. In fact, Fairer demonstrates that Sterne's fictions collapse divides between both body/mind *and* text/reader: we, too, are invited to feel the electricity. The final two essays pick up on this suggestion, extending part II's concerns about persons and things out towards fundamental questions of reading and thinking. Joshua Swidzinski argues for an important similarity in the formal techniques of Edward Young's *Night Thoughts* (1742-6) and Samuel Richardson's *Clarissa* (1747). In both cases, complex formal structures and difficulty in the reading experience encourage a mode of attention that has real ethical stakes as well as a model of individuality that stays in touch with collectives. Shifting registers in homiletic blank verse and contradictory narrative viewpoints in epistolary fiction both "enable an orthodox mode of self-reflection designed to temper solipsism."[29] Natalie Phillips grapples with related issues of attention, difficulty, and form, though for her poetry's capacious embrace of multiple foci existing in rhythmic tension with one another actually runs counter to novelistic absorption. Exploring the models of focus assumed in eighteenth-century couplets and in contemporary experimental neuroscience, she proposes that eighteenth-century poetry engaged an older rhetorical tradition to require a mode of attention that seems, somewhat counter-intuitively, *more* relevant to our current moment than ones associated with the novel and Enlightenment. Our volume thereby entertains multiple models for the eighteenth-century self: people are marked by heightened, almost solipsistic states of consciousness, or their ethical well-being requires facing obstacles to interiority that help fend off such solipsism. They slip smoothly between alternate and sometimes incompatible identities, or they are bundles of inconsistent parts in motion. They are porous, excitable, and omnivorous in their ability to take energy from everything, and they are—like us—distractable, necessarily divided in their attentions.

In the coda, Margaret Doody reflects on future work that might be done on this volume's questions: she points out, for example, that several contributors underscore "the omnipresence of forms of poetry in eighteenth-century life" and that we should revisit canonical works with an awareness of this stubborn fact of lived experience, as well.[30] Her own contribution situates the concerns of this volume in a historical sweep that includes ancient Greek novels and Horatian poetry, and she offers compelling ruminations on the ways that different literary forms help us think about time, space, objects, and ourselves.

In sum, *Eighteenth-Century Poetry and the Rise of the Novel Reconsidered* takes seriously some of the simple realities of eighteenth-century bookstalls: poetry and novels co-existed and commingled, and the poetry predominated. The readers lingering at these stalls and taking these books home were not constrained by our retrospective understandings of the genres or our retrospective assumptions about people and things. We offer, in a spirit of genuine discovery, meditations on why this matters for our understanding of the period and its literature.

Notes

1. John Brewer, *The Pleasures of the Imagination: English Culture in the Eighteenth Century* (New York: Farrar Straus Giroux, 1997), 172. Brewer draws on John Feather, "British Publishing in the Eighteenth Century: A Preliminary Subject Analysis" *The Library*, 6th series, 8 (1986): 41, which notes that the broad category of "Fiction" accounts for 11 percent. See also James Raven: "The proportion of all fiction (new titles and reprints) to total book and pamphlet production" is "1.0% for 1700–09, 1.1% for 1720–29, 2.2% for 1730–39," "4.0% for 1740–49" and "about 4%" for "the 1750s and 1760s." James Raven, *British Fiction 1750–1770: A Chronological Check-List of Prose Fiction Printed in Britain and Ireland* (Newark: University of Delaware Press, 1987), 10. Related statistics about provincial print markets in particular prompted Jan Fergus to remark, "at least," that "the often-proclaimed 'rise' of the novel looks unimpressive between 1740–1780." In Jan Fergus, *Provincial Readers in Eighteenth-Century England* (Oxford: Oxford University Press, 2007), 6.

2. Jane Austen, *Northanger Abbey*, ed. Marilyn Butler (London: Penguin, 2003), 36. Paula Backscheider notes Defoe worked on *Jure Divino* for longer than anything else he wrote in his career, including "his 1200-page *Tour thro' the Whole Island of Great Britain*. Even his longest works were usually written in less than a year; on *Jure Divino*, he spent five." In Paula Backscheider, "The Verse Essay, John Locke, and Defoe's *Jure Divino*" *English Literary History* 55, no. 1 (1988): 99. If—given how difficult it is to come by the exact dates for the composition of Defoe's texts—these estimates might be called into question, we can say with certainty that "Defoe's career as a poet was longer and more prolific than his career as a novelist"; that he "wrote more than a dozen long poems totaling some 20,000 lines, and for much of his lifetime was far better known as a poet than a novelist"; and that even in the later eighteenth century he was more "'famous for politics and poetry'" than novels—see, respectively, Paula Backscheider, *Daniel Defoe: His Life* (Baltimore: The Johns Hopkins University Press, 1989), 54; J. Paul Hunter, "Defoe and the Poetic Tradition," in *Cambridge Companion to Daniel Defoe*, ed. John Richetti (Cambridge: Cambridge University Press, 2009), 216; and *The Preceptor* (1776), 353, quoted and discussed in Ashley Marshall, "Fabricating Defoes: From Anonymous Hack to Master of Fictions," *Eighteenth-Century Life* 36, no. 2 (2012): 4.

3. Margaret Doody, *The Daring Muse: Augustan Poetry Reconsidered* (Cambridge: Cambridge University Press, 1985), 199.

4. Ibid., 199.

5. The best recent work on poetry includes Suvir Kaul, *Poems of Nation, Anthems of Empire: English Verse in the Long Eighteenth Century* (Charlottesville: University Press of Virginia, 2000); Kevis Goodman, *Georgic Modernity and British Romanticism: Poetry and the Mediation of History* (Cambridge: Cambridge University Press, 2004); Paula Backscheider, *Eighteenth-Century Women Poets and Their Poetry: Inventing Agency, Inventing Genre* (Baltimore: The Johns Hopkins University Press, 2005); Sandro Jung, *The Fragmentary Poetic: Eighteenth Century Uses of an Experimental Mode* (Bethlehem, PA: Lehigh University Press, 2009); David Fairer, *English Poetry of the Eighteenth Century, 1700–1789* (London: Longman, 2003) and *Organising Poetry: The Coleridge Circle, 1790–1798* (Oxford: Oxford University Press, 2009); Patricia Meyer Spacks, *Reading Eighteenth-Century Poetry* (Maldan, MA: Wiley-Blackwell, 2009); and John Sitter, *The Cambridge Introduction to Eighteenth-Century Poetry* (Cambridge: Cambridge University Press, 2011). See below for more on recent revisionary work on the novel's rise.

6. John Gay, *Trivia: Or, the Art of Walking the Streets of London,* in *John Gay: Poetry and Prose,* ed. Vinton A. Dearing and Charles E. Beckwith, vol. 1 (Oxford: Clarendon Press, 1974), book 2, lines 551–2, 557.

7. Ibid., 2.557 and Jonathan Swift, *Battel of the Books,* in *A Tale of a Tub,* ed. A.C. Guthkelch and D. Nichol Smith, 2nd ed. (Oxford: Clarendon Press, 1958), 234–5.

8. Gay, *Trivia,* 2.544, 546–8, 540.

9. Mikhail Bakhtin, "Epic and Novel: Toward a Methodology for the Study of the Novel," in *The Dialogic Imagination: Four Essays,* ed. Michael Holquist and trans. Caryl Emerson and Michael Holquist (Austin: The University of Texas Press, 1981), 5.

10. "Rise of the novel" narratives sometimes foster such temporal displacement by figuring epic poetry as the backwards-looking foil to the novel or by featuring poets primarily as important voices of resistance to the cultural forces cohering into the novel—see, for example, Georg Lukacs, *The Theory of the Novel,* trans. Anna Bostock (Cambridge: Massachusetts Institute of Technology Press, 1971) and J. Paul Hunter, *Before Novels: The Cultural Contexts of Eighteenth-Century English Fiction* (New York: Norton, 1990). A complement to this approach is work that finds in both eighteenth-century poetry and novels important sources of Romanticism—for a thoughtful consideration, see Marshall Brown, *Preromanticism* (Stanford: Stanford University Press, 1991).

11. Anthony Low, *The Georgic Revolution* (Princeton: Princeton University Press, 1985).

12. Brean Hammond, *Professional Imaginative Writing in England, 1670–1740: 'Hackney for Bread'* (Oxford: Clarendon Press 1997), 107. Hammond here draws interestingly on Bakhtin's work.

13. Blanford Parker, *The Triumph of Augustan Poetics: English Literary Culture from Butler to Johnson* (Cambridge: Cambridge University Press, 1998), 3, 18.

14. Ian Watt, *The Rise of the Novel: Studies in Defoe, Richardson and Fielding* [1957], 2nd ed (Berkeley: University of Los Angeles Press, 2001).

15. John Sitter, *Literary Loneliness in Mid-Eighteenth-Century England* (Ithaca: Cornell University Press, 1982), 111, 174, 218.

16. G. Gabrielle Starr, *Lyric Generations: Poetry and the Novel in the Long Eighteenth-Century* (Baltimore: The Johns Hopkins University Press, 2004), 7, 14, 198. For another take on the relationship between Romantic lyric and novels—focused especially on the kind of transcendent or visionary experience that centers on and "expands the self"—see Jay Clayton, *Romantic Vision and the Novel* (Cambridge: Cambridge University Press, 1987), 7.

17. Starr, *Lyric Generations,* 199.

18. Julie Park, "Introduction: The Drift of Fiction," *The Eighteenth Century: Theory and Interpretation* 52, nos. 3–4 (2011): 243–8, and Clifford Siskin, *The Work of Writing: Literature and Social Change in Britain, 1700–1830* (Baltimore: The Johns Hopkins University Press, 1998), 2.

19. Park, "Introduction," 247.

20. Adela Pinch, *Strange Fits of Passion: Epistemologies of Emotion, Hume to Austen* (Stanford: Stanford University Press, 1996); Deidre Shauna Lynch, *The Economy of Character: Novels, Market Culture, and the Business of Inner Meaning* (Chicago: University of Chicago Press, 1998); Dror Wahrman, *Making of the Modern Self: Identity and Culture in Eighteenth-Century England* (New Haven: Yale

University Press, 2004); Nancy Yousef, *Isolated Cases: The Anxieties of Autonomy in Enlightenment Philosophy and Romantic Literature* (Ithaca: Cornell University Press, 2004); Helen Thompson, *Ingenuous Subjection: Compliance and Power in the Eighteenth-Century Domestic Novel* (Philadelphia: University of Pennsylvania Press, 2005); Sandra Macpherson, *Harm's Way: Tragic Responsibility and the Novel Form* (Baltimore: The Johns Hopkins University Press, 2010); Julie Park, *The Self and It: Novel Objects in Eighteenth-Century England* (Stanford: Stanford University Press, 2010).

21. Wolfram Schmidgen, *Eighteenth-Century Fiction and the Law of Property* (Cambridge: Cambridge University Press, 2002); Cynthia Sundberg Wall, *The Prose of Things: Transformations of Description in the Eighteenth Century* (Chicago: University of Chicago Press, 2006); Lynn Festa, *Sentimental Figures of Empire* (Baltimore: The Johns Hopkins University Press, 2006); Mark Blackwell, ed. *The Secret Life of Things: Animals, Objects, and It-Narratives in Eighteenth-Century England* (Lewisburg: Bucknell University Press, 2007); Joanna Picciotto, *Labours of Innocence in Early Modern England* (Cambridge: Harvard University Press, 2010); and Jonathan Lamb, *The Things Things Say* (Princeton: Princeton University Press, 2011).

22. Jonathan Kramnick, *Actions and Objects from Hobbes to Richardson* (Stanford: Stanford University Press, 2010), 233.

23. Sophie Gee, *Making Waste: Leftovers and the Eighteenth-Century Imagination* (Princeton: Princeton University Press, 2010).

24. A complement to Park's work on the novel, focused on the lyric as dominating genre, can be found in Ann Wierda Rowland, "Romantic Poetry and the Romantic Novel" *Cambridge Companion to British Romantic Poetry* (Cambridge: Cambridge University Press, 2009): 117–35. Mary Favret, in "Telling Tales about Genre: Poetry in the Romantic Novel," *Studies in the Novel* 26, no. 3 (1994): 281–300, provides an eighteenth-century model for our method. She demonstrates that later eighteenth-century writers themselves found it helpful to mix poetry and novels as they attempted to influence the stories their contemporaries were telling about these different genres.

25. On the "new formalism," see, for example, Susan Wolfson's edited special issue of *Modern Language Quarterly* 61, no. 1 (2000) and Marjorie Levinson, "What Is New Formalism?" *PMLA* 122, no. 2 (2007): 558–69. The continued excitement around these questions is attested to by the popularity and multiplicity of panels on such questions at the 2012 and 2013 ASECS meetings.

26. Parker in this volume, 37.

27. Schmidgen in this volume, 96.

28. Keenleyside in this volume, 112.

29. Swidzinski in this volume, 164.

30. Doody in this volume, 207.

Part I

HEROIC COUPLETS AND
EIGHTEENTH-CENTURY HEROISM:
POPE'S COMPLICATED CHARACTERS

Sophie Gee

OPE STOLE BELINDA, THE HEROINE of *The Rape of the Lock* (1714), from Eve in *Paradise Lost* (1674), but in his haste to get away from the scene of the crime, left all Milton's good bits behind. Where we cared deeply for Eve and sympathized intensely with each stage in her tragedy, we find ourselves barely caring at all for—or about—Belinda. She's modern, she's superficial, she's socially ambitious, she's unreflecting: a parody, travesty, even, of Milton's heroine. Where Eve was all depth, Belinda is all surface. Belinda's a glassy, glittering imitation of the rich original, manifestly a forgery. But Pope is a good writer; some would say he's as good as Milton. So what is he up to in creating a heroine who fails to appeal? One thing he's doing is making Eve new, an eighteenth-century character. Belinda belongs to a world that's primarily communal, commercial and social, not private and inward-looking. Her selfhood is visible on the surface, it doesn't go much deeper. It's constituted by her world rather than being innate and individuated.

Belinda belongs, in short, to the reality in which the earliest experiments in novelistic realism take place: the world of Moll Flanders or Lemuel Gulliver. Pope steals from a poet to write like a novelist. But he never quite leaves Milton's Eve behind; he never entirely throws off that often-sad, thoughtful, always-wistful woman whom we remember from *Paradise Lost*. He never forsakes his privileges as a poet to work the gaudier effects of his prose-writing contemporaries. Instead what he leaves us with is a hybrid of the most fascinating kind. A poem that's part-novel, a typological heroine with glimmerings of a deep interior life, a realistic setting that never settles into the stable idioms of realist fiction. We see a writer performing experiments in genre and technique that will play out across the eighteenth century—across the entire evolution of the modern novel.

In her landmark monograph *The Economy of Character*, Deidre Lynch remarks that Captain Wentworth's censure of Anne Elliot's inconstancy is like Pope's opening sally in "Epistle to a Lady: of the Characters of Women" (1735). Both speakers imagine characters as marks imprinted in the surface of a person's face and affect.[1] Captain Wentworth declares, "It is the worst evil of too yielding and indecisive a character, that no influence over it can be depended upon.—You are never sure of a good impression being durable." In the same spirit, Pope's speaker begins:

> Nothing so true as what you once let fall,
> "Most Women have no Characters at all."
> Matter too soft a lasting mark to bear,
> And best distinguish'd by black, brown or fair.[2]

The problem, as Lynch says, is that Captain Wentworth and Alexander Pope shouldn't think alike. Wentworth deploys a metaphor that belongs to the beginning of the eighteenth century, not the end (thus revealing that he has yet much to learn about Anne Elliot). He uses "character" in the sense of a typographical mark that "exceeds its meaning" by being "fleshed out": a person in the place of a letter.[3] That is, Wentworth wishes Anne's character was both permanent and immediately legible. But this isn't how characters worked by the time *Persuasion* was published. Instant legibility was no longer enough to constitute selfhood. As Dror Wahrman has charismatically shown us, a radical shift took place some time in the later part of the eighteenth century and "identity became personal, interiorized, essential, even innate. It was made synonymous with self."[4] Before that, identities were "fluid and mutable," belonging to surfaces, not depths. Characters whose selves exist in their interior lives, not their outward manner, belong to what Warhman calls "the modern regime of selfhood," a regime that begins around about the time of the French Revolution or the British Romantic movement (in Lynch's version of the same story). Almost invariably, such characters exist in novels, not poems. In Nancy Armstrong's provocative phrasing, "The history of the subject and the history of the modern novel are, quite literally, one and the same."[5]

Pope, unlike Austen, is writing under the *"ancien regime* of identity," in which characters were still external, not innate. If we accept Wahrman's argument, the expression "know thy self" in Pope's day meant "knowing the generic type to which you belong and abstracting yourself, as it were, into a collective category: its imperative was outward, not inward."[6] So Pope is faithful to his aesthetic and cultural moment in assuming that characters are composed of what we would call *characteristics*, that people's identities can be known from their faces and their affects, that idiosyncratic hidden emotions weren't something one paid attention to and that selfhood was mutable. Plus, he's writing poetry, which had been, in sixteenth- and seventeenth-century lyric, the genre for "constructing shared emotional experience between characters and from character to reader," but in the early eighteenth century increasingly avoided representing "individual experience in isolation."[7] In summary, it wasn't Pope's job to write about people's deep emotional lives and hidden selves.

If we look carefully, however, we actually see a tension in Pope's writing between the idea that identity is mutable and superficial and an acknowledgment that selfhood is innate and private. There's ambiguity as to whether we should read character as his fellow Augustans were doing, or as his Romantic heirs would do. And my own argument is that the unresolved tension between interior and exterior, between surface and depth isn't a carelessness on Pope's part, or some sort of literary coincidence. It's an account of selfhood that we've always assumed depended for its development on the narrative resources of prose fiction.

In "Epistle to a Lady" Pope is speaking to his old friend Martha Blount, who, we're told, has spoken disparagingly of the female character by saying that "most women have no characters at all" (presumably Martha didn't literally say *that*). By starting the poem with her purported remark, Pope immediately tells the reader he's construing character in the early eighteenth-century sense, as identity marked on people's exteriors, not as innate, internal selfhood. In his own note to the line, Pope makes this explicit by clarifying: "[women's] particular Characters are not so strongly mark'd as those of Men, seldom so fixed, and still more inconsistent with themselves." He accepts, in other words, rules for describing character that Deidre Lynch identifies as typographical in nature:

> Eighteenth-century culture . . . made *person* both a word for someone's physical appearance and a word for someone. It made *trait* signify a minimum unit of the stuff of personality, one of the identifying marks that set persons apart, and it made *trait* cognate with words such as stroke or line—words for the graphic elements from which both pictorial and written representations are composed and through which they are identified. It is punning like this that dictates that reviewers in the eighteenth century will talk about how characters are "drawn," "coloured," "marked with traits," and made diverting through "strokes of fancy, gaiety, or humour."[8]

We soon learn why Pope is interested in characters as "fleshed out" typographical markings. The image gives him his first joke, the line "matter too soft a lasting mark to bear." Women are like wax tablets or some other unsuitable surface—nothing like the sturdy paper of Pope's real-life print market—unable to "bear" the permanent mark of identity. The joke, obviously, is that Pope has literalized the expression "softer sex." Not just figuratively gentle, he makes women literally viscous, their outsides inconstant and melty. The problem with this, for an ambitious commercial poet looking for subjects, is that women are unreliable, both as people and as surfaces on which representations might be made.

At the end of "Epistle to a Lady," however, Pope does an about-face and re-imagines character as innate and internal. The poem closes with a panegyric to Martha Blount, whom he describes as a "contradiction," but a pleasing, not an infuriating one. Whereas other women have changeable, inconstant identities—"All how unlike each other, all how true!"⁹—Martha's many parts together make up a varied and delightful self. So, Pope tells us that she "blends" many characteristics at once:

> Your love of Pleasure, our desire of Rest,
> Blends, in exception to all gen'ral rules,
> Your Taste of Follies, with our Scorn of Fools,
> Reserve with Frankness, Art with Truth ally'd,
> Courage with Softness, Modesty with Pride,
> Fix'd Principles, with Fancy ever new;
> Shakes all together, and produces—You.¹⁰

(Pope wants his women like James Bond wants his cocktail: shaken, not stirred.) The difference between Martha and the other ladies in the poem, it turns out, is that Martha's self lies inside her, not on her surface. We learn this in the last lines of the poem, at once touching and arch. Read carefully, they reveal a transformation in Pope's understanding of character:

> The gen'rous God, who Wit and Gold refines,
> And ripens Spirits as he ripens Mines,
> Kept Dross for Duchesses, the world shall know it,
> To you gave Sense, Good-humour, and a Poet.¹¹

To paraphrase: Martha's character is like a goldmine, ripened by Phoebus the sun-God. Since Phoebus is also the God of poetry, Pope's devoted friendship is part of the total package Miss Blount receives. Pope really shows his chops here. By using the image of gold, he takes us back to the metaphor of his opening—soft matter, capable of being engraved—but because it's nice Martha, it's precious metal, not ordinary wax. The "gold" from which Martha's selfhood is cast isn't mere sheet metal adorning the surface of an eighteenth-century beauty, it's gold in an actual goldmine. Martha's character is private and hidden, ripened internally. In other words, Pope has turned away from surfaces and toward interiors to represent his friend. As Pope thinks more deeply about character, and what constitutes a self, we learn that he becomes less interested in the image of legible, exterior markings and more attuned to the possibilities of private, unseen depths. We learn that Pope turns to the model of character that we've assumed that it requred the institution of the novel to develop.

Critics disagree about when characters start being defined by their inner lives. The best we can say is that it happened some time between when Locke wrote the *Essay Concerning Human Understanding* (1689) and Wordsworth wrote *The Prelude* (after 1798). Pretty much everyone accepts that by the time Jane Austen was working, novelists had acquired the power to look into their characters' hidden selves, and to represent people endowed with what Sandra Macpherson calls "interiority, affect and assent."[12] For Ian Watt, characters being defined by private, personal interiority began with Locke and evolved over the course of the century in novels from Defoe to Austen. It happened in novels because novels are the genre in which exteriors and interiors are simultaneously, equally, portrayed: "The delineation of the domestic life and the private experience of the characters who belong to it: the two go together—we get inside their minds as well as inside their houses."[13] Nancy Armstrong takes the view that novelists "sought to formulate a kind of subject that had not yet existed in writing," one who "acquired social experience and converted those encounters with the world at large into self restraint and good manners."[14] The key to novelistic subjects, for Armstrong, is that "feelings well up from within the subject in response to sensations and acquire the form of ideas."[15] It's because novelistic characters have interior lives that they can process social experience.

Interiority had previously been the province of poetry, especially sixteenth- and seventeenth-century lyric. To some extent this remained the case in the eighteenth century. But early eighteenth-century poems are often narrative-based and satirical, and, like novels of the same period, tend to eschew interiority in the interests of representing speakers in social worlds. In *Lyric Generations*, Gabrielle Starr argues that novels get more like poems and poems get more like novels. Or, in her elegant phrasing: "novels exhibit two concurrent movements: one in which lyric conventions were reorganized and adapted in concord with emerging theories of aesthetics, another in which private experience and the inner world were given new shape and a new set of literary markers."[16] In Starr's view, this is because poets after the Glorious Revolution needed to produce a fiction of community to counter "'the haunting fear that one's own consciousness is all there is' . . ."[17]

The crucial thing about the way novels represented interiority, which made them different from poems, is that insides were always being threatened by out-sides. And this is the threat that I'm arguing Pope notices and exploits. To put it very simply: novels have settings and things in them as well as characters, and characters have affects as well as consciousnesses. Novelists are interested in the expressive possibilities of material, visible things, places, objects, affects, as well as their characters' hidden selves. When Defoe publishes *Robinson Crusoe* (1719) this balance is strongly weighted toward the material, the visible, the external. When Austen's *Persuasion* is published (1818), the balance has tipped and the inner lives of characters become more powerful devices for achieving representation. But there's always a struggle going on. Individual consciousnesses always struggle to retain their place amid the demands of objects, social worlds and other people's affects. Pope pays attention to that struggle, merging techniques that Renaissance poets used to represent character with devices that would come to distinguish characterization in the novel.

For Catherine Gallagher, this oscillation between insides and outsides, be-tween surfaces and depths, is precisely what novelistic fiction—fictionality, in her parlance—*is*. Hence she's able to claim aphoristically that fiction is invented in the eighteenth-century; it didn't exist prior to the realist novel. Gallagher's chief in-sight is that realism is, paradoxically, the sign of fiction: "the novel could be judged generally true even though all of its particulars are merely imaginary."[18] Plausibility is what keeps fiction safe; an experience that readers need not confuse with reality. "Disbelief is thus the condition of fictionality, prompting judgments, not about the story's reality, but about its *believability*, its plausibility."[19] In Gallagher's words, fictions are "believable stories that do not solicit belief," valuable because they can be experienced as stable representations. To sustain this safe space of fiction, Gallagher argues that novelists must manage an oscillation between dangerous over-identification and unproductive non-identification. This is what constitutes for her the story of the rise of the novel. As she writes in *Nobody's Story*, "each gen-eration of writers felt called upon to reform the genre by encouraging an affective pulsation between identification with fictional characters and withdrawal from them, between emotional investment and divestment."[20] Perhaps it goes without saying that emotional investment is generally achieved by our gaining sympathetic access to characters' feelings, while divestment is produced by the "everything else" of eighteenth-century novels—the things, the actions, the characters' "outsides."

Gallagher says there's an "affective pulsation," an "oscillation" between insides and outsides. But I think the reader's pulsation between emotional investment and divestment is most often experienced as a wrench, and that it's marked in texts by discontinuities—in style, imagery, characterization, tone or some other technique. In other words, plausibility is threatened by disturbing implausibility. Pope experiments with the traumatic discontinuity between character as a set of surface markings, and character as "personal, interiorized, essential." In the interests of focusing my argument and making a sustained reading, I'm going to talk about *The Rape of the Lock*, though I would say that these observations are true about all of the poems in which Pope develops characters, "Eloisa to Abelard" (1717), "Epistle to Dr. Arbuthnot" (1735), the *Epistles to Several Persons* (1731–5).

The main character in *The Rape of the Lock* is Belinda, and the first thing worth remarking about Belinda is her name. Remarkable because it's not her name. The original for Belinda, as we know, was Arabella Fermor, whose real-life lock was cut and who never married the Baron, Lord Petre. Pope however discards his historical heroine for a literary alternative. As he writes in the prefatory letter to Mrs. Arabella Fermor in the 1714 edition, "The Human Persons are as Fictitious as the Airy ones; and the Character of *Belinda*, as it is now manag'd, resembles You in nothing but in Beauty."[21] There couldn't be a better illustration of the fictionality that realism creates, nor a more perfect piece of evidence that Pope was thinking like a novelist. "Eighteenth-century readers identified with the characters in novels *because* of the characters' fictiveness and not in spite of it," Catherine Gallagher observes.[22] Arabella's reality is replaced by Belinda's *believability*. Belinda behaves like an ordinary girl with an ordinary name. "The way that the novelist typically indicates his intention of presenting a character as a particular individual by naming them in exactly the same way that particular individuals are named in ordinary life," Ian Watt writes.[23] But on closer inspection, Belinda involves a more complicated act of naming. When Pope chose it the name was very new, with one precedent in Vanbrugh's *Provok'd Wife* (1697). A faux-gerundive that doesn't have an agreed-upon translation, it sounds classical but doesn't mean a lot. As such, it gestures toward allegorical or epic characterization without committing Pope to fixed significance. Belinda is simultaneously a fake fictional heroine and a fake archetype, a canny hybrid for this experiment in characterization that refuses to obey the rules either of novel or epic.

There's another layer to Belinda's moniker. Arabella's nickname was Belle, often spelled Bell or Bel. The real girl endures in the fake name Bel-inda, as we're reminded when Pope asks, jokingly: "Say what strange Motive, Goddess! cou'd compel / A well-bred *Lord* t'assault a gentle *Belle*?"[24] Belinda's name gestures toward archetype but resists it both by being too real and too Realist. She seems characteristic but is actually singular; her name has the veneer of allegory but in fact encloses the familiar address of a real, fully-fledged individual. The tension in Belinda's name reveals the tension of eighteenth-century fictional selfhood. Will the subject's selfhood be allowed to emerge, or will it be constrained by a form whose demands overwhelm actual individuality and interiority? Pope gives us a heroine whom we know to have had a complicated experience in real life, whose complexity is forced into simplicity by her allegorical alter ago and by the formal constraints of the couplets and artificial narrative machinery.

Finally, as I said at the beginning, the real original for Belinda is Milton's Eve, a piece of literary thievery by Pope that's never explicitly acknowledged. Like Eve, Belinda gazes at her reflection, like Eve she's attended by invisible creatures, like Eve she receives dream-visions. And like Eve she has luxuriant hair. It's a fascinating parallel that I won't explore in detail here. For now, let me say that Belinda's status as a diminished Eve adds a layer to her ambiguous identity, further complicating the way we understand her exterior affect and interior selfhood.

Defoe starts *Robinson Crusoe* by claiming that it's true. Pope begins *The Rape of the Lock* by claiming the opposite. Written within five years of each other and yet entirely unlike, they nonetheless can be seen to be uncannily similar. Defoe's novel recognized the seductive pleasure that would be created if something untrue could be made to feel as though it were true. Pope was seduced by the inverse: that something true could be made to feel as though it were fictional. Like all seductions, the kind of pleasure both writers create provokes anxiety as well as excitement. If Pope fails to write fiction (despite his claim in the preface) because he can never let his narrative become non-referential, he fails to write the history of a real person, because he keeps incorporating elements that drive narrative away from believability. Far from failing though, the uncomfortable power of *The Rape of the Lock* comes from the fact that we keep trying to believe it, and that Pope's realism, for all its palpable authenticity, doesn't release us into stable suspension of disbelief.

Like the early experimenters with the novel, Pope makes the external world of *The Rape of the Lock* vivid. Precise physical details abound. The exact sense of color and texture we get when Belinda's combs are identified as tortoiseshell and ivory, "the speckled and the white." The chaotic mess of her things spread across the dressing table: "Files of Pins . . . Puffs, Powders, Patches, Bibles, Billet-doux."[25] The detail of how tea looks when it pours out of an expensive silver spout: "from silver Spouts the grateful Liquors glide,"[26] or the way one pinches snuff up with "one Finger and a Thumb."[27] From the start, Pope plunges us into proto-novelistic realism. Belinda, it seems, is a drawing-room Crusoe, and the poem's narrator crowds the opening with the dense textures of the everyday. Curtains, lapdogs, watches, bells, slippers, pillows construct a world as pleasantly plausible as a modern movie set. Pope fabricates the texture of real life, anticipating by nearly half a century the tricks that will make Richardson's realism seem so very believable:

> Other writers avoid details that are not necessary or impressive . . . with Richardson we slip, invisible, into the domestic privacy of his characters, and we hear and see everything that is said and done among them, whether it be interesting or otherwise, and whether it gratify our curiosity or disappoint it.[28]

So wrote Francis Jeffrey in the *Edinburgh Review* in 1804, a passage Ian Watt quotes to illustrate his point that "the novel's realism does not reside in the kind of life it presents, but in the way it presents it."[29]

Pope invests much of his imaginative energy in creating a palpably physical world for Belinda and her friends. At the beginning of the second canto, when she sails up the Thames to Hampton Court, Pope describes the effect of wind on the craft's sails and ropes ("shrouds"). His trick is to imagine that the sylphs' bodies are being touched by the wind and sun, dispersing glittering light and shivery breezes over Belinda:

> The lucid Squadrons round the Sails repair:
> Soft o'er the Shrouds Aeriel Whispers breathe,
> That seem'd but *Zephyrs* to the Train beneath.
> Some to the Sun their Insect-Wings unfold,
> Waft on the Breeze, or sink in Clouds of Gold.
> Transparent Forms, too fine for mortal Sight,
> Their fluid Bodies half dissolv'd in Light.[30]

At first glance, the passage involves the opposite of realism, since it's orchestrated by the imaginary sylphs. The remarkable thing, though, is that the sylphs make reality *more* intense here, because light and wind are made visible by the sylphs' transparent, but material, bodies. The vivacity of the picture is extraordinary (to borrow Elaine Scarry's word for palpable immediacy): we believe that the sails are luffing in the breeze and that the sun glances off the lines as though we too were on the boat. In *Dreaming By the Book*, Scarry figures out why this effect works so well, and though she's talking about a moment in Proust where a magic lantern casts light across a solid wall, her insights apply beautifully to Pope's sylphs and sails: "the transparency of one somehow works to verify the density of the other."[31] In order to believe in solidity—an object's reality—we need to be persuaded that something has touched it:

> Solidity—if we may trust Locke in consultation with our own aliveness—is the key experience for percipient creatures; solidity relies on touch to provide access not just to material surfaces but to deep haptic experience as well. . . . [S]olidity is difficult to reproduce in the imagination because it entails touch, the sense whose operation is most remote to us in imagining. It is impossible to create imaginary persons if one has not created a space for them. Speaking of the perceptible world, Locke says that "space in itself seems to be nothing but a *capacity or possibility for extended beings, or bodies, to exist*"; space is "only the consideration of a bare possibility of body to exist."[32]

Pope's commitment to verisimilitude in the creation of a fictional world that seems real is, in its way, as rigorous as Defoe's.

But Belinda herself is no Crusoe, in truth. She's a complicated individual, with a profoundly ambivalent relationship to her own desires, and an inner life that neither she nor we understand. For Belinda, unlike Crusoe, insides and outsides definitely don't match. Pope tells us this early on, but we barely notice. After asking why the Baron would reject Belinda, he reverses the question: "Oh say what stranger Cause, yet unexplor'd, / Cou'd make a gentle *Belle* reject a *Lord*?"[33] In addition to succeeding as a comic chiasmus, the line tells us something important about Pope's narrative strategy—and Belinda's self. Belinda, we understand, rejected her suitor for reasons that are "yet unexplor'd"—and their (indirect) exploration will constitute Pope's narrative. Pope's story starts with the promise that he's about to undo an upper-middle class precept: women don't reject men with titles. This set-up is very similar to a novel: what are we going to learn about the main character, that we don't yet know, to explain a socially unimaginable event? It's a premise very similar to the one Austen will use nearly a hundred years later with "it is a truth universally acknowledged that a single man in possession of a good fortune must be in want of a wife."

A few lines later Pope hints as to why Belinda's rejected the Baron. He asks:

In Tasks so bold, can Little Men engage,
And in soft Bosoms dwells such mighty Rage?[34]

This question, parallel to the first one about Belles rejecting Lords, discloses a parallel social paradox. It also reveals crucial information about Belinda. Almost inconceivably to Pope's speaker, this feminine body hides anger so immense that it seems to contradict the very fact of her being a woman. It's worth noting that Pope uses the word "soft" here with the same associations that it has in "Epistle to a Lady," about twenty years later. Softness, the defining quality of womanhood, resists clear markings or strong indications of character. In other words, Belinda's soft bosom should not be able to support mighty rage, and yet there it is. Not only is Belinda rageful, her rage is concealed, hidden beneath the surface—revealing an interior self that contradicts her exterior. Superficially, Belinda displays a seemingly implacable calm, as Pope repeatedly reminds us in lines such as "Favors to none, to all she Smiles extends, / Oft she rejects, but never once offends," and "Bright as the Sun, her Eyes the Gazers strike, / And, like the Sun, they shine on all alike."[35] But that's not what she's really like.

Why is this interesting? Because it's not the first impression we get from reading the poem. Most readers would say that Belinda's superficial, and that the mighty rage Pope alludes to here is itself mock-heroic—her rage isn't any more mighty than the "mighty Contests" of the opening couplet. But that's giving in to the misreading Pope's domineering speaker tempts us with. Belinda isn't as trivial as Pope's couplets often force her into being; her anger, grief and humiliation dominate the second half of the poem, in which her superficial composure has been lost. The Belinda of the second half of the poem is a figure of profound emotional and cognitive disorientation.

The action of *The Rape of the Lock* opens with Belinda asleep. Thus disposed, she's visited by the sylph Ariel, who causes Belinda's cheek to "glow" by showing her a tableau of images that make a big impression. Ariel appears disguised as a beautiful Youth: reading between the lines Belinda's glowing cheek tells us that she's having an erotic dream. Like Belinda's mighty rage, the glowing cheek indicates that more is going on for Belinda than she—or we—are consciously aware. Belinda has desires she's not in control of, whose nature she doesn't fully understand, to which Ariel appeals. We also learn that while Belinda can fully acknowledge her desires while asleep, she represses them when awake. Readers often think that in the dream-vision Ariel promises Belinda the material spoils of her social caste: smart carriages, success in cards, plenty of admirers, etc. Actually he promises her protection if a "dread Event" that he's been warned of should occur: that is, the theft of Belinda's hair. Belinda believes that he'll protect her if she gets into trouble because she believes Ariel's pleasing assurances that she's special: "thy own Importance know, / Nor bound they narrow Views to Things below" and "unnumber'd Sprits round thee fly / The light *Militia* of the lower Sky."[36] Being told that you have a secret admirer watching over you is every self-involved girl's dream, so it's no wonder that these promises arouse a glow while she sleeps. In addition to being flattered, she's also been warned, so the dream is both a threat and a promise.

Ariel is a bit mean, too. He says that her heart is nothing but a "moving Toyshop," where superficial preoccupations vie with one another for attention like so many mechanical toys:

> Where Wigs with Wigs, with Sword-knots Sword-knots strive,
> Beaus banish Beaus, and Coaches Coaches drive.[37]

This is harsh. The image of the moving toyshop effectively strips Belinda of the capacity to absorb and meditate on her own experiences. It's an aggressive move on Ariel's (and Pope's) part to characterize her heart, her innermost spirit, as a location that is mechanically operated and from which Belinda is consequently alienated. The very insight that she *is* mechanical is granted her while she's asleep, so she can't even keep hold of it in her conscious life. To be sure, this section of the poem is a parody of several sources: seventeenth-century Platonist arguments about the nature of matter, the debates over the status of spirituous substance between Locke, Hobbes, Stillingfleet and others, as well of course as the epic convention of the dream-vision. But it transcends these links to parody and reveals important things about Pope's fiction-making technique. He gives Belinda an interior, a spirit, and yet denies her access to it. He gives her an exterior character in conflict with her interior self, and yet she has no control over the conflict. The passage is closely parallel to the episode in *Paradise Lost* when Satan appears to Eve in the guise of a toad and promises her divine knowledge. But Belinda, unlike Eve, isn't troubled by this unlicensed penetration of her soul; she throws it off, unwilling and unable to consider the implications of what she's heard.

The couplet that brings Belinda's dream to an end is hostile in its comedy:

> He said; when *Shock*, who thought she slept too long,
> Leapt up, and wak'd his Mistress with his Tongue.[38]

Belinda's dog Shock, envious of her retreat to the private life of the dreamer, brings her back to the world of trivial things. He competes overtly with Ariel and the seductive vision that caused Belinda's blush by performing his own slapstick canine seduction, licking his mistress into consciousness. The subtleties of Belinda's inner life, where sexual feelings mix with her desires for power, are rendered instantly glib and ridiculous by Shock's mock-love making. The rhyming of "long" with "tongue" is overtly comic and covertly mean. We imagine the dog's insistent tongue forcing Belinda out of her long sleep, abruptly, and we hear a rhyme that, because it doesn't precisely work, makes her pleasure a laughing-stock.

It only took a couplet to wake Belinda from a dream that took nearly a hundred lines to unfold. And another couplet to banish Ariel's promises:

> *Wounds, Charms,* and *Ardors,* were no sooner read,
> But all the Vision vanish'd from thy Head.[39]

The very short distance between "read" and "head," and the over-simplicity of the rhyme means that the vanishing vision happens very quickly, in five perfect iambs. I draw attention to this because I'm struck by the fact that Belinda's interior life is revealed and then foreclosed, and because the closing down of Belinda's hidden self is coerced by Pope's aggressively rhymed couplets. This strikes me as a considered strategy. Deidre Lynch has pointed to the increasingly marked disconnect between characters' interior selves and exterior affects as the century wears on, showing how "psychological subtext" replaces an exterior affect as a truer reading of character. For this reason "Austen identifies to her readers the proper means of and motives for literary experience when she demonstrates that the truth of a letter is situated beneath or beyond the face of the page and when she demonstrates that character cannot be known at first sight."[40] The preference for hidden depths over immediately legible surfaces reflects a cultural shift in favor of a new kind of reading, one that valued repetition and inexhaustibility. "This postulate of a depth that could never finally be sounded ensured that aesthetic dispositions would receive repeated and regular workouts."[41] Pope also demonstrates that character cannot be known at first sight, but for different reasons. Plagued by feelings that she's unable to understand, Belinda is also unable to consent, refuse, celebrate or mourn, even as she's assailed by grief, fear and desire. The discontinuity between Belinda's inside and outside forecloses her agency. Saved from a tragic end by the robust comic framework of the story, Belinda might have been closer to Milton's Eve than Pope lets us see.

The coherence of my thinking on this point is much indebted to Sandra Macpherson, whose field-changing *Harm's Way* is concerned with the many instances of accidental harms for which their perpetrators bear "tragic responsibility" in eighteenth-century novels. She's interested, in short, in things going wrong, not right. It's hard to précis Macpherson's sophisticated argument, but here's my shot at it. Macpherson perceives that liability law, the part of English law relating to accidental harms, imagines agency not as individual but collective, "dispersed over a structure."[42] The logic of liability for accidental wrongs means that actual individuals—the parties involved—are "individuated solely *by* responsibility, and responsibility conceived against the criteria by which we tend to define individuals—against interiority, against intentionality, even, paradoxically, against agency itself."[43] The subjects Macpherson pays attention to are thus radically different from the consenting, reasoning, self-determined individuals on whom the law of contract is premised—as well as contractual agreement's bedfellow, the eighteenth-century novel. Macpherson's argument splits her apart from critics who see the novel as a technology for producing "individuality and conjugality"—that is, good outcomes, willfully chosen (this group includes all major theorists of the novel, even those whose work is counter-intuitive in other ways: Ian Watt, Michael McKeon, D. A. Miller, Ruth Perry, Deidre Lynch). Instead, she abandons "the axis of modernity, interiority and compassionate affiliation along with the premise . . . that modernity moves from status to contract."[44] While Macpherson is talking primarily about the tragedy of individuals who commit harm accidentally, the victims of such harm are of course equally bereft of interiority, intentionality and agency, since they are part of the collective "structure" of liability. Macpherson's perceptions have enabled me to explain the essential paradox of Belinda's position in *The Rape of the Lock*. In some ways fully individuated—endowed with intentionality and agency both by her social class and by her status as Pope's heroine—the circumstances of the narrative, coupled with the coercive power of Pope's couplets, take agency and individuality away, leaving her with the empty possession of mere "status."

This account of Belinda enables me to explain the residual dissatisfaction I've always experienced reading the poem's famous set-piece, the toilette scene. When we're told that Belinda "Sees by Degrees a purer Blush arise, / And keener Lightnings quicken in her Eyes,"[45] the phrase "purer blush" depends for its effect on our remembering that Belinda's cheek glowed in slumber at Ariel's vision. Here, the cosmetic blush of make-up is "purer" than the glowing cheek of the dream because it's untouched, uncontaminated, by Belinda's interior experience. My point is that Pope's insistence on Belinda's superficiality is deliberately perverse; he's set up the poem so that we know it's not a complete picture of her. We're not, therefore, gratified by Belinda's beautification, gratifying as it purports to be, because we know that it's an inadequate expression of her character. It could be argued that in 1714 the version of selfhood Pope presents in this scene is more gratifying than it appears to us now. After all, Betty's and the sylphs' preparation of Belinda gives her a fixed self that establishes her as instantly legible, devoid of interiority. But I'm suggesting that Pope's handling of Belinda would have troubled contemporary readers as much as it does moderns.

In the second canto, we're given an account of the Baron's thoughts as he prepares for the rape. He comes across as a distinctly unsavory character:

> Resolv'd to win, he meditates the way,
> By Force to ravish, or by Fraud betray;
> For when Success a Lover's Toil attends,
> Few ask, if Fraud or Force attain'd his Ends.[46]

These couplets are like a lot of moments in Pope in that they present an ironic observation as though it were a matter of fact. It's a novelist's trick, because it's in novels that we find characters whose personal needs are at odds with the social milieu in which they exist. Pope's speaker lets canny readers know he's being ironic, while suggesting that for the people in the poem there's no irony at all. In the Baron's social universe, Pope implies, fraud and force are the only options available to a lover to get what he wants—and both courses are justified by the validating importance of "success." Success here is presumably either getting married or having a sexual relationship—in the Baron's moral economy these options are also undifferentiated. Pope describes an unpleasant social code with a breezy confidence that makes us ignore how nasty it actually is. It's a technique that Austen uses too. Were Mrs. Bennet to read the opening sentences of *Pride and Prejudice* she wouldn't do a double-take because in her interior world rich single men *are* in want of wives, and nothing more. She doesn't mind about the sufferings endured by the would-be wives in the process—and, Austen's narrator implies, neither should we. We do care, though, which is why we root for Jane, who falls legitimately in love with Mr. Bingley, without being cynically interested in a "good" marriage, and Elizabeth, who, for the same reason, at first fails to fall in love with Mr. Darcy. These central characters have interior lives, have private, rational selves, that enable them to step outside the social environment Austen places them in and to think for themselves. Belinda, by contrast, is soon to become the victim of a coercive campaign involving either fraud or force, and we know she doesn't have the interior life she needs to protect herself.

The type of irony at stake in Pope's comment on the Baron's prayer pervades *The Rape of the Lock*. The celebrated zeugmas do the same:

> Whether the Nymph shall break *Diana's* Law,
> Or some frail *China* Jar receive a Flaw,
> Or stain her Honour, or her new Brocade,
> Forget her Pray'rs, or miss a Masquerade,
> Or lose her Heart, or Necklace, at a Ball . . .[47]

This passage is endlessly quoted to show how trivial things are equated with serious things, a habit of thought from which Pope's speaker remains ironically aloof—*he* knows the difference. True. I want to note that it's also a technique which collapses the distinction between interior processes, matters of feeling and cognition, and material things existing out in the world. Pope's zeugmas herd private and public happenings, objects and feelings, into the same ontological space. They do so, moreover, at a moment when Locke and his followers were working hard to distinguish them. One of the fictions of *The Rape of the Lock* is that the characters live in a world without distinctions—in reality the opposite was, almost obsessively, the case. The same is true of the zeugma at the beginning of Canto three:

> Here Thou, Great *Anna*! Whom three Realms obey,
> Dost sometimes Counsel take—and sometimes *Tea*.[48]

Pope implies that the characters in his world perceive no difference between these things, even though we do. But Belinda isn't really given a chance to prove itself against this assumption. She sustains an injury that she doesn't experience as trivial, but that she is required to treat as though it were. Or rather, there isn't a place in the world of *The Rape of the Lock* where distinctions can be preserved between a rape and a playful prank—so when the lock is cut Belinda isn't able to figure out how serious an affront it actually is. The offense against Belinda may not be a trivial matter that she takes too seriously, but a potentially serious matter that Pope demands we interpret lightly. Again, this feels like a novelist's trick: the narrator who plays down the emotional stakes for the characters. Think of the obtuse Nelly Dean and Lockwood in *Wuthering Heights* (1847), much later examples, or of the turn at the end of *Mansfield Park* (1814): "Let other pens dwell on guilt and misery. I quit such odious subjects as soon as I can, impatient to restore everybody, not greatly in fault themselves, to tolerable comfort, and to have done with all the rest."[49] Austen's narrator steps in to give her heroine a comfort that the circumstances of the plot have denied her; Pope's narrator mocks the very notion that comfort might be needed, either for the real Arabella or for the fictional Belinda.

To live in this world of collapsed distinctions—at a historical moment obsessed with the marking of difference—would, of course, be alienating. Which is why the characters in the poem are alienated, both from themselves and their capacity to feel. The losses Pope humorously aligns as being equal were not, in reality, being experienced as like. So it's no wonder that Belinda is on the edge of hysteria, and that the Baron's assault instantly tips her into madness.

The collusion against coherence is aided and abetted by the sylphs. It's they who refuse to draw a distinction between broken chastity and a broken vase. The sylphs are like bad parents, treating minor mishaps and real disasters as though they were all the same. There's an important moment before Belinda's hair is cut in the third canto when Ariel abandons his watch:

> Just in that instant, anxious *Ariel* sought
> The close Recesses of the Virgin's Thought;
> As on the Nosegay in her Breast reclin'd,
> He watch'd th'Ideas rising in her Mind,
> Sudden he view'd, in spite of all her Art,
> An Earthly Lover lurking at her Heart.
> Amaz'd, confus'd, he found his Pow'r expir'd,
> Resign'd to Fate, and with a Sigh retir'd.[50]

It turns out that Belinda has been keeping a secret all this time. The Baron is her lover, she isn't chaste. As Pope tells us in the Dedication to the poem, according to Rosicrucian doctrine of invisible spirits, "any Mortals may enjoy the most intimate Familiarities with these gentle Spirits, upon a Condition very easie to all true *Adepts*, an inviolate Preservation of Chastity."[51] This raises the stakes of the incident considerably. No idle prank, the Baron's cutting of Belinda's lock is a taunt, either intended to mock her for being his lover or to shame her by violating her in public. Belinda's extreme reaction to the incident is explained by this short account. She's at her most vulnerable when the Baron cuts her hair because she's his lover (or at the very least wants to be). She's also at her most vulnerable because Ariel is forced to abandon her.

Most interesting to me is the way Pope uses Belinda's interiority to mark off a cognitive and emotional landscape that can't be perceived or interpreted, except by an imaginary being. Ariel discovers the truth about Belinda's relationship to the Baron because he's able to see the "close recesses" of her mind, the thoughts not available to public view. The implications of this are twofold. First, because it's a secret that only Ariel knows, it guarantees that Belinda's reaction to the cutting of her hair will seem a ridiculous over-reaction to everyone around her. Her secret will make her appear more foolish, not less. And second, it's the fact that she has a private self, separate from her public persona, that means Ariel's abandonment happens at the moment of greatest need. If you think about how the inner lives of characters normally work, they generate sympathy and—perhaps most importantly—they give characters the resources to evade the stifling manners and morals of the social milieu they inhabit. Such evasion can have tragic consequences, think of Clarissa Harlowe. But interiority also offers freedom. Even if it's a tormented space, it guarantees a self that's protected from the world. Belinda's interiority isn't like this, because she's never allowed to access it. She's trapped in a superficial relationship to the events around her because her interior life is so compromised.

My reading of the poem, and of Pope's strategy with respect to characterization, moves away from certain interpretative assumptions. First, that Pope is writing from a seventeenth-century worldview, in which writers depict "general human types against a background primarily determined by the appropriate literary convention."[52] Clearly, Pope understands the literary conventions against which he's composing. But equally clearly, *The Rape of the Lock* enormously exceeds its generic frame as a virtuosic instance of the mock-heroic. Second, I'm suggesting that the speaker's aggression toward Belinda can't be explained away by the poem's epic parody. The sustained humiliation of Belinda isn't ultimately absorbed by the jokes; rather, epic parody enables cruel humiliations that aren't sufficiently recuperated. Third, I'm resisting the idea that *The Rape of the Lock* is merely a light comic poem in which we don't need to care about the characters. Obviously, the poem *is* mock-heroic in tone, structure and composition. Every moment depends on, and can be attributed to, a counterpart in epic. But Pope isn't just filling in negative space. The effects he produces by way of mock-heroic devices differ in kind from the epic originals and produce a different kind of meaning. To put it simply, the most interesting moments in this comedy happen when Pope isn't being funny.

If there's any doubting that the hostility of the Baron's attack on Belinda exceeds the satirical frame Pope places around it, let's revisit the language of the rape itself. There's dark innuendo in "The Peer now spreads the glitt'ring *Forfex* wide, / T'inclose the Lock; now joins it, to divide,"[53] where the humorously Latin "forfex" includes the *for-* prefix with its connotations of physical might. The spreading, joining and dividing trio of verbs imply the story of a forced sexual encounter. And the closing couplets of the canto finish the job, with the hilariously phallic: "What Time wou'd spare, from Steel receives its date," and "What Wonder then, fair Nymph! thy Hairs shou'd feel /The conqu'ring Force of unresisted Steel?"[54] Hilarious, that is, unless you're Belinda.

It's noteworthy that a repeated word in *The Rape of the Lock* is "anxious," a word referring specifically to an uncertain or perturbed state of mind.[55] At the beginning of the fourth canto, Belinda's interior states vex her, intellectually and emotionally, provoking her "Rage, Resentment and Despair"[56]—emotions far darker than the Belinda of Cantos 1 and 2 seems destined for. "Anxious" and "secret," these internal torments don't allow her to feel liberated from her oppressive social world, but oppressed and belabored:

> But anxious Cares the pensive Nymph opprest,
> And secret Passions labour'd in her Breast.[57]

Belinda's devastation is noticed by the "dusky melancholy Spright" Umbriel, who repairs on her behalf to the Cave of Spleen. The ostensible point of the Cave scene, like all the other set-pieces in this poem, is that it parodies epic journeys to the underworld; it's also reminiscent of allegorical caves in Spenser and elsewhere, modeled on Ovid. But it's also noteworthy as an aberration in the poem's imaginative scheme: it's the only entirely invented setting, and it's the only place that departs symbolically from Pope's emphasis on the superficial, the overtly visible, the surfaces of things. The Cave of Spleen is the allegorical representation of an internal condition, a distorted state of mind. Margaret Doody has noted that enclosed spaces frequently do the work of figuring psychological depths in the Augustan sensibility:

> In a period when English gardeners introduced open spaces and then contrasted them with closed or inverted ones, with hermitages and grottoes, the English Augustan poets seldom lose a chance of showing us what lies *medio in antro*,—though the cave may be presented as a garret room, prison cell, or room in Bedlam. What is to be found in these cavernous retreats is not emptiness but unfamiliar potencies.[58]

Although the cave scene is the closest we get to a study of Belinda's anguished mental topography, it's also the moment in which the poem's landscape switches from meticulous plausibility into absolute implausibility, interrupting the poem's realism.

It's important that the Cave of Spleen is allegorical in nature. On the one occasion that Pope offers a sustained exploration of Belinda's interior, it's a compromised landscape. I don't just mean by this that the Cave of Spleen isn't believable (though it's not; its power derives from being so gloriously surreal). I'm also adopting Gordon Teskey's argument in *Allegory and Violence* that the epistemological status of allegory changes in the eighteenth-century, rendering it a more literal, and, crucially, an hermetic literary mode—where in the Renaissance world allegory was fluid, playfully integrated with the reader's cognitive experience. Teskey writes that Enlightenment allegory was no longer "mythopoetic and visionary" but "didactic and argumentative," existing in "isolation from what it refers to."[59] The change is significant for reading the Cave of Spleen, because it meant that Pope understood his allegory to be isolated not only from the reader's mental experience, but also from Belinda's. "An allegory was an aesthetic end in itself, an artifact to be considered by the mind from a distance and appreciated for its simplicity and propriety."[60] When Pope allegorizes Belinda's distress by way of the Cave of Spleen he self-consciously alludes to the richness of Spenserian allegory, in which reader and character journey through the imagined landscape—but the allusion merely emphasizes the fact that this is *not* what will happen here. Instead, allegory is "an illusion created by the mechanics of mind," or, as Blake called it in *Europe*, "an allegorical abode, where existence hath never come."[61]

Belinda doesn't get to journey through her rage, resentment and despair either as a reader of allegory or as a character in Pope's poem. Only Umbriel can go to the Cave. Belinda's feelings therefore remain static, inaccessible emotions that she can neither fully immerse herself in nor adequately dispel. To exacerbate matters, Spleen turns out to be a joke distemper. It's a malady brought on by too much money and idleness, attended by the "handmaids" ill-nature and affectation. Though the contemporary word for what Renaissance writers called Melancholy, spleen is a much less dignified complaint in Pope's account. The hallucinations that it can cause expose its sufferers' triviality by being themselves distortions of trivial, bourgeois possessions:

> Here living *Teapots* stand, one Arm held out,
> One Bent; the Handle this, and that the Spout:
> A Pipkin there like *Homer's Tripod* walks;
> Here sighs a Jar, and there a Goose-pye talks;
> Men prove with Child, as pow'rful Fancy works,
> And Maids turn'd Bottels, call aloud for Corks.[62]

This is the closest Belinda gets to expressing real unhappiness. Umbriel begs from the Queen of Spleen "chagrin" for Belinda, the feeling of vexation or mortification. His wish granted, he collects together allegorical anger and grief to be released on the heroine, one figured as a bag of wind, the other as a vial of poison. Anger comes first, "Belinda burns with more than mortal Ire" while Thalestris, seemingly her protector, says nasty things to her. Then, when the Baron refuses to return Belinda's lock of hair, but rather displays it tauntingly as his prize, Belinda is "half-drown'd in Tears."[63] Anguish gives Belinda a power she has previously lacked and she launches a homicidal attack on the Baron, armed with a deadly bodkin.

I'm interested in the fact that Pope had already started experimenting with characterization early in the eighteenth century in ways that would prove crucial to the history of the novel. And I'm interested in what Pope's writing shows us about the process of identifying with yet feeling distanced from fictional characters, since this process is so fundamental to the experience of reading. Finally, and most importantly, I'm interested in the strategies Pope uses to construct an uneasy relationship between the reader and his characters, because the inability—and refusal—to read easily is one of the most interesting distortions fiction produces. I say this not to be counter-intuitive for its own sake, but because it seems to me that the moments when we cannot read what characters are feeling, or the moments when characters are unable to connect with the innermost selves and the insights that we want them to have, are the moments when we realize that there is very little "willing" about the suspension of disbelief required to read fiction. We're compelled to read because we want to believe in made-up stories. And because we know we won't be able to.

Notes

1. Deidre Lynch, *The Economy of Character: Novels, Market Culture and the Business of Inner Meaning* (Chicago: University of Chicago Press, 1998), 217.

2. Alexander Pope, *Epistle II. To a Lady. Of the Characters of Women*, in *The Twickenham Edition of the Poems of Alexander Pope*, ed. John Butt, vol. 3.2, *Epistles to Several Persons*, ed. F.W. Bateson (London: Methuen & Co., 1951), lines 1–4.

3. Lynch, *Economy of Character*, 78.

4. Dror Wahrman, *The Making of the Modern Self: Identity and Culture in Eighteenth-Century England* (New Haven, CT; London: Yale University Press, 2007), 276.

5. Nancy Armstrong, *How Novels Think: The Limits of British Individualism from 1719–1900* (New York: Columbia University Press, 2005), 3.

6. Wahrman, *Making of the Modern Self*, 189.

7. G. Gabrielle Starr, *Lyric Generations: Poetry and the Novel in the Long Eighteenth Century* (Baltimore: The Johns Hopkins University Press, 2004), 8.

8. Lynch, *Economy of Character*, 38.

9. Pope, *Epistle to a Lady,* 6.

10. Ibid., 274–280.

11. Ibid., 289–92.

12. Sandra Macpherson, *Harm's Way: Tragic Responsibility and the Novel Form* (Baltimore: The Johns Hopkins University Press, 2010), 29.

13. Ian Watt, *The Rise of the Novel: Studies in Defoe, Richardson and Fielding* [1957], 2nd ed. (Berkeley: University of California Press, 2001), 175.

14. Armstrong, *How Novels Think*, 3–4.

15. Ibid., 16.

16. Starr, *Lyric Generations*, 7.

17. Ibid., 9.

18. Catherine Gallagher, "The Rise of Fictionality," in *The Novel*, ed. Franco Moretti, 2 vols. (Princeton: Princeton University Press, 2006), 1:342.

19. Ibid., 346.

20. Catherine Gallagher, *Nobody's Story: The Vanishing Acts of Women Writers in the Marketplace 1670–1820* (Berkeley: University of California Press, 1994), xvii-iii.

21. Alexander Pope, *The Rape of the Lock*, in *The Twickenham Edition of the Poems of Alexander Pope,* ed. John Butt, vol. 2, *The Rape of the Lock and Other Poems*, ed. Geoffrey Tillotson (London: Methuen & Co., 1940), p. 143. Unless otherwise noted (as here), references are to canto and line numbers.

22. Gallagher, *Nobody's Story*, xvii.

23. Watt, *Rise of the Novel*, 18.

24. Pope, *Rape of the Lock*, 1:7–8.

25. Ibid., 1:136, 1:138.

26. Ibid., 3:109.

27. Ibid., 5:80.

28. Francis Jeffrey, in *Contributions to the Edinburgh Review* (London, 1844), quoted in Watt, *Rise of the Novel*, 175.

29. Watt, *Rise of the Novel*, 11.

30. Pope, *Rape of the Lock*, 2:56–62.

31. Elaine Scarry, *Dreaming by the Book* (New York: Farrar, Straus and Giroux, 1999), 12.

32. Ibid., 14.

33. Pope, *Rape of the Lock*, 1:9–10.

34. Ibid., 1:11–12.

35. Ibid., 2:11–14.

36. Ibid., 1:35–6, 1:41–2.

37. Ibid., 1:101–2.

38. Ibid., 1:115–6

39. Ibid., 1:119–20.

40. Lynch, *Economy of Character*, 131.

41. Ibid., 142.

42. Macpherson, *Harm's Way*, 30.

43. Ibid., 30.

44. Ibid., 4.

45. Pope, *Rape of the Lock*, 1:143–4.

46. Ibid., 2:31–4.

47. Ibid., 2:105–9.

48. Ibid., 3.7–8.

49. Austen, *Mansfield Park*, ed. R.W. Chapman (Oxford: Oxford University Press, 1923; repr. 1988), 461.

50. Pope, *Rape of the Lock*, 3:139–46.

51. Ibid., p. 143.

52. Watt, *Rise of the Novel*, 15.

53. Pope, *The Rape of the Lock,* 3:147–8.

54. Ibid., 3:171, 3:177–8.

55. See Ibid., 2:142; 3:139; 4:1.

56. Ibid., 4:9.

57. Ibid., 4:1–2.

58. Margaret Anne Doody, *The Daring Muse: Augustan Poetry Reconsidered* (Cambridge: Cambridge University Press, 1985), 168.

59. Gordon Teskey, *Allegory and Violence* (Ithaca: Cornell University Press, 1996), 98; 104.

60. Ibid., 99.

61. William Blake, Europe, plate 8, in *William Blake's Writings,* ed. G.E. Bentley, 2 vols. (Oxford: Clarendon Press, 1978), 1:228. Quoted in Ibid., 102.

62. Pope, *Rape of the Lock*, 4:49–54.

63. Ibid., 4:144.

2

"THE BATTLE WITHOUT KILLING":
ELIZA HAYWOOD AND THE
POLITICS OF ATTEMPTED RAPE

Kate Parker

*T*HE HISTORY OF MISS BETSY THOUGHTLESS (1751) is a novel that appears in the later stages of Eliza Haywood's prolific career, and has historically been read as the product of the author's purported "conversion" from amatory novelist to didactic writer.[1] Given that the novel is often perceived as marking a departure from Haywood's earlier, more explicit writings, it has attracted lesser and mixed attention from critics who tend to isolate her amatory works in discussions of the eighteenth-century domestic novel's "rise."[2] Yet *Betsy Thoughtless* also represents, as John Richetti notes, "[Haywood's] most mature phase as a novelist," one in which she can be seen to engage in formal and thematic experimentation, sophisticated imitation, and extended, complex parody.[3] The present essay contributes to the ongoing reconsideration of *Betsy Thoughtless* by linking its representation of persecuted female desire with earlier phases in Haywood's career as an amatory novelist—specifically, by highlighting the novel's simultaneous instantiation and critique of the mock-heroic trope of the "battle without killing" in its depictions of attempted rape.[4] The mock-heroic—a form that dominated the early eighteenth-century literary scene—reached its apex at the start of Haywood's own career and was popularized, in particular, by poets like John Dryden and Alexander Pope, as well as Jonathan Swift and Haywood's rival novelist, Henry Fielding. I contend that the mock-heroic conceit inspired Haywood's confusingly comic rendering of the "promiscuous enjoyments" of Betsy's London, where high and low life are often virtually indistinguishable. Indeed, Haywood's appropriation of the mock-heroic responds, in particular, to its inherent trivialization of often overtly gendered power dynamics, such as the "rape" of the lock in Pope. Like Belinda, Betsy suffers humiliating and traumatizing—but ultimately, "non-deadly" (because non-consummated)—sexual violence at the hands of "gentlem[e]n."[5] The repetitive and often excessive scenes of sexual violence, coupled with the dramatic irony of Betsy's overconfident ignorance in the face of such dangers, renders them both disturbingly comic and disproportionately critical, suggesting a broader cultural and political commentary rather than a specific chastisement of the heroine's own actions. And further, the novel's sprawling social apparatus often colludes to place its naïve heroine in precarious situations, suggesting a continuous critique—conspicuously carried over from Haywood's earlier amatory fiction—of the sexed institutions that permit men to freely indulge their desires while women are forced to suffer, or to submit, in silence.

Haywood's appropriation of the "battle without killing" suggests the prominence—indeed, the ubiquity—of a mock-heroic logic in the literature of the period. Claude Rawson traces the characteristic element of martial "non-deadliness" to the English epic *Paradise Lost* (1674), where angels and archangels battle violently but do not experience lasting physical harm.[6] Indeed, Milton is demonstrably fascinated by the ethereal "bodies" of angels that "mortal wound / Receive, no more than can the fluid air. . ."[7] Milton's impact on the emerging genre of mock-heroic cannot be understated; Rawson documents how the "battle without killing" becomes a kind of central mechanism for the mock-heroic's inflation of the trivial to epic significance. Jonathan Swift, in *The Battle of the Books* (1704), pits Ancients against Moderns in a raging (literary) battle to the (intellectual) death, and Belinda's lock, savagely severed by the Baron, leaves the warrior sylphs and gnomes of Pope's *Rape of the Lock* (1714) defeated. However, significantly for this essay, what Pope ultimately trivializes in his poem is not, as in Swift, an entire epistemological tradition but a more specific—indeed, historical, as Sophie Gee points out in this same volume—portrait of embodied feminine virtue susceptible to the whims and impulses of the largely fraternal culture of courtship.[8] Toni Bowers has insightfully demonstrated that "Pope's poem shows how distributions of power come to seem inevitable merely by being assumed and . . . alternatives can remain unthought (even unthinkable) if they go unrepresented." While Pope might be seen to "rich[ly] imagin[e] . . . models of gendered sexual agency besides the model of male initiatory desire and subordinate female response," this is only achieved "indirectly and obliquely," as the poem centers on the false dichotomy of "force or fraud"—the conflation of rape with seduction.[9] Richard Terry diagnoses in the mock-heroic an inherent tendency towards the misogynistic: while the mock-heroic can "provid[e] a formula for thinking through a range of personal or social issues, ones involving ideas of triviality, disproportion, condescension or degradation," there also exists a specifically gendered tint in precisely this logic.[10] Terry names this tendency "fair-sexing," noting that Pope's *Rape of the Lock* is exemplary of such a strategy, because it was "a way of elevating women, but in terms that were consistent with a general subjugation of them: women were subject to treatment rather like that of Belinda's lock in the poem itself," a treatment that "simultaneously aggrandized and trivialized them."[11] Or, to take Terry one step further, the mock-heroic strategy as exemplified by *Rape of the Lock* trivialized women *by* aggrandizing them: by making the suggestion that acts such as rape and assault are significant subjects, indeed worthy of literary epic, but only when filtered through a comic lens that minimalizes the impact for the female heroine and mocks the seriousness of sexual violence—even as the poem subtly calls into question the very separation of force and fraud.

And what we find in *Betsy Thoughtless* is that Betsy's near-constant victimization is enabled by precisely this logic: her capriciousness, simultaneously rewarded and chastised, does empower her but only within the circumscribed, limited context of a patriarchal culture that vilifies and ultimately seeks to humiliate "promiscuous" women. Thus, the repeated sexual violence that Betsy suffers throughout the novel not only serves to perversely highlight her attractiveness and refinement, but also demeans Betsy both physically and psychologically. Indeed, Betsy's beauty, wittiness and confidence are precisely what make the acts of sexual violence both trivial and acceptable in the minds of her perpetrators, because they (mistakenly, it turns out) associate such traits with freer women who lack substance and virtue. Unlike Pope, who makes this paradox the basis of his poem's ironic conceit, Haywood represents this as a chilling ideology of patriarchy in her own instantiation of mock-heroic violence.

Though I hope I have begun to demonstrate, here, how Haywood's appropriation of a mock-heroic logic reveals, at least, a conceptual engagement with the problems Pope confronts in *The Rape of the Lock*, it is true that *Betsy Thoughtless* also has a more immediate historical model for mock-epic parody in her rival novelist Henry Fielding, and this influential connection should not be overlooked.[12] Richetti, who calls *Betsy Thoughtless* a "pretty good imitation of Fielding," recognizes the many ways in which Haywood's "history" draws directly from Fielding's own formal experimentations with the mid-century novel. However, Fielding's participation in a mock-heroic tradition can be distinguished from that of Pope, as Rawson notes, by the "fiction of low life" that Fielding constructs, "equat[ing] heroes with gangsters and politicians" so that the heroic becomes a "tarnished analogue" for a "lowered" modern reality.[13] Thus, while Haywood incorporates much of Fielding's narrative and formal apparatus into her own novel, *Betsy Thoughtless*'s detailed and deliberate portrait of upper-class courtship would seem to suggest other preoccupations, many of which remain consistent with her earlier amatory fiction.[14] In short, I want to push against the tendency to see Haywood's engagement with mock-heroic as unoriginal, or even incidental, as other critics have intimated: for example, Michael McKeon, who insightfully notes the "spirit of mock heroic" that "plays about the edge" of Haywood's periodical *The Female Spectator*, ultimately dismisses it as "surely unintended."[15] Indeed, my essay will ask how we might read Haywood's novel—particularly, its disturbingly comic scenes of attempted rape—if we take Haywood's investment in a mock-heroic logic, exemplified by Pope and his gendered representation of a "battle without killing," as precisely intentional rather than accidental or coincidental, if we view it instead as a meaningful engagement with what is, according to Rawson, perhaps *the* defining mode of early eighteenth-century literature. There is every reason to believe that Haywood found the mock-heroic much more than a casual influence: every stage of her career saw her surrounded by—in fact, competitive with—writers like Fielding, Pope, and Swift. By extending the logic of Pope's mock-heroic "rape" to a disturbing extreme, Haywood can be seen as responding directly to the *Rape*'s punitive portrait of female capriciousness.

But *Betsy Thoughtless* is not the only one of Haywood's novels to grapple with these themes; Haywood's early amatory fiction also engages directly with Scriblerian politics, as Ros Ballaster persuasively demonstrates. For Ballaster, Pope's text becomes representative of an intellectual sphere hostile to female novelists and to Eliza Haywood in particular. Mock-epic allowed Pope, Swift and others to "advocate [. . .] an aesthetics of heroic masculinity," which directly engaged the "encroaching and engrossing effeminacy" of the "female-authored novel."[16] Just as Haywood becomes a scapegoat for female authorship in Pope's *Dunciad* (1729), Pope too becomes a defining figure in Haywood's early writing, as she "imitates the supernatural machinery" of his *Rape of the Lock* in works like *Memoirs of . . . Utopia* (1724/25). In appropriating Pope, Haywood "exposes the misogynist underpinnings of the aesthetics deployed by the masculinist satires that she imitates"—works like *Rape of the Lock*—which results in a "peculiarly 'double' nature" to her own "satirical enterprise, both imitation and critique."[17] *Rape of the Lock* serves as an "important intertext" for reading *Memoirs*, which adopts the "form of a repetitive series of accounts and seductions and rapes of court and country ladies by rapacious politicians and aristocrats," and thus registers in significant ways the misogyny of *Rape*'s premise in the characteristic narrative structures of Haywood's romance. As in *Betsy Thoughtless*, it is the repetitiveness of rape and sexual assault that marks Haywood's critique and that, as Ballaster concludes, "literaliz[es] the 'rape' of the lock into an account of the sexual predatoriness of a 'corrupt' court."[18] And, I argue, Haywood draws upon these same energies when she extracts her heroine from the implausibly romantic setting of *Memoirs* and sets her down in the equally precarious (if more subtly so) social scene of contemporary London. She reframes the corrupt "coquettes and beaus" as hypocritical "friends" who aim to control and manipulate Betsy as she strives to negotiate this world independently.

From her first moments in her guardian's household, Betsy—at first a relatively naïve ingénue—is initiated into Lady Mellasin's luxurious and corrupting lifestyle of gaming, intrigue and entertainment. "It cannot," the narrator observes, "seem strange, that Miss Betsy, to whom all things were entirely new, should have her head turned with that promiscuous enjoyment, and the very power of reflection lost among the giddy whirl . . ."[19] Betsy becomes, indeed, thoughtless: impulsive, easily distracted, and irresponsible, all characteristics that the narrator locates in her original, extrinsic experience of the "giddy whirl" of London society. Thus, the behaviors that ultimately endanger Betsy—her characteristic impulsiveness, her marked lack of "reflection"—become explicitly linked not only with the "promiscuous enjoyments" that she experiences in Lady Mellasin's house, but also the "friends" and "guardians" to whom she entrusts her safety and financial success. In the corrupt world of London society, it turns out, no one is safe and no one is trustworthy. What Betsy then suffers at the hands of her perpetrators, again and again, seems less an indictment of *her* particular character and behavior and more a reflection of how an unprincipled society abuses and destroys women who aim to either gain advantage or—perhaps more disturbingly—seek independence and autonomy within its bounds.

However, in the world of the novel, the attempted rapes are often interpreted as chastisement and punishment for her "thoughtless" behavior, however innocent. Like "Lady Such-A-One" in Haywood's earlier *Fantomina* (1725)—and like Pope's Belinda—these sexual assaults often perversely serve to underscore her desirability, but not her virtue in resisting.[20] In an alarmingly typical scene, Betsy leaves a group of questionable friends at the theatre and is accompanied home by a "strange" gentleman, finding herself alone in the carriage with him. Betsy, who entered the theatre in a more sober and contemplative frame of mind (having just been remonstrated by her beau Mr. Trueworth for her misguided loyalty to the disreputable Miss Forward), has her mood lifted by a scene so "brilliant" and "gallant," and "once more relapse[s] into her former self," again inspired to frivolity by the gaiety of her surroundings.[21] Like the coquettes in *Memoirs of . . . Utopia*—and, again, like Belinda—Betsy is both a glittering product and a keen observer of this frivolous world of theatre and other "promiscuous enjoyments." It is only *after* immersing herself in this dazzling fray that Betsy can easily be coaxed home by a gentleman, who touts himself as a "man of honour," "[in]capable of an ungenerous action."[22] This proves anything but true when, on the way home, he immediately accosts her:

> They were no sooner seated, and the windows drawn up, to keep out the cold, then Miss Betsy was alarmed with a treatment, which her want of consideration made her little expect:—since the gentleman-commoner, at Oxford, no man had ever attempted to take the liberties which her present companion now did:—she struggled,—she repelled with all her might, the insolent pressure of his lips and hands.—"Is this," cried she, "the honour I was to depend upon?—Is it thus you prove yourself incapable of an ungenerous action?"
>
> . . . she had not the power of interrupting him; but recovering herself, as well as she was able, "Heavens!" cried she, "what means all this?—What do you take me for?" "Take you for," answered he laughing, "prithee, dear girl, no more of these airs:—I take you for a pretty, kind, obliging creature, and such I hope to find you, as soon as we come into a proper place.—"In the meantime," continued he, stopping her mouth with kisses, "none of this affected coyness."
>
> The fright she was in, aided by disdain and rage, now inspired her with unusual strength;—she broke from him, thrust down the window,—and with one breath called him monster,—villain;—with the next screamed out to the coachman to stop, and finding he regarded not her cries, would have thrown herself out, if not forcibly with-held by the gentleman, who began now to be a little startled at her resolute behavior,—"What is all this for?" said he, "would you break your neck, or venture being crushed to pieces by the wheels?" "Any thing," cried she, bursting into tears, "I will venture, suffer any thing, rather than be subjected to insults, such as you have dared to treat me with."[23]

Again, it is Betsy's initial "want of consideration" that places her in harm's way, a relationship that the narrator takes pains to connect directly with the frivolous indulgences and vanities of both Betsy's friends and her immediate surroundings: particularly, the theatre where Betsy—like Fantomina before her—lets down her guard. Here, Haywood frames individual flaws (gambling, vanity, promiscuity—perhaps even rape?) as the result of a corrupted society that particularly renders vulnerable its female members.

Betsy responds appropriately and even virtuously in her recognition that the gentleman's forcible attempt is something dangerous and improper, and—not recognizing that the gentleman has mistaken her for a prostitute—appeals to his "honour," demanding proper treatment as a lady. Betsy, despite being called a "perfect Machiavel in love affairs," has no clue how she has misrepresented herself.[24] "What means all this?" she exclaims as the gentleman takes liberties, and he, responding perniciously, laughs that he is only taking her for what she has presented herself to be: "a pretty, kind, obliging creature," a capricious, wanton girl. Yet throughout the novel, this is precisely what Betsy has valued in herself: "the pleasure of being told she was very handsome, and gallanted about by a great number of those who go by the name of very pretty fellows," and though her "friends" have, at times, chastised her for it, they have also confusingly praised and admired Betsy for her "plurality of suitors."[25] Haywood uses this scene of attempted rape to underscore the surprising collusions between the social expectations Betsy has learned from her "friends" and those of would-be perpetrators aiming to capitalize on her weaknesses and frivolities. Following a form of the mock-heroic logic, what is touted as superior behavior and worthiness is found, paradoxically, to be precisely what is equally valued—if troublingly—by the kind of "low-life" that Betsy ostensibly aims to avoid. However, here Haywood makes the logical conclusion of these mismatched expectations an actually precarious event, one that diverges in significant ways from the stylized "rape" in Pope's poem.

Betsy, realizing her mistake, then does something unexpected. She prepares to leap from the carriage and fatally injure herself rather than suffer the disrespect of the gentleman's advances. For Betsy, the threat of violence here is two-fold: Betsy can either jump and be seriously hurt, perhaps killed, or she can be raped and destroyed. Based on the gentleman's startled reaction, Haywood construes this as an almost hyperbolic response to the intended rape, underscoring, again, the mismatch between the gentleman's expectations and Betsy's. He, startled by her willingness to injure herself, "forcibly with-[holds] her," terrified by the threat of "real" violence ("break[ing] her neck," or "being crushed to pieces by the wheels") but unable to make sense of the "why" of Betsy's behavior: the *other* form of impending violence Betsy anticipates from within the carriage. This "gentleman of honour" is as clueless about the threat of violence he imposes upon Betsy as Betsy is about what she has done to invite his attack. By heroically "saving" her from being crushed by the wheels, the gentleman immerses Betsy in an equally danger-ous situation, one in which she remains truly powerless, as Haywood emphasizes by describing him as "forcibly" withholding her; even in her heroic flight, Betsy is still firmly under his control, and thus unable to remove herself from the situation (even though she is willing to injure herself in doing so). It is in this moment of violent *non-violence*—a moment in which the threat of injury, from both fronts, is palpably felt but not actually enacted—that Haywood constructs perhaps her most persuasive critique of a society that has so skewed its own sense of morality when it comes to exerting sexual force over women. The man, shocked and ap-palled by the threat of an "actual" injury to Betsy, remains uncritical and seemingly unaware of the dangers he brings in making his assumptions about her sexual willingness, her availability, and, indeed, even her attraction to him. In situating this critique in a moment where rape is *not* committed but is seriously and pur-posefully threatened, Haywood casts aspersions, more generally, on a society that does not view sexual violence against women as an act of consequence, in essence revising the kinds of conclusions intimated by works like Pope's *Rape of the Lock*. The attempted rape—a form of the "battle without killing" in its own right—thus reveals as much, if not more, about the misguided and convoluted sexual politics of Betsy's London than would a consummated rape: an act that would likely only indict the perpetrator himself (and this remains a problem turned over and over by contemporary sexual assault advocates who repeatedly assert that it is a *rape culture* that colludes to encourage violence against women even today, as opposed to the individual aberration of the violent perpetrator).[26] And the scene ends with a moment of ultimate irony: the gentleman, seeing the disheveled and disordered heroine home, gently chastises her for her free and willing behavior, a moment that reads as rather excessively ridiculous: it being obvious that the gentleman has learned *nothing* from this encounter, remaining unconcerned and unapologetic about his own violent behavior, and further, presenting himself as a social author-ity ready to instruct Betsy in the kinds of proper "feminine" behavior that will enable her to avoid, he surmises, such an unpleasant and unfortunate situation in the future.[27]

As in the mock-heroic battle without killing, it is here the violent act without actual violence that communicates the significance and meaning of the event, and further, does so *via* a deeply disturbing comedy of errors. The tone is dramatic and urgent to emphasize the seriousness of the event, even though it is not completed: Betsy's attacker presses on even as Betsy desperately tries to convince him otherwise, and it is only after her hysterical escape attempt followed by a near-swooning that she ultimately "obtain[s his] pardon."[28] His "pardon," which is immediately followed by his chastisement of *Betsy's* behavior, is less a moment of true contrition and more an opportunity for him to instruct her in the "principles" of his libertine philosophy: "'I love my pleasures,'" he tells Betsy, "'and think it no crime to indulge the appetites of nature.—I am charmed with the kind free woman, but I honour and revere the truly virtuous, and it is a maxim with me never to attempt the violation of innocence.'"[29] In juxtaposing the "truly virtuous" against the "kind" and "free woman," Haywood again underscores the novel's constant confusion of ethics, particularly when voiced as part of a "maxim" by a libertine who presumably only sees "violation" as a problem when it involves "the truly virtuous" or "innocent," and further does not truly apologize for his own behavior despite his seeming supplication. Given the novel's emphasis on the problematic and vexed ethics of courtship, elsewhere exemplified by Betsy's "friends"—including the less-than-true Trueworth and Betsy's own hypocritical male siblings—it seems we must read Betsy's "repentance" at the end of the novel, historically seen as Haywood's open embrace of a new domestic morality, as fundamentally less definitive because it only involves Betsy's submission to the skewed and problematic behaviors valued by said "friends"—behaviors that are not principally different from those voiced by the "penitent" gentleman.[30] At the novel's end, Betsy's moment of "repentance," where the narrator reports that her "virtues" were "at length rewarded with a happiness, retarded only till she had render'd herself wholly worthy of them," must be regarded suspiciously, or at least, as a morally ambivalent moment, rather than as evidence Haywood has matured as a novelist and now walks a more definitive ethical line.[31]

The politics of attempted rape, then, are not simply evinced in scenes like the former, but also deeply tied into the novel's formal apparatus, as the novel makes use of the trope of a "repetitive series of accounts and seductions" of single women who collectively seem unable to assess the *real* stakes of sexual promiscuity outside of the institutions of courtship which pervade the novel. The novel plays with a kind of mock-heroic logic by distorting the consequences of virtuous feminine behavior. Haywood was deeply conscious and critical of the double-standard governing female sexual behavior in Betsy's London: in order, for example, for Betsy to comply with the demands of her "friends," she must simultaneously submit to her suitors (to maintain their favor) and resist their more fervent advances (to maintain virtue, mystique, power). Haywood paints this as a slippery political slope, reminiscent of her response to Pope's mock-heroic "rape" in *Memoirs of . . . Utopia.* By combining the straightforward "reformed heroine plot" popularized by domestic fiction with the fracturing and variegating effects typical of Fieldingesque mock-heroic, Haywood is able to reconstruct the convoluted and confused world Betsy must navigate in order to be "rewarded with . . . happiness." It is, again, the logic of the mock-heroic that brings together clashing contraries and disparate narrative pieces under the framework of the cohesive, dominant "happy marriage" plot. Haywood's novel thus embodies the tensions between the climactic expectations of companionate marriage and the repetitive parody of Betsy's misguided and ill-advised promiscuity in what Richetti calls its "loosely strung" form.[32]

Betsy's story is both a version of the "reformed heroine" plotline and consistently resistant to that title. It is a text composed mostly of brief episodes, divided into ninety-two relatively short chapters, and often flitting back and forth between several interrelated plots and storylines, with Betsy at the (ever-shifting, ever-tenuous) center of things. The novel enacts the kind of scandalous story-telling and practically impossible cognitive processing that is required of the distracted, "thoughtless" Betsy as she aims to navigate the revolving door of London society, with its seductive and often insidious "continual round of publick diversions" that Betsy indulges in. *Betsy Thoughtless* formalizes the tension between self-possession and promiscuous enjoyment through its stitching-together of Betsy's (often virtuous) private meditations with the frenzied and violent distractions of external "diversions," or "promiscuous enjoyments." Betsy arrives in London a social novice and, under the guardianship of the mostly apathetic Mr. Goodman and the duplicitous Lady Mellasin, quickly develops and maintains an enviable "plurality of lovers," notably including the esteemed Mr. Trueworth. Despite frequent admonitions from friends and guardians—many of whom are actively engaged in their own questionable intrigues despite outward professions of virtue—to avoid the *appearance* of promiscuity, Betsy persists in her belief that "a young woman who ha[s] her fortune" should "be allowed to hear all the different proposals . . . offered to her on that score."[33] At least ostensibly, Betsy views her promiscuous behavior as a very efficient means to an inevitable end, and remains openly "averse" to the "marriage-state," until, presumably, a mutually desirable arrangement presents itself.[34]

Yet Betsy clearly savors the powerful play of courtship and thrives on juggling her various suitors' passions, a "fault" that ultimately results in Trueworth's abandonment of his suit in favor of the bland and submissive Miss Harriot. Betsy, left to her devices, continues to encourage a wealth of suitors until she is convinced to marry Mr. Munden, largely as a result of the trauma sustained by the multiple attempted rapes she suffers; after enduring many months of his abuse in turn, she separates from him and is plunged into a state of painful self-scrutiny. She returns dutifully to care for him on his death-bed, and discovers that Trueworth's wife has also passed away in the interim. Finally admitting her real feelings for Trueworth, she is reunited with him at the novel's end, providing a sense of closure to what has stretched well beyond the typical "courtship novel" ending. However, *Betsy Thoughtless* cannot seem to stay centered on one extended domestic plot; it is digressive, distractible, and much more convoluted than is typical of, say, Richardsonian novels of virtue (with which it is also often compared). Neither is *Betsy Thoughtless* straightforwardly comic. As Andrea Austin notes, *Betsy Thoughtless* functions as more of a parody than a work of didacticism; interestingly, Austin claims that much of Haywood's use of parody can be located in the novel's formal tendencies towards digression and repetition: the repeated attacks on Betsy's virtue—the series of attempted rapes that, I argue above, represent Haywood's simultaneous instantiation and critique of the mock-heroic "battle without killing." Austin concurs with me in her recognition that "Haywood's point is not that rape is funny," but that, when "juxtaposed with the seriousness of the seduction narratives, *the humour of Betsy's exaggerated and contrived misadventures falls curiously flat.*"[35] She continues:

> With such vivid depictions as the destitution and desperation of Forward, Flora, and the others, the tragedy Betsy avoids never leaves the stage, as it were, but is continually kept before us. *This juxtaposition thus works to fundamentally redirect our notion of the scenes' farcical content— to expose, the proper sense of the word "farce" as a kind of humorous sham or absurd pretense, that the true sham(e) is belief in Betsy's culpability.* In this way, Haywood parodically takes aim at the use of this plot as stock comic theater and prose fare, suggesting that the spectacle of old men and rakes attempting to ruin vain young girls is by no means a funny one after all.[36]

I would reiterate here that Haywood's formal experimentations with parody are not straightforwardly comic, but that her development of the "battle without killing" trope into a proliferating series of violent attacks can only, at best, be seen as purposefully *half-hearted*: a comic device in which the humor "falls curiously flat" because the subject matter is fundamentally *unfunny*. Further, even as Betsy reaches crucial moments of moral epiphany throughout the novel, her newly-attained and much-desired clarity does not, in fact, protect her from rape, but perhaps even renders her *more* susceptible.[37] By giving such parodic elements less-than-comic conclusions, as I will show in my reading of another attempted rape below, Haywood manifests a critique of mock-heroic rape by adopting and embracing its conceits in a way that is, indeed, curiously ineffective in terms of the novel's moral conclusions, and by extension exposing the fallacy and inappropriateness of seeing any sexual violence as either inherently "comic" or viciously instructive—as, we have seen, is the tendency of the masculinist mock-heroic in *Rape of the Lock*.

Perhaps one of the novel's most disturbing rape scenes involves the foppish and effeminate Sir Frederick Fineer—a gentleman whose hyperbolically flattering letters and embarrassingly over-the-top wooing of Betsy makes him, according to the narrator, "[t]hat enamorato of all enamoratos."[38] Fineer, who has showered Betsy with crude and flowery poetry in several prior episodes, is indeed *such* a ridiculous character that her brother Francis (in a rare moment of perspicacity) warns Betsy that "his stupidity seems to me too egregious to be nature,—all his expressions have more the appearance of a studied affectation, than of a real folly," leading Francis to urge her to "take care sister, I have heard there are many imposters in this town, who are continually on the watch for young ladies, who have lost their parents, and who live in the unguarded manner that you do."[39] Betsy, able to see the truth of Francis's statement, remains confident that, though Fineer "is a fool indeed," he is also "a man of quality," and rightfully recognizes that such characteristics often afford married women *more* independence and freedom than would a partnership with a solemn husband: "I know several ladies who are the envy of their own sex, and the toast of the other and yet have fools for husbands."[40] For Betsy, the ultimate goal throughout the novel has been to secure a relationship that will allow her to maintain those characteristics that, fundamentally, she has always appreciated in herself—gaiety, light-heartedness, independence, power—though these characteristics have been both lauded and chastised by others. Throughout *Betsy Thoughtless*, Haywood can be seen as repeatedly questioning whether or not it is categorically wrong for women to define themselves by their conquests, to "value themselves on the number and quality of lovers, as they do upon the number of richness of their cloaths."[41] Betsy correctly recognizes, for example, that a marriage with the more sober Mr. Trueworth would require her to submit rather fully to his desires:

> . . . she thought she could be pleased to have such a lover, but could not bring herself to be content that he ever should be a husband. She had too much good sense not to know that it suited not with the condition of a wife to indulge herself in the gaieties she at present did, which

though innocent, and, as she thought, becoming enough in the state she now was, might not be altogether pleasing to one, who, if he so thought proper, had the power of restraining them.[42]

Thus, Haywood reiterates, the choices available to Betsy are both, in their own way, unappealing, and this proves prescient when Betsy does submit to her friends' desires by marrying the brutish Mr. Munden, who immediately demonstrates himself to be an abusive and withholding spouse. Given this inevitable fate, Betsy's choice to allow Fineer to pursue her—while going against the (uncharacteristically) thoughtful admonitions of her brother—is, in fact, a perfectly rational and even desirable choice, given Betsy's desire to maintain her independence and to avoid being inextricably linked to a husband who can exercise complete power over her.

Haywood does not stage this as a moment of Betsy's weakness or capriciousness. The irony of the episode with Fineer is that it rather immediately follows a scene in which Betsy openly embraces virtuous and responsible behaviors, as evidenced by her reflections after witnessing the behavior of the promiscuous Miss Airish (whose own actions mirror those of Betsy's earlier in the novel). Betsy cautiously turns down an outing with Miss Airish and two unknown gentleman, as

> . . . she knew very little of these two young nobleman, yet thought she saw enough in their behaviour to make any woman, who had the least regard for her honour or reputation, fearful to trust herself with them in any place, where both might be so much endangered;—she was, therefore, very much amazed, that Miss Airish should run so great a risk.[43]

Only *moments* before Betsy is to enter Fineer's apartment under the ruse that he is suicidal and ill, she aptly and correctly anticipates the danger to her reputation and to her person in accompanying Miss Airish on a jaunt with two unknown gentleman. It can no longer be said that Betsy is fully "thoughtless," at least not in the same way, as here she appears serious, prudent and reflective—demonstrating, in short, that she *has* found her past experiences morally instructive. After learning that Miss Airish does pass a scandalous night of "harmless libertinism," Betsy congratulates herself even further:

> Never had Miss Betsy felt within herself a greater or more sincere satisfaction, than she now did, for having so prudently avoided falling into inconveniencies, the least of which, she very rightly judged, would have been paying too dear a price for all the pleasures she could have received.

> Sweet indeed are the reflections, which flow from a consciousness of having done what virtue, and the duty owing to the character we bear in life, exacted from us, but poor Miss Betsy was not to enjoy, for any long time, so happy a tranquility;—she was roused out of this serenity of mind, by an adventure of a different kind from all she had ever yet experienced, and which, if she were not properly guarded against, it ought to be imputed rather to the unsuspecting goodness of her heart, than to her vanity, or that inadvertency, which had occasioned her former mistakes.[44]

As the narrator suggests above, Betsy's concern for Fineer arises from "unsuspecting goodness of . . . heart" rather than from "vanity" or "inadvertency"—and yet, again, it is these well-meaning, virtuous qualities that will place Betsy in a considerably more precarious situation than Miss Airish in the very next scene, suggesting again a blatant mismatch between the novel's professed expectations of virtuous women and the rewards they receive.

Driven to Fineer's apartment by the duplicitous Mrs. Modeley under the impression that Fineer is near death, Fineer first tries to compel Betsy into marrying him as his "final wish," insisting that the marriage will be immediately annulled by his impending demise. Betsy, initially confused about the appropriate response (as meanwhile a "parson" moves swiftly through the ceremony), finally refuses and tries to escape. As she flies the room, Fineer leaps from the bed, suddenly healthy, and asserts that they are, indeed married, with the only missing ingredient the consummation of the marriage. He then attacks her, and she fights back:

> 'Tis hard to say, whether rage for the imposition she now found had been practiced on her, or the terror for the danger she was in, was the passion now most predominant in the soul of Miss Betsy;—but both together served to inspire her with unusual strength and courage.
>
> 'Your resistance is in vain,' cried he, 'you are my wife, and as such I shall enjoy you:—no matter whether with your will or not.'—She made no answer to these words, but collecting all her force, sprung from him, and catching hold of one of the posts at the bed's foot, clung so fast round it, that all his endeavours to remove her thence were ineffectual for some moments, though the rough means he made use of for that purpose, were very near breaking both her arms.
>
> Breathless at last, however, with the continual shrieks she had sent out for help, and the violence she had sustained by the efforts of

that abandoned wretch, who had as little regard to the tenderness of her sex, as to any other principle of humanity, she fell almost fainting on the floor; and was on the point of becoming a victim to the most wicked stratagem that ever was invented, when on a sudden the door of the chamber was burst open, and a man, with his sword drawn, at that instant rushed in upon them.[45]

Fineer's brutality, "little regard" and lack of "humanity," juxtaposed against Betsy's goodness and generosity in tending to him during his feigned illness, highlights a drastic discrepancy between virtuous actions and rewards. Here, Betsy's more sober and serious behavior only serves to place her in the most brutish and violent situation she has had to endure throughout the entire novel—one in which she clings, humiliated and terrified, to the bedpost while Fineer violently attempts to disengage her. Haywood seems fully conscious of the profound unfairness of this situation: Betsy, in finally becoming a woman of 'worth,' is immediately debased and humiliated, while a *man* of worth—Trueworth, who bursts in at the last moment—receives a heroic welcome and reward. Betsy responds to Trueworth with effusive thanks, while simultaneously acknowledging her disempowered position: "Oh! Mr. Trueworth, how shall I thank the goodness you have shewn me!—I have no words to do it,—it is from my brothers you must receive those demonstrations of gratitude, which are not in my power to give."[46]

Betsy's words here are telling. Betsy has begun to recuse herself from the patriarchal social circle of her "guardians," who are now empowered to grant gratitude on Betsy's behalf, whereas earlier in the novel she would have sought to profess thanks (indeed, to profess *anything*) herself—a further demonstration of how Betsy's embrace of virtue is disempowering. And by whom is Betsy displaced and remanded? Trueworth and her brothers. Though Trueworth is proven throughout the text to be a reasonably virtuous and loyal character, he is responsible for the destruction and sexual exploitation of Betsy's friend Miss Flora, with whom he engages in an illicit relationship while openly courting the polite and refined Miss Harriot. And Betsy's brother Andrew Thoughtless has even more compelling parallels with the novel's rakes and libertines, and is often encouraged and rewarded in his behavior while Betsy is chastised and punished. When asked by Mr. Goodman to assume guardianship of Betsy upon his arrival in London, Andrew replies in the negative, stating:

. . . as I am a single man, I shall have a crowd of gay young fellows continually coming to house, and I cannot answer that all of them would be able to behave with that strict decorum, which I should wish to see always observed toward a person so near to me . . . In fine . . . it is a thing wholly inconsistent with the freedom I propose to live in . . . [47]

Here Haywood stringently juxtaposes the limited capacity Betsy enjoys for social pleasure against the normalized "proposed" freedoms her brother enjoys, underscoring how these behaviors are "wholly inconsistent" despite being explicitly identical. (Betsy, who values herself upon maintaining a "plurality of lovers," also enjoys being followed around by a "crowd of gay young fellows," who rarely "behave . . . with strict decorum.") Further, Andrew is willing to leave his sister in the equally (if not more) precarious and demonstrably vulnerable position of remaining under the care of Mr. Goodman and Lady Mellasin, where she has already suffered through two attempted rapes and a highly odd near-kidnapping while visiting a local monument on her own. Andrew's motives here are purely selfish; he wishes to keep enjoying his "freedoms" unchecked—an argument Betsy understandably finds "so weak, and withal so unkind, that she could not forbear bursting into tears."[48]

But, the reader discovers, this is not in fact the real story. The narrator reveals that Andrew's real motivation stems from a desire to keep secret his mistress, with whom he has traveled from France. Andrew's duplicity thus highlights the doubly-offensive nature of the sexual double-standard with which Betsy constantly must grapple: not only is Andrew permitted to enjoy such freedoms, but he is in fact permitted to enjoy them so unquestionably as to be able to use them as an acceptable front for even more morally reprehensible behavior. And, as the attempted rape by Fineer demonstrates, even so-called "virtuous" behavior on the part of women can result in abuse and sexual violence. In a recent article, David Oakleaf has presented compelling evidence that Haywood drew Betsy Thoughtless's character from that of a real-life prostitute, Betsy Careless, who worked Haywood's Covent Garden neighborhood. According to Oakleaf, she fascinated Haywood because she exemplifies the epistemological paradox that underlies the problem of virtue in *Betsy Thoughtless*: as he frames it, "How can a young woman taste the commercial delights of the city without circulating as public property (a prostitute) rather than private (wife or potential wife)?"[49] As I have argued here, one way that Haywood responds to the concern of a double-standard is by representing how these moments of comic confusion, and clashing expectations, are fundamentally *unfunny*. They are moments in which the heroine, despite her best efforts to meet the (skewed) moral expectations of her "friends" and family, is trivialized, humiliated, and degraded. They are also moments, Haywood notes, in which equally unworthy men are valorized and celebrated.

This double-standard colored Haywood's own experience as a female novelist; she was herself the victim of a scathing mock-heroic parody in Pope's celebrated *Dunciad*. The poem takes aim at "hack" writers who work for money, particularly professional women authors. Haywood is one of those writers; Pope essentially accuses her, in a notorious scene, of being a prostitute whose writings are like "bastard" children. "Dulness," the odious muse of Pope's satire, judges a pissing contest in which publishers William Chetwood and Edmund Curll compete for the rights to Haywood's bastardized literary offspring. "Two babes of love"—two of Haywood's salacious amatory novels, are named by Pope in an accompanying footnote: *Memoirs of...Utopia* (as we might expect, given the explicit overlaps explored earlier by Ballaster) and *The Count of Carimania* (1726). As Haywood "stands confess'd" in the center, Dulness decrees "His be yon Juno of majestic size, / With cow-like-udders, and with ox-like eyes," representing Haywood as a perverse mixture of cow's body and ox's perspicacity, as she clutches her "babes" and obstinately persists as the spectacle of authoress-as-whore, conflating literal with literary promiscuity by mothering texts outside of the established patrimonial bloodline.[50] Haywood is imagined as voraciously sexual—charged with writing promiscuously, not necessarily poorly. *The Rape of the Lock* also depicts a female heroine whose own copious desires—the "Earthly lover lurking at her heart"—makes her "vulnerable" to the advances of the Baron and simultaneously culpable, an active player in her own undoing.[51]

Haywood responds to this kind of charge in the first essay of *The Female Spectator* by recasting the authoress-as-whore as a productive and profitable form of engagement with her reader. She asserts that if women writers are like prostitutes, it is only because *readers* are so inconstant, and thus reframes the problem of authorial "promiscuity" as a viable—indeed, perhaps the *only* viable—response to the skewed values with which the author finds herself confronted. Haywood makes a case for promiscuous (literary) behavior as the only way of deploying female self-knowledge and exerting control over the readerly relationship—here imagined as a masculine reader who might otherwise disempower a female author—in a way that calls to mind the precise double-standard with which Betsy herself must contend. Importantly, Haywood frames this argument from the perspective of a reformed coquette, whose own pleasures and sexual play clearly anticipate some of Betsy's courtship practices by aiming to recruit a "plurality" of readers. Thus it is evident how Haywood returns to this model again and again: empowered women who try to play a game in which they don't know the rules find themselves humiliated and defeated, and often by a system that mocks their plight.

In Book I, the Female Spectator voices her ostensible penitence by replacing the "Hurry of Promiscuous Diversions" previously enjoyed with the presumably more edifying pursuit of writing. The Spectator vows that she "will draw no flattering Lines . . . no attempt to shadow over any Defect with an artificial Gloss," as she was once the "greatest Coquet of them all."[52]

Recalling the follies she once considered as pleasures, the Female Spectator now pursues gratification exclusively in the "Consolation" of educating the "Public" regarding the pitfalls of frivolity. Importantly, while she explicitly laments her naïve worship of "Dress, Equipage and Flattery," she does not actually condemn the behavior, and further suggests that these "Promiscuous Diversions" are precisely what have enabled her to become a worldly and sophisticated writer. Indeed, it is only from this cultivated perspective that the Spectator can insightfully examine the behavior of others. This is, Haywood suggests, the paradox of the reformed coquette, and it follows the same mock-heroic logic as do the attempted rapes of *Betsy Thoughtless*: knowledge can only be attained through immoral conduct, and thus authority can only be summoned and legitimated through the admission of past indiscretion.[53] The Female Spectator sees promiscuity and frivolity as a means to maintain interest and power in a fickle marketplace. By promising to appeal to both her imagined reader's particular "Curiosity" as well as the broadest possible range of "Tastes" in telling her story, the Spectator makes it repeatedly clear that she has no choice but to seduce as many readers as possible in order to ensure literary success—embracing the model of authoress-as-whore with which she is forced by authors like Pope to contend.[54] Here, Haywood openly embraces a kind of wanton persona: authorial identity is shifty, unstable; it is subject to caprice, fluctuation, whim; it is unabashedly pandering; it summons the reader openly, groping toward any possible success. But like Betsy, whose questionable and "thoughtless" ethics ultimately serve only to indict the society around her, the author of the *Female Spectator* similarly calls into question whether or not this kind of self-debasement is the only way to achieve literary success in the eighteenth-century marketplace.

And yet I am reminded that this questioning of forced debasement on a visceral level is precisely what characterizes the mock-heroic project—indeed, it is the appeal of this genre, I would contend, for both Haywood *and* Pope. As Rawson notes, it is Pope's nostalgic longing for an epic, inaccessible past that inspires the mock-heroic form, and Pope also finds himself locked out of a desirable past by virtue of an unchanging condition: the year and time of his birth. Pope thus struggles as a modern who can only content himself with rendering, as the subject of great epic, the lowly present, and it is this anxiety of lowness that repeatedly shows up throughout his poetry.[55] Haywood also sees the value of the mock-heroic in how it simultaneously diffuses and underscores the constant threat and possibility of violence: how women suffer the jeers of suitors—or the sneers of readers—simply by virtue of their sex. Betsy's is a mock-heroic predicament because it is borne of an inability to access or to control a desirable—in this case, patriarchal—system in a way analogous to the mock-heroic writer who seeks to assimilate, unsuccessfully, an inaccessible past. Haywood exploits its inherent vulnerability in a way that underscores the impossibility of female autonomy in a system that views such a proposition as fundamentally comic.

In 1752, Haywood is again charged with "Dulness," this time by Henry Fielding, who brings "B——T—" to court in *The Covent-Garden Journal*. Of this charge, Betsy is initially found guilty but—unlike the prolific Eliza and her babes—she's acquitted on the basis that "no single Instance hath been shewn where any Author of Grub-street hath paid any Tribute to the Kingdom of Wit, but have in all Ages claimed, had, and used the full Privilege of being as dull as they please."[56] In Fielding's mock-trial, Haywood is again vilified for her "Dulness"—but this charge is precisely what enables her to take an established, if unieviable, seat among the Grub-Street hacks. Unlike Pope, who in the *Dunciad* challenges the very legitimacy of Haywood's writing, Fielding places her firmly within a literary tradition—albeit a crude and popular one. Though a far cry from the excoriation she receives at the hands of Pope, the charge ultimately remains the same, and Haywood finds herself, decades later, still unceremoniously lumped in with the dunces by the triumphant mock-heroics of her rivals.

Notes

1. In 1785, Clara Reeve famously applauds Haywood in *The Progress of Romance* for "employ[ing] the latter part of her life in expatiating the *offenses* of the former." See *The Progress of Romance, Through Times, Countries, and Manners, with Remarks & Etc.* (London: Printed for the author, 1785); reproduced in Eliza Haywood, *The History of Miss Betsy Thoughtless*, ed. Christine Blouch (Petersborough, ON: Broadview Press, 1998), 642. For a nuanced reading of Haywood's later "didacticism," see Deborah J. Nestor in "Virtue Rarely Rewarded: Ideological Subversion and Narrative Form in Haywood's Later Fiction," *Studies in English Literature 1500–1800* 34 (1994): 579–98.

2. Some of the most important critical works engaged in the project of recovering Haywood as a novelist have either looked at *Betsy Thoughtless* cursorily or have omitted the novel entirely, including Ros Ballaster's *Seductive Forms: Women's Amatory Fiction from 1684 to 1740* (Oxford: Oxford University Press, 1998) and Paula Backscheider, in her essay "The Novel's Gendered Space," *Revising Women: Eighteenth-Century "Women's Fiction" and Social Engagement* (Baltimore: The Johns Hopkins University Press, 2000), 1–30. This is largely because both Ballaster and Backscheider isolate

the early 1700s as the formative moment for the eighteenth-century novel, although Backscheider is careful to provide her reader with a "good thick description[. . .] of an author's world" (2), one that admits the crucial interplay between male novelists (like Defoe, in Backscheider's example) and female novelists. I would agree wholeheartedly with Backscheider that this is a crucial and necessary project, while underscoring that this mutually-influential relationship between male and female authors carries forward into the mid-century, as evidenced by *Betsy Thoughtless*.

3. John Richetti, "Histories by Eliza Haywood and Henry Fielding," in Kirsten T. Saxton and Rebecca P. Boccicchio, *The Passionate Fictions of Eliza Haywood: Essays on her Life and Work* (Lexington, KY: The University Press of Kentucky, 2000), 248.

4. While readers of the novel can easily register a shift from the explicitly promiscuous tenor of Haywood's earlier writings towards the more 'acceptable' topics of courtship and marriage, *Betsy Thoughtless* does clearly extend some of the concerns and strategies of Haywood's other works, such as *Love in Excess* (1719) and *Fantomina; or Love in a Maze* (1725) in ways that have only recently been discussed. Critics have begun to see *Betsy Thoughtless* as on a continuum with Haywood's works rather than as a departure from it. See, for good examples of this trend, Helen Thompson's *Ingenuous Subjection: Compliance and Power in the Eighteenth-Century Domestic Novel* (Philadelphia: University of Pennsylvania Press, 2005), and Emily Hodgson Anderson, "Performing the Passions in Eliza Haywood's *Fantomina* and *Miss Betsy Thoughtless*," *The Eighteenth Century: Theory and Interpretation* 46, no. 1 (Summer 2005): 1–15.

5. For Claude Rawson, it is the "non-deadliness" of the battle without killing that marks it, even as it is seriously and graphically violent. See "Mock-Heroic and English Poetry" in *The Cambridge Companion to the Epic,* ed. Catherine Bates (Cambridge: Cambridge University Press, 2010), 172.

6. See, again, Rawson's discussion in "Mock Heroic and English Poetry," esp. pages 169–172.

7. Milton, *Paradise Lost*, bk. 4, lines 348–9.

8. See Sophie Gee's discussion of Belinda in her contribution to his volume, "Heroic Couplets and Eighteenth-Century Heroism: Pope's Complicated Characters," esp. page 10 where she also discusses the relationship of Belinda to Milton's Eve.

9. Toni Bowers, *Force or Fraud: British Seduction Stories and the Problem of Resistance, 1660–1760* (Oxford: Oxford University Press, 2011), 4.

10. Richard Terry, *Mock-Heroic from Butler to Cowper: An English Genre and Discourse* (Aldershot: Ashgate, 2005), 8.

11. Ibid., 9.

12. See Richetti, "Histories," and also Christine Blough's introduction to the Broadview edition of *Betsy Thoughtless* (see note 1), 7–18.

13. In this way, Fielding perhaps has more in common with Pope's *Dunciad* than he does with *The Rape of the Lock*, but still for Pope the "lowered reality" of the *Dunciad* is not an "analogue" for heroism but rather its "antithesis." See Rawson, "Mock-Heroic and English Poetry," 180.

14. For an excellent discussion of the continuities between Haywood's early and later fiction, see Aleksondra Hultquist, "Haywood's Re-appropriation of the Amatory Heroine in *Betsy Thoughtless*," *Philological Quarterly* 85, nos. 1–2 (Winter-Spring 2006): 141–65.

15. Michael McKeon, *The Secret History of Domesticity: Public, Private and the Division of Knowledge* (Baltimore: Johns Hopkins University Press, 2005), 408.

16. Ballaster, "A Gender of Opposition," in *Passionate Fictions* (see note 3), 147.

17. Ibid., 149, 151.

18. Ibid., 149.

19. Haywood, *Betsy Thoughtless* 36–7.

20. Haywood, *Fantomina and Other Works*, eds. Alexander Pettit, Margaret Case Croskery, and Anna C. Patchias (Petersborough, ON: Broadview Press, 2004), 42.

21. Haywood, *Betsy Thoughtless,* 236–237.

22. Ibid., 238.

23. Ibid., 239.

24. Ibid., 131.

25. Ibid., 56.

26. For recent discussions of "rape culture" not limited to literary examples, see studies like Jackson Katz's *The Macho Paradox: Why Some Men Hurt Women and How All Men Can Help* (Napierville, IL: Sourcebooks, 2006) as well as influential documentaries like *The Bro Code: How Contemporary Culture Creates Sexist Men*, DVD, directed by Thomas Keith (Northampton, MA: The Media Education Foundation, 2011).

27. "He then took the liberty of reminding her, that a young lady more endangered her reputation, by an acquaintance with one woman of ill fame, than by receiving the visits of twenty men, though professed libertines.—To which she replied, that for the future she should be very careful what company she kept, of both sexes." Haywood, *Betsy Thoughtless,* 241.

28. Ibid., 240.

29. Ibid., 240–241.

30. See my discussion of Trueworth and Andrew Thoughtless on pages 72–73 of this essay.

31. Haywood, *Betsy Thoughtless*, 634.

32. Richetti, "Histories," 248.

33. Haywood, *Betsy Thoughtless*, 127.

34. Ibid., 213.

35. Andrea Austin, "Shooting Blanks: Potency, Parody, and Eliza Haywood's *The History of Miss Betsy Thoughtless*," in *Passionate Fictions* (see note 3), 269; emphasis added.

36. Ibid., 269.

37. In this, Haywood actually aligns herself with a sentimental tradition of persecuted virtue that is often believed to originate with Samuel Richardson's *Clarissa* and manifest—as extreme parody—in works by the Marquis de Sade. See R.F. Brissendon, *Virtue in Distress: Studies in the Novel of Sentiment from Richardson to Sade* (Harper & Row, 1974).

38. Haywood, *Betsy Thoughtless*, 350.

39. Ibid., 385–6.

40. Ibid., 387.

41. Ibid., 142.

42. Ibid., 93.

43. Ibid., 419.

44. Ibid., 420.

45. Ibid., 425.

46. Ibid., 429.

47. Ibid., 276.

48. Ibid., 277.

49. Oakleaf, "Circulating the Name of a Whore: Eliza Haywood's Betsy Thoughtless, Betsy Careless, and the Duplicities of the Double Standard," *Women's Writing* 15, no. 1 (2008), 107.

50. Alexander Pope, *The Dunciad Variorum*, in *The Twickenham Edition of the Poems of Alexander Pope,* ed. John Butt, vol. 5, *The Dunciad*, ed. James Sutherland, 3rd ed. (London: Methuen & Co., 1963), 2:150–1, 2:155–6. Pope's evocative metaphor—disparaging Haywood's book as bastard children—imagines her writing as an unnatural form of sexual generation; throughout *The Dunciad*, such images of aberrant generation are deployed to malign bad writing as a form of literary parasitism and postlapsarian, even apocalyptic, moral corruption.

51. See Bower, *Force or Fraud*, page 3, where she argues that it is Belinda's "Earthly Lover" that "makes her vulnerable to the 'Fatal Engine.'"

52. Haywood, *Selections from the Female Spectator,* ed. Patricia Meyer Spacks (New York: Oxford University Press, 1999), 8.

53. See Juliette Merritt's excellent discussion of *The Female Spectator* in *Beyond Spectacle: Eliza Haywood's Female Spectators* (Toronto: University of Toronto Press, 2004), particularly the introduction, pages 3–24, in which she connects the epistemological gains of the female spectator to *Betsy Thoughtless*, albeit to different ends than I aim at here.

54. The complete passage reads: "To confine myself to any one Subject, I knew, could please but one kind of Taste, and my Ambition was *to be as universally read as possible*: From my Observations of human Nature, I found that Curiosity had, more or less, a Share in every Breast; and my Business, therefore, was to hit this reigning Humour in such a manner, as that Gratification it should receive from being made acquainted with other People's Affairs, should at the same time teach everyone to regulate their own." In Haywood, *The Female Spectator*, 9; emphasis added.

55. See, for example, Pope's *Eloisa to Abelard* (1717).

56. Henry Fielding, *The Covent Garden Journal*, ed. Gerard Edward Jensen, 2 vols. (New York: Russell, 1964), 1:229–31, quoted in Haywood, *Betsy Thoughtless*, 640.

3

THE NOVEL'S POEM ENVY:
MID-CENTURY FICTION
AND THE "THING POEM"

Christina Lupton and Aran Ruth

I N 1760 *POLLY HONEYCOMBE*, a single act play satirizing
the appetite of young women for novels, became a minor hit on the London
stage. George Colman's heroine, Polly, is presented as being overtly absorbed in
the pages of fiction: she reads from her favorite plots, preaches to her servants
of their excitement, and tries as hard as she can to live her life according to the
precepts of modern fiction. Mid-century advice literature, as we know, is full of
warnings against such an attempt being dangerous to the morality and good sense
of young women.[1] Colman's play, however, composes a somewhat unusual argument against novels by drawing out the irony, rather than the danger, of Polly's
position: the kind of adventure for which novel-reading primes her turns out to be
palpably difficult to realize as the reader of novels. During in the play, Polly must
frequently put her bound and printed books aside in order to participate in the
more interesting traffic in poems and love notes that cross her domestic threshold.
An important effect of the farce is thus to bring novels into focus as objects duller
in their paper trajectories than the more ambulatory verses that Polly and readers
of *her* narrative handle. Written by professionals for bored young women who will
consume them en masse in stifling domestic settings, novels are excluded, and exclude their readers, from the performative sphere to which occasional, ephemeral,
and materially-charged writings can claim to belong.

This is an unusual way to think about the novel, which is normally seen as
having set the mid-century literary bar low partly precisely because of the kinds of
vicarious involvement invited from its readers. If, we are trained to think, novelists
aspire to greater things than Richardson and Fielding promise, it is to the kind of
literary respectability that poetry models; one that involves sublimating the material

conditions of writing to a literary project of transcendence. But Colman's play puts novels in a new light, suggesting that for a moment they could appear disreputable partly because of their dullness as objects, sequestered from the world of circulation, and at a disadvantage against the kind of writing that solicits readers' action and attention in its materiality. Thus, *Polly Honeycombe,* written at a point when the novel had entered into common use as a form of entertainment, ridicules fiction for having become formulaic and derivative, and does so partly by pointing to the pages on which it is delivered being sterile couriers of life.

Our argument in this chapter concerns the way that poetry becomes a model for the novel at this historical juncture—not on the basis of its formal or generic distinction from prose fiction, but because of the limited action it supports at the level of its textual materiality. Novels, we will argue, may be generically superior to bits of verse, scraps of unpublished writing, but they are more inhibited than these kinds of writing when it comes to the energy of their circulation and their ability to effect people as objects. To use the terms of Bruno Latour, poems of a particular kind become actants in the networks of the novel, while novels themselves remain more difficult to conceive in these terms.[2] As actants, the poems discussed here make certain connections and events possible, providing evidence of the adventures a circulating piece of paper might have. This is not to say that poetry becomes an alternative to the novel in any simple way; rather, in the case of *Polly Honeycombe* at least, the desirability of the poem as an artifact is due to the novel's prizing of a certain kind of action. Thus, it is novel reading that makes Polly such an ardent follower and proclaimer of verse. And, as we show later in this chapter, the mid-century prose forms of the it-narrative and the sentimental novel follow the traffic in scrappy and unpublished verses.

Poetry in Motion

The fact that bits of paper become actants in the world of eighteenth-century fiction does not fully explain, of course, why it should be poetry that is written on them. Love letters and notes might do just as well. But handwritten poems are imbued with a particular liveliness as things—one that is captured both in their locodescriptive potential, and because the anthology form, in which poetry was beginning to appear in the mid-century, lends itself to the suggestion that poems are things that get arranged and collected as physical pieces of writing on the move. The most famous collection of poems from the period is Robert Dodsley's *Poems by Several Hands* (1748–58). Due to its first volume's popularity as an anthology and the individual success of several of the poems it contains, *Poems by Several Hands* is now understood as having been crucial in forming the English literary canon, providing in the form of an anthology what George Bornstein has described as a "dehistoricising field that obscures the social embedding of its own contents."[3] Yet *Poems by Several Hands* can also be seen, Michael Suarez points out, as a volume like the miscellanies popular at the time, that evidences its poems being "scavenged" and materially appropriated.[4] Many of the poems collected here were literally the remnants of other projects left on Dodsley's desk and even the title, *Poems by Several Hands*, can be seen to present the collection as more proximate to a sheaf of handwritten notes than as an edition as we now understand it.

One poem in particular suggests the attraction of seeing a poem in this way. Found in volume two of *Poems by Several Hands*, "Written on a Paper, Which Contained a Piece of Bride-Cake. Given to the Author by a Lady," describes a piece of bridal cake, left under a shepherd's pillow at night as a magic charm.[5] Only the paper wrapping remains, having been, as the title states, "given to the author by a lady." On this paper, the origins and properties of the cake are described:

> The Cyprian queen, at Hyman's fond request,
> Each nice ingredient chose with happiest art;
> Fears, sighs, and wishes of th'e enamour'd breast,
> And pains that please are mixt in every part.[6]

The second stanza begins, "This precious relick, form'd by magic pow'r." While the cake itself is the immediate referent for these lines, they also speak to the piece of paper that has wrapped it, and which is now also a "relick." The "Bride-Cake" poem illustrates the appeal of imagining paper itself having a history, and of doing this in a context where a text might claim its own status as a thing that has been used-up, or used for non-literary purposes. Once the cake has either crumbled beneath the pillow, been eaten, or decayed, its wrapper comes into focus as something that can witness its existence—not as an empty shell, but as an object that has acquired its own right to speak by virtue of its material survival. In this way, the "Bride-Cake" poem becomes what Barbara Benedict describes as a "thing-poem," a poem that "make[s] the present moment of encounter with the thing the poetic occasion."[7] Bringing wrapping paper into focus suggests poetry's place within—rather than its exemption from—the ranks of perishable and tactile objects.

Sara Dixon's "From a Sheet of Gilt Paper. To Cloe" (1740) makes this way of looking at a poem both explicit and more complicated. Here, the paper on which a love letter has been written protests against the manner in which it has been deployed. "Touch'd with Remorse, tho' guiltless, I/Approach you with Humility," says the paper to Cloe:

> With Lyes and Nonsense slubber'd o're,
> More vile by far, than heretofore,
> Take this kind Hint, despite the 'Squire,
> And gently lay me—on the Fire.[8]

Appealing to the idea of paper having a story to tell that is more authentic than the one related at its surface, the paper urges Cloe to look accordingly at the object in her hands and to respond physically to the letter as physical evidence of its author's disingenuity. Introducing this idea that paper could object to the words written on it, Dixon is also gesturing to the stories that might be gleaned at this same juncture were we all to read as Cloe does, through and around the lines addressed to her, to the object that speaks of the human condition.

One anthology, *The Merry-Thought: or, The Glass-Window and Bog-House Miscellany* (1731), is particularly insistent on the fact that its contents have been collected on this basis, as physical scraps of the situations out of which they were born. The verses tossed together there align themselves by this logic with the interest of the surfaces to which most of them refer—in this case, to the panes of glass, walls, and locations on which the fictional editor, "Hurlothumbro" claims that the graffiti in his collection has been found. This includes lines that describe themselves written on the bog-house wall as their author was using the toilet, and those that reference the glass on which they have been inscribed. "From the Playhouse Boghouse" we get:

> Good folks, sh-t and write and mend honest Bog's
> > Trade,
> For when you sh-t Rhymes, you help him to Bread:
> He'el feed on a Jest, that is broke with your Wind,
> And fatten on what you here leave behind.[9]

And "From the Bog-House at Pancras Wells," scatological scribblings that occasion a response:

> Hither I came in haste to sh—t,
> But found such Excrements of Wit,
> That I to shew my Skill in Verse,
> Had scarcely Time to wipe my A—se.
> *Underwritten.*
> D—n your Writing,
> Mind your Sh-t-ng.[10]

Hardly "reliks" of the conventional kind, the fascination of these poems is that they report in scandalous ways on their own production, but also that they turn up in a collection that preserves them as pieces of the action they describe.

Hurlothumbro makes much of his anthology as a jumbled assortment of items, collected and sent in from various locations in London, and arranged by chance in the pages of his four volumes. The introduction to part II states: "You will pardon the Editor that he does not put Things in better Order . . . he believes the Preface is in the Middle of the Book; but I dare swear you'll find it somewhere or other, and so read on."[11] The preface is indeed found after fourteen pages of miscellaneous graffiti, and it is noted that even this preface is "from a Paper found in the Street at Twelve at Night, 1708. near Covent-Garden."[12] Prefaced by and filled with found artifacts, the miscellany claims to be the kind of writing that will re-join as recycled paper the material environment from which it has been plucked. "Nay," states Hurlothumbro, "I have even found some of the *Spectator's* works in a Bog-House, Companions with Pocky-Bills and Fortune-telling Advertisements [. . .] and I dare venture to affirm, no Body shall pretend to use any of your bright Compositions for Bum-Fodder, but those who pay for them."[13]

Colman was well aware of the appeal of thinking about writing as a textual artifact. As editor of the *Connoisseur*, he had published a piece in 1755 describing the way a reader, "Orator Higgins," has learnt to write by tracing the graffiti on display around London, and to read by noticing handbills and magazine covers available on the street. Higgins shuns the idea that "learning is only to be acquired in the closet, and by turning over a great number of pages" and celebrates the way the streets teem with words.[14] Although one cannot conclude from this that Colman finds graffiti superior to printed matter, or ephemera to canonical books, the piece forecasts the mood in which he will write *Polly Honeycombe*, as a text that satirizes the novel for not being able to turn itself into an event, or offer itself up as a site of physical adventure—poems, he implies, can turn up in public spaces, while novels keep readers out of them.

The It-Narrative and the Poem

The anthology that presents itself as a collection of papers, and the poem that directs attention to the peregrinations of the material surface on which it is written, can be connected to another mid-century form important to the development of the novel: the it-narrative, or circulation narrative. These narratives document from the first-person point of view the rapid and unpredictable movement of an object or animal through the hands of a sequence of owners, from paupers, to garret poets, to professionals, to aristocrats. Typically, they include the tales of objects—corkscrews, petticoats, hackney-coaches—whose fascination as narrators lies almost exclusively in this range of movement. For this reason, these tales are oddly positioned as evidence of their own movement as texts. While some, including *History of Pompey the Little* (1751) and *Chrysal* (1760) were published as full-length, multi-volume novels, most appeared as magazine pieces, participants in the circulation of more ephemeral writing where their sensitivity to the lowest kind of paper substratum makes them a particularly reflexive kind of prose. In the same way that thing-poem or the graffito can introduce its physical substratum as the basis of its interest as an object, it-narratives such as *Adventures of a Quire of Paper* (1779) and *The Genuine and Most Surprizing Adventures of a Very Unfortunate Goose-Quill* (1751) claim the surface of the maligned, circulating, and recycled page as the one on which their characters accumulate.

Leah Price has made an important case for these narratives as inspiration for the nineteenth-century novelist to think about the circulation of books.[15] Nineteenth-century it-narratives such as "Adventures of a Bible" illustrate her point, which is that novelists are inspired in imaging the life of characters in part by the versatile positions that textual objects have in Victorian culture. But the earlier examples of it-narratives are slow to pick up on novels as things that circulate with any kind of excitement; they are more likely to introduce unpublished papers, love letters, and occasional poems as the forms of writing to which adventure accrues. *The Adventures of a Quire of Paper* (1779) would, for instance, have come to an end if the paper that speaks in it were ever to become a novel: it is precisely because it is a surface used for scribblers, kite-makers, and writers for the magazines, that the paper can keep up its satirical reports on the society through which it passes and the paper industry of which it remains a self-evident part.[16] And the narrator of *The Genuine and Most Surprizing Adventures of a Very Unfortunate Goose-Quill* (1751) fulfills its mandate as roving narrator by being used to write recipes, notes, and two dubious poems that are interpolated into the text. In this spirit, it-narratives regularly showcase poems as the kind of object to turn up within their own rapid economy of circulation. The Goose-Quill's poems, for instance, are presented as being like the quill that wrote them, objects that fly around and appear casually on display.[17] In *Adventures of a Rupee* (1782), the coin that speaks is also lined up with a poem. Dropped by a young owner into the grass of St. James' park, the Rupee is found by a poet whose lines, "To My Anna" "fell from his heart."[18] The poem, which is printed so as to appear a physical trophy of

the rupee's narrative, seems to have been exchanged for the coin as an item for exhibit. The way in which "To My Anna" shows up on display models what it would
be like for the coin itself to appear there, with both embodying at their surface the
contingency of their adventures.

More generally, it-narratives that are interested in the circulation of paper
represent scribbled verses as the form that work undertaken by tortured young
writers is likely to take. In *The Adventures of the Black Coat* (1760) the coat is
rented by a wan author and has "some detatched pieces of poetry in blank verse,
and other papers of the like nature put into my pocket."[19] The sedan, narrator of
a two-volume narrative by this title from 1757, details the different passengers it
carries, including a young author who is going to pay homage to his bookseller.
This author, another poet with "his pockets bursting with papers," is en route to
his bookseller and describes out loud a strategy he has used to promote his collection, which he has inscribed as:

> Verses sent to the right honourable the earl of—, with a present of some
> goldfish; another to lady Harriot—, with Johnson's dictionary, a third
> to Sir William—. with a Cheddar cheese, a Normandy cow, shells for a
> grotto, or a painting of Annibal Caraccio's.[20]

Pairing his poems with these luxury goods will allow him, he speculates, to suggest that he is "no common garrateer poet" struggling for money and to imply his
acquaintance with the nobility. But the pairing also promotes the idea the way that
his poems, like many of the speaking objects in these tales, are more notable for
the nature of their exchange as objects between members of different classes rather
than for anything they say.[21]

Poems also turn up in it-narratives as what Benedict calls "things-in-time."[22]
This is the kind of thing the "Bride-Cake" poem claims to be: the refuge of a context that has already past, but which remains in circulation. In the *Adventures of a
Pincushion* (1784), the pincushion is wrapped as a present to a child in what turns
out to be a fragment of poetry, which is then reproduced within the narrative.[23]
Edward Thompson's "Indusiata; or, the Adventures of a Silk Petticoat" (1773),
another narrative that embeds several examples of poetry within its text, points to
the history of these poems as key to the petticoat's own material circulation. In the
final stage of its adventures, the petticoat describes its transformation, from rags to
"a spotless, snowy sheet of paper. I was next purchased by the Stationers, who sold
me to a certain Ovidian Captain, who first stained me with a lovesick rhapsody
to his dearest *Pollia*."[24] This Ovidian Captain is Thompson, author of the poem

"Pollia" and of "Indusiata," both of which come into focus at the end of his tale as material forms in which the adventures of the petticoat are to continue. While we are vaguely led to believe that the petticoat has metamorphosed into the magazine in which "Indusiata" is published, it is the interpolated poem that seems more specifically to have been written on paper made from the petticoat.

It-narratives are important experiments in suggesting that writing, rather than being part of the life led in the closet, might be seen as a material participant in the dramas of need, commerce, and desire that propel the circulation of material objects in the eighteenth century. Their most direct gestures of self-referentiality involve the representation of magazine writers, who write prose by the page in the way it-narratives themselves were produced. But they are notably silent on the subject of their existence or reception as novels, suggesting that this is a material form of writing which would provide a limited vantage point were it to report on its own reception. In this respect, Mark Blackwell has argued, it-narratives profit at the level of their own conceit from seeing themselves as genre fiction, more likely to be passed along or recycled that bound and shelved.[25] And they are keen to register poems, particularly unpublished poems, as slipping and sliding around in the world in the same way that their narrators do. Their self-reference is skewed, not towards the world of print and preservation in which novels ideally arrive, but towards the occasional poem that travels through the world on the verge of being scrap paper.

The Thing Novel

There are several mid-century novels that interpolate texts in this mode, pointing in not-quite-self-referential moments to writing that flies low enough under the literary radar to garner attention as paper on the move. We want to end here with three cases that mark the slightly different fortunes of the story we have told, of the novel's mining the verse scribble's energy for a model of its own activity as paper: the case with which we began, of *Polly Honeycombe*; the case of Henry Mackenzie, who was inspired by graffiti to present his novels as circulating pieces of paper; and the last case of *Emma*, which suggests how a new hierarchy is established in favor of the novel as a less visibly material form.

As we have already suggested, *Polly Honeycombe* points to the limitations of novel reading in its own material history as well as in its internal debates. At the level of its plot, the heroine Polly has two lovers. The one she would like to marry, Mr. Scribble, who dashes off love ditties and letters that are secretly delivered to

Polly, and the one Polly's father would prefer Polly to wed, Mr. Ledger, the banker. These two suitors are treated according to the styles of text their names indicate: Ledger is the reasonable, dependable, and thoroughly boring option, embodying the ennui and repetitious life of marriage; Scribble is the madcap and adventurous lover. The dichotomy between them is qualified, however, by Polly herself. Because of her addiction to novels, Polly characterizes Ledger and Scribble through the lens of her favorite books. Ironically, this means that she perceives her own preference for Scribble, who embodies a form of writing unlike novels, as being scripted by novel reading, while she spurns Ledger, the character most like novels, on the same grounds. One of the things that makes Scribble so attractive is the form of his notes to Polly. Pestering her nurse for a letter from Scribble, Polly shows herself more practically interested in these papery details than in the twists of the plot she reads about: "will he write it in lemon-juice, and send it in a book, like blank paper? Or will he throw it into the house, inclosed [*sic*] in an orange?"[26] When Scribble's verse missive finally arrives, Polly is delighted, but she derives much greater satisfaction from the mystery of its arrival—from the question of how it arrived, and how it came to be in her nurse's hand—than from the formulaic protests of love it contains.

The packaging of Colman's play extends this emphasis on letters that enthrall at the level of their production and reception. While *Polly Honeycombe* was published under the satirical title "A dramatic novel," Colman invented for his text a history of reception very different to that of a novel. Appended to the play, Colman included a preface, a large part of which pretends to be a letter from his mother critiquing a rehearsal of the play that she has attended. At the end of the letter, this fictional mother concedes that, although the play itself is unsatisfactory, the point against novel-reading is well made. She then relates her own experience of visiting her creditor and finding that this gentleman's daughters have left a table piled with the remnants of their novel-reading: "the third volume of Betsy Thought-less, the New Atlantis for the year 1760, and the Catalogue of the Circulating library" lie half-bound and "much thumbed and in a greasy condition" amongst dresses, fans, and gloves.[27] Colman's preface ends by reproducing this library catalogue. The amusingly dramatic and formulaic titles of the novels on offer in 1760 are underscored by their readers being absent from the room—occupied, the scene implies, with more genuinely interesting activities than reading novels. This gives a new ring to Polly's declaration that "A novel is the only thing to teach a girl life, and the way of the world, and elegant fancies, and love to the end of the chapter," by putting emphasis on the fact that chapters, and novels themselves, are actually destined to be left behind as their readers engage in action.[28]

Poetry plays into this not only because Scribble's notes to Polly contain verse, but because it is as verse that Colman's text travels through the city that his fictional novel readers occupy. The Prologue and Epilogue to the play, spoken by Scribble and Polly respectively, appeared as advertisements to the play in the newspapers, with Scribble's satirical epilogue introducing novels as the successors to romance, inferior not only in their tempting women into sin, but also for their physical and formal predictability:

> ROMANCE might strike our grave Forefather's pomp.
> But NOVEL for our Buck and lively Romp!
> Cassandra's Folio's now no longer read,
> See, two Neat Pocket Volumes in their stead!
> And then so sentimental is the Stile,
> So chaste, yet so bewitching all the while!
> Plot, and elopement, passion, rape, and rapture,
> The total sum of every dear—dear——Chapter.[29]

Polly's epilogue, spoken as she has confounded her parents and avoided marriage to Ledger, comes as a jaunty rebuke to Scribble, announcing the victory of novel-readers:

> Let us to arms!—Our Fathers, Husbands, dare!
> Novels will teach us all the Art of War:
> Our Tongues will serve for Trumpet and for Drum;
> I'll be your Leader—General Honeycombe![30]

This victory, however, is modified by the Epilogue's performative context as verse printed in the newspaper. Its setting undermines Polly's vote of confidence in novel reading, indicating that she has only fulfilled the novel's promise of adventure by breaking its moral, formal, and generic codes. The form of writing and reading that the Epilogue promotes is so palpably occluded by its appearance in these venues that Polly's words underscore the irony which has all along been evident in Colman's play: that truly adventurous lives will be modeled on and fueled by forms of writing other than those kept in closets and contained in "Two Neat Pocket Volumes." *Polly Honeycombe* defies the rules, in other words, by making itself a novel that circulates in verse.

In contrast to Colman, who used the label "novel" to describe a text that does little else to deserve the title, Henry Mackenzie helped resuscitate the popularity of the genre by making prose fiction more like a "thing-poem" in its alignment with the paper on which it appeared. Mackenzie's strategy of presenting his sentimental novels as found documents is well known. *The Man of Feeling* (1771), *The Man of the World* (1773), and *Julia de Roubigné* (1777) are each framed by a narrative in which an editor claims to have discovered the pages of the novel as a bundle of papers, rescued from becoming wrapping paper for groceries, gunwadding, or from being abandoned pathetically in a box. What is less well-known, however, is that Mackenzie was privately quite obsessed with verse that embodied the plight of its writer, in particularly with the graffiti that he found engraved on windows as he was travelling throughout the highlands.

In 1770, Mackenzie was gratified to find the following verse engraved at an inn:

> Of all the ills unhappy mortals know,
> A life of wandering is the greatest Woe;
> On all their weary ways wait Care and Pain,
> And Pine, and Penury, a meagre Train:
> A wretched exile to his country send,
> Long with Grief and long without a friend.

Transcribing the lines into a letter to his cousin, Elizabeth Rose, Mackenzie introduces this verse as "Six lines which I met with on a window at Dalnecardoch, the only tolerable window-poetry I could find on the road." He goes on to describe the way in which he first encountered these lines as deeply moving: "If these are original, which I imagine they are, they were probably (as I devoutly belive'd at the Time I read them) the Production of some unfortunate Native of the Highlands, who had been actually in the Situation they describe."[31]

Mackenzie's package to Rose also includes his rewriting of the verse he has found. "Poor Soul!," he reflects of the original writer, "'twas all the Expression which the reality of his Greif could allow; I, who could feel it only in Idea, who had Leisure and Safety for the Task, would lengthen it out a little; and accordingly produced an Elegy, which I send you enclosed."[32] Suggesting that time and paper have allowed him to expand upon the writer's feelings, Mackenzie offers the "The Exile" as an elaboration of the window poem. This poem describes in the third person the return of a Highland native to the village in which he led a small band of Jacobites against the English. In battle, Mackenzie's clansman has seen his comrades killed and been forced to flee, leaving his village to be sacked and his new wife killed. When he returns it is with withered limbs in his "Scottish weeds" to a scene of ruin, "where half a column now derided the great/where half a statue yet records the brave" to die, in the last lines of the poem, on his wife's long neglected grave.[33]

At the level of its content, "The Exile" sentimentalizes poorly the scenario that has fascinated Mackenzie, of a writer who summons up the energy to write on a window even as he is in the throes of grief. But what makes his reworking of the poem interesting for our case is that Mackenzie then laid his own unpublished poem aside for ten years before rediscovering it as a document that had acquired some of the power he'd originally attributed to the graffito. In 1780, he published it in his own journal, *The Mirror*, along with a frame narrative that invents a history of transmission for the poem. The editor is besieged, Mackenzie begins, by contributions of poetry he cannot use. This piece, however, has merited attention because "the gentleman from whom I received it says, he has been informed that it was founded on the following inscription (probably written from real feeling) on the window of an inn, situated in the Highlands of Scotland." Mackenzie then includes the same lines he had sent ten years earlier to Rose, and follows them up with "The Exile," which, he coolly writes, "points out the fatal consequences of such treasonable attempts, and represents the distress of the person described, in a very interesting and pathetic manner."[34] As a result of this introduction, readers encounter "The Exile" as evidence of a complicated story in which many sympathetic readers have responded to each other's verses as relics. Handed down to a gentleman who is informed of its original debt to a window poem (of which he must also have a copy), the poem has supposedly been sent to the *The Mirror*. The editor has then published it neither as poetry, to which he is in principle opposed, nor as Jacobite sympathy, but as a tribute to the afterlife of the lines located on the glass of a lonely inn. In its published form, "The Exile" appears as the story of these lines' unlikely survival, but it also becomes proof of Mackenzie's attempt to make the printed text into the kind of referent that the one written on glass has been. The narrative Mackenzie tells, and in which he casts himself as slightly sentimental editor, is an object in print that speaks to a complex history of being lost and found.

Even in witnessing such print artifacts, Mackenzie implies, the reader participates in an emotional history of their being passed along; one that makes reading part of the action, rather than something that must be laid aside before the reader can act, and that affirms writing as an activity that speaks, not just through, but also as, letters on the page. This is the kind of history that Mackenzie aspires to give his own novels as he situates them as found things, manuscripts that reward responsiveness and bring deserted piles of paper into view as the conduit of distant human relationships. Polly, in other words, might have found redemption in the form of sentimental novel reading Mackenzie imagines, for here novels become "actants" in the sphere occupied by their characters. Cried over, abandoned, and treasured as evidence of the sentimental narrator's efforts, the pages of the senti-mental novel resemble more closely the graffito on the window-pane than those of the book that is unimaginable as part of the active life of romantic adventure it describes.

Our last example, Jane Austen's *Emma*, suggests a different kind of satisfac-tion that became available to the novel reader who could distinguish herself from the reader and scribbler of verses. In this novel, verses appear in the material form of the "ciphers" and "trophies" collected in Harriet's "thin quarto of hot-pressed paper."[35] The riddle represented in full is Mr. Elton's courtship poem, presented to Emma under cover of it's being a contribution to Harriet's book. Whereas this is just the kind of missive that Polly lusts after, pointed and active in its design and unworthy of posterity as anything but a keepsake, in *Emma* this verse ap-pears on a distinctly lower register than the novel itself. Austen's quick-minded heroine instantly deciphers its meaning (although she blindly sees it as an address to Harriet rather than herself) and strips it of deeper literary credibility. Harriet, meanwhile, hangs onto the verse as a trophy although its meaning has eluded her at every textual level. If the paper on which the note is written has any kudos as the protagonist of its own small drama (Mr. Elton claims deceptively that the poem has been given to him by a friend), it is clearly of a very limited kind, which Harriet will have to renounce as she learns more about human relationships and intentions. The view of paper, or any other kind of object, being an actant in the world of romance is here rendered childish and superstitious.

In the hierarchy that Austen helps to establish, the novel's power lies in its being able to register real kinds of romantic and everyday action without material involvement in their unfolding. Although letters continue to operate as key links in the chain of events, the narrator's agile perspective transcends and trumps the level at which they could be described as actants, and there is very little suggestion in later eighteenth-century fiction that novels themselves should be handled as documents with a physical history. Romantic verse, on the other hand, continues to expand creatively upon the locodescriptive promise of earlier "thing-poems" and "poems-in-time," making the scene of inscription and composition into an important point of reference in the feelings it invokes.[36] The entanglement of the novel and the poem as genres that share an interest in their own material fate passes, in other words, as more familiar generic distinctions are established. But the metamorphosis of the thing poem's particular energy into Romantic poetry cannot be distinguished entirely from the history of the novel: one of the effects of mid-century fiction was, as we have shown, to point readers quite squarely in this direction even as most novelists chose not to follow it themselves.

Notes

1. See, for instance, Jacqueline Pearson, *Women's Reading in Britain, 1750–1835: A Dangerous Recreation* (Cambridge: Cambridge University Press, 1999).

2. Bruno Latour, *Reassembling the Social* (Oxford: Oxford University Press, 2005), 54.

3. George Bornstein, *Material Modernism: The Politics of the Page* (New York: Cambridge University Press, 2001), 14. For the argument about politics of the eighteenth-century anthology see Barbara Benedict, *Making the Modern Reader: Cultural Mediation in Early Modern Literary Anthologies* (Princeton, N.J.: Princeton University Press, 1996).

4. Michael F. Suarez, "Trafficking in the Muse: Dodsley's Collection of Poems and the Question of Canon," in *Tradition in Transition: Women Writers, Marginal Texts and the Eighteenth- Century Canon*, eds. Alvara Ribeiro, S.J., and James G. Baskers (Oxford: Clarendon, 1996), 311.

5. Robert Dodsley, *A Collection of Poems in Two Volumes. By Several Hands* (London, printed for G. Pearch, No 12, Cheapside, 1768), 46.

6. Ibid., 46.

7. Barbara Benedict, "Encounters with the Object: Advertisements, Time, and Literary Discourse in the Early Eighteenth-Century Thing-Poem," *Eighteenth-Century Studies* 40, no. 2 (2007): 205

8. Sarah Dixon, "From a Sheet of Gilt Paper. To Cloe" in *Eighteenth-Century Poetry: An Annotated Anthology*, ed. David Fairer and Christine Gerrard, 2nd ed. (Oxford: Blackwell, 2004), lines 44–47.

9. Hurlothrumbo. *The Merry-Thought: or, the Glass-Window and Bog-House Miscellany*, Parts 2, 3, and 4 [1731–?] (Los Angeles: The Augustan Reprint Society, Publication Number 221–222, 1983), 5.

10. Hurlothrumbo. *The Merry-Thought: or, the Glass-Window and Bog-House Miscellany*, Part 1 [1731] (Los Angeles: The Augustan Reprint Society, Publication Number 216, 1982), 30.

11. Ibid., 1

12. Ibid., 14.

13. Ibid., vi.

14. George Colman, *The Connoisseur* 86 (September 18, 1755): 517.

15. Leah Price, *How to Do Things With Books in Victorian Britain* (Princeton, N.J.: Princeton University Press, 2013).

16. "Adventures of a Quire of Paper" in Mark Blackwell, ed., *British It-Narratives, 1750–1830*, 4 vols. (London: Pickering and Chatto: 2012), 4:23–40.

17. *The Genuine and Most Surprizing Adventures of a Very Unfortunate Goose-Quill* in Ibid., 4:1–22.

18. *Adventures of a Rupee* in Ibid., 1:27–72; 67.

19. *The Adventures of a Black Coat* in Ibid., 3:111–52; 128.

20. *The Sedan*, in Ibid., 3:79–110; 98.

21. This is the argument that Nicholas Hudson makes for the power of it-narrators in "It-Narratives: Fictional Point of View and Constructing the Middle-Class" in *The Secret Life of Things: Animals and Objects in Eighteenth-Century England*, ed. Mark Blackwell (Lewisburg, PA: Bucknell University Press, 2007).

22. Benedict, "Encounters with the Object," 199.

23. *The Adventures of a Pincushion* in Blackwell, *British It-Narratives, 1750–1830*, 4:57–78; 75.

24. "Indusiata: or, The Adventures of a Silk Petticoat" in Ibid., 3:153–180; 179.

25. Mark Blackwell, "Hack-Work: It-Narratives and Iteration," in Blackwell, *The Secret Life of Things*, 187–217

26. George Colman, *Polly Honeycombe, a Dramatick Novel of One Act* (London: Printed for T. Becket, at Tully's-Head in the Strand; and T. Davies, in Ruffel-Street, Covent-Garden, 1760), 4.

27. Ibid., vi.

28. Ibid., 4.

29. Ibid., xiv.

30. Ibid., 46.

31. Henry Mackenzie, *Letters to Elizabeth Rose of Kilravock*, ed. Horst W. Drescher (Meunster: Verlag Aschendorff, 1967), 26.

32. Ibid., 63.

33. "The Exile" in *The Mirror* 85 (1780), 167.

34. Ibid, 167.

35. Jane Austen, *Emma* (Oxford: Oxford World's Classics, 2003), 53.

36. Geoffrey Hartman suggests that Romantic "nature-inscription" poetry forms a direct link between the poetic forms we have discussed here and later Romantic verse. Hartman, "Wordsworth, Inscriptions, and Romantic Nature Poetry," *Beyond Formalism* (New Haven, Yale University Press, 1970), 207.

4

"TO DELINEATE THE HUMAN MIND
IN ITS ENDLESS VARIETIES":
INTEGRAL LYRIC AND CHARACTERIZATION
IN THE TALES OF AMELIA OPIE

Shelley King

AT THE OPENING OF THE TWENTY-FIRST CENTURY critics have searched for a language to describe the place of poetry in the novels of the long eighteenth century, seeking to understand it not simply as lyric impulse and interiority transferred to prose narrative, but as lyric verse proper. Leah Price, in *The Anthology and the Rise of the Novel: From Richardson to George Eliot* (2003), offers the term "inscribed lyric"[1] to focus attention on the way in which the verses inserted into Ann Radcliffe's Gothic fiction interrupt or delay the narrative force of the plot; Gabrielle Starr, in *Lyric Generations: Poetry and the Novel in the Long Eighteenth Century* (2004), proposes the term "absorbed lyric" to describe "fragments woven into novels, like *Love in Excess*, but also the songs of *The Beggar's Opera*," elements that she designates as moments of lyric artifice that throw into relief the "rhetorical construct of realism."[2] Although both phrases are illuminating in their contribution to our understanding of the insistent presence of poetry in novels of the Romantic period, neither quite encompasses the place of poetry in the fiction of Amelia Alderson Opie (1769–1853). In tale after tale, lyric insertions—whether as songs performed or poems read—become instruments that illuminate and propel the plot rather than interrupting or inhibiting it; in tale after tale, Opie constructs the lyric effusions of her protagonists as necessary and natural contributions to the psychological realism of their characterization rather than extraneous embellishments standing in artificial opposition to it.

Most approaches to understanding the lyric in the novel, including in an understated way those of Starr and Price, begin from the genre-based assumption that the presence of verse in a prose medium is anomalous—that it requires explanation because the apparent constructedness of verse is construed as exotic when located within the confines of a naturalized prose medium. Hence the inclusion of lyric is sometimes understood as self-interested, either because it offers an opportunity for an author who is also a poet to showcase a second artistic talent or because, in the case of the incorporation of lines written by others, it demonstrates a literary pedigree and exploits the cachet of a writer's command over cultural capital. Both interpretations could feasibly be applied to Opie's work, which sometimes quotes from contemporary sources but that increasingly features original verses of her own composition. I begin from a different premise: what if lyric performance were regarded as a natural rather than an artificial human activity? What if people sang songs, quoted verses to each other, and wrote poetry as part of their ordinary human existence? That, I argue, is the case in Opie's fiction. The "reality" she chooses to represent is inhabited by characters who live rich aesthetic lives—they paint and draw, they sing and play music, and yes, they even read and write poetry. Such a representation reflects both the author's own lived experience and that of her imagined subjects. Thus, in working with Opie's fiction, the phrase I would suggest is not the "inscribed" or "absorbed" lyric, but rather the "integral lyric," so central is poetry to the development of realist characterization in her tales.

The inner complexity of Opie's protagonists reflects an emphasis on psychological realism that has been recognized as a dominant feature of the novel as it developed at the end of the eighteenth century. In *The English Jacobin Novel 1780–1805*, Gary Kelly establishes two key features of the fiction produced by the proponents of modern philosophy including Opie's circle of friends in the 1790s—Mary Wollstonecraft, William Godwin, Thomas Holcroft, and Mary Hays in particular: "The English Jacobin novels were doubly 'philosophical' . . . . they contained many dialogues, monologues, and 'perorations' on serious and weighty topics," and they were "philosophical in structure and technique"—that is, "they tried to show how their characters had been formed by circumstances, and how character and incident were linked together like the parts of a syllogism."[3] This concept is perhaps expressed most clearly by Opie's contemporary Mary Hays in her 1798 essay "On Novel-Writing," in which she describes the social value of the novel as a literary form: "The business of familiar narrative should be to describe life and manners in real or probable situations, to delineate the human mind in its endless varieties, to develop the heart, to paint the passions, to trace the springs of action, to interest the imagination, exercise the affections, and awaken the powers of the mind."[4] For Opie, the lyric impulse formed part of that "endless variety" of the human mind, and she frequently relies on poetry as an index of emotional response—a means of revealing and developing the subjectivity of her characters, both those who read and those who write, and especially those who perform and those who listen, activities that she represents as belonging to "life and manners in real or probable situations." Her work suggests that, by the end of the eighteenth century, poetry and the novel had developed a symbiotic relationship in which the fiction of sensibility incorporated the powerful effect of lyric verse as a recognizable aspect of individual character. Perhaps even more intriguingly, life borrowed from fiction as verses written and performed by characters in Opie's tales were sometimes set to music for performance in the "real" world. Opie's works thus provide an opportunity to consider not only the function of poetry in the context of the rise of realism and the novel but also the reintegration of the lyric elements derived from fiction into contemporary cultural performance. This paper will look first at the role of poetry and song in the daily life of Amelia Opie, then turn to her increasingly complex use of lyric verse as an element of realist characterization in her fiction before concluding with an examination of the reciprocal transfer of her verses between fiction and life.

The Poetry of Everyday Life

Opie's correspondence and related memoirs demonstrate repeatedly the casual interweaving of poetry, song, and fiction in her daily life. In one of her earliest extant letters a youthful Amelia Alderson writes to Mary Wollstonecraft regarding her own initial disappointment on meeting philosopher William Godwin and her subsequent appreciation of his better qualities. To illustrate her point she paraphrases a popular song: "I am reconciled even to *flattery*, Horne Tookian flattery from his lips, & in the words of a charming song 'I fear him less, but love him more' (Do you know the next lines? Don't laugh if I transcribe them—.)"[5] She goes on to quote the next eight lines of a poem that first appeared as "To *****" in the volume *The Muse's Blossoms* (1769), but that had been recently republished as "To S—a R—s" in *The Ladies Magazine* in 1791:

> When with licentious boldness fired
> I dared to clasp what I admired
> Dared round thy neck my arms to twine
> And press thy balmy lips to mine,
> Then thro' my soul sharp poison ran
> Twas then my keenest pangs began
> For by the dangerous bliss half slain
> I drag a life of ceaseless pain.[6]

If Wollstonecraft was familiar with the lyrics, then the lines offered a shared laugh at Alderson's cheeky reversal of a young man's lament over the power of his nymph; if not, they provided a means of using verse to communicate a ruefully erotic playfulness. A few months later she describes for Wollstonecraft an evening's visit to a friend in the country:

> Part of our amusement was painting or working, while the master of the house read to us Mrs. Radcliffe's Italian! Mem: when I marry to have it inserted in the marriage articles that my husband shall read to me in an evening while I work &c. God grant he may also be able to converse well on the merits of the work he has just read, for at least two hours after supper. Then my greatest idea of domestic happiness will be realized.[7]

Amelia Alderson's letters to Wollstonecraft reflect the casual ease with which literature, which doubtless on occasion included lyric verse, was integrated into her daily experience, and the degree to which both private reading and aural reception of public literary performance form an important element of her cultural life in the 1790s.

The correspondence of the first decades of the following century similarly demonstrates the ways in which poetry and song formed an integral part of Opie's subjectivity and thus might also be understood as central to her understanding of the production of fictional character. Her memoir of John Opie, published with his lectures for the Royal Academy following his early death, draws a portrait of a domestic life that hints that the wish she had expressed to Wollstonecraft of a marriage imbued with literary performance was fulfilled. John Opie, she writes, "delighted in Italian music and Italian singing . . . and though he had not the smallest pretension to voice, he sung comic songs to me occasionally; and repeated comic verses with such humourous and apt expression" that she was persuaded that he might have been an actor rather than a painter.[8] More common are accounts of Amelia Opie's own penchant for lyric performance, both public and private. Harriet Martineau records an anecdote of the domestic life at the studio *cum* home of the Opies at Berners Street: "Once at a morning party where Mrs Opie was charming her guests by her singing, he put his head in at the door with, 'Amelia, don't sing; I cannot paint if you do,' and she immediately obeyed."[9] Her proclivity for performance even extended to the streets of Paris. During a brief visit to that city following the Peace of Amiens in 1802, a companion recalls "how she sat on the Boulevards and sang with heart and voice, 'Fall, tyrants fall.'"[10] Perhaps the most detailed account the degree to which the composition and performance of poetry might structure the author's life derives from a visit to Holkham Hall, the seat of Thomas Coke, MP for Norfolk. In a letter to her cousin Eliza, Opie relates how she entertained her hosts:

> After breakfast I sung several songs to Miss Coke, Miss Auson, & the Blackwell's—I then *wrote* and read to them 12 lines to *Mr. Coke*. I then read my *epistle* from Mary aloud. . . . After dinner Lady Andover who is ill, begged *she* might hear the *epistle*—I went to her bedside, & read it to her & sung two songs besides & repeated the lines.[11]

For Opie as a practicing poet, a country house party provided an excellent opportunity both to repay the kindness of her hosts by singing and composing celebratory verses, and to test out works in progress—in this case, her series of verse epistles written in the voice of Mary, Queen of Scots.[12] Lyric composition here hints at the importance of Romantic sociality in literary production, while lyric utterance transcends the solipsism of its usual associations with purely subjective experience and it becomes instead a mode of social integration. It is from this background of lyric community that Opie constructs her increasingly realist fiction.

Character, Context, and Shared Lyric Experience

In her analysis of the function of lyric in Charlotte Smith's *The Old Manor House*, Ann Wierda Rowland identifies two related strategies in the deployment of lyric verses in the novel: the first, quotation of poetry drawn from world of the reader, Rowland characterizes as "invaluable to the novel's project of representing and inserting itself into a recognized cultural field."[13] That is, poetry becomes primarily a means of connecting real readers with fictional characters whose "interiority is, in fact, a communal construct crafted in a series of movements out into a shared social world" marked by verse. Rowland's second category includes original verses inserted into the text, usually figured as the work of a principal character: "Poetic effusion . . . not only gives form to emotion and memory; it also gives embodiment and place to [a character's] emotional life."[14] These two strands offer a useful entry point for discussion of Amelia Opie's incorporation of lyric in her fiction. In my discussion of *The Father and Daughter* (1801), I trace Opie's use of the first category, the quoted lyric familiar to the reader, where poetry serves as a remedy for psychic disorder, and as a touchstone of authentic connection between characters; in "The Orphan," from *Simple Tales* (1806), I look at Rowland's second category, original lyric composition, which serves as both symptom of psychic disorder and necessary means of communicating culturally unspeakable interior truths. Together these examples demonstrate the degree to which Opie conforms to the emerging norms of Romantic fiction in her use of lyric, but also the degree to which she renders lyric utterance as integral to the realist representation of character in her fiction.

Starr comments in *Lyric Generations* that "[c]oncerns over how to make personal experience available—meaningful, affective, comprehensible, communicable—would find a different set of answers in novels than in poetry."[15] In Opie's novels, however, poetry becomes the answer, a central vehicle for making personal experience "meaningful, affective, comprehensible, [and] communicable" both to other characters and to the reader. We encounter the affective power of lyric poetry and its particular ability to communicate individual subjectivity in Opie's first acknowledged novel, *The Father and Daughter*. It is perhaps difficult for modern readers to comprehend the popularity of this brief, melodramatic tale of Agnes Fitzhenry, the beloved daughter seduced by Clifford, and of her doting father, who descends into madness when his only child elopes. The seduction plot has run its course by the first quarter of the novel, and the remaining pages focus on Agnes's attempts to redeem her sexual error by caring for her demented parent who no longer recognizes her as his daughter. After realizing that the madman roughly dragged away by keepers from their initial meeting on the moor is in fact her father, Agnes pleads her case for access to Fitzhenry to the governors of the asylum. When she is given permission to see him, the first significant encounter between father and daughter is shaped by remembered lyric song and the connection it provides:

> When they had made one turn round he garden, he suddenly stopped, and began singing—"Tears such as tender fathers shed," that pathetic song of Handel's, which he used to delight to hear Agnes sing: "I can't go on," he observed, looking at Agnes; "can you?" as if there were in his mind some association between her and that song; and Agnes, with a bursting heart, took up the song where he left off.
>
> Fitzhenry listened with restless agitation; and when she had finished, he desired her to sing it again. "But say the words first," he added: and Agnes repeated—
>> "Tears such as tender fathers shed,
>> Warm from my aged eyes descend,
>> For joy, to think, when I am dead,
>> My son will have mankind his friend."

> "No, no," cried Fitzhenry with quickness, "for joy to think when I am dead, Agnes will have mankind her friend." I used to sing it so; and so did she, when I bade her to do so. O! she sung it so well!—But she can sing it no more now, for she is dead; and we will go look for her grave."[16]

Part of what makes this lyric inclusion integral to the narrative is its ability to draw together both thematic and contextual elements. Published just a decade after George III's very public mania, *The Father and Daughter* is grounded in new approaches to dealing with mental disorders. Agnes's care for her father resembles the "moral management" that had begun to displace more brutal treatment in asylums. And just as modern neuroscience has found that music offers therapeutic benefits for patients with a wide range of psychiatric disorders, so the physician in Opie's tale advises "Let him resume his usual habits . . . let him hear his favourite songs . . . and if you should not succeed in making him rational again, you will at least make him happy."[17] Here the lyric fragment, in Rowland's terms, "insert[s] itself into a recognizable cultural field" of shared lyric experience in that the reader may recognize Handel's song, but it is also implicated in the broader cultural field of contemporary medical discourse.

Beyond these contextual gestures, however, the lyric articulates a shared past specific to Agnes and her father, illuminating the way in which their connection to Handel's song transcends simple domestic performance, as the language of the lyric is reshaped to reflect their unique individual circumstances. In their collaborative revision of the phrase "my son shall have mankind his friend" to "Agnes shall have mankind her friend," father and daughter mark the common cultural artifact as a lyric performance specific to their own lives. By inserting Agnes's name into the song, they revise its circumstances to reflect their own, and in so doing incorporate its affect as an aspect of their own relationship. The inclusion of the lines thus becomes more than a calculated expenditure of cultural capital as the rendering of this moment of lyric engagement not only evokes a powerful affective response in both characters and readers, it also models the permeable boundaries of art and life.

Subjectivity, Interiority, and Connection

If *The Father and Daughter* is deftly sparing in its integration of four brief lines of poetry familiar to the reading audience, focusing on the importance of that shared lyric experience to Agnes and her father, Opie's later narratives frequently include lengthy original verses whose composition is ascribed to her fictional characters.[18]

The four poems included in "The Orphan. A Tale. Founded on a Well-known Fact" from *Simple Tales* (1806) demonstrate the degree to which Opie could make lyric production central to both plot development and characterization. Published five years after *The Father and Daughter*, *Simple Tales* is a collection of twelve tales in four volumes, in which Opie developed and extended her exploration of psychological realism.[19] Reviews of *Simple Tales* were mixed, but most placed the work in the context of the development of a new emphasis on what might be termed "domestic realism" in prose fiction. The review in *Literary Journal* opens with an anecdote illustrative of this point:

> Before these tales came into our hands, we accidentally heard a lady in conversation criticising them. They were, in her opinion, very common place things. They contained nothing sublime, nothing striking, nothing wonderful, but consisted of every day transactions which every one knew and every body might write. She gave Mrs. Opie no credit for invention, and concluded that she would make a very bad romance writer. We instantly recollected Partridge's remarks on Garrick, and could not but consider the lady's observations as an unintentional eulogium on the composition whose value she endeavoured to depreciate.[20]

Although contemporary readers might still expect to encounter the conventions of romance in their fiction, many reviewers recognized the important shift taking place. The writer for *Literary Journal* continues "Mrs. Opie agrees with us that simple tales ought to be simple, and that it is much better to afford *a correct picture of the real manners of life* than to fill volumes with extravagance and absurdity," arguing,

> When fiction is employed to represent human nature, as it is to give an accurate view of characters and manners, to trace the means by which they have been formed, and the consequences naturally resulting from them to point out the real causes by which virtue and vice are generated and fostered, and consequently to enlighten mankind with respect to the proper mode of cherishing the one and avoiding the other, then a simple tale may justly be considered as an apt and pleasing illustration of the soundest philosophical reasoning.[21]

Significantly, the tendency of Opie's characters to write and read verses seems not to have struck the lady reader as "wonderful," nor does the reviewer classify it as a form of "extravagance and absurdity," suggesting that such activities might readily fall under the classification "real manners of life." The integration of lyric verse would appear to be "an every day transaction."

"The Orphan" brings together Opie's growing reputation as a writer of both sentimental fiction and popular lyric verse by including four original poems totaling some eighty lines on the subject of "Secret Love."[22] The female protagonist, Jane Vernon, is the ward of adoptive parents Mr. and Mrs. Hanbury. Their son, George Douglas, becomes the object of Jane's affections over a series of vacations taken at home during his years at Cambridge. As her unrequited passion deepens, Jane falls into what today might be recognized as a clinical depression, characterized by headache, lethargy, and physical decline. Jane's worsening condition is diagnosed by her physician as arising from "mental uneasiness. 'She has something on her mind,' said he; 'and unless you can prevail on her to disclose what it is, believe me, it is not in the power of medicine to save her.'"[23] He proposes a diagnosis of "secret and unrequited love," and offers as evidence her manuscript poems: "'Nay, madam, if you require any further proof,' said the physician, 'read these verses, which, as she lay in a restless sleep just now, dropped from her pillow. They are torn through, you see, and she was probably going to destroy them entirely, when some one came in and interrupted her.'"[24] At this point the reader is not given access to the verses, and can gauge their force only indirectly from the responses of the physician and the Hanburys. Not until the "good old folks" attempt to persuade Douglas on his next visit home to reciprocate her love are we—and he—privy to the lines.

Sent to his room that he might "read them when he was alone," Douglas gradually unveils the lyrics that lay bare Jane's heart and an emotional connection she has been too modest and too properly feminine to reveal by word or gesture. The first poem opens "Not one kind look—one friendly word!" and closes with Jane's sense that her "timid, hopeless passion" bids her heart "*silence* keep, and *break*."[25] The second poem, "To me how dear this twilight hour," expresses Jane's contentment with Douglas's mere occasional proximity and her realization that his scholarly ambitions eclipse any interest in her domestic presence. The third poem details her efforts to disengage her mind from its fascination with Douglas. Her lyric utterance is effective, sending Douglas into a frenzy of remorse: "'I will read no more,' said Douglas, pacing the room:—'Oh! What a monster I was to be blind and insensible to so true and delicate an attachment! And yet, what a coxcomb must I have been, had I thought myself capable of inspiring such a passion as this!'"[26] Despite his resolution to "read no more!" one final song falls from the manuscript pages and Douglas cannot resist perusing the lines. In the verses opening "One little moment, short as blest" he is reminded of the single instance of tender physical contact between them, when, astonished by her physical decline, he carried her from the coach to the house:

> His frame with strong emotion shook,
>   And kindness tun'd each falt'ring word;
> While I, surpris'd, with anxious look
>   The meaning of his glance explor'd.
>
> But soon my too experience'd heart
>   Read nought but generous pity there;
> I felt presumptuous hope depart,
>   And all again was dark despair.[27]

Such is the power of Jane's lyric verse to communicate her passion and her pain that Douglas resolves instantly to marry her. In the cold light of morning, however, he recognizes that although he is sufficiently moved to save her life, he does so from compassion rather than love: "That man is a contemptible being who lives for himself alone, and I have it in my power not only to save the life of one of the most amiable of human beings, but bid her live for happiness dear as unexpected.—No: mine she shall be; and I doubt not but that in a short time my love will fully equal hers."[28] Having thus rationalized his course of action, Douglas proposes marriage, but his protestations of affection prove too much for the weakened Jane, and she succumbs to the excess of feeling attendant upon requited love.

"The Orphan" concludes with an exhortation from the narrator to young women to eschew allowing themselves to embrace hopeless passions, no matter how worthy the object. In this tale lyric verse becomes a plausible index for the expression and communication of intense emotions. However, Jane's poems are cast as the private effusions of a diseased mind, and though they may stir pity and compassion in the sensitive and reflective reader, they are thus regarded more as symptoms of psychic disorder than evidence of complex virtue. Here lyric verse is less the expression of an admirable affection than a means of articulating the heightened psychological states of grief and despair. They may express the force of deep personal feeling, but they also reveal the dangers attendant upon unregulated affection.

Permeable Boundaries

Perhaps the most compelling evidence of the permeable boundaries between lyric in realist fiction and lyric in real life may be found in the ease with which poetry initially published as song lyrics for contemporary performance found its way into Opie's fiction, and poetry initially ascribed to her fictional characters was subsequently set to music for performance in life. *Tales of the Heart* (1820) provides examples of both practices. In 1806 Opie wrote the lyrics for "Mad Song," one of the *Eight Ballads* set by Wesley Doyle and published in London by Chappell, a company known for its sheet music for domestic performance. Some fourteen years later Opie places this song on the lips of a character in "Love, Mystery and Superstition" from *Tales of the Heart*. Similarly, her "Henry, a Song" first published with sheet music in 1818 is described as the character Laura's "favourite song" and incorporated into the tale "After the Ball."[29] In these tales, songs familiar from contemporary performance play a significant role in suggesting the character of fictional figures, but more frequently the lyric progression moves in the opposite direction. Of particular interest are three songs performed by characters in "A Wife's Duty"—"Oh! That I could Recal the Day," "Fairest, Sweetest, Dearest," and "The Heart's Dearest Pleasures Await Thee at Home"—which begin as songs performed by fictional characters and are later set to music. All three are framed by the first-person narrator in terms of the powerful connection between heard lyric performance and its ability to speak to individual circumstances. The preamble to the first poem, "Oh! That I could Recal the Day," connects the individual state of mind to the subjective interpretation of texts:

> But as the hypochondriac, when he reads a book on diseases, always finds his own symptoms in every case before him, so I in the then existing state of my feelings always brought home every thing I heard or read to my own heart; and two of the songs which were sung that night accorded so well with my own state of mind, that I felt the tears come into my eyes as I listened; and during the following one Pendarves sighed so audibly, that I imagined *he* felt great sympathy with the sentiments; and that idea increased my suffering.[30]

The analogy establishes the practice of interpreting textual encounters through personal experience. The songs produce in the protagonist, whose "feelings always brought home every thing [she] heard or read to [her] own heart," both an emotional release through tears and a sense of shared response in Pendarves' sighs. The next song, "Fairest, Sweetest, Dearest," is similarly framed:

> The other song was only in unison with my feelings in the last lines of the last verse. Still, while my morbid fancy made me consider them as the expression of my own sentiments, I listened with such a tell-tale countenance, that my delicacy was wounded; for I saw that my emotion was visible to those who sat opposite to me.[31]

Lyric performance produces visible signs of emotion in the listener, allowing an interior emotional state to become readable by the sensitive observer. This use of inserted lyrics is common enough in the fiction of the period, but action that follows is certainly less frequently found, and points to an important but often overlooked lyric economy underlying such depictions of social performance.

Helen, the protagonist, interrupts her narrative to comment on what the reader might perceive as the unrealistic memory she demonstrates regarding the lyrics:

> You will not, I conclude, imagine that I remember these songs only from having heard them that night, especially as they have very little merit; but the truth is, I was so pleased with them, because I fancied them applicable to my own feelings, that I requested them of the gentlemen who sung, and they were given to me.[32]

Lyric possesses exchange value within this culture, and here the song circulates within the tale as a mark of social favour and connection. The subsequent lyric, however, moves from the represented social world of the tale immediately into the social—and economic—world of the reader. When the final song, "Duet" ("Say, why art thou pensive, beloved of my heart," later published as "The Heart's Dearest Pleasures Await Thee at Home"), appears in the tale, it is accompanied by a footnote reading "This duet is set, and about to be published, by Westley Doyle, Esq."[33] The lyric just read was soon to be available for purchase so that readers might perform it within their own circles.[34] We know that Doyle also set the previously mentioned *O! That I Cou'd Recall the Day, a Ballad, Written By Mrs. Opie* in 1821, and it is possible that the 1825 date assigned by cataloguers to "The Heart's Dearest Pleasures" in *One Duet & Six Ballads . . . By Wesley Doyle* is somewhat late, and that the publication of the lyrics with score was designed to accompany the release of the collection.[35]

Opie even goes so far as to model the purchase of songs for just such affective personal purpose within the tale itself. Seymour Pendarves, the male protagonist, recognizes the appropriateness of the duet's discussion of potential infidelity and domestic happiness to their own situation, and suggests to his wife that they purchase it to perform themselves:

> "That is a charming duet," cried Seymour when it was ended. Then leaning behind Lady Martindale and Lord Charles, and calling to me, he said, with a look from which my conscious eye shrunk, "Helen, I admire the sentiment of that duet. I think, my love, we will get it—we should

sing it *con amore*, should we not?" I could not look at him as I replied, "*I* could, I am *sure.*"

"Silly girl," he added in a low and kind tone, "and so, I am sure, could I."

I then ventured to raise my eyes to his; and his expression was such, that I felt quite a different creature, and was able to enjoy the rest of the evening.

But why do I enter into these minute and unimportant details? Let me efface them—but no, perhaps they may chance to meet the eyes of some whose hearts have felt the anxieties and the vicissitudes of mine, and to them they may be interesting.[36]

"A Wife's Duty" thus offers evidence of a cultural expectation that lyrics would circulate between the real world and the world represented in realist fiction, that the presence of lyric poetry in fiction was neither necessarily a mark of high culture or self-conscious literariness within the prose medium, but rather a natural appropriation and incorporation of lyric by both readers and authors. Readers of Opie's novels and tales might well recognize fictional characters performing songs that were familiar from their own lived experience, and others might recognize friends and relatives performing songs first associated with figures drawn from her fictional works.

This interplay of the real, the lyric and the realist proclaims a relationship more complex and more compelling than arguments based on difference in genre assert regarding the function of poetry in the novel. One explanation of the close ties between fiction, poetry and readers can be found in studies of the idea of the audience and the public sphere in this period. Jon Klancher, in *The Making of English Reading Audiences, 1790–1832*, suggests ways in which this relationship develops. Klancher explores the connection between regarding oneself as an individual reader and being aware of oneself as part of an audience, a collective he describes as "complicated social and textual formation" with "interpretive tendencies and ideological contours."[37] As he notes, "the terms 'reader' and 'audience' are hardly neutral; they have come to mean in post-Romantic critical discourse, two contradictory and seemingly irreconcilable intellectual frameworks: the one hermeneutic or 'critical,' the other empiricist or 'sociological.'"[38] Klancher's study aims to bring these concepts into conversation by invoking Bakhtin and Voloshinov to explain the emergence of a readerly subjectivity that understands itself in relation to a social group:

Recognizing the trace of a socially alien discourse in the language I read, I must also recognize evidence of a relationship to that discourse different from mine: competitive with mine, perhaps antithetical to mine. I thus become aware of myself as a reader situated in a particular social space—a reading space among differing reading acts. But I do not recognize this merely as an individual reader. This awareness dawns on me by putting me in the realm of a *kind* of reading act that I share with some but decidedly do not share with others.[39]

Klancher's focus in this passage lies in explaining the ways in which readers come to a sense of community through a recognition of difference. Concomitant with this awareness of difference, however, is the consciousness of similarity: readers develop a sense of community through recognition of specific shared discourses and experiences. In the case of Opie's works, they recognize that her songs express shared social experience both through the subjective emotions they chart, the shared affect they produce, and the cultural performances they represent. Her fictional characters are rendered more realist because they, too, participate in lyric utterance shared by her readers.

Opie also uses lyric to explore connections between identity, affect and performance, in the process constructing a surprisingly complex subjectivity that incorporates sophisticated understanding of ideology and cultural position. "The Hindustani Girl's Song" was one of Opie's most popular lyrics written early in her career, and it was one that the author herself was famous for performing. As the biographical sketch of Opie published in *The Cabinet* in 1807 notes,

> Mrs. Opie . . . may be said to have been unrivalled in that kind of sing-
> ing in which she more particularly delighted. Those only who have heard
> her, can conceive the effect which she produced, in the performance
> of her own ballads. Of these, "*The Poor Hindu*," was one of her chief
> favourites, and the expression of plaintive misery, and affectionate sup-
> plication, which she threw into it, we may with safety affirm, has never
> been surpassed, and very seldom equalled. Mrs. Opie may fairly be said
> to have created a style of singing of her own, which though polished and
> improved by art and cultivation, was founded on that power which she
> appears so pre-eminently to possess, of awakening the tender sympa-
> thies, and pathetic feelings of the mind.[40]

Like many of her songs, this one provided the singer with the opportunity to per-form the abject Other, a recurring strategy in Opie's lyrics whether the speaking subject of the song were a poor girl selling lace, as in "Fatherless Fanny," or a young woman driven mad by the death of her lover in "Mad Song." In this poem the girl is abandoned—sent up county—by her British lover when his bride arrives in India from Britain. The song articulates her love and longing as she is carried to her banishment, but also offers a critique of her lover's ranking of cultural differences through a comparison of the imagined conduct of the "British fair" with her own:

> Born herself to rank and splendour,
> Will she deign to wait on thee,
> And those soft attentions render
> Thou so oft hast praised in me?[41]

In its recognition of the ways in which cultural norms can both shape and challenge individual conduct, this song expresses an awareness of the impact of broader national and political forces on the feeling subject.

In her last acknowledged novel, *Madeline* (1822), Opie introduces a fragment of this song to comment on the unequal relationship between the protagonist and her aristocratic Scottish lover. At the nadir of the romance when the couple has been secretly wed according to the Scottish tradition, Madeline, the cottage girl raised by British minor gentry, begins to imagine herself as the abject Other of an imperial union, and Opie signals her protagonist's condition by integrating the early lyric into a journal entry:

> Day-break—still he has not been here! Well then, when next he comes
> he shall seek for me in vain. That song of the poor Hindoo, which you
> and he are so fond of, has been haunting me all day!
>
> "'Tis thy will and I must leave thee.
> Oh then best belov'd farewell!"
> Little did I ever think this song would be so applicable to my feelings!

Madeline subsequently returns her wedding ring and the only paper record of their Scottish union, with "written in the cover—'Thou are free!' 'Thy Poor Hindoo.'"[42] Nor is the comparison unprepared for, given that in the opening pages of her journal Madeline had previously recognized in accounts of colonial experience an analogue of her own return to Scotland from her adoptive home in England:

> How often have I pitied those poor Hindoos, who, if they leave their
> country, forfeit their caste, and wander unacknowledged and degraded
> ever after! *I* quitted my country and my family, and I am forced to return
> to them: and, spite of the caresses of my kindred when I left them, fear
> that they consider me as having forfeited my caste, and that their hearts,
> though not their tongues, disown me.[43]

Such levels of abjection affirm the parallels between Scottish and Indian colonial experience, and reveal the insufficiency of the Scottish marriage, provoked by jealousy and possessiveness and entered into under an act of filial disobedience contrary to edict of her Calvinist father. Rather than reflecting a more egalitarian Scottish tradition of cross-class marriages like that of Madeline's parents, it instead enacts an unequal union of colonially confused identities.[44] By invoking her own lyrics, sung by herself and scores of young women in the drawing rooms of British society to perform an abject feminine desire expressed through the voice of colonized subject, Opie connects readers to specific emotions of loss and abjection through the recollection of shared lyric moments. The affective power of lyric to simulate/stimulate emotional states blurs the boundaries between real and imagined experience.

Conclusion

The Father and Daughter, "The Orphan," "A Wife's Duty," and *Madeline* are but four among many tales in which Opie experimented with the inclusion of lyric verses in her prose narratives. And while doubtless, as Rowland notes of Charlotte Smith's insertion of original verses, such a strategy allows her "to showcase her own poetical work,"[45] the featured verses frequently contribute more than poetic ornament or the simple demonstration of a character's sensibility. More work, of course, remains to be done in exploring archival evidence of the application of literary paradigms to personal experience. For the most part we catch only occasional documentary glimpses of the ties between poetry and lived experience from letters, diaries, and memoirs, though with increasing digitization and search capabilities more intersections of art and life will undoubtedly be found. Sufficient evidence exists, however, to suggest that in Opie's fiction the verses are neither mere ornaments nor supplements to the real business of prose fiction in realist representation; rather, lyric verse is integral to the delineation of both individual character and social experience.

Notes

1. Leah Price, *The Anthology and the Rise of the Novel* (Cambridge: Cambridge University Press, 2000), 93.

2. G. Gabrielle Starr, *Lyric Generations: Poetry and the Novel in the Long Eighteenth Century* (Baltimore and London: Johns Hopkins University Press, 2004), 74.

3. Gary Kelly, *The English Jacobin Novel 1780–1805* (Oxford: Oxford University Press, 1976), 16.

4. Mary Hays, "On Novel Writing," *Monthly Magazine* 4 (1798), 181.

5. Amelia Alderson to Mary Wollstonecraft, 28 August 1796 (Abinger Collection, Bodleian Library, Oxford).

6. "To S——a R——s," *The Ladies Magazine* (1791), 48.

7. Amelia Alderson to Mary Wollstonecraft, 18 December 1796. Abinger Collection, Bodleian Library, Oxford.

8. Amelia Opie, "Memoir of John Opie," in *Lectures on Painting* (London: Longman, Hurst, Rees and Orme, 1809), 34–5.

9. Harriet Martineau, *Biographical Sketches 1852–1875*. 4th ed. (London: Macmillan & Company, 1876), 74.

10. Cecelia Lucy Brightwell, *Memorials of the Life of Amelia Opie: Selected and Arranged from Her Letters, Diaries, and Other Manuscripts* (Norwich, U.K.: Fletcher and Alexander, 1854), 117.

11. Amelia Opie to Eliza Alderson, n.d. Huntington Library, California.

12. In 1823 Opie published a series of eleven "Epistles Supposed to be Addressed by Mary, Queen of Scots, to her Uncles the Duke de Guise and the Cardinal of Lorrain" in the *European Magazine*. Interspersed with the narrative epistles are inset lyrics in which Mary intensifies personal affect. In this sequence, Opie combines the modes Starr sets in antithesis in her discussion of the place of lyric in the eighteenth century: "Accordingly, lyric gave way to the verse epistle as the dominant form of Augustan poetry. With its concentration on two civilized people speaking a common language of morality and discipline, the verse epistle produces a fiction of community to counter 'the haunting fear that one's own consciousness is all there is, and that the world and other people may be no more than figments of the solitary mind' (Dowling, *The Epistolary Moment*, 11). Poetic discourse takes place in a community of speakers, of friends exchanging letters in public and private." Starr quotes William C. Dowling, *The Epistolary Moment: The Poetics of Eighteenth-Century Verse Epistle* (Princeton, N.J.: Princetown University Press, 1991) in her *Lyric Generations*, 8.

13. Ann Wierda Rowland, "Romantic Poetry and the Romantic Novel," in *The Cambridge Companion to British Romantic Poetry* (Cambridge: Cambridge University Press, 2008), 130.

14. Ibid., 130, 131.

15. Starr, *Lyric Generations*, 13.

16. Amelia Opie, *The Father and Daughter, a Tale, in Prose*, 5th ed. (London: Longman, Hurst, Rees, and Orme, 1806), 113.

17. Ibid., 145.

18. These lyrics are incorporated in a variety of ways—in *Temper* (1812), the conniving Mrs. Felton passes off two songs by her ex-lover as her own in performance in hopes of impressing St. Aubyn with her vocal and compositional talents; in the epistolary *Madeline* (1822) the heroine sends five lyrics to her former governess to convey the state of her heart, as well as one fine elegy supposedly written by her spurned suitor that accentuates his character.

19. The terms "novel" and "tale" were often used interchangeably at the beginning of the nineteenth century, though Gary Kelly argues for the importance of the "tale" as a distinct fictional genre, with aims and techniques recognizably different from those associated with the novel at the end of the

eighteenth century: "to readers of this time this designation [as tale] would suggest a short narrative, probably dealing with rustic or provincial life and with daily and domestic reality, celebrating values of simplicity, naturalness, and candour, and perhaps featuring an eccentric storyteller as mediator of the simple matter." In Gary Kelly, *English Fiction of the Romantic Period 1789–1830* (London: Longman, 1989), 64–5. Kelly argues for the recognition of Opie's significance as an author of tales whose grasp of psychological realism makes her an important precursor of the later nineteenth-century novel. For the purposes of the present study, however, I will regard the tale as analogous to the novel in its use of lyric poetry to enhance psychological realism.

20. *Literary Journal, A Review* 2, no. 2 (August, 1806), 159. The reviewer goes on to suggest that although Opie is not thoroughly exemplary in her constructions, she nevertheless exceeds the common mark: "But to construct tales of this sort requires no ordinary share of judgment, discrimination, and accurate knowledge of human nature, and therefore it is, that so few have succeeded in this way. In the tales before us we meet with many things which serve to shew that Mrs. Opie does not possess the proper requisites to the extent that might be wished, but at the same time they in general furnish ample proof that she possesses them in a much higher degree than the ordinary writers of fiction." In Ibid., 160.

21. Ibid., 159.

22. To complicate matters, the poems would subsequently be republished two years later in her verse collection *The Warrior's Return and other Poems*, without any indication that they had first been part of her tale.

23. Opie, *Simple Tales*, 4:257.

24. Ibid., 4:260.

25. Ibid., 4:267–68.

26. Ibid., 4:270.

27. Ibid., 4:270.

28. Ibid., 4:242–43.

29. Amelia Opie, "After the Ball; or, The Two Sir Williams," *Tales of the Heart*, 4 vols. (London: Longman, Hurst, Rees, Orme & Browne, 1820), 1:306.

30. Amelia Opie, "A Wife's Duty," *Tales of the Heart*, 3:239–40.

31. Opie, "A Wife's Duty," 3:241.

32. Ibid., 3:243.

33. Ibid., 3:244.

34. The reach of Opie's lyrics is perhaps indicated by what the New York Public Library catalogue describes as "an unidentified miscellany of piano music and songs" published in Charleston by J. Siegling between 1819 and 1825; the collection includes the earlier song "Fairest, sweetest, dearest; [with] music by an amateur." Opie's songs had a transatlantic appeal, both to amateur composers and domestic performers.

35. See *O! That I Cou'd Recall the Day, a Ballad, Written By Mrs. Opie, the Music by Wesley Doyle Esqr.* (London: Chappell & Co., 1821) and *One Duet & Six Ballads ,with an Accompaniment for the*

Piano Forte, Composed and Inscribed to Thomas Moore, Esqr. By Wesley Doyle, Esqr. (London: Chappell & Co., [1825?]).

36. Opie, "A Wife's Duty," 3:245–6.

37. Jon Klancher, *The Making of English Reading Audiences, 1790–1832* (Madison: University of Wisconsin Press, 1987), 6.

38. Ibid., 9.

39. Ibid., 12.

40. *Cabinet, or, monthly report of polite literature, 1807–1808* 1 (June 1807), 218.

41. "A Hindustani Girl's Song," Music by Edward Smith Biggs. In *A Second Set of Hindoo Airs with English Words Adapted to Them by Mrs. Opie, And Harmonized for One, Two, Three, and Four Voices (or for a Single Voice) with an Accompaniment for the Piano Forte or Harp, by Mr. Biggs* (London: R. Birchall, 1800), Air 3.

42. Amelia Opie, *Madeline, A Tale,* 2 vols. (London: Longman, Hurst, Rees, Orme and Brown: 1822), 2:210–11.

43. Ibid., 1:35.

44. At this point Madeline flees once more to London, where she is "so fortunate as to hire a Scotch maid, well-recommended, to wait on [her child]" (Ibid., 231). Two months later Glencarron finds her and convinces her that she was "blinded by temper and jealousy" and that he had "rather played on [her] feelings to punish [her] injustice" (Ibid., 236). In order to forestall future evasion, this time Glencarron purchases a licence and vows to marry her "according to the laws of this country." Accordingly, "The Scotch maid went with us, and in an English church, and at an English altar, we vowed eternal fidelity" (Ibid., 237). This English marriage, however, for all its publicity in the anonymity of the metropolitan centre, offers little change for Madeline, as the secrecy continues and Glencarron's imperial nature is made ever clearer: "He says that I am now a wife, and a *slave* also, for never till now did I vow obedience to him; and never yet have obeyed him; but he declares he will make me better behaved now, for he knows I am too scrupulous not to act up strictly to vows made at the altar" (Ibid., 237).

45. Rowland, "Romantic Poetry," 131.

Part II

5

UNDIVIDING THE SUBJECT OF LITERARY HISTORY:

FROM JAMES THOMSON'S POETRY TO

DANIEL DEFOE'S NOVELS

Wolfram Schmidgen

L ET ME START BROADLY, even a little abstractly. Ian Watt established the arrival of the early English novel as a serious and exciting intellectual problem. In the decades following the publication of *The Rise of the Novel* (1957), the grand puzzle of the novel's emergence and development became one of the most compelling problems for literary historians working in the eighteenth century. The early English novel presented a unique opportunity. It allowed us to observe, seemingly for the first time in literary history, the formation of a genre in the broad light of historical day. While the beginnings of other genres were irretrievably lost in the mist of ancient time, the novel came into existence in a vividly documented environment: the sprawling print culture of the seventeenth- and eighteenth centuries. The early novel presented a privileged object not only in eighteenth-century English studies, but in the study of literature as such. Its analysis promised rich insights into the process of genre formation and literature's interaction with social, political, and intellectual history. Here, in the early eighteenth century, in an increasingly enlightened, commercial, and expansive Britain swayed by an emboldened parliament, literary form could be witnessed in the fullness of its interaction with history. It might even be possible to catch literary form at the very moment it crystalized out of the liquid mass of concrete human practice.

Heady prospects. They prompted us to place the novel at the literary center of the social, scientific, political, economic, and religious processes that reshaped European societies between 1500 and 1800. The novel became "the quintessentially modern genre," expressing the sweeping modernization of European society.[1] Socially, the novel was affiliated with class mobility; scientifically, with the close observation of particulars; politically, with liberalism and individualism;

economically with commercial society and exchange relations; religiously with Protestantism. Our stories about the origins and the effects of these affiliations prominently relied on a central narrative paradigm: the paradigm of differentiation. Differentiation came to assume its paradigmatic role in the eighteenth century, when thinkers such as Jean-Jacques Rousseau, Adam Ferguson, Adam Smith, and eventually Karl Marx began to argue that modern society came about through the differentiation of various kinds of labor, of persons and things, public and private spheres, male and female, individual and society, nature and society, and so on. In the nineteenth- and twentieth centuries, anthropologists, sociologists, and historians made differentiation the fundamental figure of modernization. They looked at differentiation positively and negatively, as gain or loss or a bit of both, and literary historians followed suit, building the case of the early novel's alliance with the history of European modernization.

Since the political and historical turn of the 1980s, literary scholars have deepened their attachment to the notion that the rise of the novel is the central literary episode in the story of modernization. The novel has become the protagonist in our literary histories, embodying the modern not only formally, by its loose and leveling combination of various modes and materials, but also thematically, through its portrayal of interiority and individualism, of the materials and routines of daily life, of social mobility, and of carefully situated manners, be it spatially, socially, or sexually (typically, the tension between a heterogeneous form in which various materials mingle freely and the differentiating work happening at the level of content goes unnoticed).

Claiming the novel, that quintessentially modern creature, as our own has given eighteenth-century studies extensive cultural capital. We may not always have known this, but we have all felt it. Many a graduate student (myself included) has been gained by exposure to the exciting story of the rise of the novel and the birth of the modern. The novel has given us a precious public legitimacy. I have found it tempting, for example, to tell non-academics who blank when they hear I'm working on the British eighteenth century that it is the period when the novel was begun or (dare I say it?) invented. The cachet is palpable. It represents a rare moment of validation in the public square, which has been a tough spot for us since we decided, sometime in the 1980s, that "the enlightenment" was no longer a category that could inspire, in any straightforward way, feelings of scholarly relevance or pride. For many years now, our narratives of modernization have privileged loss, repression, and alienation as the central heritage of enlightenment culture. It has been hard to feel good about the period we study. But while a majority of critical studies associated the novel with the negative version of enlightenment and modernization, we could still claim the novel as the unique and distinguishing problem of our field.

It's a good problem to have, but do we still care? Is there still more to be said about the novel? There are signs that the novelism that has distinguished and distorted our literary histories is losing its once irresistible lure. Perhaps we have done enough about the novel. Over the last twenty years, more and more scholars have remembered that poetry is the dominant literary genre of the eighteenth century and have devoted their energies to the recovery, construction, and analysis of an immense archive of poetic writing. A quick glance at the books about poetry that have been published since 1990 indicates a significant increase in the number of anthologies, companions, introductions, and guides to eighteenth-century poetry. The recovery of poetry by women has been an especially important aspect of these developments. Arguably, eighteenth-century poetry today is more accessible than perhaps at any time over the last one hundred years. A driving force in the reviving interest in poetry is the realization that our poetic canon was narrow and lopsided. It was skewed toward Tory satire in the first half of the eighteenth century and echoed the account of literary history and taste advocated by the Scriblerians (at the expense of the Kit-Cats). Even more importantly, we have been late to realize how popular an art poetry was in the eighteenth century. Until fairly recently, we had little idea of how many threshers, milkmaids, cobblers, and servants wrote poetry. After the massive recovery of lost and unheard poetic voices that has taken place over the last twenty years or so, it can sometimes seem as if everyone—*everyone*—was scribbling poetry in the eighteenth century. There is still much to be discovered and argued about as this reclamation of lost voices continues, including an issue that could command scholarly attention for decades: why is it that so many people from so many different groups and classes were drawn to writing poetry? And why did this happen in the eighteenth century? Is there anything like it in France or elsewhere in Europe?

Much of the new work on poetry that has appeared since 1990 has been committed to recovery and re-discovery. Paula Backscheider's 2005 *Eighteenth-Century Women Poets and Their Poetry* represents a late example of this tendency. Her book is of interest here because it comes from a scholar who has spent much of her time studying the fiction of the period. Backscheider offers a spirited attack on the closedness of the poetic canon, hoping to open it up to known and unknown female poets (signaling the reclamatory nature of her project, she adds a section of short biographies of female poets). The inclusion of women poets in the history of eighteenth-century poetry, she predicts, will trigger a "structural reorganization and reconception" of this history that would match the transformation that has already occurred in novel studies.[2] Novel studies, in fact, is repeatedly appealed to as a model for the transformation of our histories of poetry. I'm a little nervous about this appeal. That's because the appeal accepts as true assumptions that today can be recognized as the rather specific result of a kind of literary history that is coming to an end, a literary history that was animated, in various ways, by the story of modernization.

Backscheider indicates that her account of poetry is animated by this story as well. She appeals, for instance, to a thoroughly modern notion of authorship. To remake eighteenth-century literary history through female poets, she argues, we need the idea of an original, self-possessed author.[3] Yet this idea of authorship is unlikely to fit most early eighteenth-century authors—male or female—because it established itself broadly only in the late eighteenth- and early nineteenth centuries. This argument about authorial identity is related to another Backscheider makes. In this related move, she argues that the transformation of novel studies through the inclusion of women authors has given us a better model for understanding the novel's "dynamic contributions to shaping the modern mind."[4] Such a mind, our modernization narratives tell us, is self-possessed and original—and thus clearly differentiated from its environment. When Backscheider appeals to novel studies as a success story whose lessons can be exported to other fields, she is mistaking the exhaustion of a critical paradigm (novelism-modernism) for its completion.

For those of us who have grown up academically with the story of the novel it surely is tempting to use this story to approach the still underexplored waters of poetry, but it's probably even more tempting to approach the relationship between novel and poetry in this way. We should resist the temptation. Having novel studies provide the conceptual grid to study the relationship between poetry and novel may produce some interesting results, but it will not move literary history forward. It will keep us inside novelism. It will make us feel at home, in the worn-out, but still comfortable furnishings of modernization. Are we not ready to leave this place behind? I propose a different response to the opening of poetry in eighteenth-century studies. I believe we should take this occasion to demote the novel from its dominant position, undo its ancient alliance with modernization, and begin to develop a literary history that is no longer tied to an idea of the modern in which differentiation is the organizing paradigm.[5]

There are some broad, powerful historical reasons to do so now. These reasons have ultimately to do with the accelerating speed of globalization and technological innovation. The objects that today we are willing to host in our bodies; the electronic mediation of intimacy, sociability, and political action; the restless circulation of commodities and capital around the globe; the splicing of corporations across multiple nations; the increasing contact among people from different cultural and ethnic backgrounds—we surely live in a period of weakening boundaries and increasing mobilities. The basic paradigm of our modernization narratives, differentiation, can no longer capture such a world. That's why we increasingly resort to concepts such as hybridity to explain the life of culture under postcolonial, global capitalism. Conceptually, hybridity moves us in a direction directly opposite from differentiation: it explains culture not by highlighting the separation of kinds, spheres, and functions, but by stressing their blending. Today, we are much more willing to consider such blending as productive, not transgressive. We have become more aware—and overall less afraid, despite some anxiety flares—of the positive transformations that can be triggered when political, geographic, aesthetic, ethnic, or species boundaries are crossed. By contrast, narratives of modernization track the development of civilization and culture in the opposite direction, from indistinction to distinction, impure to pure, mixed to differentiated.

Because we occupy a historical moment of increasing boundlessness, the logic of modernization narratives has become much more visible and, to some of us, burdensome.[6] If such narratives can no longer describe our own historical moment, we have begun to ask, can we trust their account of earlier historical periods? I would go further, push past such questions and argue that global capitalism and technological innovation have changed our relationship to the past. I say this in the belief that present and past are not separable, that they always exist in dialectic relation to each other. As a result, when the present changes, we see different things in the past, ask different questions about it. If we continue to inhabit the fraying tent of modernization, we are insulating ourselves from our present and miss how that present is reshaping the past. If we stay where we are, we are inviting irrelevance because we will not testify to the life that pulses between past and present. And without such testimony, the public square is an awkward place indeed.

Our doubts about modernization as a paradigm for literary history present a precious opening. It should allow us not only to shake off the novelism/modernism yoke, but help us rethink in more basic ways our approach to the production of culture in eighteenth-century Britain. I think we would be well-advised to heed the kind of argument Stephen Greenblatt has recently offered when he noted that all cultures make themselves by crossing boundaries and by drawing boundaries.[7]

Cultural, regional, ethnic, and personal identities are not made by processes of differentiation and purification. They're just as much, if not more, made by the mixture of different ingredients. To understand the life of culture in any period, I believe we need to study the different kinds and degrees of differentiation and mixture that characterize a particular historical moment. There is a lot of work that waits for us here, even in those areas of literary studies that seem to have recognized the importance of mixture. The field of genre studies provides one example. It has embraced the assumption that all genres are always mixed. But while this insight has produced careful analyses of the combination of different poetic genres, not much nuanced historical work has been devoted to the modes of mixture that are sanctioned or censured in a given cultural moment and assist writers in the forging of literary works. A fully historicized and theorized understanding of how mixture works is absent in the field of genre studies.[8]

Because it is more challenging than the investigation of generic mixture in poetry alone, the investigation of the links between poetry and novel holds a special promise. It could lead us to a more unified literary history in which the crossing of boundaries is fully recognized as a productive force.[9] Unburdened from the paradigm of modernization, such recognition would correct the novelistic exceptionalism that has distorted our literary histories by making the novel the primary vehicle of modern culture; it would bring together the most prestigious and the least prestigious literary forms; and it would force a more concerted historicist account of generic interaction (simply because, unlike poetry, the novel has not been around forever).

But let me try to be more concrete. How might we approach rethinking the relationship between novel and poetry in the early eighteenth century? I propose an experiment that is designed to resist the influence of the novelism-modernism paradigm. My starting point will be James Thomson, a poet who shares at least some of the values we have associated with the novel. Thomson was not only Whiggishly inclined, but also promoted empiricism and the new science. In fact, some of the contemporary complaints about Thomson's poem as lacking design, plan, or unity echo comments that have also been made about the early novel.[10] Daniel Defoe's novels provide a case in point. One of the founding figures of the novel, Defoe shared Thomson's inclinations. His Whiggism and his empiricism have shaped our understanding of his novels. In the following, I will propose that Thomson and Defoe not only shared these broad inclinations, but also a corresponding aesthetic. What can seem formless in their works is, in fact, design. I would like to start by spending some time with Thomson's *Spring* (1728–44).

I'm quoting a familiar passage in which Thomson celebrates his patron and fellow patriot oppositionist, George Lyttelton. It's a traditional scene of the landlord on his estate:

> O LYTTELTON, the Friend! thy Passions thus
> And Meditations vary, as at large,
> Courting the Muse, thro' HAGLEY-PARK you stray,
> Thy *British Tempe*! There along the Dale,
> With Woods o'er-hung, and shag'd with mossy Rocks,
> Whence on each Hand the gushing Waters play,
> And down the rough Cascade white-dashing fall,
> Or gleam in lengthen'd Vista thro' the Trees,
> You silent steal; or sit beneath the Shade
> Of solemn Oaks, that tuft the swelling Mounts
> Thrown graceful round by Nature's careless Hand,
> And pensive listen to the various Voice
> Of rural Peace: the Herds, the Flocks, the Birds,
> The hollow-whispering Breeze, the Plaint of Rills,
> That, purling down amid the twisted Roots
> Which creep around, their dewy Murmurs shake
> On the sooth'd Ear. From these abstracted oft,
> You wander thro' the Philosophic World;
> Where in bright Train continual Wonders rise,
> Or to the curious or the pious Eye.
> And oft, conducted by Historic Truth,
> You tread the long Extent of backward Time:
> Planning, with warm Benevolence of Mind,
> And honest Zeal unwarp'd by Party-Rage,
> BRITANNIA's Weal; how from the venal Gulph
> To raise her Virtue, and her Arts revive.
> Or, turning thence thy View, these graver Thoughts
> The Muses charm. . .[11]

At the risk of seeming tedious, I would like to tend to the use of the conjunction "or" in these lines. In lines 911–913, the waters initially play "on each hand" "Or gleam in lengthen'd Vista thro' the Trees." This is followed by human activity: "You silent steal; or sit beneath the shade" (914). And in line 923, "continual Wonders rise, / Or to the curious or the pious Eye." Finally, we get line 932: "Or, turning thence thy View, these graver Thoughts / the Muses charm." Three times in this passage does the word "or" stand at the beginning of lines. Despite the concrete location (Hagley Park) and the actual human being running around in it (George Lyttelton), this is not a particularized setting and Thomson doesn't present us with anything that we would recognize as a personality. The scene and its occupant are thoroughly idealized. Objects do not receive marks of individuation. This, it seems to me, is the point. We are not meant to get absorbed by concrete particulars; we are to experience movement and the crossing of boundaries.[12]

The use of the conjunction "or" crucially contributes to such crossing. Its frequent insertion suggests that we are in a potential rather than an actual scene, that we're witnessing a sequence that does not want to resemble actual behavior on a cloudy spring afternoon, but aspires instead to something like an ideal fullness in which various possibilities are realized, but without being tied to the "here" and "now" of a particular point in time, space, and development. This removal from the particular and the concrete—this embrace of the general and the abstract— enables, for example, a representation of sensual plenitude in which several senses quickly succeed each other. We move from the rich textures and varied surfaces of the mossy rocks that roughen the wood-covered dale to the "gushing waters" playing (literally and figuratively) "on" each hand to the less tactile and more distant visual "gleam" that the water produces when seen through a "lengthen'd Vista." The "or" that moves us so swiftly from touch to sight places the observer in different positions in the landscape, but without worrying about their geographic coherence. Instead, we're immersed in a dream-like scene of effortless alternation where each sense can be awakened by a simple turn of the head or a sudden shift of perspective. All of this isn't grounded in a coherent center of perception and experience. It's the hands, eyes, and ears that matter here, not the person that they are attached to. The verb and the subject come late, in line 914, barely able or willing to accommodate the preceding five lines of landscape description. While the landscape is active and full, the figure is empty and passive. Its actions—stray-ing, stealing, sitting, listening, wandering, treading—are so many ways of bringing the landscape to reveal its plenitude and its ability to affect the walker, whose own thoughts unfold like a walk.

The narrative action in these lines, then, produces an increasing dispersal that dissolves the physical and psychological coherence of the protagonist, whose outline and experience is, in the end, only vaguely held together by the name "Lyttelton." The passage deliberately shirks differentiations between ground and figure, setting and self. By loosening the usual boundaries of inside and outside, the limits of time and space, Thomson's poem generates variety, an important principle of his poetics. The narrative action produces a maximum of indirection while maintaining a minimum of directedness to gather and collect a sensual plenitude that exceeds the limits of the probable, the particular, a single body, and a specific experience. Dispersal is in a productive relationship with collection, which generates variety, but a variety that defies limits and crosses boundaries.

It seems uncontroversial to note that the relationship between ground and figure in Thomson's poetry does not resemble the relationship between ground and figure in the early novel. In the tradition of the rise of the novel, the modernity of prose fiction is pegged to its solidification of individual experience against socially, politically, or epistemologically more incorporating forms. From the perspective of this tradition, Thomson's portrayal of Lyttelton can only read like an allegory of traditional ways of being in which individual experience is defined and contained by surrounding forms and institutions (patronage, property, landscape gardening, etc.). Instead of particulars and a probable report of the individual's interaction with such particulars, we get something general, vague, and (deliberately) improbable. Seen from this perspective, poetry like Thomson's just isn't "modern."

I would like to pull us in a different direction, away from the contrast between novel and poetry toward similarity. Thomson's aesthetic shares considerable ground with Defoe's. Defoe's fictions have long been seen as irregular, as lacking a tangible commitment to unity. Following apparently hardwired instincts, Defoe produced expansive episodic sprawl frequently relieved by repetition. But if Defoe thus seems unselfconscious about questions of design, that's not exactly how he saw it. In preface after preface, Defoe declared that his narratives were governed by a principle that also shapes Thomson's aesthetic. That principle is "variety."

In the brief preface to *Robinson Crusoe* (1719), for example, Defoe states that "the wonders of this man's life exceed all that . . . is to be found extant; the life of one man being scarce capable of a greater variety."[13] Defoe makes good on this promise: from being the son of a middle class father with a clear place in the world, Crusoe turns sailor, slave, planter, slave trader, jack-of-all trades on a desert island where he makes umbrellas, bread, pots, boats, and ends up a rich trader whose fortunes exceed all that one would expect after twenty-eight years of total isolation. Defoe's faith in variety (and the way it pays off) also inspired the novel's ending and sequels. To the consternation of many readers, *Robinson Crusoe* spins out in a fight with "monstrous wolfs," a hasty settlement in England (for seven years), a brief marriage, a return to his island at the ripe age of sixty-two, and a sequel in which Crusoe sets out again on a seafaring life, undeterred by the fact that he is now in his seventies. One is tempted, in fact, to include in this pursuit of variety Crusoe's mind, whose wide vacillations between opposing viewpoints are a characteristic feature (I have the right to kill cannibals/I do not).

Defoe's push beyond the probable bounds of individual experience can also be observed in Moll Flanders or Roxana, both of whom move through what Defoe calls "vast variety of fortunes" without too much regard for probability.[14] Moll still makes money in exchange for sexual favors when she is forty, at which point the narrator insists that she is as attractive as when she was sixteen. The half-dozen or so marriages she tumbles through may say something about the limits of female agency at this time, but they also display the incidental multiplicity Defoe craves. Defoe's pleasure in such multiplicity is tangible when he praises the "infinite variety" of Moll Flanders, its "abundance of delightful incidents."[15] Defoe's endorsement of variety as the governing aesthetic principle of his novels substantially modifies, and perhaps even violates, our assumptions about this supposedly first realist novelist. The rendering of experiences that *belong* to a single individual is not really Defoe's goal in such novels as Robinson Crusoe or Roxana. Defoe disregards the limits of the individual body, the individual mind, and the probabilities of a career. His real goal is to represent the heterogeneity and multiplicity of experience itself.

Defoe's commitment to a variety that exceeds the limits of time and space, the bounds of the single individual, is something he shares with Thomson. Defoe and Thomson realize this commitment by means similar and different. In Defoe, Thomson's cultivation of variety through rapid alternation and substitution is not located on the level of potentiality, not tied to the conjunction "or." In Defoe's novels, Thomson's plenitude is realized on the level of actuality, straining probability even more severely. The "or" becomes an "and," the potential becomes the actual in Defoe's profoundly episodic narratives. As a result, unremitting transformation is central in Defoe's texts, which push against the unifying fictions of the name, the sameness of identity, and the coherence of a mind—and therefore against much that we have been told about realism's way with character.

The most instructive example of all of Defoe's narratives in this regard is *Roxana*, which I'm inclined to see, somewhat anachronistically, as resisting and fighting off, in the name of transformation and change, the threat of realism: the threat of identity, continuity, interiority, development, and boundedness. In some ways, Defoe's novel might seem initially to go in the opposite direction. Its title page, bearing the usual emphasis on variety, announces the following:

Roxana the Fortunate Mistress, or, a History of the Life and Vast Variety
of Fortunes of Mademoiselle de Beleau, Afterwards Call'd the Countess
de Wintselsheim, in Germany. Being the Person Known by the Name of
the Lady Roxana in the Time of King Charles II.[16]

Defoe's title page points to the way in which Roxana has destabilized the name
as a reliable indicator of identity. Defoe uses temporal and spatial markers to motivate her multiple identities: Roxana is first called Mademoiselle de Beleau and
later (but only in Germany) the Countess de Wintselsheim (a name that manages
to combine English, French, and German elements). She is also known as Lady
Roxana, but only during the restoration in England. Spatial and temporal markers
thus go hand in hand with nominal difference. In this way, the title page associates
Defoe's text with the secret history and the roman à clef. It gives the reader the
knowledge that these different names, signifying different characters at different
times and in different places, refer to the same person. The various identities of
Roxana are announced to be one, and the following narrative, one is likely to assume, will thrive on an initial exultation and eventual reduction of difference to
identity.

But this is not quite how it works out. Roxana's story is not a case of narrative action taming the powers of transformation and alterity, even as the title page
announces such reduction as the narrative occasion. Enormous pressures mount
at the end of the novel, but Roxana ultimately defeats the threat of identity and
continuity. Roxana isn't fixed. Her shape-shifting career is never brought back to a
point of origin, and the murder of her daughter Susan by her trusty servant Amy
indicates her determination, despite confessed horrors and doubts, to escape the
reduction of identity promised on the title page. Though the ending isn't happy,
Roxana has transformed herself once again by the end, this time into a Dutch
noblewoman.

There is in Defoe's novel something I'm tempted to call a strange anticipa-
tory nostalgia for a stable self and a continuous relationship with the past. Such
nostalgia is perhaps most dramatically realized in the encounter Roxana has late in
the novel with her daughter, whom she greets unrecognized and under profound
emotional distress.[17] Yet this contradictory emotional formation can only emerge
under the signs of threat and self-destruction. Though Defoe cannot have been
conscious of this and though he couldn't have used these terms, Roxana shows that
realism contradicts the basic tendencies of Defoe's narratives. Up to the very end of
his career as a fiction writer, Defoe had little to do with the rise of the novel as we

know it. In *Roxana*, identity, continuity, and interiority are forces that beleaguer and haunt the heroine.

Thomson's use of the potential "or" and Defoe's of the actual "and" say something about the difference of poetry and prose, but "realism" is not concerned in this difference. If anything, Defoe's novels strain the canons of probability and individualism even more than Thomson's description of Lyttelton's potential stroll. Nor does the contrast between Defoe's use of narrative conjunction and Thomson's indicate that Defoe's novels are modern whereas Thomson's poetry isn't. The impulse toward a differentiation of figure and ground, toward a portrayal of self-possessed individuals whose clearly delineated contours set them off from the settings in which they act does not exist in either writer. We are dealing instead with writers who consider permeable boundaries, uncertain limits, and smudgy contours as enabling. Both Thomson and Defoe join dispersal and collection to create a dynamic relational structure characterized by a variety that ignores the chaste demands of differentiation, demands that always rely on the drawing of boundaries and the imposing of limits. In this sense, they share an aesthetic—a cultural form that cuts across generic difference.

Obviously, this cultural form is not modern in the sense in which we have come to understand that concept. But it is modern in the sense in which many seventeenth- and eighteenth-century thinkers understood that term. As I show elsewhere in some detail, early eighteenth-century Englishmen were familiar with an alternative tradition of theorizing modernity that emerges out of the scientific and political revolutions of the seventeenth century.[18] In this alternative tradition, mixture, not differentiation, is the primary driver of English culture and civilization. In the face of recurrent threats of absolutism and arbitrary government, an array of seventeenth-century thinkers sought to overcome ideas of natural and political order that privileged strong boundaries, clear forms, and sovereign essences. Political and scientific writers such as Henry Parker, Philip Hunton, Robert Boyle, Nehemiah Grew, and John Locke did so by giving mixture something it rarely possesses in Western culture: ontological and epistemological dignity. They argued that mixture was a legitimate and even privileged cause, a cause that could produce superior languages, new species, flawless ideas, and resilient civil societies.

This alternative theory of modernization informs and energizes the debates about naturalization and toleration in early eighteenth-century England. In these debates, many Whigs viewed the religious and ethnic variety they observed in Holland as a recipe for the creation of prosperity and refined culture. Many Tories, meanwhile, were fearful of turning Dutch and preferred national recipes that included fewer and purer ingredients. Such writers as William Temple, John Locke, John Toland, and Daniel Defoe promoted the Dutch model and praised variety and mixture as certain means of advancing English culture.[19] Their position chimed with the emergence in the early eighteenth century of so-called mixed government—a blend of democratic, aristocratic, and monarchical forms—as the canonical theory of British government. Having weak boundaries between kinds, spheres, and functions was a plus. This extension of variety into the realm of political order is also visible in Thomson, whose poem "Liberty" embraces the mixture of different forms of government.[20]

While Defoe and Thomson can be associated with this general outlook on modernization as a process in which mixture, not differentiation, dominates, a more concrete source of their aesthetic of variety may be seen in the literary reorientation that Whig patrons and writers sought to promote after the revolution of 1688.[21] Thanks to such figures as Lord Somers, John Toland, John Dennis, Joseph Addison, Jonathan Richardson, and Richard Blackmore, John Milton became central to this reorientation.[22] As is well known, Milton had a significant influence on Thomson's poetics.[23] In fact, I would argue that Thomson's reliance on the conjunction "or" is indebted to Milton, who realized the expansionist and inclusivist ambitions of his epic poetry in part through boundary-crossing shifts from one potential figure or scene to another.[24] The effects Milton achieved in this manner were recognized as manifestations of the sublime, an aesthetic category that became a central plank in the Whig platform of literary renewal. It is here, in the Whig promotion of the sublime as an aesthetic category deeply allied with a politics of liberty, that we find unexpected common literary ground for the boundary-crossing aesthetic of variety I have described in Thomson and Defoe.

I cannot make the case for the relationship of this aesthetic to the Whig sublime at the length or depth it deserves, and refer readers instead to Abigail Williams and David Womersley, who have done important work on this issue.[25] For the purposes of this essay, it may be best to go straight to Alexander Welsted's 1712 translation of Longinus's treatise on the sublime (Welsted was another Milton-adoring Whig, whose store of examples for sublime effects drew heavily on "our great Master, Milton").[26] In chapter eight, Longinus addresses the power of circumstances in the creation of sublime effects. "The choice of Circumstances," he points out, and "the throwing them together when chosen, bear very forcibly upon the imagination."[27] His example is Sappho's description of the effects of love. The lines Longinus quotes—which capture the pains of love by depicting a variety of psychological and physiological effects—are less important here than his commentary. "Are you not in Admiration," Longinus addresses his interlocutor after citing Sappho's verses,

> to see how she accumulates all these things, the Soul, the Body, the Ear, the Tongue, the Colour, as if they were so many different Persons ready to expire? And do you not observe with how many contrary Motions or Impulses she is agitated? She Chills, she Burns; she's Foolish, she's Wise; or she's entirely out of her Wits, or she's upon the point of Death: In a word, one would say, that she was not possesst with any one single Passion, but that her Soul was the Rendezvous of all Passions. . . . Here you observe then, as I have already said, that all those great Circumstances introduced properly, and put together with judgment, are what create the main Beauty of her Poem. In like manner, when Homer gives us the Description of a Tempest, he takes care to express every thing which can appear Terrible in a Tempest.[28]

The sublime is allied with a logic of crowding that exceeds the boundaries of the probable because it collects and accumulates all the accidents that could describe a mental or a natural state. Perhaps not surprisingly, Longinus's effort to represent Sappho's crowded lines relies on the conjunction "or" and suggests that her combination of different organs and contrary impulses gives the impression of multiple persons. Sappho's circumstantiality achieves sublime effects by creating a variety that strains the bounds of probability. Taking the perspective of realism, we may well ask: can one person really be subject to so many different physiological and psychological responses? Can a particular storm really have all of these characteristics? Are we not dealing here with the extraordinary rather than the probable? Questions like these point to a divide between the sublime representation of mental or natural states and the mandates of empiricist philosophy. We are familiar with this divide. We tend to see empiricism's characteristic achievement as a drawing of boundaries between observer and observed and between the different things of nature. Realistic writing such as Defoe's, we have been told many times, responds to such mandates. The sublime would seem to move in the opposite direction. But this picture isn't quite right. I contend that the empiricist impulse in the 1690s and beyond effected an opening toward boundlessness.[29] Empiricism and realism may have more in common with certain aspects of the sublime than we are used to admitting.[30]

Let me explain this a bit more. One of the fastest-spreading claims circulated by John Locke's *An Essay Concerning Human Understanding* (1690) is the insistence on our ignorance about the ultimate reality that endows things with their specific identity.[31] According to Locke, the identity of a thing cannot be decided by distinguishing between accidental and essential characteristics. For the purpose of our lives on this planet and our inquiries about it, we only have accidents: various qualities and parts whose careful recording and collecting is our only path to delineating the identity of a thing. But this path, Locke realizes, is endless. We may wind up with an extraordinary collection of details about a thing and may have a sense that we know its nature pretty well, but we can never arrive at a definitive collection, never be entirely sure. There may always be qualities that we have not yet discovered and that may emerge in the process of removing a thing to a different location or of combining this thing with another. The collection of empirical data, we might say, disperses the sameness and oneness of the single thing. Infinity and multiplicity are therefore built into our most straightforward attempts to establish the nature or identity of a thing by collecting empirical details. Complete knowledge, final knowledge is not possible. The identity of a thing is always preliminary, never fixed, always evolving. There is no essence that articulates a stable identity across time and place. Identities are collective/dispersive and their formation never really ends.[32]

At the heart of the empirical inquiry into the nature of things stands thus a sublime infinity that contradicts the idea that an individual is single (it is always a collection of parts and qualities), that identity is stable, and that our definition of identity can proceed by reduction, by peeling away what's inessential and revealing the core. Identity is not that which is one and the same. It is, rather, that which accumulates and shifts and always is, in Robert Boyle's words, "one *collective* Thing."[33] For this reason, empiricism in the tradition of Boyle and Locke shares with Sappho's, Thomson's, and Defoe's representational strategies a profound respect for the sublime multiplicity and openness that constitutes any single thing. In Thomson and Defoe, the sublime is not necessarily the experience that disrupts and shakes the boundaries of the self. It is not clear to me that for them there is such a self, a figure that would be clearly defined, safely differentiated from a ground. If that is true, the sublime will not be the exceptional experience that challenges the boundaries of the self or the limits of ordinary life. In Thomson and Defoe, I see writers who intuit a kinship between empiricism's anti-essentialism and the sublime's hospitality toward multiplicity and heterogeneity. Their representation of life does not consider the transgression of boundaries as a threat to some pre-established coherence of self or experience. Instead, they see the crossing of boundaries as the process by which life reproduces itself.

And if the representation of life in Defoe and Thomson does not rely on the consolidation of boundaries, we should extend this insight to the question of literary form. As part of his critique of Aristotelian definitions of identity, Locke's *Essay* offers a withering critique of the idea of species, a term that in eighteenth-century Britain is still widely used to describe literary genres.[34] In this way, Locke contributes forcefully to the destabilization of generic categories Michael McKeon has described in *The Origins of the English Novel, 1600–1740* (1987). What has been lacking, however, is a clearer understanding of the positive formal program that must accompany or perhaps even prompt such destabilization. My essay has begun to respond to such lack by presenting the sublime's revival between 1680 and 1720 as a possible contributor to such a positive program. But there must be more. We must find ways to formulate a more comprehensive and positive response to J. Paul Hunter's call for the reconstruction of the "anti-essentialist aesthetic" that he sees dominate these decades.[35] We need a unified narrative about literary innovation that manages to recover the positive program nestled inside the anti-essentialist impulse. The historical conditions for such a recovery continue to be very good. Living in our own increasingly boundless historical moment, we are more attuned to the potential and the advantage of crossing boundaries than previous generations of scholars. We are more likely to see things that were not visible previously: including, hopefully, the growing contours of the relationship between poetry and novel.

Notes

1. The sentiment that the novel is the quintessentially modern genre is widely shared. I refer here specifically to Michael McKeon, "Introduction," *Theory of the Novel: A Historical Approach* (Baltimore: The Johns Hopkins University Press, 2000), xv.

2. Paula R. Backscheider, *Eighteenth-Century Women Poets and Their Poetry: Inventing Agency, Inventing Genre* (Baltimore: The Johns Hopkins University Press, 2005), xiv.

3. Ibid., 22–26.

4. Ibid., xiv.

5. The call for a literary history that does not treat differentiation as its central narrative paradigm is also the motto of Clifford Siskin's *The Work of Writing: Literary and Social Change in Britain, 1700–1830* (Baltimore: The Johns Hopkins University Press, 1998). Unlike Siskin's, my argument relies on a hermeneutic model.

6. One of the more spirited recent attempts to exorcize differentiation from modernization is Bruno Latour's *We Have Never Been Modern*, trans. Catherine Porter (Cambridge: Harvard University Press, 1993).

7. Stephen Greenblatt, "Cultural Mobility: An Introduction," in Stephen Greenblatt, with Ines Županov, Reinhard Meyer-Kalkus, Heike Paul, Pál Nyíri, Friederike Pannewick, *Cultural Mobility: A Manifesto* (Cambridge: Cambridge University Press, 2010), 1–23.

8. For the argument that all genres are mixed, see Alistair Fowler, *Kinds of Literature: An Introduction to the Theory of Genres and Modes* (Cambridge: Harvard University Press, 1982). See also Ralph Cohen, "On the Interrelations of Literary Form," in *New Approaches to Eighteenth-Century Literature: Selected Papers from the English Institute*, ed. Phillip Harth (New York: Columbia University Press, 1974), 33–78. Cohen recognizes the need to situate historically different modes of mixture: he suggests, for example, that the primacy of mixed forms in early eighteenth-century England has something to do "with religious and political factionalism" (Ibid., 73).

9. Margaret Doody presciently called in 1985 for a more unified literary history that recognizes boundlessness and mixture as central forces in the literary production of the early eighteenth century: *The Daring Muse: Augustan Poetry Reconsidered* (Cambridge: Cambridge University Press, 1985).

10. Ralph Cohen records some of the comments about the lack of design and unity in Thomson's *Seasons*, in *The Art of Discrimination: Thomson's Seasons and the Language of Criticism* (London: Routledge and Kegan Paul, 1964), 86, 119.

11. James Thomson, *Spring*, lines 906–933. I quote from *Eighteenth-Century Poetry: An Annotated Anthology*, ed. David Fairer and Christine Gerrard (Oxford: Blackwell, 2008), 233.

12. Doody has emphasized "character in appropriate setting," "individual point of view," and "inner life" as characteristic achievements of Augustan poetry, achievements that she argues precede and match the novel's (*Daring Muse*, 202–204). Her comments are intriguing, but they also betray their origin: our understanding of the novel as a modern genre concerned with a self-reflexive individual placed in believable settings.

13. Daniel Defoe, *Robinson Crusoe*, ed. John Richetti (London: Penguin, 2001), 3.

14. Daniel Defoe, *Roxana*, ed. David Blewett (London: Penguin, 1987), 3.

15. Daniel Defoe, *Moll Flanders*, ed. David Blewett (London: Penguin, 1989), 39–40.

16. Defoe, *Roxana*, 3.

17. Ibid., 323.

18. For the argument that early eighteenth-century Englishmen were familiar with a theory of modernization that relied on mixture, see my *Exquisite Mixture: The Virtues of Impurity in Early Modern England* (Philadelphia: University of Pennsylvania Press, 2012), 1–23.

19. For the argument that the early-eighteenth-century debate over toleration and immigration was influenced by the Dutch model, see my *Exquisite Mixture*, 8–12.

20. Thomson embraces mixed government in "Liberty," in *Works of Mr. Thomson*, 2 vols. (London, 1738), 2:144–145; lines 813–821.

21. On the renewal of the arts pursued by Whigs after 1688, see Ophelia Field's excellent *The Kit-Cat Club: Friends Who Imagined a Nation* (London: Harper Press, 2008).

22. Though he does not attend to the partisan appropriations of Milton, Dustin Griffin has effectively described the emergence of Milton as a commanding poetic presence in the early eighteenth century

in *Regaining Paradise: Milton and the Eighteenth Century* (Cambridge: Cambridge University Press, 1986), 33–44.

23. For Milton's influence on Thomson, see Griffin, *Regaining Paradise*, 179–202.

24. For an example of Milton's reliance on the conjunction "or," see the following lines from book one of *Paradise Lost*: "Thus Satan talking to his nearest mate/ With head uplift above the wave, and eyes/ That sparkling blazed, his other parts besides/ Prone on the flood, extended long and large/ Lay floating many a rood, in bulk as huge/ As whom the fables name of monstrous size,/ Titanian, or Earth-born, that warred on Jove,/ Briarios or Typhon, whom the den/ By ancient Tarsus held, or that sea-beast/ Leviathan . . . " (bk. 1, lines 192–201, in Milton, *Paradise Lost*, ed. Alistair Fowler [London: Longman, 1998]).

25. Abigail Williams, *Poetry and the Creation of a Whig Literary Culture* (Oxford: Oxford University Press, 2005) and David Womersley, "Introduction," in *Augustan Critical Writing*, ed. Womersley (London: Penguin, 1997), xi–xliv. See also *Cultures of Whiggism: New Essays on English Literature in the Long Eighteenth Century*, ed. David Womersley (Newark: University of Delaware Press, 2005).

26. *The Works of Dionysius Longinus*, trans. Alexander Welsted (London, 1712), 158.

27. Ibid., 35.

28. Ibid., 37.

29. In arguing for boundlessness as an empiricist impulse, I build on Barbara Shapiro's and Richard Kroll's insight that seventeenth-century culture was concerned with finding ways to justify greater complexity, cooperation, and uncertainty. See Shapiro, *Probability and Certainty in Seventeenth-Century England* (Princeton: Princeton University Press, 1983) and Kroll, *The Material Word: Literate Culture in the Restoration and Early Eighteenth Century* (Baltimore: The Johns Hopkins University Press, 1991). I believe that Kroll's and Shapiro's arguments align with Doody's argument about literary culture in the Augustan age.

30. Grudgingly accepting the validity of Kroll's and Shapiro's arguments, James Noggle has claimed that the sublime in early eighteenth-century culture is "the exceptional mode of experience that justifies the system of liberal probabilism in terms unavailable within the system itself." In *The Skeptical Sublime: Aesthetic Ideology in Pope and the Tory Satirists* (Oxford: Oxford University Press, 2001), 26. Against such an ideological view of the sublime, I raise here the possibility of an open and more directly collaborative relationship between the sublime and empiricism, between the aesthetic and science.

31. John Yolton has shown the controversial force of Locke's claims about the unknowability of the essence of things in *John Locke and the Way of Ideas* (Oxford: Clarendon, 1968), 126–147.

32. For a more patient exposition of Locke's views and its connection to Boyle's, see my *Exquisite Mixture*, 101–145.

33. Robert Boyle, *The Origine of Formes and Qualities* (Oxford, 1666), 102; emphasis in original.

34. John Locke, *An Essay concerning Human Understanding,* ed. Peter H. Nidditch, Clarendon Edition of the Works of John Locke (Oxford: Oxford University Press, 1975), 402–524.

35. J. Paul Hunter, "Serious Reflections on Farther Adventures: Resistances to Closure in Eighteenth-Century English Novels," in *Augustan Subjects: Essays in Honor of Martin C. Battestin*, ed. Albert J. Rivero (Newark: University of Delaware Press, 1997), 288–289.

6

THE RISE OF THE NOVEL AND
THE FALL OF PERSONIFICATION

Heather Keenleyside

ECIL DEANE BEGINS HIS 1935 *Aspects of Eighteenth-Century Nature Poetry* with a discussion of personification, the better to dispense with it quickly: "We have dwelt on the subject of personification partly lest it be thought that in the ensuing pages . . . the case is overstated, and insufficient attention is paid to the less defensible aspects of [this poetry]."[1] In the section of his 1762 *Elements of Criticism* devoted to "Figures," Lord Kames also begins with personification, but his rationale is rather different: "I begin with Prosopopoeia or personification which is justly intitled to the first place."[2] This essay takes its cue from the striking shift from Kames to Deane, and from the question it raises: how and why did the figure most associated with the poetry of the eighteenth century become an embarrassment? In his 1947 essay, "Personification Reconsidered," Bertrand Bronson put the same question in world-historical terms: "Why did the eighteenth century derive such extreme satisfaction from a device which the nineteenth and twentieth centuries have joined to execrate as frigid and lifeless? Fully to answer this query would require a better history of the last three hundred years in Western Europe than has yet been written."[3] Somehow, Bronson suggests, the fate of personification—and with it, of eighteenth-century poetry—is tied to the history of Western modernity.

Bronson's essay became the opening salvo in a short-lived mid-century effort to rehabilitate or at least explain this favorite of eighteenth-century figures; it was followed by Earl Wasserman's essay, "The Inherent Values of Eighteenth-Century Personification" (1950), and Chester Chapin's monograph, *Personification in Eighteenth-Century Poetry* (1954). Together, the work of these critics comprises the most sustained and illuminating reflection on eighteenth-century personification;

it remains a touchstone for important recent studies by Stephen Knapp and Adela Pinch.[4] There are significant differences between the accounts of Bronson, Wasserman, and Chapin, but all hold at least one fundamental point in common. For all three, the fate of eighteenth-century personification indicates a crisis in the relationship between concrete particularity and abstract generalization, which accompanies a transformation in the relationship between the individual and society.[5] Twentieth-century readers no longer know how to appreciate personification, Bronson argues, because "[w]e have moved from a taste for the abstract . . . to a preference for the concrete," and Wasserman agrees, "[t]oday we have so dedicated ourselves to the representational force of the particular that only with difficulty can we realize how intimately the eighteenth century lived with personified abstractions."[6] Chapin quotes Donald Davie to make a similar point. Unlike modern readers and writers, the Augustans were not "'concerned with those features which make a man unique, but with those which he has in common with his fellows'"; Chapin urges us to recognize that "although 'the two sorts of concern are different,' there 'are no *a priori* grounds for thinking one less interesting or less moral than the other.'"[7] For all of these twentieth-century critics, recuperating personification (and much of eighteenth-century poetry) involves explaining the period's peculiar fondness for abstractions, and defending its antiquated interest in the traits and experiences common to all human beings. Each critic turns to some wider context—Newtonian science, neoclassical decorum, empiricist philosophy—to help twentieth-century readers see personification as "something more than an 'empty abstraction,'" typically locating the origin of personification (and its unexpected "quality of concrete force") in the personal experience of "particular individuals."[8] As Adela Pinch points out, this mid-century defense of neoclassical generality has a distinctively modern ring, not least because its "understanding of the neoclassical is trapped in an opposition between the personal and the general."[9] Which is also to say that it is trapped in an opposition cemented, in eighteenth-century studies, at precisely this mid-century moment, by Ian Watt's 1957 *The Rise of the Novel.*

Watt's formulations of the particularizing tendencies of the novel are familiar enough to need little rehearsing. Watt begins his account of the novel's rise by contrasting the "individualist and innovating" orientation of the novel with "the dominant literary outlook" of the early eighteenth century, "still governed by the strong classical preference for the general and universal."[10] The dominance of this preference did not last: "In the literary, the philosophical and the social spheres alike the classical focus on the ideal, the universal and the corporate has shifted completely, and the modern field of vision is mainly occupied by the discrete particular, the directly apprehended sensum, and the autonomous individual."[11] Watt's story of the rise of the novel shares its logic with Bronson's account of the fall of personification, which charts the same narrative of literary, philosophical and social modernization. Neoclassicism, Bronson maintains, was "the last historical effort to stave off the collapse of those sustaining postulates which for centuries had given dignity and importance to mankind."[12] What is left, after the collapse, is the "inordinate egocentricity" or "absolute individualism" of Watt's Robinson Crusoe.[13] Bronson puts the point this way: "Preoccupation with individual experience became the rule and the egocentricity of the last century and a half bears witness to our all but universal inability to reach any compelling generalizations."[14] In the modern world of which Crusoe is both effect and sign, it is little wonder that we can no longer make sense of the poetry of personified abstractions.

In the context of Watt's roughly contemporaneous account of the novel, the mid-twentieth-century interest in personification appears a retrograde position in the soon to be settled "controversy between neo-classical generality and realistic particularity" (the phrase is Watt's).[15] Eighteenth-century poetry is thus set on the wrong side of literary, intellectual and cultural history, as the last bearer of aesthetic and ethical values that are on the wane. Along such lines, Clifford Siskin identifies personification as the key figure for what he, after M. H. Abrams and A. O. Lovejoy, calls the myth of "Uniformitarianism"—the Augustan fiction of "a given, uniform human community."[16] Personification plays the same role for the neoclassical "myth of uniformitarianism" that the novelistic character plays for Watt's modern "myth of individualism." Latter-day Augustans like Bronson, Wasserman and Chapin seek to restore human vitality to what can seem a "frigid and lifeless" figure, assuring their readers, with Wasserman, that "[a]lthough we today tend to feel that the personified abstraction is bloodless and lacking in human individuality, the eighteenth century invested its interpretation of personification with a still-vital humanism."[17] Despite this assurance, Wasserman concedes that the humanism of uniform values and common virtues is no longer ours; it has been replaced by the humanism of "human individuality." Together, Watt, Wasserman, Bronson and Chapin tell twin stories of rise and fall: the rise of the novel, realism, the human individual, the literary character; the fall of poetry, neoclassicism, common virtues, personification. So the story goes.

This is a familiar story, and it has been subject to trenchant correction and critique on a host of fronts. I return to it for a couple of reasons. First, because I suspect it still shapes the teaching of eighteenth-century literature, at least at the college level. In his afterward to the anniversary edition of Watt's monograph, W. B. Carnochan recalls that as an undergrad at Harvard in the 1950s, he had "never read a novel in a course, unless one counts *Gulliver's Travels* or *Rasselas*."[18] Most undergraduates now would, I think, say the same of eighteenth-century poetry. Watt's 1957 publication of *The Rise of the Novel* moved the novel to center stage in eighteenth-century studies, linking eighteenth-century literature to a narrative of modernization and individuation that has had tremendous staying power. In doing so, it established coordinates that can make central features of eighteenth-century poetry seem vestigial, holdovers from a passing world. My sense is that personification is one such feature, and that it need not be so—that putting things this way tells us at least as much about the 1950s as it does about the 1750s.[19] The rise of the novel need not mean the fall of personification.

I return to the story of poetry, personification, and this mid-century moment because I share Bronson's sense that this humble and apparently outmoded literary figure has a good deal to tell us about our own cultural and intellectual history. In our twenty-first century moment of new materialisms and impersonality, of posthumanism, animal studies, and thing theory, it may be time to return to and even rehabilitate personification on somewhat different grounds—not as the bearer of an alternate form of humanism, but as a figure attuned to ties that extend beyond human being.[20] In what follows, I turn from twentieth-century critics like Bronson and Wasserman to eighteenth-century critics like Lord Kames and Hugh Blair to elaborate a different story about the figure, one in which familiar terms (like community and abstraction) operate in ways we may not expect. Blair opens his discussion of personification this way: "One of the greatest pleasures we receive from poetry, is, to find ourselves always in the midst of our fellows; and to see every thing thinking, feeling, and acting, as we ourselves do. This is, perhaps, the principal charm of this sort of figured style, that it introduces us into society with all nature."[21] On this formulation, personification is a figure of commonality and society; it is not as clearly a figure of human being. As Kames and Blair proceed through their extended and often puzzling accounts of the figure, it turns out that "to see every thing thinking, feeling, and acting, as we ourselves do" is often as perplexing as it is pleasurable. A figure that "introduces us into society with all nature," they suggest, can very quickly unsettle our sense of ourselves.

Living Hands

Moving from mid-twentieth century to mid-eighteenth century accounts of personification, a number of things are immediately striking. The first is that what counts as personification widens considerably. Wasserman is representative of his contemporaries when he writes interchangeably of "the eighteenth-century affection for personification" and "the eighteenth-century use of personified abstractions."[22] For him, as for Bronson and Chapin (and more recently, for Siskin, Pinch and Knapp), personification means personified abstractions.[23] By contrast, eighteenth-century rhetoricians like Kames and Blair do not exclusively or even primarily focus on the personification of abstract ideas (like Fear, or Observation, or Dullness). Both Kames and Blair grant personification pride of place in their discussions of rhetoric, and both are, as Kames puts it, "profuse of examples" of the figure.[24] Very few of these examples are abstract ideas. Kames devotes only four of thirty-two pages to personifications of this kind; Blair, only one paragraph in fifteen pages. Both define personification as the figure, in Kames' words, "which gives life to things inanimate."[25] Abstraction only comes into play when Blair elaborates on this first definition, identifying personification with "the facility with which the mind can accommodate the properties of living creatures to things that are inanimate, or to abstract conceptions of its own forming."[26] The "or" that yokes objects and ideas troubles Blair remarkably little, and it is often left out of his extensive lists of all the inanimate things that might be personified—like the "War, peace, darts, spears, towns, rivers, every thing" that Homer brings to life.[27]

In these eighteenth-century accounts, personification appears first as a figure of animation, rather than of abstraction or generalization.[28] It affects "things in-animate" (sometimes including ideas), attributing to such things the properties of living creatures, or of sensible beings. It does so by way of a corresponding anima-tion of its personifying subject, a point that Kames underscores when he classifies two types of personification according to the degree of animation of both person and thing. Kames's first type is "complete" or "passionate" personification, which is "derived from an actual conviction, momentary indeed, of life and intelligence;" the second is descriptive personification, which involves imaginative supposition rather than belief: "[t]he inanimate object is imagined to be a sensible being, but without any conviction . . . that it really is so." In the second sort of personifica-tion, Kames continues, "[t]he elevation . . . is far from being so great as when the personification arises to an actual conviction; and therefore must be considered of a lower and inferior sort."[29] Kames's distinction between an actual conviction of the passions and a supposition of the imagination is a roughly Humean one—conviction is a matter of animation, of greater liveliness or vivacity. And much like Hume, Kames acknowledges that the distinction is not absolute. Someone "endued with a sprightly imagination," or whose "present state of the spirits" is "lively," will see personification where another does not.[30]

Noting that Kames privileges personifications that are prompted by passions, readers like John Sitter and Stephen Knapp suggest that he anticipates a Romantic and particularly Wordsworthian understanding of the figure, in which personification indexes the power of the imagination, the life or soul of the poet.[31] At times, Kames does suggest such a sense of the figure, arguing that "A poet of superior genius hath more than others the command of this figure; because he hath more than others the power of inflaming the mind." A poet of great genius like Homer thus succeeds in personifying darts and arrows, much as James Thomson does winds, rain, the seasons, even a diamond.[32] But Kames's discussion quickly takes a different turn when he proceeds to catalogue unsuccessful personifications from Shakespeare, Virgil, and Thomson again, cautioning that "there are things familiar and base, to which personification cannot descend."[33] Kames's caution becomes the second of Blair's "two great rules" for personification. Blair's first rule, "never to attempt it, unless when prompted by strong passion, and never to continue it when the passion begins to flag," suggests that successful personification depends on the mental powers or affective state of the poet. By contrast, Blair's second rule, "never to personify any object in this way, but such as has some dignity in itself and can make a proper figure in this elevation to which we raise it" suggests that it is the object that determines the success of the figure.[34] These seem contradictory claims: if personifications depend on the passions or imagination of the poet, why should there be any limits to what can be personified? According to Stephen Knapp, Wordsworth favors the quasi-allegorical personification of natural objects (including human beings) precisely because of the "curious inappropriateness" of the figure to its objects: "the discrepancy between the agent's natural status and its sudden acquisition of a quasi-allegorical resonance . . . becomes, for Wordsworth, a formal index of imaginative power."[35] On Knapp's view, such personification is central to the Wordsworthian sublime, which "depends on the recognition of some disparity between the mind's exertions and the objects in which its energies are invested."[36] The personification of "familiar and base" objects like darts and rain, or a leech-gatherer and a blind beggar, effectively brings such disparity into view.

When Kames and Blair worry about personifying something without "natural dignity," they seem attuned to the limits of the poet's mind, rather than to its power.[37] Explicitly, they cite the risk of boldness, ridiculousness, extravagance, or absurdity: "If extraordinary marks of respect put upon a person of the lowest rank be ridiculous, not less so is the personification of a mean object."[38] When personification stoops too low, Blair cautions, the result is not an inflamed mind or an elevated object, but laughter:

> if the orator fails in his design of moving our passions by them [his personifications], he is sure of being laughed at. Of all frigid things, the most frigid, are the awkward and unseasonable attempts sometimes made toward such kinds of Personification . . . We remain not only cold, but frozen; and are at full leisure to criticize the ridiculous figure which the personified object makes.[39]

Described in this way, the laughter Blair worries about sounds Bergsonian—the effect of "something mechanical encrusted upon the living."[40] This is an understanding of laughter that Bergson elaborates by picturing a falling man: "Perhaps there was a stone on the road. He should have altered his pace or avoided the obstacle. Instead of that, through lack of elasticity, through absentmindedness and a kind of physical obstinacy, *as a result, in fact, of rigidity or of momentum*, the muscles continued to perform the same movement when the circumstances of the case called for something else. That is the reason of the man's fall, and also of the people's laughter."[41] We laugh, Bergson suggests, when we see life arrested by "the deep-seated recalcitrance of matter"—when the animate body becomes its opposite.[42]

At stake in Bergsonian laughter is the distinction between the living and the nonliving—a point that Sianne Ngai emphasizes when she links this laughter to the "crucial ambivalence embedded in the concept of animation."[43] Ngai suggests that animation "commingles antithetical notions of physical agency"—moving from within, and being moved from without. In doing so, it gives rise to a "surprising interplay between the passionate and the mechanical."[44] Ngai is primarily interested in the aesthetics and politics of animation in an era of technological reproducibility, but her notion of animation is useful for thinking about eighteenth-century personification—not least, because the interplay between the passionate and the mechanical looks less surprising in a period in which the passions were routinely described as Joseph Priestley describes them, as "blind and mechanical principles."[45] In his own lectures on rhetoric and criticism, then, Priestley follows Kames in splitting personification into two, but he demotes Kames's passionate personification (which Priestley calls "real" or "serious") as a lesser form of the figure, "the mechanical effect of a strong and serious passion."[46] Priestley prefers Kames's descriptive personification (which he calls "rhetorical" or "ideal") because it is under the poet's control:

> Such personification as this is the exercise, or rather the *play*, of a mind at ease, which first of all seeing things to be what they really are, is afterwards struck with their resemblance in point of form, situation, cause, effect, &c. to thinking beings, and amuses itself with completing the resemblance, and thus transforms them, as it were, by a voluntary effort of imagination, into real persons. Whereas in the *serious personification* the mind is under a temporary deception, the personification is neither made nor helped out by the speaker, but obtrudes itself upon him.[47]

Priestley may reverse the hierarchy of aesthetic and affective values held in common by Kames and Blair, but he works from the same logic as they do, in which passions—the life and soul of both poetry and persons—are also mechanical effects. Finally, then, Blair's laughter may sound like Bergson's: we laugh, in Blair's words, when we are "not only cold, but frozen," rather than "considerably heated and agitated" by "a strong passion."[48] But Blair's world is not ordered as Bergson's is. For Blair, as for Priestley and Kames, the terms that Bergson and Ngai take to be "antithetical notions"—person and machine, vitalism and mechanism, moving and being moved—are not so clearly opposed.

As a result, when Bergson's comic scenario of a falling man appears in eighteenth-century discussions of personification, it functions to different ends and effect. "Let a man by an unwary step, sprain his ankle, or hurt his foot upon a stone," Blair writes, "and in the ruffled, discomposed moment, he will sometimes feel himself disposed to break the stone in pieces, or to utter passionate expressions against it."[49] James Beattie gives a similar instance of the personification prompted by everyday life: "when things inanimate make a strong impression upon us, whether agreeable or otherwise, we are apt to address them in terms of affection or dislike. The sailor blesses the plank that brought him ashore from the shipwreck; and the passionate man, and sometimes even the philosopher, will say bitter words to the stumbling-block that gave him a fall."[50] The falling bodies in Blair and Beattie work differently than they do in Bergson. Rather than prompt the laughter of onlookers, they transform "things inanimate" *into* onlookers (or interlocutors, or antagonists). Recounted from the point of view of falling bodies rather than passers-by, what is represented in such scenes is less physical obstinacy than it is material impressionability or passion—terms that cross would-be divides between the living and the nonliving, between animate bodies and inanimate matter. These falling, passionate, and sometimes even philosophical figures (Blair's man, Beattie's sailor and philosopher) register the feeling of being an object among others, of acting and being acted upon in turn.

To say that rhetoricians like Kames, Blair, and Beattie take personification to be a figure that registers the feeling of simultaneously moving and being
moved is not to say that they are comfortable with this feeling. This is evident
in Kames's concerns about the "things familiar and base, to which personifications cannot descend," lest we are moved to laughter. He continues this way:
"to animate a lump of matter even in the most rapid flight of fancy, degenerates
into burlesk."[51] Kames turns to the *Aeneid* for an example of such degeneration,
and he cites the personification of a hand that has been cut off in battle—"your
right hand, Laridus, sought its owner."[52] Kames comments: "The personification here of a hand is insufferable, especially in a plain narration; not to mention that such a trivial incident is too minutely described."[53] It is a strange
comment—in what sense is death and dismemberment a trivial incident? And
it is a stranger scene, which recounts the battlefield deaths of twin brothers who
were "so alike" in life that they were "indistinguishable to kin, and a dear confusion to [their] parents." In death, they undergo "a cruel separateness" from one
another and from themselves, as a sword severs the head from one and a hand
from the other, which lingers on as the only thing living on the scene: "the dying fingers twitched and clutched again at the sword."[54] Raising questions about
the relationship between life and lifelessness, as well as between persons, parts,
and other people, this peculiar scene condenses anxieties that recur throughout
eighteenth-century discussions of personification. Of all the "things familiar
and base" to which personification can or ought not descend, first and foremost
is the "lump of matter" that is "a part or member of a living creature."[55] If the
hard case for Wasserman, Bronson and Chapin's accounts of personification is
the abstract idea like Hope or Pity or Liberty, for Kames and for Blair, it seems
to be the body part: the hand, or eye, or arm.

Kames returns to personified body parts three times, in what becomes an
anxious refrain of his discussion of personification. His next example comes from
Dryden's *All for Love* (1678); it is spoken by Cleopatra, just before she commits
suicide by stabbing herself with a dagger. Rather than a personified appendage
seeking its owner, this scene features a would-be owner addressing an appendage
that seems to be something else altogether:

> Haste, bare my arm, and rouze the serpent's fury
> Coward flesh—
> Would'st though conspire with Caesar, to betray me,
> As thou wert none of mine? I'll force thee to it . . . [56]

In his commentary on this example, Kames does not complain about triviality or burlesque degeneration. He complains instead about realism, about Dryden's lack regard for the way things—or persons—really are: "the different parts of the human body are too intimately connected with self, to be personified by the power of any passion; and after converting such a part into a sensible being, it is still worse to make it be conceived as rising in rebellion against self."⁵⁷ Kames makes a similar charge in his gloss on his third example, from Giovanni Guarini's *The Faithful Shepherd* (1590), in which a woman's mouth and eyes envy each other's beauty. This is an instance, Kames writes, "stretched beyond all resemblance. It is bold to take a part or member of a living creature, and to bestow upon it life, volition, and action: after animating two such members, it is still bolder to make them envy each other; for this is wide of any resemblance to reality."⁵⁸ Kames levels a number of different charges at the personifications of Virgil, Dryden, and Guarini: of triviality and boldness, of extravagance and a disregard for the real. In each case, the charge seems to indicate its opposite. Something "trivial" to one's person (like a hand) comes to seem utterly central when it has been cut off—if Larides's hand cannot find its owner, this is because in some sense, it has taken his place. In the case of Cleopatra, it seems that parts "too intimately connected with self" may not be so intimate after all—or, that intimacy may not take the form of instrumentality, and that property may be an imprecise figure for persons, whose parts act as if they were "none of mine." Kames's complaint that personified body parts bear little resemblance to reality begins to indicate the contrary. Personified body parts register the uncomfortable reality that persons may be both more and less whole than we might like.

Blair picks up on this strain of Kames's thought and condenses it in one extended example. He begins in a familiar key, warning that "addressing the parts of one's body, as if they were animated, is not congruous to the dignity of passion."⁵⁹ His example comes from the opening of Pope's *Eloisa to Abelard* (1717):

Dear fatal name! rest ever unreveal'd,
Nor pass these lips in holy silence sealed.
Hide it, my heart, within that close disguise,
Where, mixed with Gods, his lov'd idea lies:
Oh! Write it not, my hand!—his name appears
Already written—Blot it out, my tears!⁶⁰

In the commentary that follows, Blair lays out precise rules for the body parts that are and are not amenable to personification. A name can be personified, he begins,

because it "often stands for the person himself" and so "can bear this personification with sufficient dignity." He also permits personified hearts, since the heart
is "a dignified part of the human frame." A hand, however, is not: "a personified
hand is low, and not in the style of true passion."[61] Blair's careful if curious reasoning signals the sort of trouble that David Hillman and Carla Mazzio discuss
in the context of the early modern fascination with "the body in parts." Hillman
and Mazzio argue that the (early) modern rise of individualism—the social and
epistemic shift to Watt's trio of "the discrete particular, the directly apprehended
sensum, the autonomous individual"—"put increasing stress on the possibility
of the recuperation of part into whole."[62] This stress increases, it would seem,
depending upon the part: a quasi-figurative heart may stand in for the person as a
whole; the more material and putatively peripheral hand may not.[63]

What Hillman and Mazzio characterize as an early modern crisis in syn-
ecdochal thinking casts a long shadow, and in the eighteenth century, it receives
its most famous poetic formulation in Pope's *Essay on Man* (1733–4): "can a part
contain the whole?"[64] Pope's answer seems clear, at least in an epistemological
register, and clearly negative: "'Tis but a part we see, and not a whole."[65] Yet in
Pope, this insistence on partiality—both the partialness of our view and our status
as part—becomes a complicated affirmation of unity:

> What if the foot, ordain'd the dust to tread,
> Or hand to toil, aspir'd to be the head?
> What if the head, the eye, or ear repin'd
> To serve mere engines to the ruling Mind?
> Just as absurd for any part to claim
> To be another, in this gen'ral frame:
> Just as absurd, to mourn the tasks or pains
> The great directing MIND of ALL ordains.[66]

Pope's quasi-Pauline analogy figures every individual as a part in some greater
whole, which her partial view both affirms and renders incomprehensible. Put in
somewhat different terms, the poem's well-known assurance that "Whatever is, is
RIGHT," becomes the injunction to "Act well your part."[67]

Kames's and Blair's preoccupation with personified body parts registers the
difficulty of "acting your part" in a way that links the issue of animation (acting,
being acted upon, and trying to tell the difference) back to the question of abstraction (parts and wholes) that so preoccupied twentieth-century critics. But rather
than move up from individuals to genera and species (in the vein of Bronson,

Wasserman, and Chapin), Kames and Blair move downward, to the parts that compose individual persons in the first place. In doing so, they follow Kames's more capacious sense of abstraction, which he outlines in the Appendix to the *Elements of Criticism*. There, Kames identifies three different types of abstraction. The first and most common is the process of generalization that interests Bronson, Wasserman, and Chapin, which distributes individuals into classes by identifying qualities common to all. Kames then goes on to identify a second sort of abstraction, which "comprehends a number of individual objects considered as connected by some occasional relation," like a crowd, a nation, or an army. In this case, abstraction is a product of the Humean relations of causation and contiguity, as well as of resemblance. Kames's third type of abstraction is the inverse of his first: the operation in which "a single property or part, which may be common to many individuals, is selected to be the subject of our contemplation; for example, whiteness, heat, beauty, length, roundness, head, arm."[68]

All of Kames's abstractions begin from "individuals," but put together, they suggest some uncertainty about what counts as an "individual object," as well as the logic that holds together part, individual, and species. Viewed in light of Kames's discussion of abstraction, one might understand the problem with Eloisa's hand (or Larides's, or Cleopatra's arm) in a couple of ways. The problem is not that of Pope's ambitious foot, which aspires to act the part of another part (the head). For Eloisa's parts act much as they ought: the heart hides, the hand writes, the tears blot. Most obviously, the problem is that her hand aspires to act not as a part but as a whole. It aspires to the condition of a person or agent, instead of serving as an engine or instrument of her ruling mind. As Eloisa stands by and observes actions that both are and are not her own—Abelard's "name appears / Already written"—the individual person seems less an integrated system of interdependent parts than an onlooker or perhaps an assemblage, a collection of semi-autonomous agents connected by what Kames calls "occasional relations" like causation and contiguity.

The second problem that Kames's threefold sense of abstraction intimates is that a part might belong less to an individual than to a species—a point that Adela Pinch makes about passions, but which Kames extends quite explicitly to the parts of the body: hands and arms, like Hope or Fear or Virtue, might be "genuinely transpersonal."[69] In other words, the part may be recuperated into the whole, but this whole may not be an individual person. In Kames, at least, there are a host of other candidates for what we might call, after Pope, the "gen'ral frame": species, nation, crowd, army, perhaps the couple. In Kames's examples of personified body parts, all of these wholes are in potential conflict with the individual person. Cleopatra's flesh seems to conspire with Caesar against her, to serve Rome rather than herself; it is, perhaps, more properly part of the nation than it is part of her self. Larides's cut off hand likewise underscores questions about individuation raised by the "cruel separateness" of "indistinguishable" twin brothers. Whether they depict parts that are not recuperated into wholes, or parts that are recuperated into wholes that are not individual persons, the personification of body parts cited by Kames and Blair signal the difficulty of discerning part from whole, inside from outside, oneself from another. These are distinctions on which the notion of animation, in the sense of self-motion, depends—if one cannot confidently sort inside from outside, how does one sort animate from inanimate, moving (from within) from being moved (from without)? Making trouble for one sense of animation (as self-motion), these personifications give rise to another—a sense of animation that is not the property of particular beings (humans, animals, living creatures) but a common feature of living in what Blair calls "society with all nature," in which "every thing" is both moving and being moved.

O Lumpish Heart

While both are wide-ranging in their sources, neither Kames nor Blair draw examples of personification, or of personified body parts, from novels. If they had, they might have looked to *Pamela* (1740). There, they might have noticed the prominent role Pamela's hands play in her story, which begins, as Pamela tells it, when Mr. B "took me by the Hand before them all."[70] But unlike Eloisa's oddly autonomous appendage, Pamela's hands are everywhere moved from without, the objects rather than subjects of action: they are "snatch'd," "grasp'd," "clasp'd," "lifted up," "held," "press'd," "breathed upon," "blister'd" and "squeez[ed]."[71] Kames and Blair might have noticed, too, the way that Pamela continues to sort agents from instruments when she begins to picture her tongue speaking of its own accord, but then brings it under the direction of her ruling part (in this case, not her mind but her heart): "I am ready, on the Apprehension of this, to bite my forward Tongue, (or rather to beat my more forward Heart, that dictated to that poor Machine) for what I have said."[72] Finally, Kames and Blair might have noted that Pamela's heart appears here as a conventional, even clichéd figure for her person, the sort of figure that Blair approves in Pope's Eloisa and that Watt uses to praise Richardson's epistolary form, for offering a "short-cut, as it were, to the heart."[73] Pamela's forward heart seems a straightforward instance of the sort of romance and sentimental conventions that recur frequently throughout her letters. "I know I wrote my Heart; and that is not deceitful," Pamela insists; or, to Mr. B, "you know best your own Heart and Designs."[74] In a perfectly familiar way, Pamela's heart stands in for her self. It is by turns glad or broken or full; it sinks, misgives, or fails her; it is, above all, innocent. Mr. B's heart figures his person in much the same way: it has mischief in it and above all is proud; sometimes, as Pamela charges, it seems simply "the worst Heart in the World."[75]

Rhetoricians like Kames and Blair may not have found much to hold their attention in these utterly conventional hearts. But they might have been more interested in the extended dialogue Pamela holds with her personified heart at the center of the novel, which stages, over three long speeches, her decision to return to Lincolnshire. This decision transforms Pamela's forced captivity into her own free choice, and it has long dissatisfied readers of the novel—who frequently suspect that Pamela's change of heart in fact disguises desires that had been there all along. Pamela herself wavers between locating her heart inside and outside her self:

> O my treacherous, treacherous Heart! to serve me thus! And give no Notice to me of the Mischiefs thou wast about to bring upon me! But thus foolishly to give thyself up to the proud Invader, without ever consulting thy poor Mistress in the least! But thy Punishment will be the *first* and the *greatest*; and well deservest thou to smart, O perfidious Traitor, for giving up so weakly, thy *whole Self*, before a Summons came, and to one too, who had us'd me so hardly![76]

In her extended elaboration on the conventional figure of the treacherous heart, Pamela insists on holding open the question of whether her heart belongs to her ("thy Mistress") or she to it—it is the heart, after all, that is figured here as a "whole Self." She also displaces this question altogether, turning away from her self and her heart to a clearly alien agent: "the proud Invader" who is both Mr. B (the one "who has us'd me so hardly") and "Love," an allegorical personification that comes from without: "creep, creep it has, like a Thief upon me."[77]

In large part, Pamela's personifications appear a familiar strategy for externalizing and obfuscating agency, creating new persons in order to exonerate those actually on the scene. Mr. B's attacks are thus cast as the effects of a personified abstraction ("Love"); Pamela's desires as the work of a deceitful betrayer ("my treacherous, treacherous Heart!"). This reading is also available in Pamela's response to Mr. B's second letter, which entreats her to return of her own free-will:

O my exulting Heart! how it throbs in my Bosom, as if it would reproach me for so lately upbraiding it for giving way to the Love of so
dear a Gentleman!—But take care thou art not too credulous neither, O
fond Believer! Things that we wish, are apt to gain a too ready Credence
with us. . . . Therefore will I not acquit thee yet, O credulous, fluttering,
throbbing Mischief! that art so ready to believe what thou wishest: And I
charge thee to keep better Guard than though hast lately done, and lead
me not to follow too implicitly thy flattering and desirable Impulses.
Thus foolishly dialogu'd I with my Heart; and yet all the time this Heart
is *Pamela*.[78]

Once again, Pamela's apostrophized heart seems a familiar if extended rhetorical
figure, of the sort that appears in more condensed form when Mr. B "takes his
proud Heart to Task," or talks about the "Fondness that my foolish Heart entertained for you."[79] Pamela's dialogue with her heart is striking for its loquaciousness
and its rhetorical self-consciousness, for the repeated insistence that this heart
both is and is not Pamela's (or simply, *Pamela*). But ultimately her heart seems a
straightforward synecdoche, a figure for her true if divided self: what she both does
and does not want, or what she wants but can or should not admit to wanting.

Read in this way, Pamela's heart figures the problem of Pamela's volition in
wholly recognizable ways, as a problem of exercising free-will amidst passions that
are patently not, as Pamela says of Love, "a voluntier Thing."[80] Mrs. Jewkes makes
this sort of point when she chides Pamela about Parson Williams: "*Nought can restrain Consent of Twain*."[81] On the face of it, Mrs. Jewkes confesses her inability to
stop a union to which both parties have consented—there is no restraining union,
she shrugs, when two have consented. But her saying also and equally makes a
different point, one which Mrs. Jewkes repeatedly puts to Pamela and Mr. B: there
is no restraining consent, where there are two. The novel makes both very much
and very little of the distinction between these two ways of reading Mrs. Jewkes's
phrase, the latter of which takes the couple rather than the individual person as
its fundamental unit. Pamela and Mr. B may both have a great deal to say about
the value of Pamela's free-will.[82] But when it comes time to exercise this freedom,
it looks remarkably like acquiescence to what Pope might call "acting well your
part": "Should I go back, or should I not?—I doubt he has too great Hold in my
Heart, for me to be easily presently, if I should refuse: And yet this Gypsey Information makes me fearful. Well, I will, I think, trust in his Generosity!" Pamela
follows this declaration—her astonishingly swift decision to trust Mr. B—with her
own formulation of the Popean affirmation that "whatever is, is right": "I have no

Notion of obliging by Halves; but of doing things with a Grace, as one may say, where they *are* to be done."[83]

Pamela's extended dialogue with her personified heart is certainly a conventional rhetorical gambit, with a long life both before and after the eighteenth century. But Richardson lingers at some length over this conventional figure in ways that link a fairly commonplace point about unruly passions to the questions about animation and abstraction that will preoccupy Kames and Blair. Staged in a series of dialogues with her personified heart, Pamela's return to Lincolnshire recalls the set of possibilities signaled by Kames's and Blair's examples of personified body parts. On the one hand, this treacherous or exulting heart is Pamela's, or simply Pamela, her own true self. On the other hand, its actions are conspicuously autonomous—this heart acts more like an agent than an engine or instrument of Pamela's ruling mind. And finally, it seems, there is a third possibility: that Pamela's heart is not so much part of her self as it is part of someone or something else—of Mr. B, whose "hold in [her] Heart" returns her to him; of the species more generally, as Mrs. Jewkes suggests with her indiscriminate and putatively naturalist imperative to couple; of an abstraction like Love, which moves beyond as well as through both self and species. Like the personified hands, eyes and arms that trouble critics like Kames and Blair, Pamela's heart suggests that like passions or ideas or attributes, body parts are not easily enclosed within the bounds of individual persons.

It might seem strange to describe Pamela's heart as a body part in the first place, since it is so clearly and so conventionally metaphorical.[84] But Pamela's personified heart does, I think, belong to the eighteenth-century discourse on personified body parts, for reasons that emerge most clearly in the first of her three addresses to it. Pamela is first prompted to apostrophize her heart when Mr. B at long last sends her home to her parents, and she discovers that she is loath to leave:

> What could be the Matter with me, I wonder!—I felt something so strange, and my Heart was so lumpish!—I wonder what ail'd me!—But this was so *unexpected*!—I believe that was all!—Yet I am very strange still . . . I'll take thee, O lumpish, contradictory, ungovernable Heart, to severe Task for this thy strange Impulse, when I get to my dear Father's and Mother's; and if I find anything in thee that should not be, depend upon it, thou shalt be humbled, if strict Abstinence, Prayer and Mortification will do it![85]

Reading this passage against the backdrop of eighteenth-century concerns about personifying "a lump of matter," we might wonder what it means for a heart to be "lumpish"—for a body part to be likened to a lump of matter. For if an organ indicates organization and a part points to some whole, a lump moves in the opposite direction: it is a shapeless, brute, or formless mass. A lump of matter is almost redundant, connoting matter at its most material, without animation even in the most basic sense of having been shaped. To be lumpish is to be material in this most inanimate way: "cumbersome . . .; not apt to be moved easily; heavy and unwieldy"; "sluggishly inactive." The *OED* cites Pamela's "lumpish heart" as an instance of a quasi-figurative sense of feeling like matter, inanimate and weighed down: "low-spirited, dejected, melancholy."[86]

To attend to the lumpishness of Pamela's personified heart is to note its oscillation between the metaphorical and the material. It is guilty of treachery, mischief, foolishness, perfidy, weakness, credulity, pride and vanity, but it also throbs, is lumpish, has impulses. Moreover, the material and metaphorical properties of Pamela's heart are not clearly sorted, but often pass quickly from one to the other. Throbs thus become a sort of speech—"how it throbs in my Bosom, as if it would reproach me"—and Pamela's reply to this reproach transforms her address into a full-fledged "dialogue."[87] If Pamela's heart is metaphorical, it is also material; or, it is a metaphor for materiality, and for the materiality of the self. In this, Pamela's lumpish, impulsive, and ungovernable heart draws not only on the conventions of romance, but also on the tradition of politico-physiological representation that goes back at least to William Harvey, whose material and metaphorical hearts unsettled traditional understandings of bodily motion, reconfiguring the relationship between part and whole, mover and moved.[88] Viewed in this light, Pamela's lumpish heart does not figure what Bergson would call the "recalcitrance of matter"—the resistance of brute matter to the activity of the mind or soul. Pamela's heart may be lumpish and "not apt to be easily moved," but it is nevertheless in motion. Fluttering and throbbing, it is not inert but "wayward," moved by or as what Pamela calls "Impulses."[89] This is the final sort of animation figured by Pamela's heart: animation that is proper neither to oneself nor to other people, that is not transpersonal so much as simply material. In *Pamela*, to be lumpish, like matter, is to be in motion.[90]

Pamela follows her apostrophe to her lumpish heart with a lament for her own condition, on finding that being set free feels much like being carried against her wishes: "here I am again, a pure Sporting-piece for the Great! a mere Tennis-ball of Fortune!"[91] Representing herself as "a mere Tennis-ball of Fortune," Pamela turns a characteristically spirited phrase. She also takes up a figure with considerable philosophical pedigree.[92] The same figure features prominently in

Locke's chapter on "Power" in the *Essay Concerning Human Understanding* (1690), which begins by distinguishing the active power of persons from the passive power of tennis balls. On Locke's account, our idea of active power (or simply, action) comes from our everyday experience of ourselves, in which "barely by a thought of the Mind, we can move the parts of our Bodies, which were before at rest."[93] By contrast, our idea of passive power (or, passion) comes from observing a ball struck by a stick or a foot: this sort of motion, we conclude, "is not any action of the Ball, but bare passion."[94] Locke goes on to explain that unlike "bare passion," action depends upon thought: "A Tennis-ball, whether in motion by the stroke of a Racket, or lying still at rest, is not by any one taken to be a *free Agent* . . . because we conceive not a Tennis-ball to think, and consequently not to have any Volition, or preference of Motion to rest."[95]

Having set up the opposition between acting persons and passionate things, Locke proceeds to detail the many ways and situations in which human beings, like tennis balls, are the objects of passion rather than the subjects of action. Such is the case for "a Man falling into the Water, (a Bridge breaking under him)," as well as for "a Man striking himself, or his Friend, by a Convulsive motion of his Arm."[96] Such is the case for all of us, all of the time, at least in some respects: "A Man's Heart beats, and the Blood circulates, which 'tis not in his Power by any Thought or Volition to stop; and therefore in respect of these Motions . . . he is not a *free Agent* . . . but under as much Necessity of moving, as a Stone that falls, or a Tennis-ball struck with a Racket."[97] More troublingly still, for Locke, is that this is the case for the motions of our minds as well as of our bodies, since our "Volition, or preference of Motion to rest" is itself determined by passions that we are not free to choose at will.[98] Locke acknowledges that in most respects, we are not acting, but we are also not at rest. Locke's word for this is passion.

Locke's chief task, in the moral-philosophical chapter on "Power," is to explain and perhaps strengthen our capacity to scale the chain of being that he charts from moved to mover, passion to action, tennis ball to human being—a process we might conceive of as a sort of personification.[99] He insists that "we are endowed with a power to suspend any particular desire, and keep it from determining the *will*, and engaging us in any action. This is *standing still*, where we are not sufficiently assured of the way."[100] Locke is quite clear that motion is very often, perhaps even essentially, unfree:

> [H]e that is at liberty to ramble in perfect darkness, what is his liberty better than if he were driven up and down, as a bubble by the force of the wind? The being acted by a blind impulse from without, or from

within, is little odds. The first therefore and great use of Liberty is to hinder blind Precipitancy; the principal exercise of Freedom is to stand still, open the eyes, look about, and take a view of the consequence of what we are going to do.[101]

On Locke's account, the power proper to the human person—what Locke calls active power or free agency rather than "bare passion"—is the power to stop. This makes for a striking and somewhat strange account of freedom, not least because it is wholly satisfied by the preference of one who "has his Chains knocked off, and the Prison doors set open to him . . . [even] though the desire of some convenience to be had there, absolutely determines his preference, and makes him stay in his Prison."[102] It is also an account of freedom that takes the perplexity of animation seriously. In a world of matter in motion, in which one is always at once moving and being moved, freedom consists not in movement, but in its arrest.

Readers have often noted Pamela's debt to and difficulty with Locke's notion of freedom. She certainly does not succeed in suspending motion when she makes her remarkably swift decision to return to Mr. B, which appears more an effect of "blind Precipitancy" than an "exercise of Freedom": "Should I go back, or should I not? . . . Well, I will, I think, trust in his Generosity!"[103] Pamela's narrative does feature one extended and successful Lockean moment, and I want to turn to this moment in closing, with the issue of animation and personification in view. Pamela's Lockean moment comes after her failed attempt to escape from Lincolnshire, when she considers drowning herself in the pond. The scene begins with her semi-personified heart, perhaps propelling her forward or perhaps beating in protest, as if it wanted no part of her actions: "my poor Heart beating all the Time against my Bosom, as if it would have forc'd its way out."[104] Pamela finds that the lock to the gate has been changed—"O then how my Heart sunk!"—and her body springs into action:

> I clamber'd up upon the Ledges of the Door, and the Lock, which was a great wooden one, reaching the Top of the Door with my Hands; and little thinking I could climb so well, made shift to lay hold on the Top of the Wall with my Hands; but, alas for me! nothing but ill Luck!—no Escape for poor *Pamela!* The Wall being old, the Bricks I held by, gave way, just as I was taking a Spring to get up, and down came I, and received such a Blow upon my Head, with one of the Bricks, that it quite stunn'd me; and I broke my Shins and my Ancle besides, and beat off the Heel of one of my Shoes. In this dreadful way, flat upon the Ground, lay

poor I, for I believe five or six Minutes; and when I would have got up, I could hardly stand; for I found I had bruis'd my left Hip and Shoulder, and was full of Pain with it; and besides my Head bled, and ak'd with the Blow I had with the Brick.[105]

Pamela's fall is not an occasion for Bergsonian laughter, nor is it the sort of fall that Blair or Beattie picture as a prompt to personification. She does not bring the brick to life, venting her passions by creating a person to blame for her own inanimation. But Pamela's falling body does occasion a personification scene of a quite different and Lockean sort. The scene that follows brings a person into being neither as a sympathetic onlooker or a blamable antagonist (an apostrophized brick), nor as an assemblage of heart and hand and tongue. It brings a person into being as an active and deliberating mind.

Pamela's fall precipitates what Mark Kinkead-Weekes calls "the first important and sustained self-analysis in English fiction."[106] It is indeed a remarkable scene: three pages of Pamela's minutely detailed reflections, punctuated by the activities of her mind: "I reason'd . . . I then consider'd . . . said I to myself . . . thinks I . . . thought I"—the last locution repeated five times in two pages, emphasizing the ongoing presence of her mind in motion.[107] As Kinkead-Weekes and others have noted, this is a landmark scene in the narrative of the rise of the novel, and it is framed in distinctly Lockean terms: "Pause here a little, *Pamela*, on what thou art about, before thou take the dreadful Leap, and consider."[108] Here, Pamela quite properly exercises the sort of freedom that Locke describes, when he enjoins readers "to stand still, open the eyes, look about, and take a view of the consequence of what we are going to do." At least, she does something close. For Pamela "could hardly stand," let alone stand still—"flat upon the Ground, lay poor I":[109]

It was well for me, as I have since thought, that I was so maim'd, as made me the longer before I got to the Water; for this gave me some Reflection, and abated that Liveliness of my Passions, which possibly might otherwise have hurry'd me, in my first Transport of Grief . . . to throw myself in without Consideration; but my Weakness of Body made me move so slowly, that it gave Time for a little Reflection, a Ray of Grace, to dart in upon my benighted Mind; and so, when I came to the Pondside, I sat myself down on the sloping Bank, and began to ponder my wretched Condition: And thus I reason'd with myself.[110]

Locke insists that unlike tennis-balls and other objects, human beings have a power to suspend motion, to stand still and think. He does not detail precisely how this power works. How are we to interrupt the course of animation, to hold ourselves apart from the world of matter in motion? In its elaborate disabling of Pamela's body, the pond scene proposes one answer. Pamela's paradigmatically Lockean moment repeatedly presents thinking as a consequence of bodily debilitation: "It was well for me . . . that I was so maim'd . . . for this gave me some Reflection"; "my Weakness of Body made me move so slowly, that it gave Time for a little Reflection"; "my Bruises made me slow; and I thought."[111] As *Pamela* stages it, the deliberation that secures what Locke calls "freedom" depends upon a body that has been rendered immobile, not only inanimate but inanimable, even broken. Free agency does not only depend upon thought, on this formulation—it is available only to and as thought.

In this scene, Pamela comes into being as a deliberating mind, what she and the novel call a "free Person."[112] I have proposed that we might think of this as a process of personification, and it is the sort of personification—not usually so called—for which the novel is best known. It has been the aim of this essay to suggest that reading eighteenth-century novels alongside eighteenth-century poetry—and, reading Watt alongside Wasserman, Bronson and Chapin, as well as Kames and Blair—might help to make visible the other sorts of personification alive in a work like *Pamela*, like that of her lumpish and wayward heart. For Pamela's heart does not register her capacity to stand still and apart so much as her embeddedness in a world of matter in motion, an embeddedness underscored by the elaborate lengths Richardson takes to extract her from it. Reading *Pamela* alongside eighteenth-century poetry and criticism might also help to make visible how fleeting the more "novelistic" or Lockean type of personification seems to be. As soon as Pamela regains mobility by the side of the pond, she enjoins herself to flee, lest she be moved again: "Quit with speed these guilty Banks, and flee from these dashing Waters, that even in their sounding Murmurs, this still Night, reproach thy Rashness! Tempt not God's Goodness on the mossy Banks, that have been Witnesses of thy guilty Intentions."[113] Pamela's personification of the pond's waters and banks is straight out of the literary tradition that interests Kames and Blair, and this too, is part of the literary tradition to which *Pamela* belongs. It is a tradition with its own sort of realism: neither the formal realism that faithfully records the material world of things nor the realism of assessment that wisely evaluates the social world of persons, but a realism true to our experience of being objects among others, some of which are at once intimate and oddly alien.[114]

This literary tradition has a good deal to interest twenty-first century readers, alert to recent calls to distribute agency more widely—to cultivate a sense of self "as itself an impure, human-nonhuman assemblage," just as we learn to "take seriously the vitality of (nonhuman) bodies . . . the capacity of things . . . to act as quasi agents or forces with trajectories, propensities, or tendencies of their own."[115] With their capacity to "introduce [. . .] us into society with all nature,"[116] eighteenth-century personifications might help us to imagine the sort of world that scholars like Bruno Latour and Jane Bennett envision: one that is not divided into persons and things, agents and instruments, animate and inanimate beings.[117] At the same time, the personifications so prominent in eighteenth-century novels, poetry, philosophy and criticism bring a different set of exigencies and issues into view. These are visible in Kames and Blair's soft policing of the ontological decorum of a rhetorical figure; in Pamela's dialogues with her heart and her fortunate fall; in Locke's effort to suspend the animation we share with tennis balls. From Locke to Richardson, Kames and Blair, the literature of this period certainly shares the new materialist question of how best to recognize or represent the agency of objects, including ourselves. But in a world that so readily apprehends "every thing thinking, feeling, and acting, as we ourselves do," the question is not how to distribute agency more widely. It is how to come to a stop.

Notes

1. Cecil Deane, *Aspects of Eighteenth-Century Nature Poetry* (Oxford: Blackwell, 1935), 11.

2. Henry Home, Lord Kames. *Elements of Criticism.* 3 vols. (Edinburgh: Millar, Kincaid and Bell, 1762), 3:54.

3. Bertrand H. Bronson, "Personification Reconsidered," *English Literary History* 14, no. 3 (1947): 171.

4. See Stephen Knapp, *Personification and the Sublime: Milton to Coleridge* (Cambridge: Harvard University Press, 1985); and Adela Pinch, *Strange Fits of Passion: Epistemologies of Emotion, Hume to Austen* (Stanford: Stanford University Press, 1996). For a fine account of the role of personification in the period, see also Clifford Siskin, "Personification and Community: Literary Change in the Mid and Late Eighteenth Century" *Eighteenth-Century Studies* 15, no. 4 (1982): 371–401. For some time, John Sitter has been leading the way in urging us to take seriously the work of eighteenth-century personifications, and demonstrating what we might learn by doing so. See especially his wonderful *Cambridge Introduction to Eighteenth-Century Poetry* (Cambridge: Cambridge University Press, 2011), 157–215.

5. Somewhat schematically, the main differences between their accounts run as follows. Bronson aims to uncover the personal grief behind the decorous generalizations of Samuel Johnson's "On the Death of Dr. Robert Levet." Wasserman looks instead to critics and rhetoricians (including Kames and Blair) in order to link personification to the period's pictorial imagination; he goes on to argue that personification plays a similar role for the Augustans as the symbol does for the Romantics.

Finally, Chapin resists the telos that leads from neoclassical personification to the Romantic symbol by emphasizing the rhetorical as much as the passionate use of the figure.

6. Bronson, "Personification," 165. Earl Wasserman, "The Inherent Values of Eighteenth-Century Personification," *PMLA* 65, no. 4 (1950): 437. The shift from neoclassical generalization to modern particularity has a different tenor for each critic. It becomes an increasingly emotional strain in Bronson's essay, which invokes its own personified abstraction to lament "the intellectual drift of the last hundred and fifty years toward Egocentricity" (165). (The phrase, "the egocentricity of the past century and a half" is repeated three times in as many pages, to become a curious and anxious refrain [172, 174, 176].) Wasserman is less worried than Bronson about this shift, not least because he sees the eighteenth-century personification and the Coleridgean symbol as different means to a similar end: both figures render reality intelligible by unifying particularity and generality. Wasserman points out that Bronson's preference for generality depends on a sense of the priority of the personal or the particular, which needs to be worked up into a general class. (As Bronson puts it, "we are so constituted that we have to make generals of particulars or be drowned in the flood of phenomena" [168].) Wasserman argues that personification "performed its poetic function so long as man assumed that all human knowledge is empirical and that abstractions are fabricated by mind to unify human experience"—an assumption shared by Bronson and by the Augustans, but not by a Romantic poet like Coleridge or an idealist philosopher like Kant (437). Wasserman concludes that "the truly fundamental processes of poetry have not changed; in the transition from personification to symbolism we have substituted one counter for another to provide for the shift in metaphysics" (463). For an illuminating approach to the aesthetics of neoclassical generality that proceeds through Bronson and especially Wasserman, as well as through Locke's epistemology, see William H. Youngren, "Conceptualism and Neoclassic Generality" *English Literary History* 47, no. 4 (1980): 705–40.

7. Chester Chapin, *Personification in Eighteenth-Century English Poetry* (New York: Octagon, 1974), 111.

8. Ibid., 114.

9. Pinch is commenting in particular on Bronson's reading of Johnson's "Death of Dr. Levet," which argues that Johnson begins with personal feelings, abstracts them into general statements, and then reparticularizes those statements by means of personification. Pinch writes, "This rather contorted account reveals the extent to which twentieth-century discussions of neoclassical feeling depend on a postromantic notion that feelings are, in their origins, at 'first' personal"—a point that "might suggest to us that our understanding of the neoclassical is trapped in an opposition between the personal and the general: it cannot admit the possibility of feelings that are genuinely transpersonal" (*Strange Fits*, 46).

10. Ian Watt, *The Rise of the Novel: Studies in Defoe, Richardson, and Fielding* [1957], 2nd ed. (Berkeley: University of California Press, 2001), 13, 16.

11. Ibid., 62.

12. Bronson, "Personification," 177.

13. Watt, *Rise of the Novel*, 86, 92.

14. Bronson, "Personification," 174.

15. Watt, *Rise of the Novel*, 17.

16. Siskin, "Personification and Community," 375, 396.

17. Wasserman, "Inherent Values," 455.

18. W. B. Carnochan, "Afterward," in Watt, *Rise of the Novel*, 302.

19. For fascinating accounts of the gestation of *The Rise of the Novel* during the 40s and 50s, and out of Watt's own wartime experiences, see Ian Watt, "Flat-Footed and Fly-Blown: The Realities of Realism," *Eighteenth-Century Fiction* 12, nos. 2–3 (2000): 147–66; and Marina MacKay, "The Wartime Rise of *The Rise of the Novel*," *Representations* 119, no. 1 (2012): 119–43.

20. This sort of return is already well under way in the work of Stephen Knapp and Adela Pinch, and in a different vein, in a work like Sarah Guyer's *Romanticism After Auschwitz* (Stanford: Stanford University Press, 2007), esp. 104–140. The broader connections between eighteenth-century studies and critical movements like thing theory, new materialisms, or posthumanism are evident in a number of recent works in the field, including Jonathan Kramnick's study of the period's literature and philosophy of action, *Actions and Objects from Hobbes to Richardson* (Stanford: Stanford University Press, 2010); Julie Park's work on animation, objecthood and the novel, in *The Self and It: Novel Objects in Eighteenth-Century England* (Stanford: Stanford University Press, 2010); Sandra Macpherson's account of the materialist and tragic logic of strict liability in *Harm's Way: Tragic Responsibility and the Novel Form* (Baltimore: The Johns Hopkins University Press, 2010); and Jonathan Lamb's work on the curious and often hostile literary relationships between persons, things, objects and authors, in *The Things Things Say* (Princeton: Princeton University Press, 2011).

21. Hugh Blair, *Lectures on Rhetoric and Belles Lettres*, 3 vols. (Dublin: Whitestone, Colles, Burnet, et al.), 3:391.

22. Wasserman, "Inherent Values," 435.

23. These critics do acknowledge the wider world of personification in the period, but they restrict their attention to the apparently more significant or difficult case of the personified abstraction. John Sitter's *Cambridge Introduction* is an exception in this regard, reflecting widely and variously on the figure.

24. Kames, *Elements*, 3:62.

25. Ibid., 3:54.

26. Blair, *Lectures*, 3:383–4.

27. Ibid., 3:390.

28. On personification as a figure of animation, see also Heather Keenleyside, "Personification for the People: On James Thomson's *The Seasons*," *English Literary History 1500–1800*, 76, no. 2 (2009): 447–472.

29. Kames, *Elements*, 3:62, 3:64.

30. See Ibid., 3:72. Kames identifies both passionate and descriptive personifications as "figures of thought" rather than "figures of speech," which simply compare two entities that remain entirely distinct. Kames argues that in figures of thought like both passionate and descriptive personification we really believe, or actually suppose, that inanimate objects have life, sense, or intelligence. See Ibid., 3:70.

31. Sitter argues that Kames's preference for passionate personification moves him closer to a Romantic view of the figure because it defines "*real* personifications—the only kind to be taken seriously—as dramas of intrapersonal voices in the poet's head." See *Cambridge Introduction*, 169. Knapp makes a similar point, but also emphasizes that for a poet like Wordsworth, personification indexes the power of a curiously autonomous imagination or mind, one that does not necessarily belong to the poet, or to anyone in particular. See Knapp, *Personification*, 109.

32. Kames, *Elements*, 3:77.

33. Ibid., 3:78.

34. Blair, *Lectures*, 3:394, 3:395.

35. Ibid., 107.

36. Ibid., 106.

37. Kames, *Elements*, 3:79.

38. Ibid., 3:77.

39. Blair, *Lectures*, 3:397.

40. Henri Bergson, *Laughter: An Essay on the Meaning of the Comic*, trans. Cloudesley Brereton and Fred Rothwell (Mineola, NY: Dover, 2005), 19.

41. Ibid., 5.

42. Ibid., 13.

43. Sianne Ngai, *Ugly Feelings* (Cambridge: Harvard University Press, 2005), 101.

44. Ibid., 101, 100. For Ngai, animation gives rise to a surprising set of "counterintuitive connections . . . between the organic-vitalist and the technological-mechanical, and between the technological-mechanical and the emotional" (95).

45. Joseph Priestley, *A Course of Lectures on Oratory and Criticism* (London: J. Johnson, 1777), 80.

46. Ibid., 251.

47. Ibid., 254.

48. Blair, *Lectures,* 3:392.

49. Ibid., 3:384.

50. James Beattie, *Essays on Poetry and Music, as they affect the mind; on Laughter, and Ludicrous Composition; On the Usefulness of Classical Learning* (London: E. and C. Dilly and W. Creech, 1779), 255.

51. Kames, *Elements*, 3:78.

52. Kames gives the lines in Latin: "Te decisa suum, Larides, dextera quaerit: / Semianimesque micant digit; ferrumque retractant" (bk. 10, lines 395–6, as quoted in Kames, *Elements*, 3:78). The English translation of these and the surrounding lines come from Virgil, *Aeneid*, trans. A. S. Kline, 2002. Online at http://www.poetryintranslation.com/PITBR/Latin/VirgilAeneidX.htm

53. Kames, *Elements*, 3:79.

54. Virgil, *Aeneid*, bk. 10, lines 390–6.

55. Kames, Elements, 3:84.

56. John Dryden, *All for Love*, Act 5, sc. 1, lines 565–8, quoted in Kames, *Elements*, 3:75.

57. Kames, *Elements*, 3:75.

58. Ibid., 3:84.

59. Blair, *Lectures*, 3:395.

60. Pope, *Eloisa to Abelard*, lines 9–14, quoted in Blair, *Lectures*, 3:395.

61. Blair, *Lectures*, 3:395–6.

62. David Hillman and Carla Mazzio, eds. *The Body in Parts: Fantasies of Corporeality in Early Modern Europe* (New York: Routledge, 1997), xiii. Watt's quote comes from *Rise of the Novel*, 62.

63. For a different version of this stress on the possibility of recuperating part into whole, see Kramnick's discussion of Rochester in *Action and Objects*, 99–140; and Macpherson's discussion of Frances Sheridan in *Harm's Way*, which concludes with a discussion of Pope's "formal commitment to synecdoche" in *The Rape of the Lock*, 133–74; esp. 169–74.

64. Alexander Pope, *An Essay on Man*, in *The Twickenham Edition of the Poems of Alexander Pope*, ed. John Butt, vol. 3.2, *An Essay on Man*, ed. Maynard Mack (London: Methuen & Co., 1950), 1:32.

65. Ibid., 1:60.

66. Ibid., 1:259–66.

67. Ibid., 1:294, 4:194.

68. Kames, *Elements*, 3:405.

69. Pinch, *Strange Fits*, 46.

70. Samuel Richardson, *Pamela; or, Virtue Rewarded* (Oxford: Oxford University Press, 2001), 11.

71. See Ibid., 34, 49, 66, 24, 66, 77, 108.

72. Ibid., 219.

73. Watt, *Rise of the Novel*, 195.

74. Richardson, *Pamela*, 230, 229.

75. Ibid., 60.

76. Ibid., 249.

77. Ibid., 248.

78. Ibid., 251.

79. Ibid., 219, 247.

80. Ibid., 248. For the wider context of Pamela's predicament, see Kramnick's *Actions and Objects*, especially his account of the debates over free-will and necessity from Hobbes to Hume, 27–60. On Kramnick's account, the compatibilist position seeks to reconcile our everyday feeling of being free with the fact of being determined, a material object that is moved like any other (see, for example, his discussion of Hobbes's concession to "our naïve intuitions . . . that agents tend to think of themselves as having a will under their control" [38]). In this essay, I am interested in the strain of eighteenth-century thought that is also attuned to our feeling of being unfree, in the sense of being moved from without—or, to our inability to clearly distinguish the feeling of moving from the feeling of being moved.

81. Richardson, *Pamela*, 147.

82. See for example Mr. B's insistence on the "Value I set upon the Free-will of a Person already in my Power" (Richardson, *Pamela*, 190), and Pamela's plea to "let my Assent be that of a free Person" (Ibid., 139). The question of Pamela's free will has long disturbed readers of the novel, who often charge Richardson with presenting, in Michael McKeon's formulation, a view of "freedom as a truckling matrimonial subservience" (380). McKeon's own reading is an important counter to this view, since it takes the novel's commitment to Pamela's freedom as a serious if troubled position. See McKeon, *The Origins of the English Novel, 1600–1740* (Baltimore: The Johns Hopkins University Press, 1987), 357–81.

83. Richardson, *Pamela*, 252, 253.

84. For a related discussion of Clarissa's heart and hymen, see Park, *The Self and It*, 51–76.

85. Richardson, *Pamela*, 244–45.

86. See the *OED* entry for "lumpish"; the citation from *Pamela* is the last historical example it gives of this quasi-figurative usage.

87. Richardson, *Pamela*, 251.

88. On Harvey's heart, see John Rogers, *The Matter of Revolution: Science, Poetry, and Politics in the Age of Milton* (Ithaca: Cornell University Press, 1996), 16–27.

89. Richardson, *Pamela*, 245, 251.

90. On the vitalism of eighteenth-century materialism (or, of the inoperability of the mechanist/vitalist opposition in the period), see Catherine Packham, *Eighteenth-Century Vitalism: Bodies, Culture, Politics* (Houndsmills, Basingstoke: Palgrave MacMillan, 2012). For two important recent essays that draw on some of the same texts or contexts as I do here, see Helen Deutsch, "Dismantl'd Souls: The Verse Epistle, Embodied Subjectivity, and Poetic Animation," in *Vital Matters: Eighteenth-Century Views of Conception, Life and Death*, ed. Helen Deutsch and Mary Terrall (Toronto: University of Toronto Press, 2011), 50–65; and Joseph Drury, "Haywood's Thinking Machines," *Eighteenth-Century Fiction* 21, no. 2 (2009): 201–28.

91. Richardson, *Pamela*, 245.

92. The philosophical pedigree of Pamela's tennis-ball of fortune goes back before Locke to Hobbes, whom Joseph Bramhall accused of picturing man as "no more than a tennis-ball, to be tossed to and fro by the rackets of the second causes." See Bramhall, *Hobbes and Bramhall on Liberty and Necessity*, ed. Vere Chappell (Cambridge: Cambridge University Press, 1999), 55–56. This passage is quoted by Drury in his "Haywood's Thinking Machines" (208), which also reflects more widely on what it means to be a thinking being in a world of material causes.

93. John Locke, *An Essay concerning Human Understanding*, ed. Peter H. Nidditch, Clarendon Edition of the Works of John Locke (Oxford: Oxford University Press, 1975), 235. Locke presents the power of thought to move the body as an undeniable feature of our everyday experience, which nevertheless defies our powers of explanation: "We cannot conceive how any thing but impulse of Body can move Body; and yet that is not a Reason sufficient to make us deny it possible, against the constant Experience, we have of it in our selves, in all our voluntary Motions, which are produced in us only by the free Action or Thought of our own Minds; and are not, nor can be the effects of the impulse or determination of the Motion of blind Matter, in or upon our Bodies; for

then it could not be in our power or choice to alter it. For example: My right Hand writes, whilst my left Hand is still: What causes rest in one, and motion in the other? Nothing but my Will, a Thought of my Mind; my Thought only changing, the right Hand rests, and the left Hand moves. This is matter of fact, which cannot be denied: Explain this, and make it intelligible, and then the next step will be to understand Creation" (Ibid., 629).

94. Ibid., 238.

95. Ibid., 238.

96. Ibid., 238.

97. Ibid., 239.

98. In Locke's empiricist epistemology, the mind's determination begins with the very fact of receiving ideas from outside. Along these lines, he notes the misleading use of active verbs in phrases such as "I see the Moon" or "I feel the heat of the Sun." In both cases, Locke argues, "I am not active but barely passive, and cannot in that position of my Eyes, or Body, avoid receiving them" (Ibid., 286). Ideas continue to elude our control even after they have entered our minds, something that Locke coins the phrase "the association of ideas" to describe. In doing so, he constructs his own curious scene of personification: "*Ideas* that in themselves are not at all of kin. . . always keep in company, and the one no sooner at any time comes into the Understanding but its Associate appears with it; and if they are more than two which are thus united, the whole gang always inseparable shew themselves together" (Ibid., 395).

99. See Helen Thompson's *Ingenuous Subjection: Compliance and Power in the Eighteenth-Century Domestic Novel* (Philadelphia: University of Pennsylvania Press, 2005), which argues that Locke's moral philosophy takes as its starting point the sort of materialist physiology articulated by Mary Astell, in which the task of morality cannot be to deny desire or the passions, but to direct them.

100. Locke, *Essay,* 266.

101. Ibid., 279.

102. Ibid., 266.

103. Richardson, *Pamela,* 252.

104. Ibid., 170.

105. Ibid., 171.

106. Mark Kinkead-Weekes, *Samuel Richardson: Dramatic Novelist* (Ithaca: Cornell University Press, 1973), 47.

107. Richardson, *Pamela,* 172–74.

108. Ibid., 172.

109. Ibid., 171.

110. Ibid., 172.

111. Ibid., 172–173. In *The Discourse of the Mind in Eighteenth-Century Fiction* (The Hague: Mouton, 1974), John A. Dussinger also remarks on the important connection between body and mind in this scene, writing that "bodily pains and discomforts are oddly juxtaposed with existential anxieties and moral platitudes in this romance of adolescent wish-fulfillment" (Ibid., 62). For

Dussinger, the adolescence of the scene stems from the indecorousness of its figurative logic—on his view, Pamela acts as though her physical fall were "tantamount to a moral fall," and her physical pain were equivalent (or at least analogous) to a more general and existential sense of human suffering. But pain seems to me rather beside the point in this scene. Once she begins her deliberations, Pamela does not mention her physical sensations or discomfort; indeed, her reflections are remarkably cogent and untroubled by the serious injuries she has sustained. Throughout the scene, her fall seems less significant as the source of pain than as the cause of immobility, the material rather than sentient condition required to transform her from a moving body into a thinking mind.

112. Richardson, *Pamela*, 139.

113. Ibid., 174.

114. The terms "formal realism" and "realism of assessment" come from Watt's *Rise of the Novel*—the former associated with Defoe and Richardson, the latter with Fielding.

115. Jane Bennett, *Vibrant Matter: A Political Ecology of Things* (Durham, NC: Duke University Press, 2010), xvii, x. See also Bruno Latour, especially *Reassembling the Social: An Introduction to Actor Network Theory* (Oxford: Oxford University Press, 2005).

116. Blair, *Lectures*, 3:391.

117. Both Latour and Bennett are sensitive to the role of figuration in shaping our conceptions of agents and actions, and both argue that we need to make innovative use of rhetorical figures in order to dislodge our usual ways of carving up the world. Bennett makes a case for the strategic use and anti-anthropocentric consequences of anthropomorphism; Latour, for the critical value of narratology's figure of the actant. See Bennett, *Vibrant Matter*, especially 98–99, 120; and Latour, *Reassembling*, especially 52–8.

7

"LIGHT ELECTRIC TOUCHES":
STERNE, POETRY, AND EMPIRICAL EROTICS

David Fairer

F OR ANNA LETITIA BARBAULD there was something surreptitious about the way Laurence Sterne had worked his way into the history of the novel. In her essay, "On the Origin and Progress of Novel-Writing" (1810), she finds it hard to fit him legitimately into her scheme. For her, *Tristram Shandy* (1759–67) is not so much a novel as a *novel-in-disguise* (that "very singular work," she says, had appeared "somewhat in the guise of a novel"), and along with *A Sentimental Journey* (1768) the Sterne phenomenon seemed to demand a different set of generic characteristics and critical expectations. In Sterne's hands the very notion of "progress," whether in narrative fiction or literary history, was diverted, impeded, broken off, even reversed. Rather than engaging the reader in an unfolding story and keeping hold of their attention, Sterne worked more elusively with discrete moments and sudden stimuli; and in trying to capture the effect of this Barbauld turns from the novelist as traditional story-teller to a distinctly modern, even risky, figure:

> It is the peculiar characteristic of this writer, that he affects the heart, not by long drawn tales of distress, but by light electric touches which thrill the nerves of the reader who possesses a correspondent sensibility of frame.[1]

It is as if Sterne's reader is being subjected to titillation at the hands of a scientific experimenter, with the novelist as the equivalent of a Benjamin Franklin or a James Graham, harnessing a power that could tap into the hidden secrets of Nature, or suggest arousals of a more chancy kind.[2]

Barbauld seems to be recognizing here the readerly equivalent of the novel's modernizing moment, in which the genre is not conventionally "rising" or "progressing," but suddenly finds a new energizing mechanism, a distinctive mode of animation, which it can exploit. It works as a discovery rather than a development. To use the scientific language of the age: within a field of *irritability* the reader is being excited to vital action by the application of some physical stimulus,[3] an experience that at once places the novel within the discourse of empirical science, specifically alongside the not-fully-understood excitations of electro-magnetism. Experiment in the novel is thus linked to the newer empirical investigation of the physical and mental worlds, especially to mechanisms of stimulus and response. But the history of the novel, as Barbauld conceives it, cannot quite assimilate Sterne's contribution, and it is included as exceptional, as "odd" in Dr. Johnson's famous characterization.[4]

The difficulty of incorporating novelty within the eighteenth-century novel suggests that in that field, unlike the field of science, experimentation was yet to be seen in developmental terms.[5] For modern literary historians too it has proved difficult to fit Sterne into a "rise of the novel" narrative. In his hugely influential study Ian Watt confined *Tristram Shandy* to a final "Note" as an ironic, parodic text.[6] It was easier to place Sterne within a philosophical/satiric tradition and see him as continuing a "line of wit" or inheriting the mantle of Swift, instead of taking further the work of Defoe, Fielding, and Richardson.[7]

In fact it is in comparison with Richardson that Barbauld, in the very next sentence, characterizes Sterne's handling of character:

> His characters, in like manner, are struck out by a few masterly touches.
> He resembles those painters who can give expression to a figure by two
> or three strokes of bold outline, leaving the imagination to fill up the
> sketch; the feelings are awakened as really by the story of *Le Fevre*, as by
> the narrative of *Clarissa*.[8]

The surer novelistic ground has always been the connected narrative, the "long drawn tale;" but Sterne's art exhibits the flair of the rapid drawing, the brilliant character-sketch in which the reader's imagination comes into play. In those two adjacent sentences Barbauld herself catches a likeness between the "light electric touches" of the electrical experiment and the "masterly touches" of the sketch. The link is one of animating discontinuities, an ability to bring life to moments of uncertainty.

If we have heard something like this before, it has not been in terms of the novel but with reference to a particular kind of poetic art, one that "tricks off," seemingly in air, the characteristic detail:

> Pictures like these, dear Madam, to design,
> Asks no firm hand, and no unerring line;
> Some wand'ring touches, some reflected light,
> Some flying stroke alone can hit 'em right . . . [9]

The multi-faceted, mobile art of Pope's *Epistle to a Lady* (1735) is closer to Sterne's art, as Barbauld characterizes it, than is any defining feature of the novel. Pope's self-consciously light, sketch-book handling in this poem offers vivid character sketches rather than composed characters,[10] and the erotic hint in *wand'ring touches*, licensed by the imagination, makes the air itself complicit: an ambience in which touching and stroking just flicker into metaphor.[11] The *firm hand* lies still; indeed in this scenario firmness itself seems to dissipate in air:

> Come then, the colours and the ground prepare!
> Dip in the Rainbow, trick her off in Air,
> Chuse a firm Cloud, before it fall, and in it
> Catch, e'er she change, the Cynthia of this minute.[12]

Pope's weightless art momentarily holds off gravity. In his imagination the *firm Cloud* might in an instant fall back to earth, into the material *ground* it only seems to have transcended.[13]

Using terms similar to those in Pope's poem, Tristram Shandy recognizes that his own art of touching and stroking is the privilege of familiarity:

> you perceive that the drawing of my uncle *Toby's* character went on gently all the time;—not the great contours of it,—that was impossible,—but some familiar strokes and faint designations of it, were here and there touch'd in, as we went along . . . [14]

However directly Sterne draws from Pope here, the two writers share a sense of excitement at the power of light touches to convey essential elements. In place of an art of realization, an embodying of fictions through sustained narrative and direct description, we have something that is more hit-and-miss (this is the game it plays), but which while discontinuous, even discomposed, trusts its *faint designations* to convey something true to life—not truths *of* life, but things more immediate and transient, true to the activity of the modern, lively, Lockean mind.

It is my contention that in this aspect of his writing Sterne is working in an earlier poetic tradition which, unlike the early novel, had responded imaginatively to the erotic implications of empiricism. By the first decade of the eighteenth century, experimental science and a new epistemology offered models of activity within physical and mental space which overlapped and interpenetrated in fascinating ways; and it was the poets who first recognized elements of the coy, suggestive, and playful in these empirical scenarios. To place Sterne in this poetic context is to move him from a narrative of rise and progress to a scene of novelty and modernity. The erotic quality lies not in the subject matter but in the lively play itself, in which things are hinted, colored, caught, touched, joined, released. It is a field of curiosity as much as knowledge. Therefore, in using the term "erotic" here I am not making it a euphemism for "sexual;" indeed I want to distinguish my "empirical erotics" from the descriptions of sexual situations in the so-called "amatory fiction" of the first decades of the century.[15] It is Sterne's manifest difference from these earlier texts that is so interesting. What he took from poetry was a responsiveness to, and fascination with, the psycho-physical world, which the writings of Eliza Haywood and others lacked. In their novels, narrative description may realize a scene for us, but without the elements of ambient vitality and tangential association that were at the heart of mind-body interaction at this period.[16] It was these elements, exploited in some of the poetry of the early decades of the century, which gave Sterne's novels the textual equivalent of a nervous system, as Barbauld pictures it. For her, Sterne's writing showed how both a fictional text and its responsive reader might share a "correspondent sensibility of frame."

It is in terms of space, specifically ambient space, that the erotic potential of empiricism is evident. Eighteenth-century poets loved exploring the sublime reaches of the universe; but what is relevant here is their very different fascination with those intimate spaces in the human world, in and between minds, and around bodies, where ideas, thoughts, and emotions are communicated. In the work of both Newton and Locke it is possible to detect an element of uneasiness, even coyness, about space. Without a Cartesian *plenum* to bind the material world together, Newton's gravitational force has to work between bodies at a distance with no intervening element to conduct it;[17] and without a dualism of matter and spirit, the Lockean *idea* has to negotiate the gap between an objective external world and the internalized image in the mind.[18] What happens in those spaces? How does bodily attraction work? How does a Thing become an Idea? How does an emotion trigger a physical response? Both thinkers are coy about where they stand between substance and abstraction—Newton hesitating about how far to justify his mathematics in terms of physics, and Locke locating himself problematically between idea and matter.

It is this area of uncertainty within the empirical project, with its ambiguous implications, which fascinated both scientists and poets, and which Sterne happily exploited.[19] Writers and experimenters of the period became intrigued with the space around and between things, with those points of intimacy where forces impinge, and where "thing" shades into "idea," sensation into emotion. This ambivalence is often spatially conceived. Around a physical object, or present within a scene (hanging in the air, or moving amongst the furniture) is something at the boundary of the tangible, interfused with sense perception but not dependent on the physical senses. In Locke's uneasy negotiation between the objective and subjective areas of experience, and in Newton's enigmatic attraction between bodies, is a perceptual field with erotic potential.

An important concept in this enmeshing of the phenomenal with the noumenal during the period is *atmosphere*, a word that links notions of "mood" and "ambience" to the air itself, and which at the end of the century was developing our modern figurative sense.[20] It is not a term that springs immediately to mind when discussing eighteenth-century texts, but it is an idea that interested both writers and scientists; and for my purposes it has erotic possibilities in that it can surround bodies with atmospheric qualities, which may be exploited to charge a scene with feeling. With this idea in mind it is possible to extend the term "erotic" to a certain textual toying with a thing, fancying it (in the eighteenth-century sense of "playing with it in the imagination"), and exploiting various arousal techniques like a minute responsiveness, a delicacy of stimulation, or an emotional dynamics of inviting, demurring, promising.

A helpful visualization of a highly charged atmosphere of this kind is James Gillray's satiric cartoon, "Harmony before Matrimony," which, although dating from 1805, draws directly from the eighteenth-century tradition of empirical erotics. (See figure 7.1)

The young couple are surrounded by the age-old emblems of love: red roses, the vase shaped into a swelling heart, and between them a picture of Cupid discharging what seems to be a hand-held rocket-launcher at a couple of birds billing and cooing on top of their nesting-box. The teasing play of the two cats tells us this is a scene of sexual arousal; but what is particularly striking is the atmosphere. What we see in this picture is the ambience these besotted creatures are creating

Figure 7.1.   *Harmony Before Matrimony* (1805), James Gillray

around themselves. Alongside the old imagery is an expressive tonal register. Her hands caress the harp strings, and the sweeping shape of the instrument picks up the arabesque of her dress to supply a vortex of feeling—suggestively echoed in the diaphanous, foliated pillar to the right which hints at an exotic space just out of view, an inviting bower waiting to be explored. It is partly concealed by the curtain, which hints at a voyeuristic element to our viewing. The space around the lovers is emotionally palpable. As they sing in harmony, their bodies, caught in a physical rhythm, are pulled almost magnetically towards each other, and the charge between them appears to irradiate the air round their heads, as it erects his coiffure. Their blushes seem mutually responsive. The effect spreads through the room: in the bowl to the left a pair of goldfish are practicing synchronized swimming, their tails in the air, and a butterfly dances with its reflection in the mirror. What Gillray has created, in my terms, is an erotic space, one in which feeling circulates around objects and bodies, and meaning draws on nuanced elements that move us into an expressive mode. The couple are creating waves through the air: sound waves, magnetic waves, and waves of feeling which evoke visually the subjective, the suggestive, and the intangible. The woman is not so much playing the harp as becoming an expressive instrument herself. The remarkable thing is that in this picture of 1805 we have the visual equivalent of a scene evoked almost a century earlier by Aaron Hill in his poem "Bellaria, at her Spinnet" (which may be as early as 1720):

> See! with what blushful bend the doubting fair
> Props the rais'd *lid* – then *sits* with sparkling air,
> Tries the touch'd notes – and, hast'ning light along,
> Calls out a short complaint that speaks their wrong.
> Now back'ning, aweful, nerv'd, erect, serene,
> Asserted *musick* swells her heighten'd *mien*.
> Fearless, with face oblique, her formful hand
> Flies o'er the ivory plain with stretch'd command;
> Plunges, with bold neglect, amidst the keys,
> And sweeps the sounding range with magic ease.[21]

The erotics of this passage come from its refusal to contain the experience within prescribed bounds. In this scene anything may potentially embrace anything else, and as Bellaria plays, the material and immaterial engage with each other in the music-filled atmosphere. The vocabulary of sensibility highlights the delightful ambiguities as words flicker between the concrete and the abstract: her *sparkling air* makes the air sparkle. The *touch'd notes* are material ones, but they are also intangibly touched by emotion. This eloquent hesitation between matter and spirit extends to her own body, which becomes an affective medium: not only does it mediate the music, but the music mediates her body. Her gestures make her grow before us like a materializing goddess: "Now back'ning [drawing back], aweful, nerv'd, erect, serene, / Asserted *musick* swells her heighten'd *mien*." There is a lighthearted suggestion of divine *afflatus* here (not for nothing was Aaron Hill one of the dunces in Pope's *Dunciad*), and Hill enjoys playing poetically with her playing; he toys with the scene, turning it into an *ecstasis*, a release of soul from body. The space around Bellaria (the *ambient air*, as Hill calls it) becomes filled with love—not symbolic cupids but responsive presences that hover on the very edge of perception. They are liminal ecstatic spirits:

> Oh! far-felt influence of the speaking string!
> Prompt at thy call, the mounting soul takes wing;
> Waves in the gale, fore-runs th'harmonious breeze,
> And sinks, and rises, to the changeful keys....
> Throng'd in bright lines, or wing'd in ambient air,
> Spirits, in fairy forms, inclose the fair.
> Some, on the *keys*, in am'rous ambush lie,
> And kiss the tune-tip'd fingers, dancing by.[22]

We emerge into an eroticized airy space where the rising and falling notes seem to create a palpable breeze. But then we are promptly drawn back to the keyboard, to the point of contact between the finger and the key—a reminder that this is a world of the senses as well as imagination, a scene where fact and fancy flirt with each other, and where mechanisms of many kinds, physical and emotional, are in operation. That is where the excitement lies. In this empirical world, matter and spirit do not merge together: they touch one another excitedly. And if there is a gap to be crossed, then it becomes a space of arousal, of charged feeling. Hill's spirits kiss the *tune-tip'd fingers* as they dance by, and the erotic wit of that phrase comes from a recognition that a tune and a finger might for the briefest magical moment be contiguous. In this writing, metaphor stands at the edge of perception itself. It flirts with the literal.

What I am calling "empirical erotics" insists on the possibility of a force exerting itself through space. Hill's phrase "far-felt influence" was, after all, the great mystery that Newton had uncovered, and which to this day remains a problem in physics: force exerted at a distance. It was what baffled Newton's critics.[23] The sound waves generated by "the speaking string" were a known phenomenon in 1720, and it was being disputed whether light travelled as waves or particles,[24] but Newton's attractive force raised a seemingly intractable problem: how was gravity mediated through empty space? Today the *graviton*, the particle that conveys the gravitational force between masses, has been hypothesized but not yet discovered. We are familiar with the *photon,* the equivalent intermediary particle of both light and electromagnetism, which has no mass and travels infinite distances through space at the speed of light, but the graviton remains an enigma.[25] To ask how universal attraction works through space is opening up large issues, but the key point for this essay is that ambient space had by the 1720s become a medium of wonder and excitement, hence the particular interest that some eighteenth-century writers show in the space around and between people and objects.

This can become hysterically charged, as it does in the figure of Faulkland, the sentimental lover in Sheridan's *The Rivals* (1775). At a distance from his absent Julia, Faulkland becomes increasingly disturbed while Bob Acres tells him of her recent behavior in the country. He hears how Julia has been playing in public: "she is so accomplished," Acres tells him, "so sweet a voice—so expert at her harpsichord—such a mistress of flat and sharp, squallante, rumblante, and quiverante!" (these could be the names of the spirits that hover over Bellaria's keyboard). As Acres reveals how he has been charmed by Julia's talents, Faulkland becomes aroused by jealous desire, and the climax comes when he hears of her country dancing. This is just too much for the frustrated lover, who in Elijah Moshinsky's 1988 production was by this point crouched on top of the dining-table tearing apart a roast chicken with his hands:

> *Country dances*! Zounds! . . . If there be but one vicious mind in the set, 'twill spread like a contagion—the action of their pulse beats to the lascivious movement of the jig—their quivering, warm-breathed sighs impregnate the very air—the atmosphere becomes electrical to love, and each amorous spark darts through every link of the chain! I must leave you—I own I am somewhat flurried . . . [26]

By 1775, during the decade of Franz Mesmer's early experiments, the magnetic force was becoming associated with physical and emotional disturbance;[27] but sixty years earlier this idea of an electrical atmosphere conducive to erotic stimulation was being exploited by English poets. In *The Rape of the Lock* (as expanded in 1714), Pope creates a world where "Beauty draws us with a single Hair." The charming Belinda moves through the scene accompanied by her sylphs, the elusive spirits of coquetry that "sport and flutter in the Fields of Air," toying with her admirers. Their "fluid Bodies" hover on the brink of the palpable, and they surround her with charisma, a force-field that enhances her physical charms: "Some, Orb in Orb, around the Nymph extend, / Some thrid the mazy Ringlets of her Hair, / Some hang upon the Pendants of her Ear."[28]

Here we are at the heart of early eighteenth-century empiricism, perhaps watching Francis Hauksbee, demonstrator of experiments to the Royal Society, as he hunts a piece of brass-leaf around his room with an electrified tube, noting the strange manner in which the airy material floats away from his tube each time he brings it near; and yet after letting it touch another object the leaf returns to the tube "with great swiftness." In his *Physico-Mechanical Experiments* (published in 1709) Hauksbee describes how

> [T]hey would often *repeat this alternate rising and falling*, the *Attractive* and *Repulsive* forces (whatever they are,) exerting themselves as it were by turns; the one drawing up, and the other beating down these light bodies; and that for several times one after the other.[29]

It could almost be a demonstration of coquetry. In fact, he was discovering the directions of the electrical fluid, and his resulting theory of electrical *effluvia* was accepted until the mid-1740s. Hauksbee was fascinated by the palpable effects of these *effluvia*, which he noticed could flow through glass, and he was able to sense them caressing his skin:

> They . . . were also plainly to be *felt* upon the Face, or any other tender part, if the rubb'd Tube were held near it. And they seem'd *to make very nearly such sort of stroaks upon the Skin, as a number of fine limber Hairs pushing against it* might be suppos'd to do.[30]

Very nearly—the sensation scarcely registers, but is undoubtedly there, seemingly without any immediate touching. It is like brushing against Pope's sylphs:

> Transparent Forms, too fine for mortal Sight,
> Their fluid Bodies half dissolv'd in Light.
> Loose to the Wind their airy Garments flew,
> Thin glitt'ring Textures of the filmy Dew. . .[31]

The ethereal was an important concept in empiricism because it offered a potential continuum between the physical and non-physical; and it is not surprising that Hauksbee's work interested Newton and may have led him to a renewed interest in the *aether* as a mechanism for transmitting his natural forces.[32] Pope's sylphs float at the boundary between the imagination and the senses; they "impregnate the very air," creating a charged, expectant atmosphere, where ideas are erotically sensitized, and thought made tangible.

The discovery of conductivity in the late 1720s takes us further toward a language of eroticized sensibility, in which the "far-felt influence" became physicalized. In 1729 Stephen Gray began experiments to carry the electric force over long distances, and he succeeded in conducting a charge through two hundred yards of string suspended from the trees in his orchard. But Gray's most influential experiment, performed in 1730, was the electrified charity boy, who was suspended by silk cords and given an electric charge, and could be seen to have the power of attracting light objects—paper, feathers, and brass-leaf—to himself.[33] Benjamin Franklin's encounter with this experiment in Boston in 1743 prompted the researches that led to his theory of "electrical atmosphere," which assumed that the "electrical fluid" existed not only in the charged body itself, but in the space around it, a fact that could be detected visibly by the use of smoke or a fine powder.[34] In 1746 William Watson reported on his experiments in measuring what he called "the electrical aether," "that atmosphere which surrounds both excited originally-electrics and excited non-electrics. That this is extended to a considerable distance," he notes, "appears from a fine thread or piece of cotton-grass-seed being attracted at some feet distance from them, as far as which, it is presumed, this atmosphere extends."[35]

It is this potential for ambient excitability that is the premise for Sterne's comedy of empiricist sensibility. In the sentry-box at Shandy Hall the Widow Wadman seizes her opportunity to arouse Uncle Toby's response mechanisms and create a channel for sentimental conductivity:

> [I]n following my uncle Toby's forefinger with hers, close thro' all the little turns and indentings of his works—pressing sometimes against the side of it—then treading upon it's nail—then tripping it up—then touching it here—then there, and so on—it set something at least in motion.[36]

Mrs. Wadman is an experimenter with electricity. In the 1740s she and her husband could have bought one of the electric machines being sold to the public by Francis Watkins from his shop "at Sir Isaac Newton's Head" in Charing Cross. In 1747 Watkins, "Optician to their Royal Highnesses the Prince and Princess of Wales," issued a pamphlet "to direct such private persons as are provided of . . . a requisite apparatus, how to put them in order, and perform with them." We can imagine the Wadmans being especially intrigued by Experiment Fifteen:

> Let a person standing on the ground offer to kiss another electrify'd on the stand, and 'tis ten to one if he executes his purpose, tho' the other be as willing as he, unless they are both appris'd of the smartness of the snapp with which each will be affected on the near approach of their lips, and resolve not to be startled at it. In order to manage this experiment properly, each person should bend a little forwards, and lean their heads towards the same shoulder (that is, each to the right or to the left) so as to prevent any other parts besides the lips coming within the sphere of their respective electrical effluvia.[37]

Watkins choreographs his scene with care, and his couple negotiate their postures as if anticipating an encounter from *A Sentimental Journey*. What is so Sternean is the disingenuous way Watkins explains how they can maximize what he terms "the communicated electric virtue." His electrical kiss is touchingly innocent. He even adds a romantic postscript: "If a rose-bud will be presented to the nose in the like manner, the sensation will be much the same." This is a concept that adds a new angle to Pope's image of an over-excited sensitivity, to "Die of a rose in aromatic pain."[38]

For Pope, this extreme responsiveness to the "quick effluvia darting thro' the brain"[39] was a troubling one; but not so for Henry Jones, the "Bricklayer Poet," who delighted in the idea that electricity not only suggested, but even encouraged, sexual arousal—of body and mind simultaneously:

> Lo! to the Brain the bright Effluvium flies,
> Glows in the Heart and flashes from the Eyes:
> Here the fond Youth with raptur'd Eye shall gaze,
> And proudly warm, enjoy th'extatic Blaze:
> See the proud Nymph partake his Flame by Turns,
> See! like a Seraph, how she smiles and burns.[40]

Here in his poem *Philosophy* (1745) Jones is addressing the polite ladies who attended John Booth's science lectures. Booth specialized in exciting his extremely fashionable Dublin audiences with practical demonstrations, including electricity and magnetism, and the language Jones uses in this passage shows that he saw electricity as mimicking the power of poetry itself:

> quick as Thought th'Electric Vigour springs,
> Swifter than Light'ning on its rapid Wings,
> A Flight so instant to no Space confin'd,
> Eludes Ideas, and outstrips the Mind.[41]

Jones's electrical stimulus is akin to the poetic genius, carried on the wings of imagination, *quick as Thought*, as if modern experimentation reflected the poet's inward eye glancing "from heaven to earth, from earth to heaven," and instantly turning "airy nothing" into reality.[42] Sterne shared the delight in experiential mental triggers of this kind. His fascination with the "Electric Vigour" of the imagination is evident throughout his fiction, not least in the disconcerting rapidity of Uncle Toby's Fancy, which operated "quick as a note could follow the touch."[43]

It is common to talk about the "mechanisms" of Sensibility; but as Jessica Riskin has shown in her study of French experimental science in the second half of the century, we need to distinguish between the "mechanists" and those she terms the "sentimental empiricists," the heirs respectively of Descartes and of Newton.[44] The Cartesian complete system of mechanical causation, with its implications of materialism and determinism, was set against the Newtonian enigma that left the physical mechanisms of his theory in question, and gave room, as Hume remarked, for Nature's "ultimate secrets."[45] In science the battle was fought out between the followers of the Abbé Nollet, for whom electricity was merely "the action of a matter in motion," and the Franklinists who saw electricity differently.[46] As Riskin says: "Franklin's electrical matter did not act by a standard mechanics of matter in motion, by momentum and impact. Instead, it influenced the world it saturated by means of its own idiosyncratic preferences and tendencies."[47] Riskin does not discuss Sterne, but his two novels beautifully fit her analysis of what she identifies as "the new, moralized epistemology, in which sensations were undetachable from sentiments, and ideas inseparable from emotions."[48] What I am arguing is that this embracing of ambivalence about the body-mind divide is at the heart of British empiricism, and of the literary tradition that grows out of it from the beginning of the century. Pope's Belinda and Aaron Hill's Bellaria are already moving through that world, and it is the one inhabited in the 1760s by Sterne's Yorick and Tristram.

The Cartesian materialists of course had their erotics too, but of a different kind, typified by *Thérèse philosophe* (1748), the porno-erotic autobiography of someone who is persuaded, after a series of solemnly energetic copulations, that she is a material girl. The Count instructs her: "Let's ask these gullible men just what the spirit is. Can it exist and yet have no location? If it is located somewhere, it must occupy space, and, if it occupies space, it has extension, and, if it has extension, it must have parts, and, if it has parts, it is matter."[49] For Thérèse, the Count's inductive logic is impeccable. Their world has no ambiguity, no awkward elisions between matter and spirit, or playful uncertainties. Such coyness and coquetry are not to be encouraged: bodies occupy and extend in response to desire. But who is the "gullible" one here? Nothing could be further from Sterne's many delightful, enigmatic arousals, like that Corporal Trim describes to Uncle Toby:

> The fair Beguine, said the corporal, continued rubbing with her whole hand under my knee . . . I perceived, then, I was beginning to be in love—As she continued rub-rub-rubbing—I felt it spread from under her hand, an' please your honour, to every part of my frame—The more she rubb'd, and the longer strokes she took—the more the fire kindled in my veins—till at length, by two or three strokes longer than the rest—my passion rose to the highest pitch—I seiz'd her hand—
>
> And then, thou clapped'st it to thy lips, Trim, said my uncle Toby—and madest a speech.
>
> Whether the corporal's amour terminated precisely in the way my uncle Toby described it, is not material . . . [50]

Not material. Exactly—love is in the air as well as the veins. Sterne's innocents move around in a world of mechanism, but they are continually, comically, set astride the threshold between matter and spirit, animated by their "idiosyncratic preferences and tendencies."

It is in this area of uncertainty that we can see a divide between Sterne's poetically alive writing and the staple narrative styles of earlier "amatory fiction." Eloquent in this regard are two contrasting prefaces. In the preface to her "little *Novel*," *Lasselia: or, the Self-Abandoned* (1724), Eliza Haywood describes her "Design" as one that consciously wishes to avoid the *inadvertent*:

> without the *Expression* being invigorated in some measure proportionate to the *Subject*, 'twou'd be impossible for a Reader to be sensible how far it touches him, or how probable it is that he is falling into those Inadvertencies which the Examples I relate wou'd caution him to avoid.[51]

Here the phrase "touches him" appears to mean "is relevant to his case." The verb lacks the tactile suggestiveness of Sterne's many *touchings* along the boundary of emotive response. The syntactical deliberation of Haywood's sentence betrays embarrassment at the necessary *invigoration* of her text. In contrast to Sterne's continual manic *inadvertencies*, Haywood's project attempts to preclude them. In her narratives, moments of potential electric suggestion and spontaneous response tend to be embedded in description, held in their proper place—as in this novel at the moment when Lasselia takes delivery of a love letter from her beloved de l'Amye:

> It wou'd have been impossible for *Lasselia*, had she endeavoured it, to conceal the swift Vicissitudes of her rolling Thoughts while reading; alternate Joy and Shame, Surprize and Fear, and sometimes a Start of virtuous Pride and Indignation, sparkled in her Eyes— a thousand different Passions succeeded one another in their turns . . .[52]

It is an intensely emotional situation; but there is no atmosphere, nothing like those instantaneous bursts of energy scattered through Sterne's text. The shapeliness of Haywood's sentence is indicative of a narrative that retains its balance, complete with a rhetorical *tricolon auctum*. The voice of the novel locates everything with care and discrimination. We are told about "the swift Vicissitudes of her rolling Thoughts" without experiencing any dizziness ourselves. In her text the well-behaved *Passions* pair up before forming an orderly queue. The *sparkle* is clearly not an electric one—indeed the result of Haywood's careful word order is more one of protective insulation. An appropriate comment on this effect is offered by Tristram Shandy, when he finally writes his own Preface in the middle of Volume 3:

> I hate set dessertations,————and above all things in the world, 'tis one
> of the silliest things in one of them, to darken your hypothesis by *placing*
> *a number of tall, opake words, one before another, in a right line, betwixt*
> *your own and your readers conception,*————[53]

Sterne seems to have had in mind the way that a descriptive narrative can effectively insulate the reader from a direct experience.

This is what repeatedly tends to happen in Haywood's novel. A representative example is the moment of high emotion as she reads that *billet doux*:

> Again she attempted to read over the dear surprizing Lines, but had not
> power; the strange Disorder of her fluttering Heart, depriving the Blood
> of its usual Circulation, all her Limbs forgot their Function, and she
> sunk fainting on the Bank, in much the same Posture she was in before
> she had rais'd herself a little to take the Letter.[54]

The reader follows everything clearly: all is material, and the mechanism is explained.[55] Lasselia's sentimental posture ("extended at her length on a fine grassy
Bank") is decorously re-composed. The *opake words* unroll, with subordinate
clauses in place and everything successively ordered, *one before another, in a right*
line. In Haywood's narrative we are being told things, with little suggested to the
imagination, and the result is to obstruct that vital transparent space "betwixt
your own and your readers conception," a gap that throughout his fiction Sterne
energises and animates in remarkably lively ways.

Sterne's "sentimental empiricism," to use Riskin's terminology, acknowledges fact and fancy simultaneously. His human scenes occasionally seem like
playful philosophical experiments conducted in ambivalent spaces where mental
and emotional processes are entwined with physical phenomena. His bodies move
through an atmosphere, taking color from things around them. In *A Sentimental*
Journey "The Temptation" leads us into a darkened room—not the blacked out
space into which Newton led his tiny beam of sunlight, but one that nonetheless
illustrates beautifully the mechanisms of refraction and reflection:

> As the fair *fille de chambre* was so near my door she turned back, and
> went into the room with me for a moment or two whilst I wrote a card.
>> It was a fine still evening in the latter end of the month of May—
> the crimson window curtains (which were of the same colour as those
> of the bed) were drawn close—the sun was setting and reflected through
> them so warm a tint into the fair *fille de chambre*'s face—I thought she

blush'd—the idea of it made me blush myself—we were quite alone; and that super-induced a second blush before the first could get off.

There is a sort of a pleasing half guilty blush, where the blood is more in fault than the man—'tis sent impetuous from the heart, and virtue flies after it—not to call it back, but to make the sensation of it more delicious to the nerves . . .[56]

Yorick's blush is "half guilty" because it is enigmatically located within the air and within the mind. The room is not a space of materialist determinism, but a kind of matrix of his own brain where the ideas of the girl's face, the closed curtains, and the bed intermingle no less suggestively than the redness which circulates between them. The beam of rosy light through the air meets the swell of feeling within—the objective material world and the subjective world of idea blush in unison. *Pace* Keats, there is no "touch of cold philosophy" in this place.[57] The "haunted air" is filled with a Newtonian blush, and the room is a Lockean sensorium come to life.

The implications of Locke's distinguishing between "primary" and "second-ary" qualities, the latter being those qualities (like color) which are registered within the perceiving mind in response to a "power" in the material object, was an idea that stimulated Joseph Addison in his *Spectator* essays on "The Pleasures of Imagination" (1712).[58] At the end of paper 413, where he has been discussing why colors "are so pleasing and beautiful to the Imagination," he remarks that he supposes his readers to be

acquainted with that great Modern Discovery, which is at present uni-versally acknowledged by all the Enquirers into Natural Philosophy: Namely, that Light and Colours, as apprehended by the Imagination, are only Ideas in the Mind, and not Qualities that have any Existence in Matter . . . if the *English* Reader would see the Notion explained at large, he may find it in the Eighth Chapter of the Second Book of Mr. *Lock's* Essay on Human Understanding.[59]

Locke's distinction also gave philosophical warrant for opening up a subjective frequency in the mind. It suggested that the mind was a highly sensitized response-mechanism that could realize qualities of things within itself. The *OED* records Locke's friend Joshua Oldfield in 1707 as first using the term *subjective* to mean "relating to the thinking subject, having its source in the mind."[60] By 1725 the poet Isaac Watts could write that "*Objective Certainty* is when the Proposition is certainly true in it self; and *Subjective,* when we are certain of the Truth of it," adding significantly: "The one is in *Things,* the other is in our *Minds.*"[61] During the early decades of the eighteenth century, therefore, a "subjective" space was being opened up for exploration. Sterne's temptation-scene plays with these notions in the 1760s; but poets of earlier decades were also interested in this enigmatic continuity between the outer world and the space of the mind.

Within the poet's imagination the ambient landscape tends to become, under emotional pressure, a sensorium that breathes, sighs, murmurs, whispers, and trembles in tune with the subjective consciousness. In Pope's "Eloisa to Abelard" (1717) long hoarded images with their emotional associations filter into Eloisa's visions, replacing the convent walls by a landscape of brooding melancholy exuded from herself: "The dying gales that pant upon the trees, / The lakes that quiver to the curling breeze."[62] In an effect of almost suffocating subjectivity Eloisa's ambient world delivers back her own projected emotions, panting and quivering. Poetry found itself well equipped to explore such areas of suggestion and association, where through the force of words "[t]he Reader finds a Scene drawn in stronger Colours, and painted more to the Life in his Imagination."[63] The age-old imaginative confidence of poetry seized on the possibilities for exciting a synaesthetic response. In his poem "The Court of Venus" (1728), William Pattison describes a love-garden filled with the disembodied intimate sounds and secret meanings that have seeped out of lovers' hearts into the air around:

> Here warming Whispers propagate Replies,
> Sweet-melting Murmurs, soft-consenting Sighs;
> With all the Eloquence that Hearts confess,
> With all the Harmony that Eyes express . . .[64]

Pattison's amorous landscape stores the emotionally charged language of love, almost like an allegorical electric battery waiting to be connected up to the next willing victim.

One poem that draws poignantly on these elements, and hints at their erotic possibilities, is Aaron Hill's "Alone, in an Inn, at Southampton. April the 25th, 1737," in which as a widower he revisits the room where he had once lodged with his wife:

> *That* glass, she dress'd at, keeps her form no more;
> Not one dear foot-step *tunes* th'unconscious *floor*,
> *There* sat she—yet, those *chairs* no sense retain,
> And busy *recollection* smarts, in vain.
> Sullen and dim, what faded scenes are here!
> I wonder, and retract a starting tear.[65]

In several of these poems, as here, objects have a potential consciousness interwoven with human perceptions and associations. In this room the floor, the mirror, and the chair had once composed a scene like that Gillray would picture, but the romantic space has gone dead and is no longer responsive to her presence. The slight erotic nuance is in Hill's mind, which thinks of the *tune* of her footsteps, imagines her dressing at the mirror, and occupying the chair. The poet of "Bellaria, at her Spinnet" is here evoking an absence that is simultaneously a haunting presence.

For the poet, an empty physical space and an achingly full memory make for an unsettling disproportion. One is longing to pour out and fill the other. The irony only emphasizes the subjective, which now has no receptive object with which to engage. A similar haunted scene is evoked when Thomas Gray writes to his young protégé Charles Victor de Bonstetten, expressing his sense of loss now that his friend has returned to Switzerland. The furniture is missing something:

> My life now is but a perpetual conversation with your shadow – The known sound of your voice still rings in my ears. – There, on the corner of the fender you are standing, or tinkling on the Pianoforte, or stretch'd at length on the sofa. . . . I can not bear this place, where I have spent many tedious years within less than a month, since you left me.[66]

Gray is conscious of how quickly immediate perception has become fading memory. The disturbance is still felt, like the sound-waves on the threshold of hearing that impossibly circle round his room. He is conscious simultaneously of space and time: in one Bonstetten is intimately close, in the other so distant. In space he seems still there, in time now years away.

The fictional world into which Sterne's readers enter, conscious of the ironic rhythms of time, also has this potentially tantalizing atmospherics, where subject and object share the same space, and human emotions seep out into the scene, not in a symbolic way but as something expressive that gives the feeling a physical shape. In his wild grief at the crushing of Tristram's nose, Walter Shandy returns to his room and flings himself across the bed; and at that moment the writing assumes a kind of sympathetic intimacy as we trace the contours of his convoluted body, no longer just a body but a study in sorrow itself:

> The palm of his right hand, as he fell upon the bed, receiving his forehead, and covering the greatest part of both his eyes, gently sunk down with his head (his elbow giving way backwards) till his nose touch'd the quilt;—his left arm hung insensible over the side of the bed, his knuckles

reclining upon the handle of the chamber pot, which peep'd out beyond the valance,—his right leg (his left being drawn up towards his body) hung half over the side of the bed, the edge of it pressing upon his shin-bone.—He felt it not. A fix'd, inflexible sorrow took possession of every line of his face.—[67]

Sorrow *takes possession* of the scene. The familiar objects in his bedroom touch him, press against him, take the weight. As on other occasions in Sterne's novel, gravity's laws exert themselves at an emotional moment, as if the physical co-ordinates are working in support of the feeling.[68] We ourselves are made to feel our way round the shape on the bed. Objective and subjective worlds come together. In Walter's case, an hour and a half (and fifteen chapters) later, the frozen posture of grief begins to thaw:

> My father . . . began to play upon the floor with the toe of that foot which hung over the bed-side. . . . In a few moments, his left-hand, the knuckles of which had all the time reclined upon the handle of the chamber-pot, came to its feeling—he thrust it a little more within the valance—drew up his hand, when he had done, into his bosom—gave a hem!—[69]

The scene, like his body, *comes to its feeling*. In Sterne's fiction minds are furnished (in the sense of "stored") as well as rooms, and where Locke presides over the one, Newton rules the other. Doors creak on their hinges; whistled tunes accompany the knocking out of a pipe on the fender; hot chestnuts slip through unbuttoned flies and warmth becomes pain; buckets, as well as memories, leak; clocks are wound and life germinated; things slip through the mind; spiders webs and mental associations form. The air is always potentially alive in Sterne's world, as it most definitely is at the instant of love, when at the end of his exhausting flight from Death in Volume Seven Tristram finally dismounts his recalcitrant mule and joins in the dance of life, hand in hand with Nanette—she of the slit petticoat, and the unraveling hair—who holds his hand and guides him:

> *Viva la joia!* was in her lips— *Viva la joia!* was in her eyes. A transient spark of amity shot across the space betwixt us————She look'd ami-able!————Why could I not live and end my days thus? . . . capriciously did she bend her head on one side, and dance up insidious————Then 'tis time to dance off, quoth I . . .'[70]

The air through which the *transient spark of amity* shoots is sustained by Newton's physical laws; but it is simultaneously emotionally electric, and Sterne's fiction finds both comedy and feeling in this idea.[71]

Empirical erotics are generated in the play between mind and body; and they are only heightened by the thought that a mysterious law is operating, by which the trajectories of our thoughts or feelings are liable at any moment to intersect and find a response linking the excitements *out there* and *in here*. It may seem an impossible leap from these eroticized spaces to Newton's inverse square law, but in Count Algarotti's witty dialogues, *Newtonianism for the Ladies*, the transition is a natural one. In the final scene of this popular work, headed "An Exposition of Sir Isaac NEWTON's universal Principle of Attraction. The Application of this Principle to Optics," the young Venetian *philosophe* coaches the beautiful Marquesa about the law of universal attraction. He explains, for example, that at night reading a letter at twice the distance would require four times the number of candles, given that "the Law requires that the Light should grow weaker in Proportion, as the Square of the Distance increases." The Marquesa coyly intervenes:

> I cannot help thinking, said the Marchioness, that this Proportion in the Squares of the Distances of Places, or rather of Times, is observed even in Love. Thus after eight Days Absence, Love becomes sixty four Times less than it was the first Day, and according to this Proportion it must soon be entirely obliterated.[72]

Algarotti, who for three hundred pages has been conducting a flirtatious one--to-one tutorial on the erotics of empirical philosophy ("You give me Lessons of Philosophy and Love both at once, replied the Marchioness"), softens at last, and tells her romantically:

> You alone have Power to reverse this Theorem, and make the Remembrance of you, and with that a Desire of seeing you, instead of diminishing, increase according to the Squares, or rather the Cubes of the Times.

A new Newtonian law seems about to come into being. But the Marchesa will have none of it: "No! no! said the Marchioness, Gallantry must never destroy a Theorem."[73]

As the pair sit alone together in her dressing-room conversing about the play of light through the diamond around her neck, or refute Descartes by focusing their eyes simultaneously on the same point in the air between them, they create a playful romantic atmosphere such as Gillray caught generations later. But these are also occasions of empirical excitement, and it is the dynamic relation between bodies in space and ideas in the mind that gives such scenes their erotic potential. This excited atmosphere, explored eagerly by poets in the early decades of the century, also animates Sterne's texts. Placing his fiction within the ambit of poetry and experimental science, and specifically viewing it in relation to the new atmospheric excitements to which the poets had responded, inevitably raises questions about "realism v. romance." This old binary, which has enlivened many a debate on the early novel, breaks down in a context where empirical experience offered not an alternative to, but a fascinating confirmation of, romance. In the animated imagined world of Sterne's fiction, these two concepts overlap, even tease each other, and perhaps a realization of this can help break down some of the critical categories that never seem to do justice to the resourcefulness of the eighteenth-century novel.

Notes

1. Anna Letitia Barbauld, "On the Origin and Progress of Novel-Writing," in *The British Novelists*, 50 vols. (London: F.C. and J. Rivington, 1810), 1:40.

2. On Franklin's electrical experiments, see I. Bernard Cohen, *Benjamin Franklin's Science* (Cambridge, MA and London: Harvard University Press, 1990), 40–109; on James Graham's electro-magnetic "Celestial Bed," see Lydia Syson, *Doctor of Love: James Graham and his Celestial Bed* (Richmond: Alma Books, 2008).

3. The latest theory of physiological *irritability* ("the capacity of being excited to vital action (*e.g.* motion, contraction, nervous impulse, etc.) by the application of an external stimulus," *OED* "irritability," *n.*, 3) had been expounded by Robert Whytt, *Physiological Essays . . . Observations on the Sensibility and Irritability of the Parts of Men and other Animals* (Edinburgh, 1755).

4. "Nothing odd will do long. 'Tristram Shandy' did not last," in *Boswell's Life of Johnson*, ed. George Birkbeck Hill, rev. ed. L.F. Powell, 6 vols. (Oxford: Clarendon Press, 1934–64), 2:449. Johnson is using "odd" in his own sense 3: "not like others; not to be numbered among any class." In Samuel Johnson, *A Dictionary of the English Language*, 2 vols. (London: W. Strachan, 1755), n.p.

5. The close links between *Tristram Shandy* and experimental novels of the 1750s are discussed by Thomas Keymer in *Sterne, the Moderns, and the Novel* (Oxford: Oxford University Press, 2002), esp. pages 49–63. The fullest discussion of the complex problem of the novel's "newness," in formal and historical terms, is J. Paul Hunter, *Before Novels: The Cultural Contexts of Eighteenth-Century English Fiction* (New York and London: W.W. Norton & Company, 1990), 3–58. See also Michael McKeon, *The Origins of the English Novel 1600–1740* (Baltimore and London: The Johns Hopkins University Press, 1987).

6. "But, of course, *Tristram Shandy* is not so much a novel as a parody of a novel . . . [Sterne] achieves a *reductio ad absurdum* of the novel form itself," in Ian Watt, *The Rise of the Novel: Studies in Defoe, Richardson, and Fielding* [1957], 2nd ed. (Berkeley: University of California Press, 2001), 291–2. The logic of this has been fascinatingly pursued by Warren L. Oakley, *A Culture of Mimickry: Laurence Sterne, His Readers and the Art of Bodysnatching* (London: Modern Humanities Research Association, 2010).

7. Classic studies are: Douglas Jefferson, "*Tristram Shandy* and the Tradition of Learned Wit," *Essays in Criticism* 1 (1951), 225–48; John Traugott, *Tristram Shandy's World: Sterne's Philosophical Rhetoric* (Berkeley and Los Angeles: University of California Press, 1954); and Michael V. DePorte, *Nightmares and Hobbyhorses: Swift, Sterne, and Augustan Ideas of Madness* (San Marino: Huntington Library, 1974).

8. Barbauld, "Origin and Progress," 40–41.

9. Alexander Pope, *Epistle II. To a Lady. Of the Characters of Women*, in *The Twickenham Edition of the Poems of Alexander Pope*, ed. John Butt, vol. 3.2, *Epistles to Several Persons*, ed. F.W. Bateson (London: Methuen & Co., 1951), lines 151–4.

10. The exception is Pope's "one certain Portrait," Queen Caroline, who is "varnish'd out" with all her vices fixed (ll.181–6).

11. Cf. Addison's suggestion that "[o]ur Sight . . . may be considered as a more delicate and diffusive kind of Touch, that spreads it self over an infinite Multitude of Bodies," in *Spectator* 411, 21 June 1712, in *The Spectator*, ed. Donald F. Bond, 5 vols. (Oxford: Clarendon Press, 1965), 3:536.

12. Pope, *Epistle to a Lady*, ll.17–20.

13. Pope's primary meaning of *ground* is of course "The first stratum of paint upon which the figures are afterwards painted" (Johnson, *Dictionary*, "ground," *n.*, 8).

14. Sterne, *The Life and Opinions of Tristram Shandy*, eds. Melvyn New and Joan New (Gainesville: University Presses of Florida, 1978–84), vol. 1, ch. 22.

15. An exception is the lyric exuberance evident in John Cleland's *Memoirs of a Woman of Pleasure* (1748–9). On Cleland and Sterne, see Florian Werner, "Kindred Spirits? John Cleland's *Fanny Hill* and Laurence Sterne's *A Sentimental Journey*," *Zeitschrift für Anglistik und Amerikanistik*, 48, no. 1 (2000), 17–30; and Leo Braudy, "*Fanny Hill* and Materialism," *Eighteenth-Century Studies*, 4, no. 1 (Autumn 1970), 21–40; pages 39–40.

16. I use "tangential" in Hazlitt's literal sense when he writes of Coleridge: "Our author's mind is . . . *tangential*. There is no subject on which he has not touched, none on which he has rested." *The Spirit of the Age* (1825), in *The Complete Works of William Hazlitt*, ed. P.P. Howe, 21 vols (London/Toronto: J.M. Dent and Sons, 1930–4), 11:29.

17. See Derek Gjertsen, *The Newton Handbook* (London and New York: Routledge & Kegan Paul, 1986), 239–41; see also note 23 below.

18. See John W. Yolton, *Thinking Matter: Materialism in Eighteenth-Century Britain* (Oxford: Basil Blackwell, 1983), 64–89. This problem was at the core of George Berkeley's famous challenge to Locke: "It is evident from what we have already shewn, that Extension, Figure and Motion are only Ideas existing in the Mind, and that an Idea can be like nothing but another Idea." In George Berkeley, *A Treatise Concerning the Principles of Human Knowledge. Part I. Wherein the chief Causes of Error and Difficulty in the Sciences, with the Grounds of Scepticism, Atheism, and Irreligion, are inquir'd into* (Dublin: Aaron Rhames, for Jeremy Pepyat, 1710), 50. See also Georges Dicker, "An Idea Can Be Like Nothing But An Idea," in *George Berkeley: Critical Assessments*, 3 vols., ed. Walter E. Creery (London and New York: Routledge, 1991), 3:162–76.

19. For a more detailed discussion, see David Fairer, "Sentimental Translation in Mackenzie and Sterne," *Essays in Criticism* 49 (1999), 132–51.

20. The earliest figurative use, "pervading tone or mood; characteristic mental or moral environment" (*OED*, "atmosphere," *n.*, 4a) dates from 1797–1803. On the developing concept of the "atmosphere" of literary texts, see the recent study by Jayne Elizabeth Lewis, *Air's Appearance: Literary Atmosphere in British Fiction, 1660–1794* (Chicago: University of Chicago Press, 2012). Sterne is not mentioned, but Lewis has much of interest to say about the airiness of Pope's *The Rape of the Lock* on pages 61–91. See also Leo Spitzer, "Milieu and Ambiance," in his *Essays in Historical Semantics* (New York: Russell and Russell, 1948), 202–7.

21. Aaron Hill, "Bellaria, at her Spinnet," *Works*, 4 vols. (1753), 3:141–5, lines 3–12.

22. Ibid., lines 23–46.

23. In his defence of Newton against the Cartesians, Voltaire tackled this objection head-on: "Those who cannot conceive a *Void*, object, that this Void must be nothing, that nothing cannot have Properties, and therefore, that there can be no Operation in the Void. We answer, It is not true that a Vacuum is nothing; it is the Place of Bodies; it is Space; it hath Properties; it is extended in Length, Breadth, and Depth; it is penetrable, inseparable, &c . . ., " in *The Elements of Sir Isaac Newton's Philosophy. By Mr. Voltaire. Translated from the French. Revised and Corrected by John Hanna, M.A.* (London: Stephen Austen, 1738), 180.

24. See G.N. Cantor, *Optics after Newton: Theories of Light in Britain and Ireland, 1704–1840* (Manchester: Manchester University Press, 1983), 11–15. For a digest of contemporary theories of both light and sound, see Ephraim Chambers, "Light," *Cyclopædia* (London, 1728), 1:454–6; and "Sound," Ibid., 2:99–101.

25. See Tony Rothman and Stephen Boughn, "Can Gravitons be Detected?", *Foundations of Physics*, 36, no. 12 (Dec. 2006), 1801–1825.

26. Richard Brinsley Sheridan, *The Rivals,* ed. Elizabeth Duthie (London: A.C. Black; New York: W.W. Norton, 1979), 37–8, 40; Act 2, sc. 1, lines 195–8, 259–64.

27. See M.L. Goldsmith, *Franz Anton Mesmer: The History of an Idea* (London: Arthur Baker, 1934).

28. Alexander Pope, *The Rape of the Lock*, in *The Twickenham Edition of the Poems of Alexander Pope,*ed. John Butt, vol. 2, *The Rape of the Lock and Other Poems*, ed. Geoffrey Tillotson (London: Methuen & Co., 1940), 2:28, 1:66, 2:62, 2:138–40.

29. Francis Hauksbee, *Physico-Mechanical Experiments on Various Subjects* (London: R. Brugis, 1709), 43.

30. Ibid., 46. On Hauksbee's electrical experiments, see J.L. Heilbron, *Elements of Early Modern Physics* (Berkeley, etc.: University of California Press, 1982), 168–71.

31. Pope, *The Rape of the Lock*, 2:61–4.

32. See "Introduction," *Conceptions of Ether: Studies in the History of Ether Theories 1740–1900*, eds. G.N. Cantor and M.J.S. Hodge (Cambridge: Cambridge University Press, 1981), 19–24.

33. On Gray's "Charity Boy" experiment, see Heilbron, *Elements of Physics,* 171–4. On that and similar entertainments, see Patricia Fara, *An Entertainment for Angels: Electricity in the Enlightenment* (Cambridge: Icon Books, 2002), 42–50. These early experiments by Hauksbee, Gray, and others are described in detail by Joseph Priestley, *The History and Present State of Electricity* (London: J. Dodsley, etc., 1767), 1–79.

34. See Cohen, *Benjamin Franklin's Science*, 53–5. "The form of the electrical atmosphere is that of the body it surrounds. This shape may be rendered visible in a still air, by raising a smoke from dry rosin, dropt into a hot tea-spoon under the electrified body,'" in Benjamin Franklin, *Experiments and Observations on Electricity* (London: E. Cave, 1751), 55.

35. William Watson, *Experiments and Observations tending to illustrate the Nature and Properties of Electricity. The Third Edition* (London: C. Davis, 1746), 45.

36. Sterne, *Tristram Shandy*, vol. 8, ch. 16.

37. Francis Watkins, *A Particular Account of the Electrical Experiments Hitherto made publick, with Variety of new ones, and full Instructions for performing them* (London, 1747), 3, 30.

38. Ibid., 31, 30, and Alexander Pope, *An Essay on Man,* in *The Twickenham Edition of the Poems of Alexander Pope,*ed. John Butt, vol. 3.2, *An Essay on Man,* ed. Maynard Mack (London: Methuen & Co., 1950), 1:200.

39. Pope, *Essay on Man,* 1:199.

40. Henry Jones, *Philosophy. A Poem Address'd to the Ladies Who attend Mr. Booth's Lectures* (Dublin: S. Powell, 1746), 5. Jones is echoing Pope's "the rapt Seraph that adores and burns" (*Essay on Man,* 1:278).

41. Jones, *Philosophy,* 5.

42. See William Shakespeare, *A Midsummer Night's Dream,* ed. Harold F. Brooks (n.p.: Methuen & Co. Ltd., 1979), page 104, Act 5, sc. 1, lines 12–17.

43. Sterne, *Tristram Shandy,* vol. 3, ch. 41.

44. See Jessica Riskin, *Science in the Age of Sensibility: The Sentimental Empiricists of the French Enlightenment* (Chicago: University of Chicago Press, 2002), 73–87.

45. David Hume, *The History of England, from the Invasion of Julius Cæsar to The Revolution in 1688,* 8 vols. (London: A Millar, 1763), chapter 71, 8:323.

46. Sterne's Yorick is evidently a Franklinist: "I felt such undescribable emotions within me, as I am sure could not be accounted for from any combinations of matter and motion." Laurence Sterne, *A Sentimental Journey through France and Italy,* in *The Florida Edition of the Works of Laurence Sterne,* eds. Melvyn New and W.G. Day, 8 vols. (Gainesville: University Presses of Florida, 2002), 6:151.

47. Riskin, *Science in the Age of Sensibility,* 85.

48. Ibid., 73.

49. Robert Darnton, *The Forbidden Best-Sellers of Pre-Revolutionary France* (New York and London: W.W. Norton, 1996), 294. See also 85–114.

50. Sterne, *Tristram Shandy,* vol. 8, ch. 22.

51. Eliza Haywood, *Lasselia: or, the Self-Abandon'd. A Novel* (London: D. Browne and S. Chapman, 1724), vi-vii. The instructional aims of the novel are examined by Kathleen Lubey, "Haywood's Amatory Aesthetic," *Eighteenth-Century Studies,* 39, no. 3 (Spring 2006), 309–22.

52. Haywood, *Lasselia,* 23.

53. Sterne, *Tristram Shandy,* vol. 3, ch. 20; emphasis added.

54. Haywood, *Lasselia*, 23.

55. The materialist philosophy underpinning Haywood's scenarios has been well analyzed. See Joseph Drury, "Haywood's Thinking Machines," *Eighteenth-Century Fiction*, 21, no. 2 (Winter 2008–9), 201–228; page 202; Helen Thompson, "Plotting Materialism: W. Charleton's *The Ephesian Matron*, E. Haywood's *Fantomina*, and Feminine Consistency," *Eighteenth-Century Studies*, 35, no. 2 (Winter 2002), 195–214. On the implications of materialist theories in this period, see Yolton, *Thinking Matter: Materialism in Eighteenth-Century Britain* (Oxford: Blackwell, 1984); and Richard W.F. Kroll, *The Material Word: Literate Culture in the Restoration and Early Eighteenth Century* (Baltimore: The Johns Hopkins University Press, 1991), 1–27.

56. Sterne, *A Sentimental Journey*, 6:121–2, "The Temptation, Paris."

57. "Do not all charms fly / At the mere touch of cold philosophy? /. . . Philosophy will clip an Angel's wings, / Conquer all mysteries by rule and line, / Empty the haunted air, and gnomèd mine— / Unweave a rainbow . . ." John Keats, *Lamia*, in *The Poems of John Keats*, ed. Miriam Allott (London: Longman, 1970), 645–6; pt. 2, lines 229–37.

58. John Locke, *An Essay concerning Human Understanding*, ed., II. 8, Peter H. Nidditch, Clarendon Edition of the Works of John Locke (Oxford: Oxford University Press, 1975), 132–43.

59. Addison, *The Spectator*, 3:547. On Addison and the erotic, see Kathleen Lubey, "Erotic Interiors in Joseph Addison's Imagination," *Eighteenth-Century Fiction*, 20, no. 3 (Spring 2008), 415–44.

60. Joshua Oldfield, *An Essay Towards the Improvement of Reason* (London: T. Parkhurst, etc., 1707), 216; pt. 2, ch. 19, sec. 22.

61. Isaac Watts, *Logick: Or, The Right Use of Reason in the Enquiry after Truth* (London: John Clark and Richard Hett, etc., 1725), 276; pt. 2, ch. 2, sec. 8.

62. Alexander Pope, "Eloisa to Abelard," in *The Twickenham Edition of the Poems of Alexander Pope,* ed. John Butt, vol. 2, *The Rape of the Lock and Other Poems*, ed. Geoffrey Tillotson (London: Methuen & Co., 1940), lines 159–60.

63. Addison, *The Spectator*, no. 46 (27 June 1712). Bond, edn, 3:560.

64. William Pattison, "The Court of Venus," in *The Poetical Works of Mr. William Pattison* (London: H. Curll, 1728), 134.

65. Aaron Hill, "Alone, in an Inn, at Southampton," in *Eighteenth-Century Poetry: An Annotated Anthology*, ed. David Fairer and Christine Gerrard, 2nd ed. (Oxford and Malden, MA: Blackwell, 2004), 198; lines 23–8. See Christine Gerrard, *Aaron Hill: The Muses' Projector 1685–1750* (Oxford: Oxford University Press, 2003), 140–1.

66. Thomas Gray to Charles Victor de Bonstetten, 19 April 1770, in *Correspondence of Thomas Gray*, eds. Paget Toynbee and Leonard Whibley, 3 vols. (Oxford: Clarendon Press, 1935), 3:1127.

67. Sterne, *Tristram Shandy*, vol. 3, ch. 29.

68. On the motif of gravity in the novel, see Michael Seidel, "Gravity's Inheritable Line: Sterne's Tristram Shandy," in his *Satiric Inheritance: Rabelais to Sterne* (Princeton: Princeton University Press, 1979), 250–62.

69. Sterne, *Tristram Shandy*, vol. 4, ch. 2.

70. Ibid., vol. 7, ch. 44.

71. Cf. Yorick's encomium to Sensibility: "eternal fountain of our feelings—'tis here I trace thee . . . all comes from thee, great—great SENSORIUM of the world! which vibrates, if a hair of our heads but falls upon the ground." In Sterne, *Sentimental Journey*, 6:155, "The Bourbonnois."

72. *Sir Isaac Newton's Theory of Light and Colours, and his Principle of Attraction, Made familiar to the Ladies in several Entertainments,* 2 vols (London: G. Hawkins, 1742), 2:155.

73. Ibid., 2:78, 2:155–6.

8

"GREAT LABOUR BOTH OF MIND AND TONGUE":
ARTICULACY AND INTERIORITY IN
YOUNG'S *NIGHT THOUGHTS* AND
RICHARDSON'S *CLARISSA*

Joshua Swidzinski

IN THE SUMMER OF 1750, corresponding over the topic of much-beloved books, Hester Mulso and Elizabeth Carter discovered anew that there is no disputing in matters of taste. Evidently, Carter found something to be lacking in the prose fiction that Mulso held dear. Mulso, meanwhile, offered some choice words concerning the apparent inarticulacy of one of Carter's favorite poets:

> I am reading Doctor Young's *Night Thoughts*; I must own, with great labour both of mind and tongue. Every word you say against my Mr. Richardson I will revenge myself for upon your Doctor Young . . . Sure never was sense so entangled in briars as his! Instead of the flowers of language, his thoughts are wrapt up in thorns and thistles. I am sure it has cost me much toil and pain to untwist them; and, to say the truth, I do like them as I do gooseberries, well enough when they are picked for me, but not well enough to gather them.[1]

Novelist Samuel Richardson and poet Edward Young tend to figure in rather distinct literary conversations: the former plays the role of an innovator in a rising genre, while the latter often seems the practitioner of a declining one. Nonetheless, in the middle of the eighteenth century, their literary fates appeared conjoined to Mulso and Carter, and by no means in a flattering manner. For these readers, the seemingly distinct forms of writing practiced by these authors—namely, the immersive epistolary prose exemplified in Richardson's *Clarissa* (1747–8) and the meditative, consolatory verse of Young's *Night Thoughts* (1742–6)—nonetheless yield a shared experience: one of sense *impeded* by form, of literary "gooseberries" too deeply buried in metrical briars or thorny prolixity to be worth the picking. In this moment of disconnect between literary correspondents, and between readers and their books, the genres of poetry and novelistic prose are most alike when they are least digestible.

I stress this moment of readerly difficulty only because so much of the scholarship addressing the relationship between poetry and prose in the eighteenth century seems to focus upon readerly ease. Whereas it was once a matter of critical orthodoxy that the literature of this period rivaled all others in its obedient submission to generic distinctions, scholars such as Ralph Cohen, Clifford Siskin, and G. Gabrielle Starr sketch a literary landscape wherein supposedly distinct genres mingle with and re-fashion one another, wherein to be a reader is necessarily to be "steeped in seeming generic heterodoxies."[2] Siskin and William Warner have recently argued that the development of just such an ability to read across distinct and proliferating genres and media—to read, as it were, trans-generically—represents a constitutive aspect of the Enlightenment.[3] In this regard, to reconsider the relationship between eighteenth-century poetry and the novel is to recover a revealing strand of Enlightenment history.

Nonetheless, and notwithstanding the fruitfulness of this scholarly approach, one must be careful lest an eye focused squarely on relationships across genres become blind to the intended literary effects of formal distinctions between them. Recent scholarship concerned with the relationship between verse and prose in the eighteenth century often takes as its object of study the experience of "intersubjectivity" or perspective-taking—namely, the process by which a reader or listener assumes the perspective of an interlocutor, whether real or imagined.[4] Siskin categorizes such an experience as a kind of transferable "data"; eighteenth-century essays and lyrics marshal empirical detail in order to generate general and generalizable propositions.[5] Starr echoes this logic; at mid-century, poetic and novelistic genres are engaged in "an affective program, an attempt to frame sense and make it not just understandable but shareable, to offer up personal experience as more than individual—as participatory."[6] In this line of criticism, seemingly distinct genres demonstrate their affinity by fashioning shareable experiences of interiority—experiences enabled, in a great measure, by the apparent transcendence of generic frames.

However, it is precisely at such moments of transcendence that considerations of literary form seem to fall away. The lyric, at its most prophetic and free, exceeds its metric frame and "lends itself to absorption in prose"; blank verse, at its most meditative, evinces a "conspicuous formlessness" and thus a likeness to unmeasured speech; mid-century works of devotion "seem to be trying to escape from the limitations of their own literary form by breaking down the barrier between author and reader and the distinction between reading and doing."[7] In this line of criticism, literary form often seems to become essentially inimical to the untrammelled expression of interiority, as when Shaun Irlam suggests that mid-century literature of sensibility and enthusiasm functions especially as an "instrument for contesting hegemonic Augustan discursive forms."[8] Ultimately, accounts of eighteenth-century literature that privilege interiority as a trans-generic goal tend to construe generic distinction as merely ornamental, or positively detrimental, to this literary phenomenon—a particular paradox in the case of poetry, where the 'hegemony' of metrical form constitutes the genre's enabling condition. (As Tzvetan Todorov remarks, "in the doctrine of naturalism, there is no place for the poem."[9])

Lurking here is the assumption that literary form successfully represents interiority only by *de*-forming itself, or minimizing its literary conventionality in order to render the private mind wholly legible to the reader. This chapter asks how we might interpret relationships between genres while simultaneously foregrounding the diverse effects produced by generic particularities, especially as they relate to the expression—as well as the restraint—of interiority. This chapter takes as its focus the two authors who spurred Mulso's and Carter's disagreement. At first glance, Richardson's and Young's respective modes of writing could not appear more distinct: *Clarissa* is a skein of letters unspooled through a vast labyrinth of domestic violence, whereas *Night Thoughts* is a theodicy in blank verse, a seeming monument of epigrams and orthodoxy. Nonetheless, a well-documented, if underremarked, working relationship existed between these authors, one that evinces a shared moral program.[10] So routine was the observation of a thematic conjunction between the works of Richardson and Young that critics such as Samuel Taylor Coleridge could charge them as jointly liable for the same aesthetic crimes.[11] Despite their apparent generic disparity, both works are concerned with the manifestation in literary form of what Clarissa calls the "*inwardest* mind"—not simply with representation of the self *in* form (a controversial phenomenon in the eighteenth century) but also with the manner in which the self is enabled *by* form.[12] In light of these ties, it behooves us to ask how Young's verse may illuminate the workings of Richardson's prose, particularly its understanding of how literary form fashions interiority. I suggest that both texts locate a homiletic value in the literal and figurative labors of *articulation*—in what Mulso characterizes as the "toil and pain" of untwisting, speaking, and digesting words and thoughts. For Young and

Richardson, habits that attend, and that frequently seem to restrain and impede, self-articulation in prose or verse—habits of versification and elocution, composition and transcription—actually enable an orthodox mode of self-reflection designed to temper solipsism. In a word, Young and Richardson often model a poetics of *mediacy* rather than immediacy, discovering a similar moral worth in the alienating constraints of poetic measure and epistolary media. *Night Thoughts* and *Clarissa* both seek to exploit this disjunction between the inward mind and its outward expression in order to fashion and regulate a socially and spiritually desirable concept of interiority.

For the vast majority of readers in eighteenth-century England, the most familiar accounts of interiority emerge from a religious discourse and are grounded upon a relationship with literary—initially scriptural—form. Michael McKeon suggests that the modern, "distinctly internal" concept of consciousness finds its origins amid sixteenth- and seventeenth-century religious debates concerning liberty of conscience, or the freedom to appeal to an inward understanding of scripture and revelation. These debates, which made "conscientious self-scrutiny central to salvation," increasingly located authenticity in the internalization of scriptural language by means of its recitation and re-articulation.[13] Voltaire could remark that the force of the English idiom "is wonderfully heighten'd . . . by the Liberty of Conscience, which makes them more conversant in the Scripture, and hath rendered the Language of the Prophets so familiar to them, that their Poetry savours very much of that Eastern out of the way Sublimity."[14] This deeply Protestant link between one's scriptural fluency and the concept of interiority quickly migrated to the realm of non-scriptural literature. Early in the century, critic John Dennis likens the function of poetry to that of "the True Religion" on the grounds that they both "make Happy the whole Man, by making Internal Discord cease."[15] Dennis's argument for the moral efficacy of poetry is predicated upon the concept of an interiority that makes itself home to, and is reformed by, an expressly literary presence.

However, as Misty G. Anderson and Thomas Keymer have shown, the pervasive association of interiority with religious revelation proved problematic for early practitioners of the domestic novel such as Richardson whose works were contemporaneous with the controversial rise of Methodism. Henry Fielding found Richardson's *Pamela* (1740) distasteful, in a great measure, due to the Methodistic quality of the heroine's "spiritual self-absorption": her familiar letters seemed to enable a solipsistic world of inwardly authenticated meaning at the expense of publicly minded conduct.[16] Moreover, this worrisome solipsism correlated with an apparent and controversial lack of form. Anderson notes that Richardson's narrative strategy shared with early Methodist tracts and confessional writings an intention to transport readers "to the 'real' beyond language and representation in an increasingly textual world."[17] Because the familiar letter seemed to offer a means of escaping its own formal and social conventions amid its representation of the "inwardest mind," Richardson's signature experimentation with this literary mode effectively rendered the author's novel part of a religious dispute. As Keymer notes, in the controversy over *Pamela*, issues of narratology and theology often prove coterminous.[18] Richardson took these charges to heart and was keen to avoid them when it came time to write *Clarissa*, remarking in a letter to George Cheyne that many readers had perceived him to be "too much of a Methodist" after the publication of *Pamela*.[19] Exhibiting "fairly orthodox religious views," Richardson generally sought to avoid religious controversy.[20] If Clarissa were to be a Christian of unimpeachable piety, her epistles would have to fashion interiority without indulging in solipsism or risking charges of heterodoxy.

It is in this regard that Richardson's editorial relationship with Young and the formal example of *Night Thoughts* become germane to the composition of *Clarissa*. The polyvocality of *Clarissa*'s epistolary form and the challenges of dialectic reading that such a form prompts have garnered much critical discussion; however, few remark that a model for such a dialectic existed for Richardson in Young's poem. *Night Thoughts* is rivaled only by Thomson's *The Seasons* (1726–30) for the title of the century's most popular poem.[21] In a series of nine "Nights," its speaker meditates upon religious doubt, theodicy, and death, and finds comfort in orthodox Anglican faith. Despite the monolithic appearance of its nearly ten thousand lines of verse, Young's work exhibits a preoccupation with multiple registers of address. Much like Richardson, Young is concerned with the formal problem of transforming ostensibly private discourse (prayer or meditation) into public instruction consonant with Anglican orthodoxy. For the modern reader of Young, the transition between these registers of address can seem jarring. Effortlessly conversational moments of introspective soliloquy, spurred "by what spontaneously arose in the author's mind," jostle up against a monotony of apothegms as well as grandiloquent attempts to reform a rakish addressee named Lorenzo:

How Great, in the wild Whirl of *Time*'s pursuits
To stop, and pause, involv'd in high Presage,
Through the long Visto of a thousand Years,
To stand contemplating our distant Selves,

As in a magnifying Mirror seen,
Enlarg'd, Ennobl'd, Elevate, Divine?
To prophesy our own Futurities?
To gaze in Thought on what all Thought transcends?[22]

Wrong not the Christian, think not Reason *yours*;
'Tis *Reason* our great *Master* holds so dear;
'Tis *Reason*'s injur'd Rights his Wrath resents;
'Tis *Reason*'s Voice obey'd His Glories crown;
To give lost *Reason* Life, He pour'd his own:
Believe, and show the Reason of a Man;
Believe, and taste the Pleasure of a God;
Believe, and look with Triumph on the Tomb.[23]

Such lability of address, ranging from the contemplative to the dictatorial, has facilitated a radical disparity amongst critical assessments of Young's poem. Depending on the passages one cites, the verse may exemplify a proto-Romantic "egocentricity of perspective" or an Augustan "habit of pedagogic moralizing," an enthusiastic fideism or a Newtonian seclusion.[24] In light of this multiplicity of views, Samuel Johnson's assessment of *Night Thoughts* seems prescient: "The excellence of this work is not exactness, but copiousness; particular lines are not to be regarded; the power is in the whole, and in the whole there is a magnificence like that ascribed to Chinese plantation, the magnificence of vast extent and endless diversity."[25] For Johnson, the poem's variegation—like the array of voices found in Richardson's novel—constitutes an enabling condition of the work as a whole. Discursive tensions and disjunctions within the poem (what David B. Morris calls its "[c]hiaroscuro" quality) ought not to be minimized or passed over in silence but rather assessed with regard to the complex, seemingly contradictory model of interiority that they fashion for the reader.[26]

I suggest that Young is keen to exploit apparent tensions between private and public forms of address—indeed, that his poem's concept of interiority is largely enabled by these tensions. Due both to the legacy of seventeenth-century radical religious dissent and to the more recent stirrings of Methodism, the relationship between private belief and public discourse continued to prompt cultural anxiety in mid-century England.[27] For the early Hanoverians, keeping certain thoughts private is as much a matter of public duty as it is one of personal liberty. One of the more memorable statements of this anxiety arises in Johnson's *Rasselas* (1759) when Imlac remarks that "[a]ll power of fancy over reason is a degree of insanity; but while this power is such as we can control and repress, it is not visible to others nor considered as any depravation of the mental faculties; it is not pronounced madness but when it comes ungovernable, and apparently influences speech or action."[28] Doubt—the offspring of inward "fancy" and the target of Young's theodicy—only becomes a political and social reality once it pronounces itself in discourse. In this light, normative discourse is not simply a barrier beyond which heterodox thought cannot pass, but also something of a compromise *with* heterodoxy: madness, treason, or heresy can dwell untouched in the realm of thought just so long as it stays quiet. This is the line crossed by Christopher Smart when he began to pray loudly in the streets; as Hester Lynch Thrale commented, "While *Kit Smart* thought it his Duty to pray in *Secret*, no living Creature knew how mad he was."[29]

Young's equivocal treatment of "fancy" explicitly positions his work upon this discursive fault-line. As John Sitter notes, the mere premise that the poem constitutes a set of nightly meditations effectively adduces fancy as "the necessary means to ideal truths."[30] Thus one must grant, with Sitter, that Young regards the literary fashioning of interiority to be a good *per se* lest the coherence of the entire work be called into question. Nonetheless, the question remains whether it is a qualified good, and, if qualified, in what manner. For Young, like Johnson, also detects in the private workings of thought the twin threats of self-delusion and solipsism. Although the poem may be called *Night Thoughts*, it does not follow that "thought" is necessarily a positive term for Young. He calls it a "tyrant" and a "murderer" who leads man astray.[31] Early in the poem, Young likens solitary thought to a mode of confinement:

> How, like a Worm, was I wrapt round and round
> In silken thought, which reptile Fancy spun,
> Till darken'd Reason lay quite clouded o'er
> With soft conceit.[32]

In a seeming paradox, Young's poetry privileges solitude while evincing distrust of the mind's ability to reach truth on its own. It wishes both to bask in reflection and, ultimately, to transcend such reflection. As Sitter cogently argues, one solution to this spiritual and literary problem involves an experience of conversion.[33] However Young also posits another mode of escaping the cocoon of "soft conceit," a mode that garners less critical treatment because it seems to contradict the work's essential investment in solitude and interiority. This mode involves forms of forthrightly public address—such as conversation, declamation, and, most intriguingly, what I will shortly characterize as a certain strain of homiletics. In the poem's second "Night" in particular, the poet is keen to explain the process by which the tangled thoughts spun by fancy may be made socially and spiritually useful. For Young, the solution is not self-censorship but rather self-measure through utterance. The mere act of conforming thought to discourse plays a pivotal role, garnering from the poet a spate of analogies:

Thoughts disentangle passing o'er the Lip;
Clean runs the thread; if not, 'tis thrown away,
Or kept to tie up Nonsense for a Song.[34]

Thoughts shut up want Air,
And spoil, like Bales unopen'd to the Sun.[35]

'Tis Thought's exchange, which like th'alternate Push
Of waves conflicting, breaks the learned Scum.[36]

According to Young, speech is not simply a forum in which the heterodox thoughts of fancy are policed; rather the very event of speech constitutes a mechanism for measuring and certifying the spiritual health of the "inwardest mind." Young characterizes speech as "Thought's Criterion"—only "When coin'd in Word" can "we know its *real* worth."[37] A thought's ability to take on normative form—to *be* disentangled, pronounced, and exchanged—indicates its moral currency, and distinguishes it from lyric "Nonsense."

The poem's investment in the moral measure of speech raises a set of questions: What sort of discursive formations does Young have in mind? And how do these advance or undermine the poem's investments in meditation and interiority? The full title of the work—*The Complaint: or, Night-Thoughts on Life, Death, & Immortality*—foregrounds the centrality of a discursive tension. Readers and critics commonly refer to the poem simply as *Night Thoughts*, thereby privileging the work's solitary, meditative character and thus its status as a species of soliloquy. However, to efface the poem's status as, in part, a "complaint" is to lose sight of its dual existence as a public and often explicitly *congregational* utterance. By the mid-eighteenth century, the "complaint" denotes a well-established lyric sub-genre in both secular and religious verse. In the former, it often makes its appearance in the eclogue when a speaker—usually a solitary, forlorn lover—pours forth his or her sorrows.[38] Arguably more prevalent, however, is the term's appearance in religious verse, where it delimits the form of utterance practiced by Job and Jeremiah: it is an audible expression of sorrow that necessarily assumes the presence of inter-locutors and auditors.[39] One suspects that Young's Anglican readers would have primarily encountered the word not amid neoclassical eclogues but rather in *The Book of Common Prayer* (1662), where it appears both as a common trope in wor-shippers' devotional armature and, often, as the explicit generic category of their morning and evening devotions.[40] In this regard, Young's title is key. It preserves the fact that the poem is as concerned with the relationship *between* the different categories of private meditation and collective utterance as it is with either of these discursive categories in isolation.

The poem's preoccupation with this discursive tension is grounded in, and illuminated by, a homiletic tradition in which *Night Thoughts* explicitly and visibly partakes. Critics rarely acknowledge the consistent and conspicuous use of blackletter to render the sub-title "Night Thoughts," and those who do sug-gest that it constitutes an early instance of the use of this typeface "to conjure up 'Gothic' or romantic ideas."[41] (See figure 8.1) However, this interpretation overlooks the well-documented tradition of using blackletter on the title pages of popular pedagogical and devotional works such as primers, hymnals, psalters, and sermons.[42] Simply put, the use of blackletter carries generic force and ap-peals to a clear constituency of readers. At the time of the poem's publication, the title page of *Night Thoughts* would have borne a telling resemblance not to long poems such as Pope's *Essay on Man* (1733–4) (to which Young's verse is of-ten considered a response), but rather to sermons such as Thomas Bradbury's *The Sin and Danger of Profane Swearing Expos'd* (1742) or to contemporary Anglican liturgies.[43] (See figures 8.2 and 8.3)

Moreover, before the appearance of Young's poem, the phrase "night thoughts" or "midnight thoughts" appears almost exclusively in devotional litera-ture and particularly in sermons.[44] Often, the term is pejorative, connoting the perils of solipsism that haunt Young's verse. Andrew Gray warns his auditors and readers to "[b]e carefull to think upon such thoughts as ye may answer for one day to the Lord, for your mid-night thoughts shall be read in the hearing of angels and men"; Samuel Rutherford lists the phrase amid the "vanity, dreams, golden imaginations & night-thoughts" of those bewitched by a "whorish world."[45] Rarely, when the phrase takes on a positive aspect, it describes a preparation for an address from the pulpit, as when Rutherford informs his congregation that "[m]y day thoughts, and my night thoughts are of you, while ye sleep, I am afraid of your souls that they be off the rock."[46] When discussing *Night Thoughts*, critics politely de-emphasize the hortatory aspect of Young's verse, which for modern readers

THE

COMPLAINT:

OR,

𝔑ight = 𝔗houghts

ON

LIFE, DEATH, & IMMORTALITY.

[Price One Shilling.]

Figure 8.1. Title page, *The Complaint: Or, Night-Thoughts* (1742). Reproduced with permission of the William Ready Division of Archives and Research Collections, McMaster University Library.

THE

SIN and DANGER

OF

𝕻𝖗𝖔𝖋𝖆𝖓𝖊 𝕾𝖜𝖊𝖆𝖗𝖎𝖓𝖌

EXPOS'D,

IN SEVERAL

SERMONS.

By *THOMAS BRADBURY.*

LONDON.

Printed for J. OSWALD, at the *Rose and Crown* in the
Poultry ; and J. BUCKLAND, at the *Buck* in *Paternoster-
Row.* 1742.

(Price One Shilling.)

Figure 8.2. Title page, *The Sin and Danger of Profane Swearing, Expos'd* (1742). Reproduced
with permission of the Thomas Fisher Rare Book Library, University of Toronto.

Evening Prayer.

Deus Mifereatur. Pfalm LXVII.

God be merciful unto us, &c.

¶ Then the *Creed*, &c. to the End of the Lord's Prayer.

¶ Then the Prieſt ſtanding up, ſhall ſay,

Prieſt. O Lord, ſhew thy mercy upon us!
Anſw. And grant us thy ſalvation.
Prieſt. O Lord, ſave the King!
Anſw. And mercifully hear us when we call upon thee.
Prieſt. Endue thy miniſters with righteouſneſs.
Anſw. And make thy choſen people joyful.
Prieſt. Give peace in our time, O Lord!
Anſw. Becauſe there is none other that fighteth for us, but only thou, O God.
Prieſt. O Lord, ſave thy ſervants!
Anſw. Who put their truſt in thee.
Prieſt. Send us help from thy holy place.
Anſw. And evermore mightily defend us.
Prieſt. Let the Enemy have no advantage againſt us;
Anſw. Nor the wicked approach to hurt us.
Prieſt. Lord, hear our prayer!
Anſw. And let our cry come unto thee.

¶ Theſe two Collects to be uſed inſtead of the firſt Collect for the Evening Prayer.

O Almighty God, who ruleſt over all the kingdoms of the earth, and on whoſe moſt gracious provi= dence they depend evermore for preſervation and proſperity; extend thine accuſtomed goodneſs to the
people·

Figure 8.3. "Evening Prayer," Church of England, *A Form of Prayer, to be Used in All Churches and Chapels* . . . (1742). Reproduced by permission of the Huntington Library.

seems to involve a "disagreeable sensation of being shouted at."[47] However, to do so is to ignore the homiletic mode that Young explicitly draws upon in both the title and the body of the poem: "Thou say'st I preach; Lorenzo! 'tis confest. / What if, for once, I preach thee quite awake?"[48] Even George Eliot's famously harsh critique of Young's "radical insincerity" takes for granted that he is working in a homiletic mode and that the poem, like a sermon, makes its essential appeal based on the *ethos* of its speaker.[49] Eliot's charge that Young is "a sort of cross between a sycophant and a psalmist" is not concerned with verse *qua* verse, but rather with the perceived failings of Young's character insofar as it subtends the moral and religious function of the poetry.[50]

To recuperate the poem's affinity with this homiletic mode is to illuminate its peculiar understanding of how address constructs interiority for the reader or auditor. Although one may initially be tempted to construe the homily as a forthrightly public mode of discourse, eighteenth-century homiletics tends to resist such categorization. In his influential *The Saints Everlasting Rest* (1650), often reprinted during the eighteenth century, Richard Baxter remarks that "Soliloquy is a Preaching to ones self. Therefore the very same Method which a Minister should use in his Preaching to others, should a Christian use in speaking to himself."[51] In the same strain—although describing a movement in the opposite direction—Bishop Gilbert Burnet contends "it is certain that a Sermon, the Conclusion whereof makes the Auditory look pleased, and sets them all a talking one with another, was either not right spoken, or not right heard . . . [b]ut that Sermon that makes every one go away silent and grave, and hastening to be alone, to meditate or pray over the matter of it in secret, has had its true effect."[52] These accounts of homiletic practice disdain labels such as "private" or "public." For Baxter, soliloquy invites the pulpit into the closet; for Burnet, preaching conjures a mentality of the closet amid the congregation. Thus, although critics often construe the closet—and, by analogy, the epistles this space enables—as a "nonpublic zone" prompting the exploration of "private consciousness," these accounts of homiletic address suggest that the discursive forms associated with the closet (such as prayer, meditation, and epistle) inform and are informed by what Johnson terms "the polished periods and glittering sentences" of pulpit oratory.[53] If the cadences of preaching structure soliloquy (and vice versa), then the homiletic form that Young adopts must be regarded as enabling and regulating the interior world of the reader in a non-trivial manner.

In this regard, Burnet's preoccupation with elocution and audition—that is, the importance of the sermon's being "right spoken" and "right heard"—is revealing because Young's eighteenth-century readership often discusses the efficacy of *Night Thoughts* in just such a context. In *An Essay on Elocution* (1748), a popular treatise directed primarily at budding preachers, independent minister John Mason raises the example of Young in order to draw an important link between the task of grappling with literary form (in this case, quite simply, the act of pronunciation) and the ability to "enter into the Spirit" of an author's words. To be "inwardly perswaded of the Truth" of a text, remarks Mason, one must internalize its formal cruces, and "hence it is that so few are able to read Milton and Young."[54] For Mason, central to the moral efficacy of Young's verse is the literal act of reading, or the "great labour both of mind and tongue" of which Hester Mulso laments. Mason insists that a poet such as Young or Milton, "by a constant Attention to his Measures and Rhime, and the Exaltation of his Language, is often very apt to obscure his Sense; which therefore requires the more Care in the Reader to discover and distinguish it by the Pronunciation." Unlike many of Young's modern critics who characterize the poet's blank verse as formless, free, and associative—and thus, implicitly, as a locus of readerly ease—contemporary writers such as Mason and Mulso routinely stress the difficulty of merely articulating Young's lines.[55] In the anthology *Beauties of Milton, Thomson, and Young* (1783), George Kearsley likewise connects the moral efficacy of verse and the habit of pronouncing it: "I thought I could not do a greater service to the rising youth of both sexes than by making such a selection as would improve the *Morals*, raise the opinion of English *Literature*, and give considerable strength to the dignity of *Elocution*."[56] In this respect, the "thorns and thistles" of Young's prosody serve a homiletic function insofar as they compel the reader to labour to internalize a difficult, often recalcitrant text:

> What, amidst
> This Tumult Universal, wing'd Dispatch,
> And ardent Energy, supinely yawns? -
> *Man* sleeps; and *Man* alone; and *Man*, whose Fate,
> Fate irreversible, entire, extreme,
> Endless, hair-hung, breeze-shaken, o'er the Gulph
> A moment trembles; drops: and *Man*, for whom
> All else is in alarm: *Man*, the sole Cause
> Of this surrounding Storm! and yet he sleeps,
> As the Storm rock'd to rest.[57]

Young's staccato verse resists easy apprehension.[58] Often, its metrical regularity and syntactic irregularity work against one another—to read for the regular pulse of the meter is to lose the complex asymmetry of the anaphora, and vice versa. This formal tension, like the broader discursive tension between meditative and didactic forms of address, is of a piece with the homiletic mode: one is consistently challenged to speak and hear its multiplicity rightly. Mason remarks that for both the preacher and lay reader "a just Pronunciation is a Good Commentary" upon a text; as such, the mere act of elocution constitutes a hermeneutical challenge.[59] Verse with homiletic ambitions such as Young's works upon the "inwardest mind" of its reader, in great measure, by *resisting* this mind's dominion.[60]

Ultimately, for Young and his more orthodox contemporaries, literary form serves a homiletic function not by facilitating a reader's or listener's experience of interiority but rather by regulating and tempering such an experience. Comparing his own night thoughts to a wild horse, Young writes that "Rude Thought runs wild in Contemplation's Field; / Converse, the Menage [*sic*], breaks it to the Bit / Of due Restraint."[61] The various "restraints" of spoken language—such as meter, cadence, and rhyme—are not simply technical regulations for Young, but moral ones. In a preface to one of his odes, Young discusses literary form in the language of spiritual trial, observing that his choice of frequent rhyme "laid me under great Difficulties. But Difficulties overcome give Grace."[62] Only in confronting norma-tive forces—be they metrical or discursive—can private thought achieve a spiri-tually useful shape. Both Isaac Watts and Samuel Johnson echo this conviction in fields as far asunder as grammar school primers and prosodic criticism. Watts warns his pupils that "[t]here are Multitudes who can read common Words true, [and] can speak every hard Name exactly," but who, "if they ever attempt to read Verse, even of the noblest Composure . . . perpetually affect to charm their own Ears . . . with ill Tones and Cadencies, with false Accents, and a false Harmony."[63] Johnson detects a note of self-delusion amongst those readers who think they hear a distinct and meaningful music in Milton's versification: "[i]t is scarcely to be doubted, that on many occasions we make the musick which we imagine ourselves to hear; that we modulate the poem by our own disposition, and ascribe to the numbers the effects of the sense."[64] Both Watts and Johnson prove wary of read-ing habits that ignore the hard, rewarding task of interpretation in favor of private affectations and solipsistic dispositions. The reader or listener who hears only what he or she wants to hear—who resides in an echo chamber of private sounds and private meanings—risks turning his or her back on the discursive community and thereby abandoning the metrical labors that teach grace.

On these grounds, Richardson's formal preoccupations in *Clarissa* reveal a deep affinity with those of Young. Richardson's epistolary dialectic, which challenges the reader to organize and interpret competing and often contradictory strands of narrative, garners much praise and scrutiny from critics. Thomas Keymer persuasively argues that "the characteristic difficulty and complexity of Richardson's narrative method, far from subverting his didactic project, may be directly attributed to it . . . [and] credited as its primary enabling means." Notably, Keymer suggests a tantalizing formal resemblance between Richardson's method and that of Milton, whose "homiletic project" in *Paradise Lost* (1667) works precisely by challenging and "entangling" its reader; however, Milton's "pervasive and complex presence," Keymer suggests, has yet to be fully understood.[65] This sense of a particularly formal link between Milton and Richardson, between verse and prose, grows at once less impressionistic and more demonstrable when the example of Young is adduced. Eighteenth-century readers and publishers such as Mason and Kearsley clearly felt that Milton's homiletic project was alive and well in Young's sermonizing verse. Moreover, when one takes Richardson's talk of his own homiletic goals at face value, the formal affinities between these works gain a sharper focus. "[N]o human being can long endure such a mixture of preaching and story-telling," remarked Leslie Stephen of Richardson's masterpiece.[66] As in the case of Young, Richardson's tendency to 'sermonize' polarizes readers; and, as in the case of Young, the explicit intentionality of such sermonizing is often overlooked. In *A Collection of the Moral and Instructive Sentiments . . . Contained in the Histories of Pamela, Clarissa, and Sir Charles Grandison* (1755), the preface foregrounds the homiletic nature of Richardson's writings:

> we cannot but greatly respect the man, who, in an age *like this*, has attempted to steal upon the world *reformation*, under the notion of *amusement*; who has found the expedient of engaging the *private attention* of those, who put themselves out of reach of *public exhortation*; pursuing to their *closets* those who fly from the *pulpit*; and there, under the gay air, and captivating semblance of a *Novel*, tempting them to the perusal of many a persuasive *Sermon*.[67]

Here the seemingly private amusements of Richardson's prose conceal, rather, what Baxter terms a "preaching to ones self": exhortation masquerades as meditation, pulpit learning as closet musing. The notion of subterfuge prevails. This poetics supposes that the reader internalizes orthodox habits of thought and conduct without ever being quite aware, and thereby construes novelistic prose as merely a more self-effacing form of homiletics—a 'plain style' whose very plainness hides its readerly challenges. Despite having the captivating semblance of a closet amusement, "reading well," insists Richardson in a letter to Mulso, is "a more uncommon excellence than preaching well"—the challenges of its articulation may manifest more subtly and elsewhere than in "great labour both of mind and tongue," but they are, implies Richardson, no less present.[68]

For Richardson, as for Young, habits of articulation prompt habits of thought: they serve interiority not by facilitating but rather by tempering and, at times, even impeding its expression. Richardson's *Letters . . . on the most Important Occasions* (1741), the work that first prompted his experimentation with the epistolary novel, argues for a direct correlation between literary form and ethical conduct. This work's sub-title insists that these model letters exemplify "not only the Requisite Style and Forms to be Observed in Writing Familiar Letters; But How to Think and Act Justly and Prudently, in the Common Concerns of Human Life." For Richardson, thought and action do not *transcend* the epistolary form, but rather are trained by it. "Letter LXXIX," entitled "A Gentleman to a Lady, professing an Aversion to the tedious Forms of Courtship," exemplifies this process of habituation. In an off-the-cuff proposal, the suitor abandons what he perceives to be the mere ornaments of epistolary address and offers what he supposes to be frank sincerity: "To try by idle Fallacies, and airy Compliments, to prevail on your Judgment, is a Folly for any Man to attempt who knows you. No, Madam, your good Sense and Endowments have raised you far above the Necessity of practising the mean Artifices which prevail upon the less deserving of your Sex: You are not to be so lightly deceived." For the lady, however, the "Artifices" of epistolary form are neither mean nor deceptive, but rather emblematic of moral seriousness. She responds: "I am very little in Love with the fashionable Methods of Courtship: Sincerity with me is preferable to Compliments; yet I see no Reason why common Decency should be discarded. There is something so odd in your Style, that when I know whether you are in Jest or Earnest, I shall be less at a loss to answer you." Unsurprisingly, the suitor soon returns a much more conventional proposal and is greeted with acceptance.[69] For Richardson (as for his imagined recipient), formless sincerity is, in a sense, illegible. Only by submitting to the measure of normative discourse can the affections of the "inwardest mind" assume social currency. In this regard, the letter serves its homiletic function of habituating the sender "To Think and Act Justly" precisely by de-individuating and regulating interiority.

Richardson's novel models a more complex mode of such habituation, particularly during Clarissa's seclusion and final days. Critics note that as Richardson's protagonist approaches her end she becomes something of a discursive absence—increasingly the object, rather than the author, of the epistolary collection that bears her name. An exception to this relative silence, however, is Clarissa's habit of compositional meditation. Belford reports to Lovelace that "Mrs Lovick obliged me with the copy of a meditation collected by the lady from the Scriptures. . . . We may see by this, the method she takes to fortify her mind, and to which she owes in a great measure the magnanimity with which she bears her underserved persecutions."[70] This meditation is one of five present in the novel proper, and is exemplary of the thirty-six such compositions appearing in Richardson's *Meditations Collected from the Sacred Books* (1750) (in which it figures as "Meditation XII"), a novelistic paratext ostensibly composed by Clarissa during her final seclusion.[71] These meditations are at once revealing and opaque. As Clarissa's private writings near the time of her death, they would seem to offer "special access to internal struggles which in the novel itself are mainly reported by uncomprehending external witnesses."[72] Yet these documents of Clarissa's "inwardest mind" consist entirely of scriptural citation. Wholly unoriginal and radically unlike the epistolary confessions that precede and surround them, they appear to be "meditations" in name only. Paradoxically, the nearer readers get to Clarissa's private devotions, the further they seem to be from any semblance of interiority.

For this reason, critics generally regard Clarissa's *Meditations* with some perplexity. Ellen Gardiner laments that Clarissa merely "copies meditations from Scripture, rather than reforming, or rewriting, them to produce new texts that she could claim as her intellectual property," while Starr suggests that these meditations employ the language of scripture as a discursive placeholder for a traumatized self temporarily unable to create its own words.[73] In this line of thought, habits of literary form become a crutch. Clarissa's meditations constitute a retreat from emotional verisimilitude, a symptom of discursive incoherence. "Caught between private prayer and public protest, [between] the devotional and the rhetorical," Clarissa sermonizes because she cannot fully soliloquize.[74]

However, this mode of interpreting Clarissa's meditations privileges their semantic content at the expense of the formal habits that they model. To overlook the labors latent in these compositions is both to misconstrue Richardson's understanding of the meditation as a mode of self-reflection and to ignore its relationship with the homiletic program exhibited in Young's *Night Thoughts*. Clarissa's meditations, particularly those featured in the novel proper, manifest a methodological complexity. Consisting of eleven lines of biblical verse without marginal gloss, the meditation mentioned by Belford can seem a single, prosaic passage of scripture that Clarissa has passively transcribed and preached to herself. This resemblance to prose is particularly prevalent in modern editions of the novel, which tend to print the meditations in smaller type in order to avoid spilling verses onto subsequent lines and producing a jagged edge of indentations. In so doing, however, such editions efface the structure of linearity clearly visible in Richardson's original settings of the meditation, which manifests a reverence for the linear integrity and discreteness of the verse; these passages are, quite visibly, measured in a way that the surrounding prose is not. (See figure 8.4)[75] Moreover, for Richardson's more scripturally minded readers, this metric differentiation would only reinforce a sense of discursive variety already latent in the meditation. Not only are these passages stitched together from more than one source within

352   *The* HISTORY *of*

mother on Saturday on her knees. It must be a very cruel one, Mrs. Lovick says, by the effects it had upon her: For, when she received it, she was intending to take an afternoon airing in a coach; but was thrown into so violent a fit of hysterics upon it, that she was forced to lie down; and (being not recovered thereby) to go to bed about eight o'clock.

On Thursday morning she was up very early; and had recourse to the Scriptures to calm her mind, as she told Mrs. Lovick: And, weak as she was, would go in a chair to Lincoln's-inn chapel, about eleven. She was brought home a little better; and then sat down to write to her uncle. But was obliged to leave off several times—To struggle, as she told Mrs. Lovick, for an humble temper. ' My heart, said she to the good woman, is a proud heart, ' and not yet, I find, enough mortified to my condition; ' but, do what I can, will be for prescribing resenting ' things to my pen.'

I arrived in town from Belton's this Thursday evening; and went directly to Smith's. She was too ill to receive my visit. But on sending up my compliments, she sent me down word, that she should be glad to see me in the morning.

Mrs. Lovick obliged me with the copy of a meditation collected by the lady from the Scriptures. She has intitled it, *Poor mortals the cause of their own misery;* so intitled, I presume, with intention to take off the edge of her repinings at hardships so disproportioned to her fault, were her fault even as great as she is inclined to think it. We may see by this, the method she takes to fortify her mind, and to which she owes, in a great measure, the magnanimity with which she bears her undeserved perfections.

MEDITATION.
Poor mortals the cause of their own misery.

SAY not thou, *It is thro' the Lord that I fell away; for thou oughtest not to do the thing that he hateth.*
Say not thou, He hath caused me to err; for he hath no need of the sinful man.
He himself made man from the beginning, and left him in the hand of his own counsel;

Miss Clarissa Harlowe.   353

If thou wilt, to keep the commandments, and to perform acceptable faithfulness.
He hath set fire and water before thee: Stretch forth thine hand to whether thou wilt.
He hath commanded no man to do wickedly; neither hath be given any man license to sin.
And now, Lord, what is my hope? Truly my hope is only in thee.
Deliver me from all my offences; and make me not a rebuke unto the foolish.
When thou with rebuke dost chasten man for sin, thou makest his beauty to consume away, like as it were a moth fretting a garment: Every man therefore is vanity.
Turn thee unto me, and have mercy upon me; for I am desolate and afflicted.
The troubles of my heart are inlarged. O bring thou me out of my distresses!

MRS. Smith gave me the following particulars of a conversation that passed between herself and a young clergyman, on Tuesday afternoon, who, as it appears, was employed to make inquiries about the lady by her friends. He came into the shop in a riding-habit, and asked for some Spanish snuff; and finding only herself there, he desired to have a little talk with her in the back-shop.
He beat about the bush in several distant questions, and at last began to talk more directly about Miss Harlowe.
He said, He knew her before her *fall* (That was his impudent word); and gave the substance of the following account of her, as I collected it from Mrs. Smith.
' She was then, he said, the admiration and delight of ' every-body: He lamented, with great solemnity, her ' *backsliding;* another of his phrases. Mrs. Smith said, ' He was a fine scholar; for he spoke several things she ' understood not: and either in Latin or Greek, she could ' not tell which; but was so good as to give her the Eng-' lish of them without asking. A fine thing, she said, ' for a scholar to be so condescending!
He said, ' Her going off with so vile a rake had given ' great scandal and offence to all the neighbouring ladies, ' as well as to her friends.'

Figure 8.4.   Richardson's typesetting for Clarissa's meditation, *Clarissa, or, The History of a Young Lady*, 7 vols. (London, 1747–8), 6.352-3. Reproduced by permission of the Rare Book & Manuscript Library, Columbia University in the City of New York.

scripture (respectively, Ecclesiasticus 15:11–12, 14–16, 20 and Psalm 39:8–9, 12, 15–16), but also from more than one biblical translation. It has gone unremarked by scholars of Richardson's *Meditations* that the psalmic verses transcribed by Clarissa originate both in the *King James Bible* (1611) and *The Book of Common Prayer*, which re-produces the psalter from Miles Coverdale's edition of the *Great Bible* (1539–40) or what Richardson in "Meditation II" refers to as "the old translation."[76] As a result, polyvocality and disjunction of form structure the eighteenth-century reader's experience of these meditations. Clarissa's peculiarly transcriptive mode of self-reflection represents not a passive recitation of holy writ but rather a methodical collation from variant translations, a deeply laborious and Protestant exercise in polyglot reading and the internalization of Scripture (or what Hester Mulso might lament as the toilsome picking of moral gooseberries). Clarissa "fortif[ies] her mind" and finds meditative grace in much the same manner as Young's speaker—by measuring and regulating self-expression to the point of apparent self-evacuation and discursive incoherence.

Soon after her departure from Harlowe Place, Clarissa looks upon the supposed "freedom" of scribbling with new eyes: "My talent is scribbling, and I the readier fell into this freedom, as I found delight in writing; having motives too which I thought laudable."[77] A tone of regret hangs over this exchange. The correspondence between Clarissa and Lovelace increasingly gives the lie to the supposition that scribbling is an unqualified freedom; as Clarissa and the reader learn, habits of writing may just as soon entrap as liberate. Clarissa's meditations capitalize on this costly lesson, seeking strength and self-possession in discursive restraint. If, as Keymer suggests, Richardson assembles the novel's letters "in such a way as to efface himself and transfer to the reader many further and more challenging tasks of organization and interpretation," then Clarissa's meditations represent a *mise en abyme* of this same poetics.[78] Effacing herself amid and beneath the polyvocality of scripture, Clarissa effectively challenges herself to read her "inwardest mind" through language untainted by solipsism. In this sense, it is precisely the mediated quality of the meditations that constitutes their devotional labour. Clarissa's ability to express her suffering in the common measure of biblical verse justifies that suffering as both a private trial and a public text, just as the homiletic habits of Young's poem work to transmute the inward gaze of fancy into knowledge worthy of a congregation. For literary allies Richardson and Young, an act of writing fashions interiority not by transcending formal restraints but rather by labouring with and in measure, by humbling thought such that it serves a community of listeners and readers.

Notes

I am grateful to Jenny Davidson for her encouragement and for her comments upon this essay.

1. Hester (Mulso) Chapone, *The Works of Mrs. Chapone*, 4 vols. (London, 1807): 3:39. The letter that prompted this exchange is not extant. However, Carter elsewhere discusses Richardson's tendency towards prolixity. See *Elizabeth Carter, 1717–1806: An Edition of Some Unpublished Letters*, ed. Gwen Hampshire (Newark: University of Delaware Press, 2005), 146.

2. G. Gabrielle Starr, *Lyric Generations: Poetry and the Novel in the Long Eighteenth Century* (Baltimore and London: The Johns Hopkins University Press, 2004), 2. See also Ralph Cohen, "On the Inter-relations of Eighteenth-Century Literary Forms," in *New Approaches to Eighteenth Century Literature: Selected Papers from the English Institute*, ed. Phillip Harth (New York: Columbia University Press, 1974), 33–78, and Clifford Siskin, *The Work of Writing: Literature and Social Change in Britain, 1700–1830* (Baltimore and London: The Johns Hopkins University Press, 1998), 130–152.

3. Clifford Siskin and William Warner, ed., *This is Enlightenment* (Chicago: University of Chicago Press, 2010), 1–33.

4. For Walter J. Ong, intersubjectivity undergirds human communication and resists explication by analogy to nature: "There is no adequate model in the physical universe for this operation of consciousness, which is distinctly human and which signals the capacity of human beings to form true communities wherein person shares with person interiorly, inter-subjectively." See *Orality and Literacy: The Technologizing of the Word* (London and New York: Routledge, 2002), 173. More recently, critics have sought to apply cognitive science to the understanding of this literary phenomenon. See, for example, G. Gabrielle Starr, "Poetic Subjects and Grecian Urns: Close Reading and the Tools of Cognitive Science," *Modern Philology* 105, no. 1 (2007): 48–61.

5. Siskin, *The Work of Writing*, 135–140.

6. Starr, *Lyric Generations*, 45.

7. Starr, *Lyric Generations*, 53; Shaun Irlam, *Elations: The Poetics of Enthusiasm in Eighteenth-Century Britain* (Stanford, CA: Stanford University Press, 1999), 3; Isabel Rivers, "Dissenting and Methodist Books of Practical Divinity," *Books and their Readers in Eighteenth-Century England*, ed. Isabel Rivers (New York: St. Martin's Press, 1982), 159.

8. Irlam, *Elations* 6.

9. Tzvetan Todorov, *Introduction to Poetics*, trans. Richard Howard (Minneapolis: University of Minnesota Press, 1981), 20.

10. By 1744, the two correspondents had entered into an editorial relationship, exchanging and commenting upon drafts of each other's works. In addition, Richardson became Young's printer. Their friendship was rooted not only in mutual regard, but also in the belief that the authors' respective works shared a moral program. In a letter explaining his desire to have Richardson review drafts of the poem, Young remarks: "Are not you in the same way of thinking? Are not virtue and religion your point of view? Who therefore can be supposed to feel wrong and right, in things of this nature, more naturally than yourself?" See *The Correspondence of Edward Young 1683–1765*, ed. Henry Pettit (Oxford: Clarendon Press, 1971), 192–3. In 1747, following his disputes with

correspondents over the structure of *Clarissa*, Richardson would remark "I wish I had never consulted anybody but Dr. Young." See Samuel Richardson, *Selected Letters*, ed. John Carroll (Oxford: Clarendon Press, 1964), 84.

11. Coleridge suggests that the rise of the much lamented and "so called *German* Drama" is in fact attributable to the conjoined influence of James Hervey's "bloated" *Meditations Among the Tombs* (1746), Young's "strained thoughts," and Richardson's "morbid consciousness" and "self-involution." See Samuel Taylor Coleridge, *Biographia Literaria*, 2 vols., ed. J. Shawcross (Oxford: Oxford University Press, 1907), 2:183–4; Chapter 23.

12. Samuel Richardson, *Clarissa*, ed. Angus Ross (Harmondsworth and New York: Penguin, 1985), 342.

13. Michael McKeon, *The Secret History of Domesticity: Public, Private, and the Division of Knowledge* (Baltimore: The Johns Hopkins University Press, 2005), 35–6. See also Misty G. Anderson, *Imagining Methodism in Eighteenth-Century Britain* (Baltimore: The Johns Hopkins University Press, 2012), 5.

14. Voltaire, *An Essay Upon the Civil Wars of France . . . and Also Upon the Epick Poetry of the European Nations from Homer Down to Milton* (London, 1727), 122–3.

15. John Dennis, *The Critical Works of John Dennis*, 2 vols., ed. Edward Niles Hooker (Baltimore: The Johns Hopkins University Press, 1939–43), 1:265.

16. Tom Keymer, *Richardson's* Clarissa *and the Eighteenth-Century Reader* (Cambridge and New York: Cambridge University Press, 1992), 27.

17. Anderson, *Imagining Methodism*, 63–4.

18. Keymer, *Richardson's* Clarissa, 27. In this regard, the problem of Methodism for early novelists such as Richardson reflects the tacit assumption of recent criticism concerned with the relationship between the novel and verse—namely, that the experience of interiority seems to transcend generic distinctions.

19. Richardson, *Letters*, 47.

20. John A Dussinger, "'Stealing in the Great Doctrines of Christianity': Samuel Richardson as Journalist," *Eighteenth-Century Fiction* 15, no.3 (2003), 458, 473.

21. Between 1742 and 1749, the as yet uncollected "Nights" of Young's poem ran through some thirty-three separate printings (either as individual "Nights" or as groupings of three to six "Nights"); between 1750 and the time of Young's death in 1762, the poem witnessed seventeen complete editions. See Henry Pettit, *A Bibliography of Young's* Night Thoughts (Boulder: University of Colorado Press, 1954). Between 1763 and 1800, at least another fifty-six editions of the poem appeared in Britain and America.

22. Edward Young, *Night Thoughts*, ed. Stephen Cornford (Cambridge: Cambridge University Press, 1989), 6:115–122. All citations from *Night Thoughts* refer to this edition.

23. Ibid., 4:755–762.

24. John Sitter, *Literary Loneliness in Mid-Eighteenth-Century England* (Ithaca and London: Cornell University Press, 1982), 163; George Eliot, "Worldliness and Other-Worldliness: The Poet Young," *Essays of George Eliot*, ed. Thomas Pinney (New York: Columbia University Press, 1963), 379; Blanford Parker, *The Triumph of Augustan Poetics* (New York and Cambridge: Cambridge University Press,

1998), 221; Marjorie Hope Nicolson, *Newton Demands the Muse* (Princeton: Princeton University Press, 1946), 149–151. On the topic of Young's "enthusiasm," see Irlam, *Poetics of Enthusiasm* in general. Sitter has recently qualified this claim regarding Young's egoism, welcoming a sociopolitical reading of Young's verse as a corrective "to earlier accounts (including my own) in which mid-century poetic solitude represents a wishful escape from the political realm." See John Sitter, "Britannia Waives the Rules: Recent Studies of English Poetry in Principle and Practice," review of *The Poetics of Enthusiasm in Eighteenth-Century Britain*, by Shaun Irlam; *Poems of Nation, Anthems of Empire: English Verse in the Long Eighteenth Century*, by Suvir Kaul; *The Triumph of Augustan Poetics: English Literary Culture from Butler to Johnson*, by Blanford Parker, in *Eighteenth-Century Studies* 35, no. 1 (2001): 133.

25. Samuel Johnson, *The Yale Edition of the Works of Samuel Johnson*, 23 vols. (New Haven and London: Yale University Press, 1958–2010), 23:1426.

26. David B. Morris, *The Religious Sublime* (Lexington: University Press of Kentucky, 1972), 146. Morris's perceptive reading of the poem's "interruptive and discontinuous sublimity" focuses primarily on the devotional function of such sublimity.

27. See Irlam, *Poetics of Enthusiasm* and Anderson, *Imagining Methodism*, particularly their introductions and first chapters.

28. Johnson, *Works*, 16:150–151. Similarly, Jonathan Swift would remark in a set of "Thoughts on Religion" unpublished until 1765 that "I am not answerable to God for the doubts that arise in my own breast . . . if I take care to conceal those doubts from others, if I use my best endeavors to subdue them, and if they have no influence on the conduct of my life." See *The Essential Writings of Jonathan Swift*, ed. Claude Rawson and Ian Higgins (New York and London: Norton, 2010), 710.

29. Katharine C. Balderston, ed. *Thraliana*, 2 vols. (Oxford: Clarendon Press, 1942), 2:728.

30. Sitter, *Literary Loneliness*, 167.

31. Young, *Night Thoughts*, 2:129, 1:225.

32. Ibid., 1:157–60.

33. Sitter, *Literary Loneliness*, 146–153, 165–170.

34. Young, *Night Thoughts*, 2:455–7.

35. Ibid., 2:466–7.

36. Ibid., 2:480–6.

37. Ibid., 2:469–71.

38. James Sambrook, *English Pastoral Poetry* (Boston: Twayne, 1983), 99.

39. See, for example, *The Complaint of Job* (London, 1734) as well as Samuel Johnson's citations of Job and Jeremiah in *A Dictionary of the English Language*, 1st ed., s.v. "complain" and "complaint." In his verse-paraphrase of Job, Young remarks that "[t]he Book of Job is well known to be Dramatick . . . like the Tragedies of old Greece." See *A Paraphrase on Part of the Book of Job* (London, 1719), 28.

40. The *Book of Common Prayer* directs Anglicans to read through the Psalter every month. Thus dutiful readers would have encountered some manner of "complaint" in psalms 17, 18, 22, 32, 77, 106, 119, 130, 142, and 144, not to mention other readings during the services proper. See Church of England, *Book of Common Prayer* (London, 1662).

41. Christine Baatz, "'A Strange Collection of Trash'? The Re-Evaluation of Medieval Literature in Thomas Percy's *Reliques of Ancient English Poetry* (1765)," *Anthologies of British Poetry*, eds. Barbara Korte, Ralf Schneider, and Stefanie Lethbridge (Amsterdam: Rodopi, 2000), 115.

42. Keith Thomas, "The Meaning of Literacy in Early Modern England," *The Written Word: Literacy in Transition*, ed. Gerd Baumann (Oxford: Clarendon Press, 1986), 99.

43. For a discussion of the aesthetic and generic force of typography in the eighteenth century, see Joseph A. Dane, *Out of Sorts: On Typography and Print Culture* (Philadelphia: University of Pennsylvania Press, 2011), 72–90. On the relationship between Young's poem and that of Pope, see Daniel W. Odell, "Young's *Night Thoughts* as an Answer to Pope's *Essay on Man*," *Studies in English Literature* 12 (1972): 481–501.

44. See for example Samuel Rutherford, *Joshua Redivivus* (Rotterdam?, 1664), 4, 318; Andrew Gray, *Directions and Instigations to the Duty of Prayer* (Edinburgh, 1669), 119; Nicholas Phillips, *The Holy Choice* (London, 1679), 22; Henry Pendlebury, *Invisible Realities, the Real Christian's Greatest Concernment in Several Sermons* (London, 1696), 53; John Scott, *Sermons Upon Several Occasions* (London, 1704), 304; John Laughton, *The Testimony of a Good Conscience* (London, 1712), 19; William Bartlet, *Barnabas's Character and Success* (London, 1716), 20; John Bisset, *A Sermon, Preached Before . . . the Presbytery of Aberdeen* (Aberdeen, 1737), 34.

45. Gray, *Directions and Instigations*, 119; Rutherford, *Joshua Redivivus*, 318.

46. Rutherford, *Joshua Redivivus*, 4.

47. Morris, *Religious Sublime*, 153, quoted in Irlam, 260.

48. Young, *Night Thoughts*, 2:62–3.

49. Eliot, "Worldliness and Other-Worldliness," 366.

50. Ibid., 337.

51. Richard Baxter, *The Saints Everlasting Rest* (London, 1650), 750. A variant of this passage is quoted in Rivers, 141.

52. Gilbert Burnet, *A Discourse of the Pastoral Care* (London, 1692), 224–5.

53. Christina Marsden Gillis, *The Paradox of Privacy: Epistolary Form in* Clarissa (Gainesville: University Presses of Florida, 1984), 21–22; James Boswell, *Life of Johnson*, ed. R. W. Chapman (Oxford: Oxford University Press, 1980), 440. Although Johnson here argues against this sort of oratory and in favour of a plain style, he later remarks approvingly that "Baxter made it a rule in every sermon that he preached to say something that was above the capacity of his audience." See Boswell, *Life*, 1209.

54. John Mason, *An Essay on Elocution* (London: M. Cooper, 1748), 28–29. (Please note that there exist two 1748 editions of Mason's treatise with different pagination.) Mason's discussion of inward persuasion is cited in part from Burnet, *Discourse*, 228.

55. Cornford, *Night Thoughts*, 3; Irlam, *Poetics of Enthusiasm*, 3.

56. *Beauties of Milton, Thomson, and Young*, ed. George Kearsley (London, 1783), iv. Intriguingly, Kearsley's selections are organized in a manner reminiscent of sermon topics under headings such as "Conscience," "Old Age," preparation for "Death," "Friendship," "Humility," "Jealously," "Self-Love," "Misfortune," "Patience," "Vanity," etc.

57. Young, *Night Thoughts*, 2:295–304.

58. Moreover, one finds much the same style (staccato clauses, clusters of spare metaphors, anaphora, and repeated questions) in Young's own sermons. Preaching before the House of Commons on the annual fast-day memorializing the martyrdom of Charles I, Young speaks of the vanity of earthly things and of the persistence of virtue in a manner that the reader of *Night Thoughts* will find familiar:

> But, Where is *Athens*? Where is *Carthage*? Where is *Rome*? The Seat of Science is *darken'd*; The Regent of the Seas is *sunk*; The Conqueror of the World is *nothing*. Their Glories are gone; They are passed by, as a Bubble on a Stream, or the Thought of a Drunken Man; as a *Post*, or a Shadow by Day, as a *Watch*, or a Vision by Night; Though their Cities were of Marble, their mighty Monuments of Brass; Though the Mountains fell, and the Rivers flow'd, as They bid them; Though their Roots struck deep in Earth, and their Heads rose high in Heaven. Of what, once, was *All*, now, *Nothing* remains, but what *Virtue* has preserv'd: Illustrious Names!

See *An Apology for Princes, or the Reverence due to Government*, (London, 1729), 51.

59. Mason, *Essay on Elocution*, 12–13.

60. Stanley Fish memorably argues that this phenomenon constitutes an essential characteristic of Milton's blank verse; see *Surprised by Sin* (London: Macmillan, 1967), 22–25.

61. Young, *Night Thoughts*, 2:490–2. The context seems to indicate that Young has in mind "manège," or the enclosed area in which horses are trained.

62. Edward Young, *Ocean. An Ode* (London, 1728), 25–6.

63. Isaac Watts, *The Art of Reading and Writing English* (London, 1721), xvi–xvii.

64. Samuel Johnson, *Rambler* 94, 4:136.

65. Keymer, *Richardson's Clarissa*, 65–8.

66. Leslie Stephen, *Works of Samuel Richardson*, 12 vols. (London, 1883–4), 1:xxix.

67. The "Preface by a Friend" at the head of the collection was composed by biblical scholar Benjamin Kennicott. For a discussion of Kennicott's role, see John Dussinger's introduction to *A Collection of Moral and Instructive Sentiments* in *Samuel Richardson's Published Commentary on Clarissa 1747–65*, 3 vols., ed. Tom Keymer (London: Pickering & Chatto, 1998), 3:xi–xix.

68. *The Correspondence of Samuel Richardson*, 6 vols., ed. Anna Laetitia Barbauld (London, 1804), 3:237.

69. Samuel Richardson, *Letters Written to and for Particular Friends, on the Most Important Occasions* (London, 1741), 111–113.

70. Richardson, *Clarissa*, 1189.

71. Tom Keymer, ed., *Richardson's Published Commentary*, 1:154–248. As Keymer thoroughly relates in his introduction to this volume, these meditations have a complex textual history. They likely consist of material written for, but ultimately omitted from, the first edition of *Clarissa*. Although Richardson clearly prepared the *Meditations* for publication, he only ever printed a small number and circulated them privately. Young was the first to receive a copy and urged Richardson to publish the work. See 1:154–160.

72. Ibid., 1:155.

73. Ellen Gardiner, *Regulating Readers: Gender and Literary Criticism in the Eighteenth-Century Novel* (Newark: University of Delaware Press, 1999), 61; Starr, *Lyric Generations*, 18–21.

74. Tom Keymer, "Richardson's *Meditations*: Clarissa's *Clarissa*," in *Samuel Richardson: Tercentenary Essays*, ed. Margaret Anne Doody and Peter Sabor (Cambridge: Cambridge University Press, 1989), 107.

75. See also Keymer, *Richardson's Published Commentary*, 1:198–9.

76. Ibid., 1:176.

77. Richardson, *Clarissa*, 408–9.

78. Keymer, *Richardson's* Clarissa, 84.

THE ART OF ATTENTION:

NAVIGATING DISTRACTION AND RHYTHMS OF

FOCUS IN EIGHTEENTH-CENTURY POETRY

Natalie Phillips

I.

When we speak of novel reading in the eighteenth century, we normally talk of absorption—of rapt, immersed readers—and of books that leave a deep impression on the mind. This vision of Enlightenment reading as being "lost in a good book" taps a tradition that stretches back to *Don Quixote* (1605–15), whose main character is so absorbed in romances that it distorts his perception of everyday life. As critics we often echo this view.[1] Yet, as distraction-conscious works such as Eliza Haywood's *The History of Betsy Thoughtless* (1751) and Laurence Sterne's *The Life and Opinions of Tristram Shandy, Gentleman* (1759–67) remind us, eighteenth-century writers were equally preoccupied with the idea of a distracted, *un*absorbed, audience. One eighteenth-century reader, Elizabeth Gurney, openly confessed to such cognitive habits in her journal: "I find it difficult to confine my attention to what I am reading; books tell us to think clearly and fix our ideas to the subject before us; I wish they would tell us how."[2] The rise in the number of works circulating in England had generated widespread anxiety about catching, much less holding, a reader's concentration. Though attacks on the dangers of novelistic absorption still ran rampant, competition for readers' focus meant writers of the period also worried deeply—and pragmatically—about inattentive readers such as Elizabeth Gurney, who might find it "difficult to confine . . . attention" to the work before their eyes.

In this sense, eighteenth-century novelists, poets, and essayists all faced a similar dilemma when it came to attention: a battle for readers' focus within an increasingly competitive economy of print. Alexander Pope's *The Dunciad* of 1729 describes a world where "Paper also became so cheap, and printers so numerous, that a deluge of Authors cover[s] the land."[3] London—and its readers' attention spans—drowns under a tidal wave of print. This well-known trope of the "groaning press," normally associated with the eighteenth-century novel, reached beyond the crowded space, or excessive weight, of books. It stretched into readers' minds, whose thoughts were imagined to be similarly crowded and over-taxed. Samuel Johnson, for instance, quipped about audiences' limited ability to concentrate amidst this barrage in his *Rambler* No. 16: readers "look into the first pages, but [are] hindered . . . by their admiration, from reading farther."[4] Eliza Haywood's opening essay of *The Female Spectator* (1744) assumes the reader will be caught or lost after "casting His eye over the four to five first pages."[5] Attention spans, most agreed, were getting shorter; and poets, like essayists, were far from immune to such concerns. While in 1694, Addison could write of Milton that "ev'ry verse . . . my whole attention draws," by 1782, William Cowper declared such "habits of close attention . . . more rare."[6]

Though poets clearly shared this concern with print overload, their discussions also tapped a distinctive thread within Enlightenment conversations about distraction: the power of literary forms to *shape* focus. Here, poetry was thought to have a distinct advantage over novels. In claiming that verse could better hold and train readers' attention, as we will see, poets drew on a long rhetorical tradition that emphasized the importance of brevity, and highly-organized structures such as rhyming verse, for improving concentration. Eighteenth-century poets tapped a set of rhetorical and pedagogical discussions of focus to describe poetry—particularly the regular meter and rhythm of Augustan rhyming couplets—as uniquely able to structure attention. Moreover, the more focused organization of verse was set repeatedly against the supposed disorder and multiplicity of narrative. Here, I investigate a series of eighteenth-century poems that take up attention and distraction from Alexander Pope's *Epistle to Arbuthnot* (1735) to John Gay's *Trivia* (1716) that illuminate this tradition, pairing them with an archive of uniquely focus-conscious verse by Christopher Pitt, John Byrom, and Erasmus Darwin. I argue that these writers used rhythm, in particular, to cast poetry as the ideal panacea to distraction, using ideas about how the regular meter of iambic pentameter couplets could improve focus to explore the larger notion of using an external structure—be it music, poetry, or a London street—to set a 'beat' to internal cognitive rhythms, or "rhythms of attention" in the mind. In their conversations about poetry, these writers highlight a key point of controversy in eighteenth-century debates over focus. In conversations *about* poetry, authors from Pope to Darwin tended to align the genre with an older, more traditional view of attention as a narrowing thought to a single object and tuning out distractions. In their actual poetry, however, they used techniques that emphasized readers' ability to maintain concentration *amidst* distraction, manage multiple information streams, and recognize layered rhythmic patterns. These formal choices supported a newer, modern view of attention as essentially multiple, coordinating many threads of focus at once. Tracing this genealogy of poetic attention alongside that of the novel—and the more familiar language of novelistic absorption—reveals important nuances in Enlightenment thinking about attention and literary reading that would be all too easily obscured in conventional novel-focused criticism. In particular, poetry helps us explore historical ideas about the intricate cognitive dynamics that arise when we engage with a unique set of literary patterns—rhythm and rhyme—and investigate more fully the play between familiarity and novelty, repetition and variation, that makes up our ongoing attention to verse.

II.

It was an accepted truth that to read in eighteenth-century London was to face a landscape of distractions. As Emily Cockayne observes in *Hubbub,* Londoners perceived their city as a maze of distractions, a barrage assailing all five senses.[7] The ears faced a melee of street criers, prostitutes, and ballad singers. Dirt, overflowing sewers, and emptied chamber-pots beset the others. As Tobias Smollett's Mr. Bramble complains in *The Expedition of Humphry Clinker* (1771), people were "everywhere, rambling, riding, rolling, rushing, jostling, mixing, bouncing, cracking, and crashing in one vile ferment'—All is tumult and hurry."[8] Such language bespeaks a sense of urban crowding, mixture, and bustle in eighteenth-century London. Yet it also it spoke to a larger sense of blurring class distinctions and aristocratic boundaries. It is not merely the rush or number of people that so bothers Smollett's misanthrope, Bramble; it is that the "different departments of life are jumbled together;" the "hod-carrier, the low mechanic, the tapster, the publican, the shopkeeper, the pettifogger, the citizen, and courtier" all *"tread upon the kibes of one another."*[9] Similar terms saturate the period's complaints about the saturation of print, particularly the entrance of Grub-Street authors into a traditionally coterie market. According to Jonathan Swift, the resulting mix was a flood of drivel—one in which work (and writers) of quality were all too easily jumbled with the haphazard prose of inattentive writers, market-driven hacks who composed hastily in "short intervals . . . stolen" from "a world of business."[10]

Carving out a place for poetic attention amidst complaints about distraction required sophisticated rhetorical maneuvering. Poets such as Pope, Swift, and Gay frequently used verse to revel in satires on the cacophony of London as well as Grub-street's chaotic flood of print. Yet even as they complained about the diversions pressing upon them, these poets repeatedly cast their verse as kind of a literary prophylactic, its ordered rhymes a genre uniquely able to set them apart from (ideally, above) this hubbub, and guide readers attentively through it. In this choice, poetry departs in important ways from the novel. A number of novelists responded to their audience's perceived mental overload by incorporating distraction *within* their works, making it their protagonist's central cognitive trait. (Think of the digressive narrator of *Tristram Shandy,* for example, or Haywood's inattentive heroine in *Betsy Thoughtless*). Eighteenth-century poets, by contrast, tended to render distraction as something that existed *outside* their verse. Though we get plenty of descriptions of distraction in eighteenth-century poetry, rarely do we get journeys inside a distracted, or chronically scattered mind. This difference emerges, in part, from the way poets sought to distinguish their brand of literary attention from that of the novel. Rather than "absorb" readers, a state that risked distraction from one's surrounding environment and duties, poetry claimed a unique ability to isolate and cocoon focus within a safe space for improved concentration. This "room," carefully carved-out for focus in poetic stanzas, was imagined to exist above the endless barrage of stimuli surrounding both poet and reader. Thus, even as they discussed distraction in verse, I suggest, poets also portrayed their works as creating a formal bulwark *against* the surrounding cacophony of cultural distractions. As we'll see, poets used three main tactics to achieve this effect: 1) imagining poetry as a space enclosed from diversion; 2) portraying the poet—and poem—as able to rise metaphorically above urban cacophony; and 3) invoking the Muse as a deity uniquely able to seize audience attention. These writers often framed their claims in verse—specifically iambic pentameter couplets—using poetry's rhythms and rhymes to both articulate and model the genre's unique claim on attention.

First, we have poetry being cast as a protected space for focus. Pope's *Epistle to Arbuthnot,* for instance, opens with a line about shutting out the distractions crowding in upon him:

Shut, shut the door, good *John!* fatigu'd I said,
Tye up the knocker, say I'm sick, I'm dead,
The Dog-star rages! nay 'tis past a doubt,
All *Bedlam,* or *Parnassus,* is let out:
Fire in each eye, and Papers in each hand,
They rave, recite, and madden round the land.

What Walls can guard me, or what Shades can hide?
They pierce my Thickets, thro' my Grot they glide,[11]

Though intrusions and diversions make up the poem's main theme, Pope's speaker remains safely enclosed. He can tell "good John" the story of distractions breaking in (a cadre of paparazzi who burst through walls, thickets, and Grots) because he has now "shut the door."[12] Moreover, the verse's intrinsic limits on meter and rhyme—five iambs, rhyming couplets—provide a structure that limits and organizes the intrusions he describes. Even as its speaker portrays a seemingly endless barrage of diversions, the poem *itself* maintains a strict, clear organization. Pope thus keeps disorder from "coming into" his verse, or allowing distractions to scatter either his mind or his crisp poetic style. J. Paul Hunter rightly describes Pope as "the craftsman who brought the couplet . . . to its most finished state of formal perfection."[13] Here, his skillful iambic pentameter couplets provide a crucial boundary, or framework, for managing distraction, creating a poetic architecture for attention.

This tradition of casting poetry as a space of enclosure (a shut door) amidst a world of diversions has a long history.[14] According to William Congreve's "Upon a Lady's Singing" (1692) the poet needs absolute concentration to write:

> Let all be husht, each softest Motion cease,
> Be ev'ry loud tumultuous Thought at Peace,
> [. . .]
> And thou most fickle, most uneasy Part,
> Thou restless Wanderer, my Heart,
> Be still; gently, ah gently, leave,
> Thou busie, idle thing, to heave.
> Stir not a Pulse, and let my *Blood,*
> That turbulent, unruly Flood,
> Be softly staid:
> Let me be all, but my attention, dead.[15]

In Congreve's ode, this stillness extends beyond the exclusion of visual and auditory distractions (the hacks that beat on Pope's door) to include internal states of mind. At the end, all but "attention" must be still and dead. The speaker, as Margaret Koehler notes, "methodically reduces himself to pure awareness" and uses the "ode to focus."[16]

In *Epistle to Arbuthnot,* Pope casts himself as a man for whom such quiet of mind—even amidst interruptions—comes naturally. This trait emerges with particular strength when set against the quick-scribbling poet who refuses to give his verse sustained attention and produces drivel: the result of a versifier who "Rhymes e're he wakes, and prints before *Term* ends."[17] Pope's speaker, by contrast, is cast as a man with an inborn gift for organized attention and well-crafted verse structures, particularly when they come in the form of poetic couplets, rhyme, and metrical feet: "Yet as a Child, nor yet a Fool to Fame, / I lisp'd in Numbers, for the Numbers came."[18] The resulting poetic structure, or cave—created by "good John," the shut door, and the architectures of focus in his carefully crafted verse—now extend to the reader. The poetic stanza, carefully framed and bound by rules of line, meter, and rhyme, helps to negotiate, and protect, our concentration amidst the diversions of London.

The second major strategy for imagining poetry as "beyond" distraction— via an imagined elevation above it—is at its height, paradoxically, in John Gay's *Trivia: or The art of walking the Streets of London* (1716). This mock-georgic poem describes the cacophony of urban life from the perspective of a pedestrian on foot. Gay's walker wakes to a London morning full of noise: "Now Industry awakes her busy Sons, / Full charg'd with News the breathless Hawker runs: / Shops open, Coaches roll, Carts shake the Ground, / And all the Streets with passing Cries resound."[19] Rather than 'shutting the door' to this hubbub, Gay casts poetry as a genre uniquely able to cordon off and manage it by producing a heightened poetic perspective that guides readers *through* the noisy throng. His poem, like Pope's, describes London's distractions in rich detail. Simultaneously, however, his speaker seeks to neutralize them, directing the vigilant walker on how to safely navigate their urban maze with due attention.

Gay's poem opens in a mode of instruction, offering the elevated perspective of an experienced urban walker to naïve pedestrians. Viewing the city as if from on high, he first presents its various distractions from a safe distance:

> Through Winter Streets to steer your Course aright,
> How to walk clean by Day, and safe by Night,
> How jostling Crouds, with Prudence, to decline,
> When to assert the Wall, and when resign.[20]

Here, we enter, not *with* or amidst the "jostling Crouds" but from a vantage point that rises above it to explain the city's patterns, ebbs, and flows. From this vantage point, Gay can see 'above' the individual to carefully categorize an otherwise chaotic throng into groups according to trade—barbers, bakers, perfumers, chimney sweepers, butchers, dustmen. This move translates an otherwise unparsable bundle of urban walkers—Bramble's gaggle of people "everywhere, rambling, riding, rolling rushing, jostling, mixing . . . and crashing,"—and separates out the "different departments of life" to be viewed "with cautious eye." Adopting this virtually heightened cognitive perspective, readers can thus navigate the distractions presented and "steer [their] Course aright."[21]

This mild elevation alternates with a more pedestrian 'on-the-ground' perspective that immerses us in the grime of the city street, a choice that has led some critics to call the mock-georgic poem a "muddled profusion;" both Gay's verses and London's streets are "are crammed with . . . a jumble of objects."[22] Yet *Trivia* uses this perspective from the street to evoke the distractions crowding in on a London walker, and expose the reader to its cognitive oversaturation. Only thus can they avoid the naiveté of the London newcomer, who "Bewilder'd, trudges on from Place to Place;" and "dwells on ev'ry Sign with stupid Gaze."[23] Like the newcomer, readers are to follow Gay's instructions, letting his perspective lead their "ventrous Footsteps" and guide them through the "the narrow Alley's doubtful Maze."[24]

Figure 9.1. An engraving of London's urban streets, from the second edition of Gay's *Trivia*, that mirrors the poem's briefly 'lifted' perspective of the city roads and walkers offered in this particular section. London, in John Gay's *Trivia: or the art of walking the streets of London* (Printed for Bernard Lintot, 1716), 69. Reproduced by permission of the British Library Board.

Trivia's second edition opens with an engraving that captures this slightly elevated point-of-view, as well as the detailed (yet detached) view it presents of urban London's "winding" ways:[25]

The artist renders the poet's view as "transported" to a spot *just* high enough to give us a perspective of the labyrinth of streets and people below. This visualization evokes a key moment later in the poem, when Gay's speaker seems to take wing. Lifted by the Muse, he glides along London's "perplexing Lanes":[26]

> I sing: Thou, *Trivia*, Goddess, aid my Song,
> Thro' spacious Streets conduct thy Bard along;
> By thee transported, I securely stray
> Where winding Alleys lead the doubtful Way,[27]

In addition to offering readers a heightened (and thus protected) view, Gay's *Trivia* uses poetic structure as a way to map the various divagations and populations London contained. As Penelope Corfield notes in her history of London streets, "At any time of day or night, some people were liable to be found in the street," with certain "thoroughfares" becoming "arteries of public communication in an expanding urban network."[28] Yet, as Claire Brant notes, "Gay's elegant couplets contain and structure the disorder: chaos is organized into energy."[29] Rhyme and meter, here, "smooth" the "broken Ways;" this stable poetic structure allows readers to "grid" the city's distractions, and, like the speaker, to "securely stray."[30]

III.

Before we turn to our final set of strategies for linking verse and focus—writers invoking the Muse to seize readers' concentration—however, we need more context; these poems draw on a series of crucial historical arguments about rhythm and attention. Over the course of the seventeenth and eighteenth century, claims about poetry's ability to capture focus grew so pronounced that one Enlightenment clergyman, John Byrom, actually argued that they should translate the Bible into rhyming couplets to get attention from the pulpit. He suggested (in a poem of course) that, for such a "Flock," translations "in *Verse* the Gospel [could] unlock:" and "flowing Numbers might th' Attention gain, / So long forbidden to his preaching Strain."[31] The idea that poetry's rhythms could well-organize concentration stretches back to the Renaissance.[32] In *De Anima et Vita* (1538), Juan Luis Vives claims poetry structured information in ways that improved attention and memory: "The stronger the associative bonds between successive elements of to-be-learned items," Vives writes, "the better the learning of them, thus verse is easier to learn than haphazard prose."[33]

Hugh Blair distills this argument about focus for eighteenth-century rhetoric in his *Lectures on Rhetoric and Belles Lettres* (1782). Concise writing produces better habits of concentration by isolating a single object for attention: "Were any object . . . to be presented to me, of whose structure I wanted to form a distinct notion," he writes, "I would desire all its trappings to be taken off [and] require it to be brought before me by itself, and to stand alone, that there might be nothing to distract my attention."[34] Short sentences pointed the mind toward a clear goal. Attention, for Blair, required strict economy and a careful organization of language. The mind thrived on brevity, which created a single line of focus.[35] So deeply did Blair believe in the rhetorical benefits of well-narrowed attention that he urged writers to eliminate all synonyms:

> Feeble writers employ a multitude of words to make themselves understood, as they think, more distinctly; and they only confound the reader . . . When an author tells me of his hero's *courage* in the day of battle, the expression is precise, and I understand it fully. But if, from a desire of multiplying words, he . . . praise[s] his *courage* and *fortitude;* at the moment he joins these words together, my idea begins to waver.[36]

According to Blair, synonyms ask the "human mind" to do an impossible cognitive task: "view . . . more than one object at a time" (i.e. *courage* and *fortitude*) without confusion. Authors prone to a "superfluity of words" make the reader's mind bounce among these options rather than focus in on one. Precise language could fix a reader's fluctuating mind.

Unsurprisingly, this idea was a mainstay for arguments about eighteenth-century poetry's claim on focus.[37] As J. Paul Hunter notes in "Couplets and Conversation," the couplet "won its dominance in the age because it was considered the single most appropriate poetic mode for . . . [developing] habits and brevity and conciseness—the art of focusing quickly on the crucial issues and terms."[38] Poet and rhetorician Christopher Pitt suggests that poetry's metrical limits helped both writers *and* readers resist the digressive multiplicity and excess of prose. In the latter case:

> Where chance presides, all *objects* wildly join'd,
> Crowd on the reader, and distract his mind;
> From *theme* to *theme* unwilling is he tost,
> And in the dark variety is lost.[39]

Poetry's bounded forms, by contrast, structured both attention and mind. Meter and rhyme keep a writer's thoughts from wandering, or sprawling, an argument for order Pitt models in his own well-ordered lines and rhyming couplets. Such constraints, for Pitt, let verse harness the mind to a single object of concentration, and thus to reason and order. Poetry maintains a "fixt design" on "just one scope," letting "sov'reign reason dictate from her throne."[40]

Such ideas about the benefits of single-minded focus in fact tapped a heated debate in Enlightenment attention theory: do we focus on just one thing at a time (*unifocal*), or on many at once (*multifocal*)? Traditionally, attention had been imagined as a single, unifocal line of sight, which was conceptualized as a thin, taut beam stretching between eye and object. Writers using this single-object model of focus, such as Pitt and Blair, cast attention as inherently exclusive. "There is nothing of more Use to the Mind," writes the unifocal John Clarke in *An Essay on Study* (1737), "than to be able to fix its *Attention* steddily upon [an] Object;" we must "[keep] out entirely . . . all foreign Ideas."[41] To concentrate, supposedly, the mind needed to stretch toward, or maintain a single line of attention upon, a single thing and to exclude all else.[42] One thus avoided distraction, a dangerous splitting, or multiplication, of thought that could lead into madness. Yet the Enlightenment also saw the rise of a competing multifocal paradigm of attention. Writers and philosophers in this group proposed that attention itself could be multiple; we think, as Gottfried Wilhelm Leibniz put it, of "many things all at once."[43] Philosophers who adopted this stance, such as Leibniz, David Hume, and Étienne de Condillac, described attention less as a mental *act* of stretching the mind toward a single object than as an ongoing—almost musical—cognitive *process* of filtering and prioritizing multiple stimuli. In the process, they also moved away from the more linear metaphors of the traditional model of concentration to adopt a rhythmic conception of focus. Whereas the unifocal view of attention was spatial, or linear, this modern multifocal paradigm imagined attention as an ongoing process of synchronizing and harmonizing many points of concentration in time, the sign of a dynamic mind in constant motion.

These debates went beyond shaping eighteenth-century arguments about poetry and focus. As we will see, the Enlightenment split between linear and rhythmic concepts of attention continue to this day. Their distinctive metaphors and contrasting arguments over multiplicity remain strikingly pertinent, shaping contemporary discussions of focus in modern neuroscience. The Enlightenment's unifocal model of attention and its linear metaphors has evolved into what cognitive scientists today describe as the "spotlight" theory of focus. This largely visual model defines attention as a selective act of concentrating on a single set of stimuli, ignoring others.[44] The Enlightenment's multifocal paradigm, with its more temporal metaphors, has become incorporated within a second movement in cognitive studies of focus, now known as *Dynamic Attending Theory* (DAT). Moving away from theories of an attentional spotlight, this contemporary model takes up a rhythmic model of concentration, exploring "how temporal structure guides attention on a moment-to-moment basis."[45] This modern theoretical divide reflects what leading neuroscientist Michael Posner calls the "long-standing controversy of whether the spotlight of spatial attention has a unitary 'beam' or [whether it can] be divided between spatially separated locations."[46] Yet Posner is thinking back only to the early twentieth century. And if modern cognitive science is replaying the very arguments, metaphors, and debates of Enlightenment debates about attention, rhythm, and poetry, eighteenth-century verse may play a larger role in shaping contemporary theories of mind than we ever would have expected, with influences on design that stretch into neuroscientific experiments themselves.

As Hunter later remarks in his article on Augustan couplets, "eighteenth-century poems . . . call a certain positive attention to formal features—conscious patterns and often ostentatious repetitions of visual or aural devices. Rhyme is a staple of eighteenth-century verse, linking particular words and syntactic arrangements so as to call special attention to word and phrase connections."[47] This eighteenth-century idea about poetry's ability to use metrical rhythms and rhyming couplets to guide focus has seen a sudden revival in modern neuroscience. The last ten years has seen a number of contemporary experiments exploring the influence of regular rhythms on attention—or as neuroscientists Schwartze and Kotz put it, how "internal attending rhythms synchronize with external event structure."[48] These studies examine the moments when our internal rhythms of thought, or focus, become aligned with the external rhythms or "beats," around us—be they that of a train horn, a metronome, a piece of music, or a rhyming couplet. Schwartze and Kotz, for example, used electro-encephelography, or EEG (a brain-imaging technology uniquely sensitive to temporal changes in neural activity) to show that providing people with regular rhythms, or beats, in time helped to structure concentration, making response times faster and memory recall more accurate. Testing how our brains process things with regular 'beats' in the background, they suggested that these stable rhythms prompt us to "predict . . . the temporal locus of future information" and prime us to move our attention there next.[49] If true, eighteenth-century claims about poetry and focus are truly prescient. Based on these studies, we may be more likely to notice words that fall on the beats established by regular poetic rhythms and rhymes.

When rhythm and rhyme interweave in iambic pentameter couplets, smaller stresses fall on the iamb, with the highest stress at the end of a line. Eighteenth-century poets experimented with, and theorized, this interplay between rhythm and focus. In arguing that poetry is superior to prose, for example, Christopher Pitt models his claims about rhythm in the very verse-structures he creates. His iambic pentameter rhythms mark key words for attention. As he describes the dangers inherent in disorderly prose, related words such as "chance," "crowd," "objects," "wild" and "join'd" are emphasized by the iamb, with the distraction such narrative causes readers reinforced by the end-stopped rhymes "tost" and "lost."[50] Here, rhythm and rhyme become tools for what Peter Stockwell calls "foregrounding," techniques that make "certain aspects of literary texts . . . more important or salient than others."[51] With this in mind, we can now turn to our final set of examples, poems that openly invoke the Muse to claim readers' focus. As we will see, eighteenth-century poets begin to use rhythm and rhyme most obviously as tools for foregrounding when they are talking *about* attentive readers. In cuing audience concentration (or describing it as already caught), these verses often amplify their use of rhyme and meter to drive home the idea that their poem has audiences completely engaged. Such choices mark the height of the rhetorical alliance between poetics, unifocal theories of attention, and eighteenth-century verse.

IV.

In this final case, poets move beyond "shutting the door" to distraction, as in Pope, or imagining themselves elevated above it, as in Gay. These verses reach still higher in their claims, calling on the Muse, or a modernized deity of love, to seize attention. Mark Akenside's *The Pleasures of Imagination* (1744), for instance, cues the attention of young, nature-loving readers: "O! attend, / Whoe'er thou art, whom these delights can touch, / Whose candid bosom the refining love / Of nature warms, O! listen to my song."[52] In John Thelwall's *The Peripatetic* (1793), the essayist suddenly breaks into poetry to sing Love's praises, declaring this modern muse will bless his verse with focused readers:

> Enchanting maid! whose voice and air
> Alike the attentive soul ensnare,
> And, with communal charm, supply
> The perfect types of harmony![53]

As he importunes his Muse for a spell of focus, Thelwall also models the notion that "harmony"—or the well-tuned patterns of a poem's rhythmic sound, particularly rhymes—are what will capture the "attentive soul." Duly enchanted by the "maid," his verse is to fully captivate us, an effect he drives home with hammer-like rhymes. (The Muse's "air," supposedly, is what "ensnare[s]" us; his charmed verse "suppl[ies]" him with our full concentration through its "harmony.")

Erasmus Darwin's *The Temple of Nature* (1803) makes a similar move as it translates scientific ideas from evolution to the creation of matter into rhyming couplets. Mid-poem, Darwin calls on the Muse (again, rendered as Love) to support a vision of rapt readerly engagement as a form of poetic binding. Drawing on his work's broader sexual metaphors for describing chemical bonds, he takes a principle used to explain how atoms attract to form molecules and how liquid matter connects and extends it to the relationship between his verse and readers' focus:

Press drop to drop, to atom atom bind,
Link sex to sex, or rivet mind to mind;
Attend my song!—With rosy lips rehearse,
And with your polish'd arrows write my verse!—
So shall my lines soft-rolling eyes engage,
And snow-white fingers turn the volant page;[54]

The Muse, fully translated from a deity *inspiring* epic song into a modern tool of focus, now she now "attend[s]" to his poem, "rehearsing," or rewriting, his lines in the form of a classical lay. Her undivided focus gives his poem the polish needed to "engage" female readers, whose fingers fly as they turn his pages. The poem's rhythmic regularity and couplet form (bind/mind, rehearse/verse; engage/page) again both foreground and model the focused attention he seeks to create. These examples, with their couplets imagining readers singularly "bound," "riveted" and "ensnared," show poetry taking Blair's idea of an object that "stand[s] alone" as the sole object of readers' focus, with "nothing to distract [the] attention," to a unifocal extreme.[55]

Yet even as poets made these claims about undivided—or "riveted"—attention to their verse, they used profoundly multifocal methods to sustain it. The very act of reading a couplet (bind/mind, engage/page) requires us to hold multiple words and sounds in mind at once. Reuven Tsur, a researcher in cognitive poetics, suggests that rhyme requires us to multi-thread, or tier, sonic information, creating resonant spaces within the memory where two words can occur "simultaneously."[56] With this, we can return to our previous examples to complicate the eighteenth-century portrayal of poetry as supporting a mode of unifocal attention. Just in claiming poetic *rhythm* as a tool of focus, poets invoked an eighteenth-century metaphor being used to support a multifocal view, in which the mind synchronizes multiple ideas in time. Poets may have used theories of single-minded concentration rhetorically to argue the genre had a unique claim on readers' attention in a competitive economy. In practice, however, poets skillfully layered and varied their rhythms in verse in order to challenge audience attention. To succeed, a good poem needed to provide unexpected novelty, sustain concentration *amidst* distraction, and interlace minute changes alongside regular rhythms. While modern studies of rhythm suggest that regular meters *do* increase our focus for words that fall on the beat, another recent set of experiments complicates this, adding another layer. Correa and Nobre's research, for example, suggests that regular patterns also strengthen our ability to process deviations *from* those rhythms, increasing our awareness of details that otherwise might go undetected.[57] Regular patterns set us up to notice change—or, pay more attention to subtle alterations in a poetic line. A stable rhythm, in other words, provides a backbeat that helps us better appreciate the complex micro-rhythms being created atop it. Eighteenth-century poets recognized that such variations on (or deviations from) a theme were critical to sustaining attention, particularly in rhyming verse. A poem that modeled perfect rhymes and strict iambic pentameter risked becoming yawningly mechanical, a sure recipe for boredom and attention lost.

As Pope notes in *An Essay on Criticism* (1711), excessive regularity produces too many "Equal Syllables" that "tire" the ear. Iambic pentameter verse, reduced to *just* its beats produces a different kind of distraction, a dullness so profound that it creates an inattention close to sleep.

> And ten low Words oft creep in one dull Line,
> While they ring round the same *unvary'd Chimes*,
> With sure *Returns* of still *expected Rhymes*.
> Where-e'er you find *the cooling Western Breeze*,
> In the next Line, it *whispers thro' the Trees*;
> If *Chrystal Streams with pleasing Murmurs creep*,
> The Reader's threaten'd (not in vain) with *Sleep*.[58]

According to Pope, the very rhymes and meter that Pitt, Byrom, and Darwin claim will seize readers' attention and use to describe their ensnared focus do exactly the opposite. Lines that "Chime" too well, or always fall on the beat, produce a "dull Line." The sure return of the "expected" (Chimes/Rhymes, Breeze/Trees) lead to an attention that "creep[s]" and readers who "Sleep."

Rather than rendering readers' focus singular, Pope uses poetic meter to provide a framework for multifocal complexity—a rhythmic structure that relies on variety and change. From the first line of *Epistle to Arbuthnot*, "Shut, shut the door, good *John!* fatigu'd, I said," Pope creates intricate micro-rhythms that move within and layer atop the regular beat. His iambic pentameter holds; simultaneously, his punctuation creates a second rhythm. The exclamation points, commas, and repeated words produce syntactic breaks ("Shut, / shut the door, / good *John!* / fatigu'd / I said,") with stresses that work *against* the iamb. These pauses move, moreover, as the verse goes on, interweaving and punctuating the iambic pentameter in unexpected places.

> Shut, / shut the door, / good *John!* / fatigu'd / I said,
> Tye up the knocker, / say I'm sick, / I'm dead,
> The Dog-star rages! / nay 'tis past a doubt,
> All *Bedlam*, / or *Parnassus*, / is let out:[59]

Placing these breaks at ever-changing points, Pope produces layered rhythms that rely on minute variations of multifocal attention, a rich interplay between expectation and diversion that actually catches and sustains us.

Gay's *Trivia* adds yet another multifocal element for eighteenth-century verse. As Koehler notes, the very blend of high and low in the mock-heroic asks readers to perform complex acts of multifocal cognition. They "must attend to the levels of mighty and trivial in turn," producing "dissonant juxtapositions" that "require parallel processing"; focus is "divided among stimuli . . . as lofty and lowly planes compete."[60] In both of these cases, rhythmic regularity does far more than guide, or "narrow," our focus to a single point in time; it draws our notice to multiple—sometime disjointed—moments that produce discordant, novel beats that stimulate our interest. In Darwin's accolade to poetic attention, these minute changes and variations on iambic pentameter are present; they simply reinforce his rhetorical message of focus. Its stable meter and end-stopped lines, as Correa and Noble's research suggests, call our attention to the mid-line breaks:

> Press drop to drop, / to atom atom bind,
> Link sex to sex, / or rivet mind to mind;
> Attend my song! /—With rosy lips rehearse,[61]

Following the regular beats and rhymes, we greet Darwin's caesuras with double-force. By pausing, unexpectedly, in the middle, he adds another layer to his metaphor of attention as coupling, already "bound" by rhyme. Even as we hold things like "bind" and "mind," the breaks mean we *also* must hold four extra sets of paired examples—1) "drop to drop"; 2) "atom [to] atom"; 3) "sex to sex;" and 4) "mind to mind"—before we reach Darwin's final cognitive declaration: "Attend my song!"

Singular attention may have been what dominated eighteenth-century *talk* about poetry, but the poems model (and demand) complex, multi-layered matching of rhythm and thought. Eighteenth-century verse invites a dynamic mode of engagement that is far more complex than merely protecting the readers' mind from distractions, or focusing in on a single line of verse. This very dissonance between poetic theory and practice in the Enlightenment also marks it as a crucial period in the history of attention, laying out critical terms of debate—as well as ongoing tensions—that have continued to shape modern cognitive studies of attention and rhythm. They have emerged, refigured, in the modern rivalry between a more linear "spotlight model" (unifocal) and the more temporal paradigm provided by "dynamic attention theory" (multifocal) in experimental neuroscience. My point is not to suggest that eighteenth-century poets simply "intuited" a modern cognitive truth regarding rhythm's influence on focus. More importantly, it is to illuminate how crucial a historical role the Enlightenment—particularly Enlightenment verse—played in the development of contemporary ideas about concentration. Recognizing this connection means not only bringing cognitive science to literature, but literature, and its history, to cognitive science. Bringing poetry into central focus as we trace this history, moreover, enhances the story we would otherwise tell about attention in the eighteenth-century based on the novel alone. Rather than merely retelling a familiar story of absorption, in which readers are inevitably "lost in a good book," we can begin to outline a far more complicated picture of attention itself—one divided into intricate styles and degrees of concentration, as well as the distinctive rhythms of focus each genre and work creates.

Notes

Sincere thanks go to Erin Beard, Katie Grimes, and Craig Pearson in the *Digital Humanities and Literary Cognition* lab for their assistance with this essay, as well as to the ACLS-Mellon foundation, the Honors College, and the College of Arts and Letters at Michigan State University for their support.

1. In *The Rise of the Novel*, Ian Watt argues that the circulation of fiction in print allowed for a new kind of narrative immersion: "[M]echanically produced and therefore identical letters set with absolute uniformity on the page," he writes, "can be read much more automatically; ceasing to be conscious of the printed page before our eyes we surrender ourselves entirely to the world of illusion which the printed novel describes." Scholarship from Michael Fried's *Absorption and Theatricality* to

¯Adela Pinch's "Lost in a Good Book" translates this into a refrain, with Fried calling absorption "a master trope" of the Enlightenment. See Ian Watt, *The Rise of the Novel: Studies in Defoe, Richardson, and Fielding* [1957], 2nd ed. (Berkeley: University of California Press, 2001), 198; Michael Fried, *Absorption and Theatricality: Painting and Beholder in the Age of Diderot* (Chicago: University of Chicago Press, 1980), 7; and Adela Pinch, "Lost in a Book: Jane Austen's 'Persuasion,'" *Studies in Romanticism* 32, no. 1 (1993): 97–117.

2. Elizabeth Fry, *Journal*, 25 April 1799, from the British Library, p. ff. 57.

3. Alexander Pope, *The Dunciad Variorum*, in *The Twickenham Edition of the Poems of Alexander Pope*, ed. John Butt, vol. 5, *The Dunciad*, ed. James Sutherland, 3rd ed. (London: Methuen & Co., 1963), page 49.

4. Samuel Johnson, *The Rambler*, vol. 3, in *The Yale Edition of the Works of Samuel Johnson*, ed. W. J. Bate and Albrecht B. Strauss (New Haven, CT: Yale University Press, 1969): 16.

5. Eliza Haywood, *Selections from The Female Spectator*, ed. Patricia Meyer Spacks (New York: Oxford University Press, 1999), 8.

6. Joseph Addison, "Account of the Greatest English Poets," *Miscellany Poems the Fourth Part* (1694), 321–23; William Cowper, "Retirement" and "Conversation," in *Poems by William Cowper* (London, 1782).

7. Emily Cockayne, *Hubbub: Filth, Noise, and Stench in England, 1600–1770* (New Haven: Yale University Press, 2007), 1–17.

8. Tobias Smollett, *The Expedition of Humphry Clinker* (Edinburgh: Printed for W. Coke Bookseller, Leith, 1788), 97.

9. Ibid., 97.

10. Jonathan Swift, *A Tale of a Tub* (London: Printed for John Nutt, 1710), 1.

11. Alexander Pope, *An Epistle from Mr. Pope to Dr. Arbuthnot*, in *The Twickenham Edition of the Poems of Alexander Pope*, ed. John Butt, vol. 4, Imitations of Horace, ed. John Butt (London: Methuen & Co., 1939), lines 1–8.

12. It is no accident that the distractors which plague Pope take the form of Grub-street writers. The "Parson, much be-mus'd in Beer," the "maudlin Poetess," the scrawling madman, and the "ryming Peer" all beleaguer him with petitions, producing a lively atmosphere of incessant disruption (Ibid., lines 15–16).

13. J. Paul Hunter, "Couplets and Conversation," in John Sitter, ed., *The Cambridge Companion to Eighteenth Century Poetry* (Cambridge: Cambridge University Press, 2001), 13.

14. Congreve's idea of an ultimate silence—an absolutely clear space—for attention stretches back to the Stoics, who believed in the necessity of a simple environment, free of distractions, for writing—the writers surrounded by nothing but chair and table. As Epictetus put it in his *Discourses*, "You cannot be continually giving attention to both externals and your own governing principle" (Book IV. X 22–29). Epictetus, *The Discourses as Reported by Arrian, the Manual, and Fragments, Books III and IV*, trans. W.A Oldfather (Cambridge: Harvard University Press, 1928), 405.

15. William Congreve, *Poems upon several occasions. By Mr. William Congreve* (Glasgow, MDCCLII [1752]), lines 1–2, 5–12.

16. Margaret Koehler, "Odes of Absorption" *Studies in English Literature, 1500–1800* 47, no. 3 (Summer 2007): 666.

17. Pope, *Epistle to Arbuthnot*, 43.

18. Ibid., 127–128. The term distraction was tightly linked to madness. Distraction, from the Latin *dis-trahere* (to pull, or drag apart) was a cognitive state in which the mind was pulled in too many directions at once, potentially fragmenting into insanity.

19. John Gay, *Trivia: or, the Art of Walking the Streets of London,* 2nd ed, (London: Bernard Lintot, 1716), pt. 2, lines 21–24.

20. Ibid., 1: 1–4.

21. Ibid., 2:29, 1.

22. Margaret Koehler, "The Filter of Attention and Indissoluble Attractors in Eighteenth-Century Mock-Heroic Poetry," *Modern Philology*, 108, no. 1 (August 2010): 79.

23. Gay, *Trivia*, 2:78–9.

24. Ibid., 2:88, 80.

25. Ibid., 1:8.

26. Ibid., 1:10.

27. Ibid., 1:5–8.

28. Penelope Corfield, "Walking the City Streets: The Urban Odyssey in Eighteenth-Century England," *Journal of Urban History* 16 (1990): 132–3.

29. Clare Brant, "Seduced by the City: Gay's *Trivia* and Hogarth," *Literary London: Interdisciplinary studies in the representation of London*, 6, no. 1 (March 2008): 7.

30. Gay, *Trivia*, 1:11, 7.

31. John Byrom, "A Letter to a Lady, Occasioned by her Desiring the Author to Revise and Polish the Poems of Bishop Ken," in *The Poems of John Byrom*, ed. Adolphous William Ward, vol. 2, *Sacred Poems* (Manchester: Printed for the Chetham Society, 1895), pt. 1, pages 124–125; lines 96–100, italics added.

32. This idea goes back as far as Lucretius, who claims verse makes hard philosophy more palatable: "To expound our doctrine unto thee in song / Soft-speaking and Pierian, and, as 'twere, / To touch it with sweet honey of the Muse—/ If by such method haply I might hold / The mind of thee upon these lines of ours." In Titus Lucretius Carus, *On the Nature of Things (De Rerum Natura)*, trans. William Ellery Leonard (Mineola, New York: Dover Publications, 2004), 28; lines 943–950.

33. Juan Luis Vives, *On Memory and Recall* (1538), trans. D.J. Murray & Helen E. Ross, *Canadian Psychology* 23, no. 1 (1982): 25.

34. Hugh Blair, *Lectures on Rhetoric and Belles Lettres* (London: W.B. Gilley, 1819).

35. The one "indispensible quality" of a good sentence, according to Blair's *Lectures,* was "Unity." It forwarded "one proposition," and "intimately knit" its clauses "so as to make the impression upon the mind of one object, not of many." Ibid., 99–100.

36. Ibid., 221.

37. Blair was so committed to this idea about brevity that he voiced concerns about poetry, believing digressive verse might rely on "superfluous words . . . to fill up the[ir] rhyme." Here, he echoes Aristotle's concerns about rhyme and meter being a distraction to content: "On account of the great importance of simplicity and conciseness," writes Blair, "I conceive rhyme in English verse, to be, if not inconsistent with the Sublime, at least very unfavorable . . . The constrained elegance of this type of verse, and studied smoothness of the sounds, answering regularly to each other at the end of the line . . . weaken the native force . . . [and] the superfluous words which the poet is often obliged to introduce, in order to fill up the rhyme, tend farther to enfeeble it." Ibid., 77.

38. Hunter, "Couplets and Conversation," 22.

39. Christopher Pitt, *Vida's Art of Poetry, Translated into English Verse, By the Reverend Mr. Christoph. Pitt* (London: Printed by Sam Palmer, 1725), 33.

40. Ibid., 50.

41. John Clarke, *An Essay Upon Study* (London: Printed by A. Bettesworth, 1731), 97.

42. René Descartes, in *Rules for the Direction of Mind*, suggested single-minded focus was key to reaching philosophical truth: "Craftsmen who . . . are used to fixing their eyes on a single point, acquire . . . the ability to make perfect distinctions between things. The same is true of those who never let their thinking be distracted. [Those who] always devote their whole attention become perspicacious." René Descartes, *Meditations on First Philosophy*, trans. John Cottingham (Cambridge: Cambridge University Press, 1988), 43.

43. See Gottfried Leibniz, *New Essays on Human Understanding*, ed. Peter Remnant and Jonathan Bennett (Cambridge: Cambridge University Press, 1996), 113.

44. For more on the "spotlight theory" of attention and its history, see Harold Pashler, *The Psychology of Attention* (Cambridge: Massachusetts Institute of Technology Press, 1999); Anthony Ward, *Attention: A Neuropsychological Approach* (New York: Psychology Press, 2004); and J. Driver "A selective review of selective attention research from the past century," *British Journal of Psychology*, 92 (2001): 53–57.

45. Schwartze, et al., "Temporal regularity effects on pre-attentive and attentive processing of deviance," *Biological Psychology* 87 (2011): 147.

46. Michael Posner, *Cognitive Neuroscience of Attention*. (New York: Guilford Press, 2004), 201.

47. Hunter, "Couplets and Conversation," 20–21.

48. Schwartze, "Temporal regularity effects," 147.

49. According to Correa and Nobre, "visual targets were detected most rapidly when their onset coincided with moments previously marked by the rhythms." A. Correa and A. C. Nobre, "Neural Modulation by Regularity and Passage of Time," *Journal of Neurophysiology* 100.3 (2008): 1654. Another study in their lab tested response times to regular rhythmic patterns, showing that response time improved (i.e., cognitive processing was easier) when the next 'beat' matched their expectations.

50. Pitt, *Vida's Art of Poetry*, 33.

51. Peter Stockwell, *Cognitive Poetics: An Introduction* (London & New York: Routledge, 2002), 14.

52. Mark Akenside, "The Pleasures of the Imagination," in *The Poetical Works of Mark Akinside* (New York: Printed for C. Wells, 1838), 95; pt 1, lines 173–175.

53. John Thelwall, *The Peripatetic,* ed. Judith Thompson (Detroit, Wayne State University Press, 2001), 198.

54. Erasmus Darwin, *The Temple of Nature: Or, the Origin of Society. A Poem* (repr., Baltimore: John Butler, Bonsal & Niles, 1804), 10; lines 25–30.

55. Blair, *Lectures*, 222.

56. Reuven Tsur, "Rhyme and Cognitive Poetics" *Poetics Today* 17 (1996): 55–87.

57. Correa and Nobre, "Neural Modulation."

58. Alexander Pope, *An Essay on Criticism,* in *The Twickenham Edition of the Poems of Alexander Pope,*ed. John Butt, vol. 1, *Pastoral Poetry and An Essay on Criticism*, ed. E. Audra and Aubrey Williams (London: Methuen & Co., 1961), lines 347–53.

59. Pope, *Epistle to Arbuthnot*, 1–4, emphasis added.

60. Koehler, "The Filter of Attention," 66, 72.

61. Erasmus Darwin, *The Temple of Nature; Or, the Origin of Society: A Poem* (1803; reprint, Baltimore: John Butler, Bonsal & Niles, 1804), 10; lines 25–28.

I AM DEEPLY HONORED TO BE ASKED *to supply a kind of "afterword" to this collection of essays. It is a privilege to be an early reader of such good works on a relatively untouched topic—the relation of eighteenth-century poetry to the eighteenth-century novel. This collection will undoubtedly figure on a number of reading lists, and both graduate and undergraduate students will be advised to turn to it. The contributions are varied, and cover a lot of ground—including literal ground made figurative (Hagley Park in Thomson's* Seasons*). We move through many spaces from the crowded city street to the shimmering attractive uncertain sylph-filled space so well treated by Sophie Gee and David Fairer. Joshua Swidzinski offers a good specific example of relating a poem and a novel to each other in discussion of Young's* Night Thoughts *and Richardson's* Clarissa. *Heather Keenleyside in discussing "Personification" offers an excellent new vision of the importance of this figure in* Pamela, *and the importance to narrative of this figure "with its own sort of realism" (125). Poetry in the novel features as well as poetry and the novel, in reference to Clarissa's "Meditations" and a full discussion of Amelia Opie's incorporation of verses into her stories. These essays do justice to something often overlooked, the omnipresence of forms of poetry in eighteenth-century life, found variously in ballad, graffito, billet-doux—or even the versified thank-you note. Male students in schools and colleges had to write Latin verses. Quotations from poems, ancient and modern, from poetic drama and hymns as well as from Scripture are woven into the fabric of common speech as well as of written works. Shelley King's interesting account of Amelia Opie's circle and their production of poems for each other can be paralleled by scenes in letters and journals, including those displaying Mrs. Thrale, Frances Burney and Johnson making up impromptu verses. Poetry was a natural activity, not formal stuff fit only for great geniuses. Wolfram Schmidgen* points out "*how many threshers, milkmaids, cobblers, and servants wrote poetry*" *(89). That knowledge must be translated to our understanding of the "great" poets, who were engaged in an activity known to many of their readers on a less formal level.*

This collection will trigger further pursuit of the topic, allowing the inclusion of more novelists—and more poets. I miss Gray—and Burns. What about hymn writers? Where's Cowper? More women poets might have been expected among those present, even if Wolfram Schmidgen discounts the discovery of women poets by announcing that we don't do traditional literary history any more. Apparently there is no need to know about individual writers, or their place in the lines of influence—though Schmidgen neglected to inform Ovid, Spenser, Milton, Gray et al. that such is the case. I find this amusing but cannot assent. Natalie Phillips' essay supplies an excellent commentary on rhythm and form, including the findings of neuroscientists of the twenty-first century regarding the attention evoked by background rhythm and variations. Her research work is noted in my own contribution. It would be possible in the future to pursue treatment of rhythm and rhyme even further. I should like to see some discussion of hip-hop and eighteenth-century poetry—two poetic and performative modes popular in their own time which stress couplet rhyme, puns and wordplay. The story is that rhyme came into European literature (oral, then written) from Africa—so a strong African element may be already present in English poetry of the eighteenth century. Be that as it may, I dream lightly of an album or at least a video with a title like "Kanye West does Pope"—although rap always prefers the 4-beat line and doesn't use pentameter. Then, how about "Jay-Z does Swift"? Butler's Hudibras *is hip-hop already—at least the beginning is, as you will find if you read it aloud with appropriate emphases and syncopations.*

Time, Space, and the Poetic Mind of the Novel

A ballad singer happening to be in the street, the first thing she heard, on her waking, was these words sung in a sonorous voice, just under her window:

> Young Philander woo'd me long,
> > I was peevish, and forbad him;
> I would not hear his charming song,
> > But now I wish, I wish I had him.

Though this was a song at that time much in vogue, and miss Betsy had casually heard it an hundred times, yet in the humour she now was, it beat an alarm upon her heart.

—Eliza Haywood, *The History of Miss Betsy Thoughtless*[1]

Poetry, sacred and profane, high and low, lies in wait for characters in eighteenth-century fiction. Already entwined about the authorial mind, it purposely entwines itself about the characters' experiences—and about the reader's separate but dangerously merging experience of participation in those characters' adventures, inner as well as outer. In the underestimated *Betsy Thoughtless* (1751)—a novel which Kate Parker has dealt with so well in this volume—the snatch of a popular song from the street suddenly evokes—even forces—a strong reaction from Betsy. She had gone to bed fearing that her lover Trueworth did not love her and had never meant to propose marriage. Her mood is no less uncomfortable on waking, and reaction to this stimulus stirs more reaction to stimuli. Haywood is one of the first novelists to delineate unintentional but deep reaction to "popular culture." Poetry high and low, classical or "pop," snags us by suddenly offering us an emotion which thus becomes more definable—but the definition does not lead to rationality or comfort. This uncomfortable emotional hearing is introduced by Haywood's narrator as an example of the way life refuses to let us know it as random.

The snatch of song comes to Betsy from a distance, from outside while she is inside. It belongs to that distracting bustle of the streets that troubled eighteenth-century commentators, as Natalie Phillips points out. That world refuses to stay outside the retired mind. This snatch of the ballad-singer intrudes through a window, a medium of useless transparency or openness which yet reveals no face of the singer who is not only outside, but below. Distance is part of the effect; the vulgar poetic intrusion is both embodied and disembodied. In this collection, David Fairer has dealt brilliantly with the effects of distances, of spaces in between. I would, however take issue with him slightly, contesting the supposition that it requires post-Lockean modernity to ratify and render possible such serious and delightful play of not-quite-inner but not-quite-outer. I too value the luminous puzzling space which becomes open to authors such as Sterne, but I see it as having been available for a long while.

Sterne's *Tristram Shandy* (1759–67), I would add, never truly escapes from linearity. Pretending to escape and disdain the straight line that is good only for cabbages is the masquerade of Tristram, who possesses or is possessed by one serious, even straightforward, objective to be served in all the apparently lighthearted or uncommitted play. Tristram is deeply committed to hiding—from himself above all—the terrible truth of linearity as lineage. He is not Walter Shandy's son, not related to Walter or Toby. As inheritor of Shandy Hall, after Bobby's death, he is a cuckoo in the nest. Moreover, the tubercular consumption he has inherited from his biological father (Yorick) sentences him to death. There is nothing Tristram can do about his bend sinister or lethal straight line—he is as doomed as

Oedipus. In order to keep personality and life going, Tristram must avoid knowing what he knows. All his defenses are at work—parallel to the defenses that emanate from Uncle Toby's conversation. Traits of apparent incompetence and incapacities are alibis for his competence in keeping the truth hidden—if but barely. Tristram's brilliant poetic smoke-screen is so impressive we may neglect to notice that the versatile and ingenious mind is devoted to evading lethal truth. Tristram is a hero—a righteous hero, moreover—of un-enlightenment.

The space Tristram has to play in we have learned from Locke to call "consciousness." Because we acquired the term around 1690 we should not think there was no such thing before the late seventeenth century, or the eighteenth-century novel. What we have been calling "consciousness," as well as the later "unconscious" or "sub-conscious" level of the "psyche," attracts the attention of authors of all kinds over millennia. Consciousness (with its layers) becomes a pet province of the Novel, though mighty work had been done by poets like Sappho. Throughout its history and adventures the Novel has proved particularly agile at connecting sense experience with what we call "mind" or" mental activity, and exhibiting the differences and relations between the two.

One of my favorite passages in the ancient novel is the scene in Chariton's *Kallirhoe* in which the heroine comes out of a coma. Mistakenly judged dead (after being kicked in the stomach by her husband), the girl has been laid to rest with pomp and ceremony in the family tomb:

> . . . as if awakening from sleep, and as if they were sleeping side by side she began to call Khaireas. But when neither her husband nor any of the servants answered and all was solitary and dark, the girl began to shiver and tremble, incapable by process of reason to guess the truth. Slowly she touched the funeral crown and ribbons. Gold and silver jingled. There was a heavy smell of aromatic spices. Then she remembered the kick and the fall that followed, and realized that because of her voicelessness she was buried in the tomb. Then she shrieked as loudly as she could, crying "I'm alive!" and "Help!"[2]

She comes first to her senses: first, smell—the pungent scent of the spices—then touch and hearing as she sets off a delicate jangle. These sensations are not unpleasant in themselves; there is an appreciable short lapse of time as she connects with the sensations as phenomena. We participate as she assembles the memory and new information, and in accelerating activity of mind realizes what the spices and the offerings signify. To know this significance is to know estrangement—even revulsion—from the objects *because* they have meaning. The cultural significance of the delicate first sensations of things invades her as idea. Kallirhoe rapidly arrives at the full horror of what has happened to her. Translators of this scene may jump the gun in using the handy modern "consciousness." Chariton has no such term available. He shows us what consciousness *is*. Ironically, in this instance, the recovery of full consciousness brings neither pleasure nor power, but terror. Kallirhoe cries out for help—"*Zöö!*" ["I live, I am alive!"] This is the statement of her primary imagination, her knowledge of herself as a living being, both object and subject. Kallirhoe is saved by grave-robbers who sell her into slavery in Asia Minor. After her resurrection and rising from the tomb, Kallirhoe takes on another identity. A false identity is forced upon her, but her own presentation of herself to herself also alters. The once naïve and open girl is secretive, introspective, and suspicious. Ultra-private, she relates to others (starting with the bandits) chiefly through irony. Kallirhoe, in short, becomes almost entirely interior self. I resist the assertions that the interior self is known to the Novel only from the "Early Modern" period.

I recognize that not everybody is such an enthusiastic advocate and enjoyer of ancient novels as myself, but the excellences and achievements we note in the poetic eighteenth-century novel are always potentially there in the ancient form— "always already," as we have been taught to say. It is accepted "historical fact" that the long prose fiction work emerged as a serious generic candidate for attention— even adulation—as a sign of modernity (as Wolfram Schmidgen notes in his article here). But the Novel is older than the English-speakers have wanted it to be. And it has certainly always been poetic—and related to poetry. The importance of epic to the novel has been dilated upon. Dramatic and epic poetry, public forms in the "ancient" world, have proved very capable of presenting complex internal relationships, exhibiting unexpected and multiple nuances of connection between the self and the not-quite-self, animate or inanimate.

In Sophocles' drama of Oedipus, as imminent full knowledge impends over the fated hero, the Chorus sings the third *stasimon*, addressed first not to Oedipus or to Apollo but to Kithairon, the mountain on which the baby was exposed and on which he should have died:

> If I am a prophet . . . O Kithairon , you shall not fail to know that tomorrow's full moon exalts you as the compatriot of Oedipus and his breast-nurse and mother . . .[3]

Oedipus himself has just wished to be the child of the *event* (solving the Sphinx's riddle) that brought him good fortune. He chooses to be the child of Fortune or

Chance—*Tyche*—an insubstantial entity. The Chorus substitutes for airy abstract Chance the substantial entity of the mountain—his mother. The third *stasimon* plays with and affects our ideas of Oedipus' consciousness—including the King's own idea of his "interiority." An idea batted between the hero and the chorus shapes the hero who comes to yearn for his earthy mountain mama. Near the very end, the blinded Oedipus himself calls out to Kithairon:

> Oh, Kithairon, why did you make room for me? Why did you not take me at once and kill me
> So that I could never have revealed my begetting to mankind?[4]

In his last dialogue with the new ruler, Oedipus asks to be allowed to live in the mountains: "Where there is my own Kithairon, famous for me, which my mother and my father while living chose to be my tomb."[5] Oedipus becomes almost obsessed by his mountain. Baby bones quietly moldering, folding into the mountain—this image offers an imagined relief. Even while desiring such anonymity Oedipus characteristically cannot let go of his terrible specialness, his celebrity, but with typical possessiveness shares it with *his* mountain. He and the mountain are always becoming one but never achieving unity. The fostering mountain betrayed Oedipus like a bad mother. It did not quietly relieve him of the burden of worldly identity; it denied the nurturing, the freedom from anxiety that he somehow should have had.

Mount Kithairon becomes an important space within the drama. It does not function as a topographical spot in a realistic geography like other places referred to such as Corinth and Delphi. The mountain shimmers in and out of the wishing mind as the ideal site where Oedipus *could have been* relieved of trauma and offense. He flickeringly repeats one of his primary taboo offences, as desire fixes on the breast and flank of the mothering mountain, one of this drama's chimeras and ghostly presences. The *stasimon* has come back to haunt the King. He has enough strength left to yearn for the lost state, a blameless innocent just lying on the mountain—another identity for Oedipus who had too many identities.

A different (and later) example of imagination turning to a mountain—or hill—is found in Horace's 9th Ode of the First Book. Horace's poem begins with the striking winter scene:

> Vides, ut alta stet nive candidum
> Soracte, nec iam sustineant onus
> silvae laborantes geluque
> flumina constiterint acuto.[6]

[You see where tall Soracte stands,
taller in white snow,
nor can the laboring woods sustain the weight,
while streams stand still in ice sharply cold.]

We don't know in this first opening whom Horace addresses. Later, an addressee is officially present as his boy servant Thaliarchus, but the "tu" implicit in "vides" seems to refer to the reader, as if the reader (singular) were standing at the window or the door beside Horace looking at this phenomenon, Soracte and the woods in the amazing fall of snow. The poet or host then urges turning away from the cold: *dissolve frigus*—break up the cold by putting wood on the fire and pouring a big cup of Sabine wine. "Let the divine powers to do what they will," says the poet, "let the winds despoil what they can; calm will follow when the cypresses and ash trees will not be moved. . . . Flee from asking what tomorrow will bring; take what Fortune provides now." Turning to his boy, the poet-speaker advises him not to spurn the dance and sweetness of love, *donec virenti canities abest/morose*— "while slow and difficult white-haired age is absent from your green youth." Take advantage of the opportunity offered by the girl laughing in the corner and playing with the ring upon her hand.

Such a summary makes a straight line of Horace's not-straight-at-all poem. The reader and Horace alike seem, at the opening, to be looking out in awe at the somewhat terrifying transformed beauty of Soracte. Senses and mind are caught by this apparition and set of sensations. Cold is to be countered by warmth, by wine and food. New physiological sensations are substituted for—or summoned to displace—the sensations that pull imagination toward white Soracte. Whether the servant-boy Thaliarchus (really a slave) will have the power to live up to the instructions is unclear. The boy has no voice here. The voice is that of the mind of "Horace" who is unable to obliterate the impressions made by Soracte, the breaking woods, the ice. He calls upon the sensory impressions of fire and wine to counteract or erase the vision of the cold mountain, but these warm sensations or ideas cannot cancel the others. The cold, the white vision, is never broken up or dissolved. The impressions of wood and fire and warmth and flamelight and wine are also present, of course. These willed and welcome things also play about the speaker's body and mind, and become part of the space between him and the mountain, between him and the boy, between him and ourselves—and between him and himself.

The speaker's injunctions are directed to a younger self who rises upon the scene while the morose white-haired age imagined as absent is already entirely present. On a literal level, there seems to be nobody in the winter-bound house save the speaker we know as Quintus Horatius Flaccus and the servant Thaliarchus. The narrative of the poem does not demand us to believe that any laughing girl lurks here in Horace's house this winter day in the corner. The girl with the ring is so specific that she seems to arise from the speaker's memory, rather than existing as a physically present prospect for Thaliarchus. Soracte, wine, youth, age, and sexual memory are all present and flicker about the entire scene, in which the speaker is hospitable to himself, amorous for himself, regretful for himself. The scene never departs from the initial effect of what was seen from a distance: the challenging tall white Soracte. It is crowned with white just as Horace in the winter of his life now has white hair. Though the full comparison is never directly made within this ode, it is indicated in *canities*—hoariness, the state of possession of grey-white hair. This is a poem about aging, as well as about memories and sensations.

Like the best lyric poems of all eras it captures ways in which the mind works—or, as we tend to say in the early twenty-first century, in which the *brain* works. Horace's space is both full and empty. Sexual hope is for someone else. He looks outward at the view; he takes in the external prospect at the same time as engaging in retrospection, resignation, pleasure and sadness. But we cannot say one of these resolves the other, or that everything can be marshaled in an orderly path of progression. Movement from one thing or topic to another is ostensibly cheerful, but causes pain. Nothing is dissolved or abandoned, but comes flickering back. Simultaneity, flickering, zigzags—these are the patterns of the brain, of the mind and personality.

This poem has attracted many admirers, among them John Dryden, whose translation simplifies the poem rather more than one would expect, although as always Dryden is good at cold and slippery things. But in Dryden's version, or perhaps the translation by Thomas Mulso, Horace's winter ode could have been known to female readers, including Jane Austen.[7] I suspect some play with this well-known winter poem in *Emma* (1816), in the Christmas Eve party given by Mr. Weston. What is connected within one flickering consciousness in Horace seems to be dissipated amongst several characters in Austen's sequence. Mr. Woodhouse (valetudinarian, nearer dying than he wants to admit) is white-haired eld, "morose" in the Latin sense of slow, impeding, cause of delay and trouble. He has the aged man's nervous fear of cold and snow, and is secretly aware that winter can press things to breaking-point. Mr. John Knightley, a healthy grumbling extrovert, dwells with grim relish on the wildness of the scene and the prospect of coachman and horses "making their way through a storm of snow."[8] Mr. Weston has provided fires and food; delighting in his own hospitality, he wishes they could all be snowed in at his house. He fully delights in defying the weather and the season: "With well heap'd Logs dissolve the Cold, / And feed the genial Hearth with Fires," as Dryden has it. Or, more expansively, Thomas Mulso:

> Pile up the chearful-blazing Wood;
> See that the life-recruiting Board
> With hospitable Plenty's stor'd
> Of racy Wines, and generous Food.[9]

"We are sure of excellent fires," says Mr. Elton "and every thing in the greatest comfort."[10] Mr. and Mrs. Weston fulfill their life-recruiting role, and their good cheer is not lost on Mr. Elton—who could have known Horace's Latin poem. He would certainly seem to take to heart the injunction: "Produce the Wine that makes us bold, / And sprightly wit and Love inspires."[11] Emma justifiably suspects that the Reverend Mr. Elton "had been drinking too much of Mr. Weston's good wine." Yet he repudiates her suggestion that he is drunk when he forces his rhetorically-amorous proposal upon her within the dark confinement of the carriage (in *angulo* indeed, in a tight corner for Emma): "Mr. Elton had only drunk wine enough to elevate his spirits, not at all to confuse his intellects."[12] After Emma's angry refusal they are beyond merely social awkwardness: "their straightforward emotions left no room for the little zigzags of embarrassment."[13] The delightful phrase, "the zigzags of embarrassment"—though officially repudiated as expressive of what goes between the rejected Mr. Elton and the infuriated Emma—begins to gather together what throughout the party sequence has been hitherto largely parceled out amongst different actors. There have been zigzags, impulsive and instinctual moves. If Mr. John Knightley had not jumped instinctively but wrongly into the other carriage after his wife, Emma and Elton would not have been alone. Throughout this engaging novelistic scene of entertainment, liveliness and mistakes, the novelist does not let go of the fundamental loneliness of the individual—a loneliness captured by Horace who makes us aware of physiological body and consciousness in the flickering of memory, the zigzags of movement between love, awe, regret, desire and hopelessness—all largely incommunicable save by indirection.

Lyric poetry has taught all writers, not just other poets, much about the connections of physiological sensations to the awareness of space and time. Horace's poem starts out with an emphasis on space—the distance between the speaker and what he is seeing in the view. The distance collapses once we realize that the aged or aging speaker feels (if he does not need to spell out) the closeness between the white-heaped mountain and his white hair. Space becomes time, and both collapse, drawing together. The season of winter belongs to public time; today, with this Thaliarchus, this fire, and this wine belongs to ongoing experience. But memory and imagination crowd in among these times that masquerade as the present, creating a unique time neither past nor present, neither here nor there.

The era (or eras) referred to by historians by the disdainful and unsatisfactory term "Early Modern" adds new elements and possibilities to the effects that can be created by stories and characters emerging toward us in words. My current research draws me to transformation and mutation as expressed in the alchemical works of Paracelsus and the spiritual-psychological adaptation of Paracelsian ideas by Jakob Boehme. (Paracelsus, by the way, is the grandfather of all "sylphs" in "Early Modern" or "Modern" Western literature.) The alchemical pattern of loss of self and reprocessing, recombination and metamorphosis, finds its way into medicine, cosmology, and psychology, creating a matrix for important ideas regarding evolution. Any one phase of a being, including a human being's personality, may be—most likely is—unstable and transitory. That is an interesting contrast to the ideal of a permanent soul-state or stable personality definitely subject to forensic scrutiny at the Last Day—or just at the Assizes. Defoe in all his novels captures the tension between the idea of a permanent self with its guilt and responsibilities and a mobile or labile alchemical self that can "morph" into different appearances, as Roxana can be courtesan or Quaker. The alchemical and scientific value of proposing a world mobile and constantly changeful, a concept or set of concepts developing from the sixteenth through the seventeenth centuries, can also seem perfectly recognizable in the manifestations of early capitalism. (Or we could say early—and late—capitalism seems like a parody of the labile self.)

Capitalist trade and consumerism accompany a sense that—inevitably—we are always in a masquerade. Whatever one is saying or doing at any moment may not be what the totality of the self is doing or would wish to be doing. Comedy of all kinds in the period from 1680–1750 deals emphatically with the unpreparedness of selves to proceed in one unified straight line. In one of the best early essays on what we call "shopping" by "Mrs. Crackenthorpe" (possibly Delarivier Manley), the blogger observes the behavior of women at a shop selling expensive fabric and gewgaws. Salesmen chant a series of seductive nouns: "Italian silks, brocades, tissues, cloth of silver . . . very fine Mantua silks, any right Geneva velvet, English velvet, velvets emboss'd . . . fine mohairs . . . and right Scotch plaids."

Consciousness is assailed and regenerated in the bewilderment of the visual and tactile: "Lady Praise-All surveyed the nick-nackatory, with an amazement, as if she had received a new sense." Customers include "quality Quakers"; precluded by their sect's belief and custom from anything but the simplest of dress, they are yet drawn to fine accessories.[14] Satire can seem judgmental and strait-laced, yet, even under the pretense of setting rules and boundaries, it is brilliantly accomplished in exhibiting what might be termed the *layeredness* of persons and phenomena. We too participate in taking in the world's variety as if we had "received a new sense."

The truly new form of the periodical essay—which stole from classical philosophical letters and from the Novel, and was stolen from in turn—centers its attention on time, on the *quidditas*, the thisness, of a particular moment. Time is always of interest to the epic, but perhaps even more to the lyric and the novel. In lyric and the novel, time is measured or marked by seasons, public festivals, and times of life. What seems genuinely new by the turn into the eighteenth century is the development of a complete notion of cultural era. Earl Miner commented many years ago on the Restoration's new use of the term "the age." I would push the emergence of an idea of cultural time further back, to the explorations of Paracelsus and his concept of the "Monarchia."[15] Each "Monarchia" is marked by its own tastes, habits, beliefs, fashions etc. The term is a half-parodic play upon common use of the reign of a monarch as a measure of time. Paracelsus' era, the "Monarchia," has in common with a king's reign as a temporal period the fact that you cannot subject it to forecast or limit it by mathematical regularity. You cannot predict while you are in it when it will end. Sterne's Tristram says "the parlour door hinges shall be mended this reign."[16] His remark is in exquisitely impossible relation to measurement of time, for a "reign"—unlike month, year or century—applies only to the past, and cannot be used to calculate or express the future. Paracelsus stresses that things happen in a particular age. Something that was invisible to people of a past age will become visible in a new "Monarchia." Time, creative time, is less a matter of regular and even-handed linear progression (as marked by sequence of calendar years) and more a matter of jumps and new visions. Paracelsus anticipates and creates the Restoration's "age" and the modern "period." By the end of the seventeenth century, the notion of a cultural period becomes something we cannot do without. The term "fashion," with its new uses, contributes importantly to the rise of the sense of "the age." The concept is now indispensable. Could any of us give an account of our own lives without invoking the sense of a "period," as a complex cultural era? Not only is this moment definable by me in terms of my status, age, income, physical appearance, etc. but in terms of the fact that I—or my parents—lived formerly in a different "period." And now I live in a different "age," freshly definable by its own characteristics. A "period" is a sort of temporal space with its peculiar bazaar of novelties, its "nick-nackatory." Like the poem and the novel, it becomes an imaginary but truthful place in which we can play with both abstract and concrete, the distant or the diurnal.

This way of thinking—or scaffolding for thought—seems one of the relatively few major elements that truly and deeply differentiate eighteenth-century literature from the classical. It has become such a dominant mode of thinking that since the late nineteenth century we have tended—for good and for ill—to regulate our studies of literature, art and philosophy almost entirely in terms of "periods." In an older world, there was some perception of difference between eras (especially in the late Roman and Christian periods) but the notion is very rough compared to our refined and defining swatches of thick time. The moment when this mode of thinking began to arise and gain power may seem to be offered in Europe by the Thirty Years' War—in England by its local branch, the Civil War. Voltaire, for instance, goes well beyond the ancients in dealing with "Le Siècle de Louis le Grand." He mediates between the old notion (king's reign) and the new idea of an "age"—a cultural period which in all its aspects (politics, architecture, literature, fashions in clothes) proclaims itself as a complex entity and object of thought. Eighteenth-century historians begin to take notice of such things. We think the arrival of newspapers and the coffee house was important for people at the turn into the eighteenth century—but so did they. The bloggers or periodical essayists—led by that genius Richard Steele in April 1709—are among the first to define new currents and movements of sartorial fashion, economics, politics— and their interrelation. Such a vision may be possible only in an era in which communication is easy and widespread (for example, after the printing press—or the Internet—has become established), and also when there is an element of the democratic in the society that observes and comments on itself. The importance of "the age" permits new emphasis upon individuals' relations to social bonds and interconnected social changes.

The Novel is always drawn towards the pressure of social bonds and ties. Thus, it has a particular job to do in redefining and sharpening our notion of the "Monarchia." The Lyric enjoys the patronage of the poet's own character, however got up for the occasion. The poet (or his/her simulacrum) may commune alone with personal thoughts—but the Novel must keep moving back into company. It needs multitudes. A novel, however, is also free to assert that bonds and ties can be questioned, even altered, as the self can be altered. Characters may hope to go through a series of creative metamorphoses, they may hope either to conform to or elude their "Monarchia." But evasion is hard. You can—like a Moll Flanders—outrun the constable, but not the culture. To be interesting and truly universal, novel characters must respond to their own cultural era, offering poetic delight in their responses to the crooked impressive world.

There is a delightful short interlude in *Moll Flanders* where she and her second husband, on a whim, spend an enormous sum of money on a pleasure trip to Northampton via Oxford—and back. He promises Moll "'you shall travel like a Dutchess,'" and she does, with a "Coach and Six":

> We had a rich coach, very good Horses, a Coachman, Postilion, and two Footmen in very good Liveries; a Gentleman on Horseback, and a Page with a Feather in his Hat . . . The Servants all call'd him [her husband] my Lord . . . and I was her Honour, the Countess; and thus we Travel'd to OXFORD, and a very pleasant Journey we had . . .[17]

This "Ramble" costs them the enormous sum of ninety-three pounds; it's no surprise that the husband is soon in debtors' prison. But the prudent moral of this story is undercut by the attraction of the journey. Moll and her man are entrapped by the Zeitgeist, subjects of their Monarchia. Yet they are also free in a new way. For they are willing to spend money on sheer experience—as distinct from possessions. Experience chosen and delighted in confers ineffable freedom. This belief is one of the marks of their time. Music, books and means of travel are all luxuries that promise experience. Rather than investing in stock or savings, one is investing in the education and evolution of the self through stimuli. Why *not* go on a week's sightseeing with "a Coach and Six"? Some people do. It would be much the same if one of us (in the middling professional professorial class) were to hire a private jet to go from Newark to Los Angeles and back. Many twenty-first century persons *can* do this. Who wouldn't like to travel like a Duchess? Should we die without the experience? Can we invoke the alibi of the "bucket list"? Eighteenth-century poetry, like the novel, communicates a great deal about social and economic experience—even at the vulgar level "how the other half"—or tenth—live. A reader of Thomson's poem may imagine how somebody like Lyttleton would wander about and enjoy his estate (see Wolfram Schmidgen's article). Vicarious experience is worth something. You can find out what unknown emotions and objects feel like—or are supposed to feel like. Bounded yourself, you might vicariously taste that boundless freedom of possession through borrowing Thomson's poem. People want to know what is "out there" or on the menu in their own Monarchia.

In the passage from *Betsy Thoughtless* quoted at the beginning of this essay, we can note Haywood's attention to multiple times at once, including the cultural period. Betsy upon awakening was subjected to the experience of popular song—an abrupt sensation not totally unlike the sensations forced upon Kallirhoe on coming to. In the whole scene, Haywood deals with Betsy rather as Pope does in bringing us Belinda at the opening of her day (see Kate Parker's comparison of the two works.) We already are aware of Betsy's youth—one level of time. Haywood gives us both the time of day at which Betsy awakes and her emotional season, the relation of her morning to the uneasy night. There is another time markedly present—a cultural period, an era of fashion, when the ballad was "at that time much in vogue." Betsy is both participant and victim of her Monarchia, her "age," the fashions of the time—which the larger novel suggests may include very defective and brutal notions of gender relations. As the song, a presence existing in fashion, had been sung so much, Betsy might have dismissed it as commonplace: "But as every little circumstance, if any way adapted to the passion that at that time we are possessed by, touches upon the jarring string, it seems a missioner of fate."[18] It is Betsy who feels the little song has meaning, that it describes the present and foretells the future. The mind can interpret anything as "a missioner of Fate." In the crowd of phenomena, we cannot choose all sensations, but we choose what we bring to ourselves as meaning.

Crowds of persons and objects feature largely in eighteenth-century literature and art. Non-fiction not only endorses, but provides a platform for conscious experimentation, as it can represent the ordinary and extraordinary life of both crowds and the individual. Hooke's *Micrographia* makes us aware of the crowd of amazing and alarming entities that compass us around. We can never opt out from sensation and what Locke calls "impression." Locke himself makes that vivid and inescapable by comically battering us with delightful word lists of disconnected terms:

> . . . 'tis past doubt, that Men have in their Minds several *Ideas*, such as are those expressed by the words, *Whiteness, Hardness, Sweetness, Thinking, Motion, Man, Elephant, Army, Drunkenness, and others* . . .[19]

Such a trope or play is congenial to poetry itself in more than one respect. Simply, poetry has been traditionally very fond of nouns. Many good poems of very different kinds have forced our attention toward noun objects and the impressions they create. This is true of the epic, which in the epic simile notoriously will remove us from an already hectic and crowded scene to provide another compet-ing set of impressions. In the second book of the Homeric *Iliad*, shortly before the famous "Ship Catalogue," the author moves us through another catalogue of various familiar or natural objects.[20] He takes us from a raging forest fire to the gleam of bronze armour (artificial and warlike) then to the light of the fire on the sky, to flights of various kinds of birds, to flowers and leaves in a meadow, and on to numerous insects. The imagination, already raised to expectation about the coming war, is diverted and slightly overloaded by numerous other impressions, curious or pretty—almost all recalling to immediacy the normal life of non-war-time which is rapidly fleeing away, subordinated to the fearful plot. The last line of this section makes clear that this great host stands facing the Trojans "eager to destroy them utterly" or (as Richmond Lattimore has it) "hearts burning to break them."[21] Nature's dynamism is co-opted by dire purpose. Natural innocent things are forced—and forced within the poem itself—to participate in the energies of war. War itself may be a terribly natural thing, a seasonal swarming. Here, Homer's vivid and varied nouns—all functioning in some sense as delayers—never permit us to withdraw our anxious attention from the hordes of armed men, the surge towards conflict. Anxiety is heightened and irritated by the assault of the nouns, unavoidable and unforgettable.

This Homeric effect is different—though never totally different—from the lyric's luxuriating in nouns:

> Mignonne, allons voir si la rose
> Que ce matin avait desclose
>   Sa robe de pourpre au Soleil
> A point perdu cettte vesprée
>   Les plis de sa robe purprée
>   Et son teint au vostre pareil.[22]

This morning's rose (a daughter of time) was found clothed (like a fine lady at court) in a new dress, a robe of deep soft red (*pourpre* is a noun), showing off before the sun—but this evening she will probably have lost the folds of her deep red robe and her color (or complexion) equal to yours. The poem, with its focus on nouns, keeps driving towards the unforgettable rose. That is more interesting than the overt conventional moral, that the "Mignonne" (Darling) who should look at the rose must make the most of her brief (sexual) bloom. The sense of passing time balances the rose's absolute beauty and intense royal color. The poetry of noun life is regulated by temporality—and "Mignonne" is a noun too. If we feel the moral here is lightly misogynistic, we may be more sympathetic to the late sonnet in which Ronsard describes his aging self:

> Je n'ay plus que les os, un Schelette je semble
> Decharné, denervé, demusclé, depoulpé,
> Que le trait de la mort sans pardon a frappé
> Je n'ose voir mes bras que de peur je ne tremble.[23]
> [I have nothing but bones, a Skeleton I resemble
> Defleshed, unnerved, demuscled, unjuiced.
> Now that the ruthless sign of death has knocked
> I do not dare look at my arms, lest I tremble.]

Ronsard plays with his own dissolution by looking and not looking at himself, his physical self which is disassembling. Reduced to a skeleton, he comically regards his own limbs as objects external to him. The nouns in the poem are parts of the personal body not usually abstracted as mere objects; bones and arms become something encountered outside the self, like the rose. Ronsard's sonnet plays on the tension between the "I" observant, ever present as always, and what *is* or *used to be* identified exactly with the "I"—this now ultra—thin fleshless body. What and where is the "I"?

Nouns are close to the center of poetry's appeal. For poetry helps us to relate our sense impressions of things to the activity of our mind which—despite brain research—must in daily experience manifest itself to us as a not-thing. Natalie Phillips in her fine article "The Art of Attention" in this volume has usefully clarified the division between those Enlightenment writers who sought unified focus and those who entertained "a competing multifocal paradigm of attention"—most notably Gottfried Leibniz who thinks us capable of attention to "many things all at once."[24] Both poetry and prose fiction of the period re-energize the attention to "many things at once." A sign of such diffuse attentiveness is the proliferation of nouns (often with striking modifiers) within poem or prose narration. A story may go in a straight line more or less—E.M. Forster was right about the basic "and then . . . and then."[25] But poetic fountains of images, posing ceaseless demands on the reader's vocabulary of sensation, must attract—even force—attention away from the linear and into the deeps. We go into sensational and emotive experience not primarily time-governed. Not just temporary, no mere passing event in a sequence, the mental image becomes a sensual and emotional event that cannot be shaken off. Like the knowledge of snow and wine and a girl with a ring, these haunting things must circulate and live in relation with each other, within the depths of narrative—within, as it were, the novel's unconscious mind. The novel (or poem) stops being forward narrative, uni-dimensional, and moves into multiple dimensions. It can move away from strict rational sense, alighting upon fears, desires and odd attractions not categorizable by worldly reason and the dictates of success.

Every noun used in a novel contributes to its sensory content at a basic absolute level. It cannot be erased. We remember Harriet Smith's inability to read the riddle proffered by Mr. Elton in *Emma*. A riddle of this kind depends on clear nouns sewn together to make another noun: "Court-ship." But Harriet's inappropriate guesses skew the meaning wildly: "Can it be Neptune? . . . Or a trident? Or a mermaid? or a shark?" Emma is impatient: "Mermaids and sharks! Nonsense! My dear Harriet, what are you thinking of?"[26] But the mermaid and the shark enter the novel and never go out of it. (And a determined unriddler might wonder if Harriet had an interior apprehension of Emma as mermaid and shark . . . .)

Poetry has been a great coadjutor in assisting the Novel and individual novelists to deal with time, memory and versions of reality. Indeed, poetry is sometimes less coadjutor than boss, especially in managing dense time. Poetic comprehension of the sliding moves of the mind is invaluable to novelists in creating "characters." There is always at least one mind exhibiting its activity—the mind of the Author—but that abstracted and familiar voice or eye is engaged with at least one and sometimes a horde of other minds, called "characters"—and these are assembled and set convincingly a-going in terms of poetic effects. Poetry is ever prepared to assault the reader with sense impressions, most powerfully conveyed in both ancient and modern instance by the presence of strong or evocative nouns. Eighteenth-century literature in general is highly noun-oriented, ready to respond to "cloth of silver . . . Geneva velvet . . . fine mohairs . . . and right Scotch plaids"— or to "elephant" and "army." So it is little wonder that the century produced fictions in which noun objects become themselves the subjects in "It-Narratives" or "Thing Poems" (discussed in this volume by Christina Lupton and Aran Ruth). Eighteenth-century poetry participates joyfully in what might be called the "strong noun catalogue." Consider the following masterly uses of the disconcerting list:

A. Lutes, Laurels, Seas of Milk, and Ships of Amber[27]

B. Nor will in fading Silks compose
Faintly th'inimitable Rose,
Fill up an ill drawn Bird, or paint on Glass
The Sovereign's blur'd and undistinguish'd Face,
The threatening Angel, and the speaking Ass.[28]

C. Sweepings from Butcher's Stalls, Dung, Guts, and Blood,
Drown'd Puppies, stinking Sprats, all drench'd in Mud,
Dead Cats, and Turnip- Tops come tumbling down the Flood.[29]

These are catalogues strong enough to astound—even assault. The reader (or hearer) will inevitably lag on first coming upon such sorted congeries. The first, from Belvidera's mad speech in Otway's *Venice Preserv'd* (1682), makes psychological sense—once one works at it quietly in a darkened room. The nouns refer us obliquely to Venice and her happier time, a time of music and poetry and unfettered trade, rich ships passing over a peaceful lagoon and calm seas, which the heroine connects with the maternal milk (in contrast to male threats, fire and bloodshed). The second example (which attracted Virginia Woolf's attention) is from Anne Finch's "The Spleen" (1709). Her list expresses wearied refusal of—even aversion to—the kind of art women are expected to go in for, embroidery and painting on glass. The anticipated results are dull figurations of hackneyed subjects, including the monarch and the biblical scene of the prophet Balaam, the warning angel and the ass. The artistry in Finch's lines lies partly in the weak aura of fatigued attractiveness that hangs about the rejected elderly images, like a stale perfume. The third example is from Swift's "A City Shower" (1710). Here nothing is attractive, unlike the faint rose or seas of milk. Everything is "low" and everything is good and dead. This is garbage—the kind of "waste" Sophie Gee discusses so well in *Making Waste*.[30] We look upon the busy kennel's mortal detritus of eating and begetting, a pile-up of mostly animal garbage. Everything in this list has already been thrown out—re-fused as *refuse*. And yet—all is energy. The divine shower brings back into the manifestation of what is dead and disgusting a kind of triumphant universal vitality. The meaningless cannot exist.

In pursuing such poetry the reader too must be plunged into the pile of things, diverted, astonished, wearied and almost—but not quite—repelled by the never-ending supply of attention-demanding objects. Literature promises to produce more nouns to love, honor and obey, to whirl us into this dangerous stimulating experience at eddying variable depths. The poetics of the pile-up of nouns appears with similar liveliness within eighteenth-century fiction. Eighteenth-century fiction is rich in pools, eddies, positive cascades of nouns.

A. . . . there was a Suit of Child-bed Linnen in it, very good and almost new, the Lace very fine; there was a Silver Porringer of a Pint, a small Silver Mug and Six Spoons, some other Linnen, a good Smock, and

Three Silk Handkerchiefs, and in the Mug wrap'd up in a Paper Eighteen Shillings and Six-pence in Money.[31]

B. . . . as the Moon shone very bright, he cast his Eyes on Stays, Gowns, Petticoats, Caps, Ribbons, Stockings, Garters, Shoes, Clogs, &c. all which lay in a disordered Manner on the Floor. All these operating on the natural Jealousy of his Temper, so enraged him, that he lost all Power of Speech.[32]

C. An old half-barred stove-grate was in the chimney; and in that a large stone-bottle without a neck filled with baleful Yew, as an Ever-green, withered Southernwood, dead Sweet-briar, and sprigs of Rue in flower.[33]

These instances of catalogue or congeries demand interpretation. But the nouns come up and hit us before we (or even the characters) are ready to interpret or connect. Perhaps nouns are particularly powerful because they require physical recollection, and introduce the earthy carnal world into the abstraction of language itself. The early eighteenth-century's extreme love of nouns—as well as their sense of what nouns can do—is expressed in the habit of giving them capital letters, making us pause and take notice.

In the passages quoted above, the first instance describes the contents of the customer's bundle taken from the shop in Moll Flanders' first theft. Moll's primary reaction on first drawing the things out of the bundle is alarm: "All the while I was opening these things I was under such dreadful Impressions of Fear, and in such Terror of Mind . . . that I cannot express the manner of it." It is only later that she "reads" the contents of her guilty bundle. A new baby has been born; its mother is sent some presents for herself and for the child. The silver objects (porringer and mug) have ritual and affectional significance far beyond the value of the silver that Moll will seek to extract. Moll has intervened in an important human and familial occasion; herself born a beggar, she has impoverished the new baby.

The second catalogue from the tenth book of *The History of Tom Jones, a Foundling* (1749) is part of the vivid sequence of events at the Inn at Upton. The promiscuous catalogue is joyful, the objects redolent of sex. Neither the reader nor the irrupting interpreter has any trouble reading the pile of female garments on the floor as a sign of hectic sexual activity. The things are sexy in themselves, each garment speaking closeness to a part of the human female body—and additionally sexually indicative in being discarded with evident haste. The list of words feels like "found poetry" (save that Fielding made it) of object names, indicating both the living body's presence and its absence. The body is tantalizingly absent but present, in an elsewhere close at hand. The use of the continuous plural in naming the objects makes it seem momentarily as if there must be a *multitude* of women in that shadowed bed. The reader who has followed the narrative will know who belongs to these metonymic objects. But the viewer who has just burst into Tom's bedroom, an infuriated "Irish Gentleman," is a personage hitherto unknown to us—and he knows nobody here. He views the objects in romantic but dim moonlight, but cannot identify the objects' particularity. He mistakenly reads the clothes as those of his absconded wife, persisting in the assumption that Tom Jones is coupling with her. "Wife" and "woman" are not to him distinguishable terms; he pursues a generic wearer of stays. In this instance the reader, not at all deceived, is happy to interpret, silently correcting the "Irish Gentleman" at every turn. The newcomer, however, encounters the objects before making any preparation for the calmer work of interpretation—rendering him comical. His wife's body, not being the individual body absent from these clothes, is the more truly an absent body, an explanation withheld.

The third of these prose-fiction examples is part of a larger catalogue, Belford's account of the objects in the wretched run-down spunging-house room in which Clarissa has been made captive. The description of the hideous bouquet follows immediately upon a clear description of the broken tiles and bare bricks of the chimney (an example of dilapidation and disuse demanding no specific interpretation). It was customary to put something in the fireplace in the summer—a paper fan, a bouquet. The broken tiles and uncovered bricks add to a tactile effect of roughness and dust, an impression which sheds itself upon the greenery in the damaged bottle. The nouns are hostile to sight and touch, and even to the sense of smell (rue having a slightly unpleasant scent). This dead and deathly bouquet is symbolic, but it will take us a moment to decode it, coming as it does between the realistic ugliness of the broken chimney preceding and the realistic "old broken-bottomed cane couch, without a squab" that follows. Yew is a sign of death, the ornament of churchyards; Southernwood or "Lad's Love" stands for affection, now withered; dead Sweet–briar is dead faithful love and Rue—the only plant flourishing—is remorse.

All of these catalogues—and hundreds or even thousands like them—add to the challenge and the pleasure of reading eighteenth-century novels. Triumphant assailing nouns are close to the essence of the poetics employed in fiction. Here we find bursts of poetry that question, even shatter, linear narrative. We go from story succession into a kind of deep present. Jumbled and intense nouns evoke a sense of the characters concerned, and the distracting objects provide their own atmosphere, stalling temporal advance. The objects strike the readers' own astonished senses and even hide out in their memories. All such passages in poetry and prose remind us that the primary work of the imagination is to take hold of the sensations of things; a secondary work is to recognize the things in words, and make the words work toward meaning. A reader puts new wine into old bottles, responding to the word as if it were the thing, smelling the violet and the orange, recoiling from the wet viscosity of blood and mud. Apparently trackers of the brain find this is what happens, that the brain lights up as if experiencing the "real thing" while reading.[34] But I don't care if I am a cerebral Christmas tree. This is the work of life that the novel holds in store for us in its poetic mind, asking us to undertake this work of life during the apparently simple linear journey which will become deep experience. We enter a thick time, sensing, interpreting. Drawing on our own bodily memories, we play them upon our own minds in a new manner. They give us what we seek—new memories. We become author and character, Defoe and Moll, each paying the tax of transformation of the self on the irresistible path to a somewhat alarming pleasure.

Notes

1. Eliza Haywood, *The History of Miss Betsy Thoughtless,* 4 vols. (London: T. Gardner, 1751), 2:215.

2. Chariton, *Callirhoe,* ed. and trans. G.P Goold, Loeb Classical Library 481 (Cambridge, MA: Harvard University Press, 1995), bk. 1, cap. 8, 56–58. This novel may have been written as early as 50 BC. As Greek does not have a letter "C" and its introduction Romanizes the work, I prefer the spellings "Kallirhoe" and "Khaireas." The translation offered here is mine.

3. Sophocles, *Oedipus Tyrannus,* ed. and trans. Hugh Lloyd-Jones, Loeb Classical Library 20 (Cambridge MA: Harvard University Press, 1997), 438–439, lines 1086–1090. Lloyd-Jones' translation is slightly altered.

4. *Ibid.,* 469; lines 1391–1393.

5. *Ibid.,* 468, lines 1391–1393; 474, lines 1451–1453. Lloyd-Jones' translation is somewhat altered.

6. Horace, *Odes,* Book I, number 9, in *Q. Horatii Flacci Carminum Liber I,* ed. T.E. Page (London: Macmillan, 1966), 10.

7. *The Works of Horace in English Verse,* collected and published by Mr. Duncombe, 2 vols. (London: R. and J. Dodsley, 1757), 1:36–39.

8. Jane Austen, *Emma,* ed. James Kinsley with intro. and notes Adela Pinch, Oxford World's Classics (Oxford: Oxford University Press, 2008), vol. I, chs. 13–15, page 100.

9. Dryden in Dodsley, *Works of Horace,* 36; Thomas Mulso in Dodsley, *Works of Horace,* 39.

10. Austen, *Emma,* 92.

11. Dryden in Dodsley, *Works of* Horace, 36.

12. Austen, *Emma,* 102–103.

13. *Ibid.,* 105.

14. "Mrs. Crackenthorpe," *The Female Tatler* no. 9 (July 25–27, 1709) and no. 67 (December 7–9, 1709), rpt. in *The Commerce of Everyday Life: Selections from "The Tatler" and "The Spectator,"* ed. Erin Mackie (Boston MA and New York NY: Bedford/St. Martin's, 1998), 294–297.

15. See Paracelsus' essay "Seven Defenses" [*Sieben Defensiones*], trans. C. Lillian Temkin, in *Paracelsus: Four Treatises,* ed. Henry E. Sigerist (Baltimore and London: The Johns Hopkins University Press, 1941; rpt. 1996), 10–41.

16. Laurence Sterne, *The Life and Opinions of Tristram Shandy, Gentleman,* 9 vols. (London: O. Lynch, 1771), vol. 3, ch.21, page 347.

17. Daniel Defoe, *The Fortunes and Misfortunes of the Famous Moll Flanders,* ed. G. A. Starr, Oxford World's Classics (Oxford: Oxford University Press, 1981), 61.

18. Haywood, *Betsy Thoughtless,* 215.

19. John Locke, *An Essay concerning Human Understanding,* ed. Peter H. Nidditch, Clarendon Edition of the Works of John Locke. 1975. Reprint. (Oxford: Oxford University Press, 1979), bk. 2, ch. 1, p. 104.

20. Homer, *Iliad,* ed. Jeffrey Henderson with trans. A.T. Murray, rev. William F. Wyatt, Loeb Classical Library 170, 2 vols. (Cambridge MA: Harvard University Press, 1999), 94–97; vol. 1, bk. 2, lines 455–473.

21. Ibid., 97; bk. 2, line 473; Richmond Lattimore, *The Iliad of Homer,* intro. Richard Martin (Chicago: University of Chicago Press, 2011), 105.

22. Pierre de Ronsard, "Mignonne, allons voir si la rose," in *Poésie Française,* http://poesie.webnet.fr/les grandsclassiques/vospoemes, lines 1–6.

23. Pierre de Ronsard, "Je n'ay plus que les os, un Schelette je semble," in *Poésie Française,* http://poesie.webnet.fr/lesgrandsclassiques/poemes/pierre_de_ronsard/je_n_ay_plus_que_les_os_un_schelette_je_semble.html, lines 1–4, translation mine.

24. See Phillip's article in this volume, page 196.

25. E.M. Forster, *Aspects of the Novel* (New York NY: Harcourt Brace, 1927), 66–67.

26. Austen, *Emma,* 58–59.

27. Thomas Otway, *Venice Preserv'd, or, A Plot Discover'd* (London: Benjamin Tooke and George Strahan, 1704), Act 5, p. 57. Belvidera picks up her own reference to milk in her earlier distressed imagining of babies killed in the revolt, their mothers' breasts dripping blood and milk. See the beginning of Act 4, *ibid.,* 44.

28. Anne Finch, *The Spleen. A Pindarique Ode* (London: H. Hills, 1709), 6.

29. Jonathan Swift, "A City Shower," *Works of Jonathan Swift,* 8 vols. (Dublin: Faulkner, 1741–46), 2:3.

30. Sophie Gee, *Making Waste: Leftovers and the Eighteenth-Century Imagination* (Princeton, NJ: Princeton University Press, 2010).

31. Defoe, *Moll Flanders,* 192.

32. Henry Fielding, *The History of Tom Jones, A Foundling,* 4 vols. (London: Andrew Millar, 1749), 3:7–8.

33. Samuel Richardson, *Clarissa,* Facsimile reprint of 3rd edition of 1751, 7 vols. (New York NY: AMS Press, 2000), 6:273.

34. Reading fiction intently stimulates brain activity, according to research of Natalie Phillips (now at University of Michigan) and others at Stanford Center for Cognitive and Neurobiological Imaging. Subjects' brains were scanned with an MRI while reading *Mansfield Park.* See "This is your brain on Jane Austen," *Stanford Report,* September 7, 2012, on Stanford Web page (www. stanford.edu). The hope that this finding will raise the study of literature in public repute seems misdirected.

Addison, Joseph. "Account of the Greatest English Poets." In *The Annual Miscellany, for the year 1694 being the fourth part of Miscellany poems*, 317–27. London: Jacob Tonson, 1694.

Addison, Joseph and Richard Steele. *The Spectator*. Edited by Donald F. Bond. 5 vols. Oxford: Clarendon Press, 1965.

Akenside, Mark. *The Pleasures of the Imagination*. In *The Poetical Works of Mark Akenside*. New York: C. Wells, 1838.

Algarotti, Francesco. *Sir Isaac Newton's Theory of Light and Colours, and his Principle of Attraction, Made familiar to the Ladies in several Entertainments*. London: G. Hawkins, 1742.

Anderson, Emily Hodgson. "Performing the Passions in Eliza Haywood's *Fantomina* and *Miss Betsy Thoughtless*." *The Eighteenth Century: Theory and Interpretation* 46, no. 1 (2005): 1–15.

Anderson, Misty G. *Imagining Methodism in Eighteenth-Century Britain*. Baltimore: The Johns Hopkins University Press, 2012.

Anon. Review of *Simple Tales*, by Amelia Opie. *Literary Journal, A Review* ns. 2 (Aug. 1806): 159–67.

Anon. "To S——a R——s." *The Ladies Magazine* (1791): 48.

Armstrong, Nancy. *How Novels Think: The Limits of British Individualism from 1719–1900*. New York: Columbia University Press, 2005.

Austin, Andrea. "Shooting Blanks: Potency, Parody, and Eliza Haywood's *The History of Miss Betsy Thoughtless*." In Saxton and Bocchicchio, *Passionate Fictions of Eliza Haywood*, 259–82.

Austen, Jane. *Emma*. Edited by James Kinsley and Adela Pinch. Oxford World's Classics. Oxford: Oxford University Press, 2003.

——. *Mansfield Park*. Edited by R. W. Chapman. 1923. Reprint. Oxford: Oxford University Press, 1988.

——. *Northanger Abbey*. Edited by Marilyn Butler. London: Penguin, 2003.

Baatz, Christine. "'A Strange Collection of Trash'? The Re-Evaluation of Medieval Literature in Thomas Percy's *Reliques of Ancient English Poetry* (1765)." In *Anthologies of British Poetry*, edited by Barbara Korte, Ralf Schneider, and Stefanie Lethbridge, 105–24. Amsterdam: Rodopi, 2000.

Backscheider, Paula R. *Daniel Defoe: His Life*. Baltimore: The Johns Hopkins University Press, 1989.

——. *Eighteenth-Century Women Poets and Their Poetry: Inventing Agency, Inventing Genre*. Baltimore: The Johns Hopkins University Press, 2005.

——. *Revising Women: Eighteenth-Century "Women's Fiction" and Social Engagement*. Baltimore: The Johns Hopkins University Press, 2000.

———. "The Verse Essay, John Locke, and Defoe's *Jure Divino*." *ELH* 55, no. 1 (1988): 99–124.

Bakhtin, Mikhail. "Epic and Novel: Toward a Methodology for the Study of the Novel." In *The Dialogic Imagination: Four Essays*, edited by Michael Holquist and translated by Caryl Emerson and Michael Holquist. 3–40. Austin: The University of Texas Press, 1981.

Ballaster, Ros. "A Gender of Opposition." In Saxton and Bocchicchio, *Passionate Fictions of Eliza Haywood*, 143–67.

———. *Seductive Forms: Women's Amatory Fiction from 1684 to 1740*. Oxford: Oxford University Press, 1998.

Barbauld, Anna Letitia. "On the Origin and Progress of Novel-Writing." In *The British Novelists*. 50 vols. London: F.C. and J. Rivington, 1810.

Bartlet, William. *Barnabas's Character and Success*. London: John Clark, 1716.

Baxter, Richard. *The Saints Everlasting Rest*. London: Rob White for Thomas Underhil and Francis Tyton, 1650.

Beattie, James. *Essays: on Poetry and Music, as they affect the mind; on Laughter, and Ludicrous Composition; On the Usefulness of Classical Learning*. 3rd ed. London: E. and C. Dilly, 1779.

Benedict, Barbara. "Encounters with the Object: Advertisements, Time, and Literary Discourse in the Early Eighteenth-Century Thing-Poem." *Eighteenth-Century Studies* 40, no. 2 (2007): 193–207.

———. *Making the Modern Reader: Cultural Mediation in Early Modern Literary Anthologies*. Princeton, N.J.: Princeton University Press, 1996.

Bennett, Jane. *Vibrant Matter: A Political Ecology of Things*. Durham, NC: Duke University Press, 2010.

Bergson, Henri. *Laughter: An Essay on the Meaning of the Comic*. Translated by Cloudesley Brereton and Fred Rothwell. Mineola, NY: Dover, 2005.

Berkeley, George. *A Treatise Concerning the Principles of Human Knowledge. Part I. Wherein the chief Causes of Error and Difficulty in the Sciences, with the Grounds of Scepticism, Atheism, and Irreligion, are inquir'd into*. Dublin: Aaron Rhames, for Jeremy Pepyat, 1710.

Biggs, Edward Smith. *A Second Set of Hindoo Airs with English Words Adapted to Them by Mrs. Opie, And Harmonized for One, Two, Three, and Four Voices (or for a Single Voice) with an Accompaniment for the Piano Forte or Harp, by Mr. Biggs*. London: R. Birchall, 1800.

Bisset, John. *A Sermon, Preached Before the Reverend, the Presbytery of Aberdeen*. Aberdeen: James Chalmers, 1737.

Blackwell, Mark, general ed. *British It-Narratives, 1750–1830*. 4 vols. London: Pickering & Chatto, 2012.

———, ed. *The Secret Life of Things: Animals and Objects in Eighteenth-Century England*. Lewisburg, PA: Bucknell University Press, 2007.

Blair, Hugh. *Lectures on Rhetoric and Belles Lettres*. London: W.B. Gilley, 1819.

———. *Lectures on Rhetoric and Belles Lettres*, 3 vols. Dublin: Whitstone, Colles, Burnet, et. al., 1783.

Blake, William. *William Blake's Writings*, edited by G. E. Bentley. Oxford; Clarendon Press, 1978.

Bornstein, George. *Material Modernism: The Politics of the Page*. New York: Cambridge University Press, 2001.

Boswell, James. *Life of Johnson*. Edited by R.W. Chapman. Oxford: Oxford University Press, 1980.

———. *Boswell's Life of Johnson*. Edited by George Birkbeck Hill, rev. L.F. Powell, 6 vols. Oxford: Clarendon Press, 1934–64.

Bowers, Toni. *Force or Fraud: British Seduction Stories and the Problem of Resistance, 1660–1760*. Oxford: Oxford University Press, 2011.

Boyle, Robert. *The Origine of Formes and Qualities*. Oxford: H. Hall, for Ric. Davis, 1666.

Brant, Clare. "Seduced by the City: Gay's *Trivia* and Hogarth," *Literary London: Interdisciplinary studies in the representation of London* 6, no. 1 (March 2008). http://www.literarylondon.org/london-journal/march2008/brant.html.

Braudy, Leo. "*Fanny Hill* and Materialism." *Eighteenth-Century Studies* 4, no. 1 (Autumn 1970): 21–40.

Brewer, John. *The Pleasures of the Imagination: English Culture in the Eighteenth Century*. New York: Farrar Straus Giroux, 1997.

Brissendon, R.F. *Virtue in Distress: Studies in the Novel of Sentiment from Richardson to Sade*. New York: Harper & Row, 1974.

Bronson, Bertrand H. "Personification Reconsidered," *ELH* 14, no. 3 (1947): 163–77.

Brown, Marshall. *Preromanticism*. Stanford: Stanford University Press, 1991.

Brightwell, Cecelia Lucy. *Memorials of the Life of Amelia Opie: Selected and Arranged from Her Letters, Diaries and Other Manuscripts*. Norwich, U.K.: Fletcher and Alexander, 1854.

Burnet, Gilbert. *A Discourse of the Pastoral Care*. London: R.R., for Ric. Chitwell, 1692.

Byrom, John. "A Letter to a Lady, Occasioned by her Desiring the Author to Revise and Polish the Poems of Bishop Ken." In *The Poems of John Byrom*, vol. 2, part 1 of *Sacred Poems*, edited by Adolphus William Ward, Litt.D., Hon. L.L.D, 124–5. Manchester: Printed for the Chetham Society, 1895.

Cantor, G.N. *Optics after Newton: Theories of Light in Britain and Ireland, 1704–1840*. Manchester: Manchester University Press, 1983.

Cantor, G.N. and M.J.S. Hodge, eds. *Conceptions of Ether: Studies in the History of Ether Theories 1740–1900*. Cambridge: Cambridge University Press, 1981.

Carnochan, W.B. Afterword to *The Rise of the Novel: Studies in Defoe, Richardson, and Fielding*, by Ian Watt, 303–21. 2nd ed. Berkeley: University of California Press, 2001.

Carter, Elizabeth. *Elizabeth Carter, 1717–1806: An Edition of Some Unpublished Letters*. Edited by Gwen Hampshire. Newark: University of Delaware Press, 2005.

Chambers, Ephraim. *Cyclopædia*. London: James and John Knapton, John Darby, Daniel Midwinter, et al., 1728.

Chapin, Chester. *Personification in Eighteenth-Century English Poetry*. New York: Octagon, 1974.

Chapone, Hester (Mulso). *The Works of Mrs. Chapone*. 4 vols. London: John Murray and A. Constable, 1807.

Chappell, Vere, ed. *Hobbes and Bramhall on Liberty and Necessity*. Cambridge: Cambridge University Press, 1999.

Chariton, *Callirhoe*. Edited and translated by G.P. Gould. Cambridge MA: Loeb Library, 1995.

Church of England. *Book of Common Prayer*. London: John Bill and Christopher Barker, 1662.

Clarke, John. *An Essay Upon Study…Wherein directions are given for the due conduct thereof, and the collection of a library, proper for the Purpose, consisting of the Choicest Books in all the several Parts of learning*. London: A. Bettesworth, 1731.

Clayton, Jay. *Romantic Vision and the Novel*. Cambridge: Cambridge University Press, 1987.

Cockayne, Emily. *Hubbub: Filth, Noise, and Stench in England, 1600–1770*. New Haven: Yale University Press, 2007.

Cohen, I. Bernard. *Benjamin Franklin's Science*. Cambridge, MA and London: Harvard University Press, 1990.

Cohen, Ralph. "On the Interrelations of Eighteenth-Century Literary Forms." In *New Approaches to Eighteenth-Century Literature: Selected Papers from the English Institute*, edited by Phillip Harth, 33–78. New York: Columbia University Press, 1974.

———. *The Art of Discrimination: Thomson's* Seasons *and the Language of Criticism*. London: Routledge and Kegan Paul, 1964.

Coleridge, Samuel Taylor. *Biographia Literaria*. Edited by J. Shawcross. 2 vols. Oxford: Oxford University Press, 1907.

Colman, George. *The Conoisseur* 86. September 18, 1755.

———. *Polly Honeycombe, a Dramatick Novel of One Act*. London: T. Becket and T. Davies, 1760.

Corfield, Penelope. "Walking the City Streets: The Urban Odyssey of Eighteenth-Century England." *Journal of Urban History* 16 (1990): 132–74.

Correa, A. and A.C. Nobre. "Neural Modulation by Regularity and Passage of Time." *Journal of Neurophysiology* 100, no. 3 (2008): 1649–55.

Cowper, William. *Poems by William Cowper*. London: J. Johnson, 1782.

Dane, Joseph A. *Out of Sorts: On Typography and Print Culture*. Philadelphia: University of Pennsylvania Press, 2011.

Darnton, Robert. *The Forbidden Best-Sellers of Pre-Revolutionary France*. New York and London: W.W. Norton, 1996.

Darwin, Erasmus. *The Temple of Nature: Or, the Origin of Society. A Poem*. 1803. Reprint. Baltimore: John Butler, Bonsal & Niles, 1804.

Deane, Cecil. *Aspects of Eighteenth-Century Nature Poetry*. Oxford: Blackwell, 1935.

Defoe, Daniel. *Moll Flanders*. Edited by David Blewett. London: Penguin, 1989.

———. *The Fortunes and Misfortunes of the Famous Moll Flanders*. Edited by G. A. Starr. Oxford World's Classics. Oxford: Oxford University Press, 1981.

———. *Robinson Crusoe*. Edited by John Richetti. London: Penguin, 2001.

———. *Roxana*. Edited by David Blewett. London: Penguin, 1987.

Dennis, John. *The Critical Works of John Dennis*. Edited by Edward Niles Hooker. 2 vols. Baltimore: The Johns Hopkins University Press, 1939–43.

DePorte, Michael V. *Nightmares and Hobbyhorses: Swift, Sterne, and Augustan Ideas of Madness*. San Marino, CA: Huntington Library, 1974.

Descartes, René. *Meditations on First Philosophy*. In vol. 2 of *The Philosophical Writings of Descartes*, translated by John Cottingham, Robert Stoothoff, and Dugald Murdoch, 1–62. Cambridge: Cambridge University Press, 1988.

Deutsch, Helen. "Dismantl'd Souls: The Verse Epistle, Embodied Subjectivity, and Poetic Animation." In *Vital Matters: Eighteenth-Century Views of Conception, Life and Death*, edited by Helen Deutsch and Mary Terrall, 50–65. Toronto: University of Toronto Press, 2011.

Dicker, Georges. "An Idea Can Be Like Nothing But An Idea." In vol. 3 of *George Berkeley: Critical Assessments,* edited by Walter E. Creery, 162–76. London and New York: Routledge, 1991.

Dixon, Sarah. "From a Sheet of Gilt Paper. To Cloe." In Fairer and Gerrard, *Eighteenth-Century Poetry,* 277–8.

Dodsley, Robert. *A Collection of Poems in Two Volumes. By Several Hands.* London: G. Pearch, No. 12, Cheapside, 1768.

Doody, Margaret Anne. *The Daring Muse: Augustan Poetry Reconsidered.* Cambridge: Cambridge University Press, 1985.

Dowling, William C. *The Epistolary Moment: The Poetics of the Eighteenth-Century Verse Epistle.* Princeton, N.J.: Princeton University Press, 1991.

Doyle, Wesley. *O! That I Cou'd Recall the Day, a Ballad, Written By Mrs. Opie, the Music by Wesley Doyle Esqr.* London: Chappell & Co., 1821.

———. *One Duet & Six Ballads, with an Accompaniment for the Piano Forte, Composed and Inscribed to Thomas Moore, Esqr. By Wesley Doyle, Esqr.* London: Chappell & Co., 1825?.

Driver, J. "A selective review of selective attention research from the past century." *British Journal of Psychology* 92 (2001): 53–78.

Drury, Joseph. "Haywood's Thinking Machines." *Eighteenth-Century Fiction* 21, no. 2 (Winter 2008–9): 201–228.

Dussinger, John A. *The Discourse of the Mind in Eighteenth-Century Fiction.* The Hague: Mouton, 1974.

———. "'Stealing in the Great Doctrines of Christianity': Samuel Richardson as Journalist." *Eighteenth-Century Fiction* 15, no. 3–4 (2003): 451–506.

Eliot, George. "Worldliness and Other-Worldliness: The Poet Young." In *Essays of George Eliot,* edited by Thomas Pinney, 335–385. New York: Columbia University Press, 1963.

Epictetus. *The Discourses as Reported by Arrian, the Manual, and Fragments, Books III and IV.* Translated by W.A. Oldfather. Cambridge: Harvard University Press, 1959.

Fairer, David. *English Poetry of the Eighteenth Century, 1700–1789.* London: Longman, 2003.

———. *Organising Poetry: The Coleridge Circle, 1790–1798.* Oxford: Oxford University Press, 2009.

———. "Sentimental Translation in Mackenzie and Sterne." *Essays in Criticism* 49 (1999): 132–51.

Fairer, David and Christine Gerrard, eds. *Eighteenth-Century Poetry: An Annotated Anthology.* 2nd ed. Oxford: Blackwell, 2004.

Fara, Patricia. *An Entertainment for Angels: Electricity in the Enlightenment.* Cambridge: Icon Books, 2002.

Favret, Mary. "Telling Tales about Genre: Poetry in the Romantic Novel." *Studies in the Novel* 26, no. 3 (1994): 281–300.

Feather, John. "British Publishing in the Eighteenth Century: A Preliminary Subject Analysis." *The Library,* 6th series, 8 (1986): 32–46.

Fergus, Jan. *Provincial Readers in Eighteenth-Century England.* Oxford: Oxford University Press, 2007.

Festa, Lynn. *Sentimental Figures of Empire.* Baltimore: The Johns Hopkins University Press, 2006.

Field, Ophelia. *The Kit-Cat Club: Friends Who Imagined a Nation.* London: Harper Press, 2008.

Fielding, Henry. *The History of Tom Jones, A Foundling.* 4 vols. London: Andrew Millar, 1749.

Finch, Anne, Countess of Winchilsea, *The Spleen. A Pindarique Ode.* London: H. Hills, 1709.

Fish, Stanley. *Surprised by Sin.* London: Macmillan, 1967.

Forster, E.M. *Aspects of the Novel.* New York: Harcourt Brace, 1927.

Fowler, Alistair. *Kinds of Literature: An Introduction to the Theory of Genres and Modes.* Cambridge: Harvard University Press, 1982.

Franklin, Benjamin. *Experiments and Observations on Electricity.* London: E. Cave, 1751.

Fried, Michael. *Absorption and Theatricality: Painting and Beholder in the Age of Diderot.* Chicago: University of Chicago Press, 1980.

Fry, Elizabeth. *Journal.* 25 April 1799. British Library. Add Mss 47456, p. ff. 57.

Gallagher, Catherine. *Nobody's Story: The Vanishing Acts of Women Writers in the Marketplace 1670–1820.* Berkeley: University of California Press, 1994.

———. "The Rise of Fictionality." In vol. 1 of *The Novel*, edited by Franco Moretti, 336–63. Princeton: Princeton University Press, 2006.

Gardiner, Ellen. *Regulating Readers: Gender and Literary Criticism in the Eighteenth-Century Novel.* Newark: University of Delaware Press, 1999.

Gay, John. *Trivia: or the Art of Walking the Streets of London.* 3rd ed. London: Bernard Lintot, 1730.

———. *John Gay: Poetry and Prose*, edited by Vinton A. Dearing and Charles E. Beckwith. 2 vols. Oxford: Clarendon Press, 1974.

Gee, Sophie. *Making Waste: Leftovers and the Eighteenth-Century Imagination.* Princeton: Princeton University Press, 2010.

Gerrard, Christine. *Aaron Hill: The Muses' Projector 1685–1750.* Oxford: Oxford University Press, 2003.

Gillis, Christina Marsden. *The Paradox of Privacy: Epistolary Form in* Clarissa. Gainesville: University Presses of Florida, 1984.

Gjertsen, Derek. *The Newton Handbook.* London and New York: Routledge & Kegan Paul, 1986.

Goldman, Corrie. "This is your brain on Jane Austen." *Stanford Report*, September 7, 2012. http://news.stanford.edu/news/2012/september/austen-reading-fmri-090712.html

Goldsmith, M.L. *Franz Anton Mesmer: The History of an Idea.* London: Arthur Baker, 1934.

Goodman, Kevis. *Georgic Modernity and British Romanticism: Poetry and the Mediation of History.* Cambridge: Cambridge University Press, 2004.

Gray, Andrew. *Directions and Instigations to the Duty of Prayer.* Edinburgh: George Swintoun and James Glen, 1669.

Gray, Thomas. *Correspondence of Thomas Gray.* Edited by Paget Toynbee and Leonard Whibley. 3 vols. Oxford: Clarendon Press, 1935.

Greenblatt, Stephen. "Cultural Mobility: An Introduction." In *Cultural Mobility: A Manifesto,* edited by Stephen Greenblatt, et al., 1–23. Cambridge: Cambridge University Press, 2010.

Griffin, Dustin. *Regaining Paradise: Milton and the Eighteenth Century.* Cambridge: Cambridge University Press, 1986.

Guyer, Sarah. *Romanticism After Auschwitz.* Stanford: Stanford University Press, 2007.

Hammond, Brean. *Professional Imaginative Writing in England, 1670–1740: 'Hackney for Bread.'* Oxford: Clarendon Press, 1997.

Hartman, Geoffrey. *Beyond Formalism: Literary Essays, 1958–1970.* New Haven, CT: Yale University Press, 1970.

Hauksbee, Francis. *Physico-Mechanical Experiments on Various Subjects.* London: R. Brugis, 1709.

Hays, Mary. "On Novel Writing." *Monthly Magazine* 4 (1798): 180–1.

Haywood, Eliza. *Fantomina and Other Works.* Edited by Alexander Pettit, Margaret Case Croskery, and Anna C. Patchias. Petersborough, ON: Broadview Press, 2004.

——. *The History of Miss Betsy Thoughtless.* 4 vols. London: T. Gardner, 1751.

——. *The History of Miss Betsy Thoughtless.* Edited by Christine Blouch. Vancouver: Broadview Press, 1998.

——. *Lasselia: or, the Self-Abandon'd. A Novel.* London: D. Browne and S. Chapman, 1724.

——. *Selections from the Female Spectator.* Edited by Patricia Meyer Spacks. New York: Oxford University Press, 1999.

Hazlitt, William. *The Complete Works of William Hazlitt.* 21 vols. Edited by P.P. Howe. London, Toronto: J.M. Dent and Sons, 1930–4.

Heilbron, J.L. *Elements of Early Modern Physics.* Berkeley and Los Angeles: University of California Press, 1982.

Hill, Aaron, "Alone, in an Inn, at Southampton." In Fairer and Gerrard, *Eighteenth-Century Poetry,* 198.

——. *The Works of the Late Aaron Hill, Esq.* 4 vols. London: Printed for the Benefit of the Family, 1753.

Hillman, David and Carla Mazzio, eds. *The Body in Parts: Fantasies of Corporeality in Early Modern Europe.* New York: Routledge, 1997.

Homer. *Iliad.* Edited by Jeffrey Henderson. Translated by A.T. Murray. Revised by William F. Wyatt. 2 vols. Loeb Classical Library. Cambridge MA: Harvard University Press, 1999.

——. *The Iliad of Homer.* Introduction by Richard Martin. Translated by Richmond Lattimore. Chicago, IL: University of Chicago Press, 2011.

Horace, *Q. Horatii Flacci Carminum Liber I.* Edited by T.E. Page. London: Macmillan, 1966.

Hultquist, Aleksondra. "Haywood's Re-appropriation of the Amatory Heroine in *Betsy Thoughtless.*" *Philological Quarterly* 85, no. 1–2 (Winter-Spring 2006): 141–65.

Hume, David. *The History of England, from the Invasion of Julius Caesar to the Revolution in 1688.* 8 vols. London: A. Millar, 1763.

Hunter, J. Paul. *Before Novels: The Cultural Contexts of Eighteenth-Century English Fiction.* New York: Norton, 1990.

——. "Couplets and Conversation." In *The Cambridge Companion to Eighteenth-Century Poetry.* Edited by John Sitter, 11–36. Cambridge: Cambridge University Press, 2001.

——. "Defoe and the Poetic Tradition." In *The Cambridge Companion to Daniel Defoe,* edited by John Richetti, 216–36. Cambridge: Cambridge University Press, 2009.

——. "Serious Reflections on Farther Adventures: Resistances to Closure in Eighteeenth-Century English Novels." In *Augustan Subjects: Essays in Honor of Martin C. Battestin,* edited by Albert J. Rivero, 276–93. Newark: University of Delaware Press, 1997.

Hurlothrumbo. *The Merry-Thought: or, the Glass-Window and Bog-House Miscellany.* Part 1 [1731]. The Augustan Reprint Society, Publication No. 216. Los Angeles: William Andrews Clark Memorial Library, 1982.

———. *The Merry-Thought: or, the Glass-Window and Bog-House Miscellany*. Parts 2, 3, and 4 [1731–?]. The Augustan Reprint Society, Publication Nos. 221–222. Los Angeles: William Andrews Clark Memorial Library, 1983.

Irlam, Shaun. *Elations: The Poetics of Enthusiasm in Eighteenth-Century Britain*. Stanford: Stanford University Press, 1999.

Jefferson, Douglas. "*Tristram Shandy* and the Tradition of Learned Wit." *Essays in Criticism* 1 (1951): 225–48.

Johnson, Samuel. *A Dictionary of the English Language*, 2 vols. London: W. Strachan, 1755.

———. *The Yale Edition of the Works of Samuel Johnson*. 23 vols. New Haven and London: Yale University Press, 1958–2010.

Jones, Henry. *Philosophy. A Poem Address'd to the Ladies Who attend Mr. Booth's Lectures*. Dublin: S. Powell, 1746.

Jung, Sandro. *The Fragmentary Poetic: Eighteenth Century Uses of an Experimental Mode*. Bethlehem, PA: Lehigh University Press, 2009.

Kames, Henry Home, Lord. *Elements of Criticism*. 3 vols. Edinburgh: Millar, Kincaid and Bell, 1762.

Katz, Jackson. *The Macho Paradox: Why Some Men Hurt Women and How All Men Can Help*. Napierville, IL: Sourcebooks, 2006.

Kaul, Suvir. *Poems of Nation, Anthems of Empire: English Verse in the Long Eighteenth Century*. Charlottesville: University of Virginia Press, 2000.

Kearsley, George, ed. *Beauties of Milton, Thomson, and Young*. London: G. Kearsley, 1783.

Keats, John. *The Poems of John Keats*, edited by Miriam Allott. London: Longman, 1970.

Keenleyside, Heather. "Personification for the People: On James Thomson's *The Seasons*." *ELH* 76.2 (2009): 447–72.

Keith, Thomas. *The Bro Code: How Contemporary Culture Creates Sexist Men*. DVD. Directed by Thomas Keith. Northampton, MA: The Media Education Foundation, 2011.

Kelly, Gary. *English Fiction of the Romantic Period 1789–1830*. London: Longman, 1989.

———. *The English Jacobin Novel 1780–1805*. Oxford: Oxford University Press, 1976.

Keymer, Tom (Thomas). *Richardson's* Clarissa *and the Eighteenth-Century Reader*. Cambridge and New York: Cambridge University Press, 1992.

———. "Richardson's *Meditations*: Clarissa's *Clarissa*." In *Samuel Richardson: Tercentenary Essays*, edited by Margaret Anne Doody and Peter Sabor, 89–109. Cambridge: Cambridge University Press, 1989.

———, ed. *Samuel Richardson's Published Commentary on* Clarissa *1747–65*. 3 vols. London: Pickering & Chatto, 1998.

———. *Sterne, the Moderns, and the Novel*. Oxford: Oxford University Press, 2002.

Klancher, Jon. *The Making of English Reading Audiences 1790–1832*. Madison: University of Wisconsin Press, 1987.

Kinkead-Weekes, Mark. *Samuel Richardson: Dramatic Novelist*. Ithaca: Cornell University Press, 1973.

Knapp, Stephen. *Personification and the Sublime: Milton to Coleridge*. Cambridge: Harvard University Press, 1985.

Koehler, Margaret. "The Filter of Attention and Indissoluble Attractors in Eighteenth-Century Mock-Heroic Poetry." *Modern Philology* 108, no. 1 (August 2010): 65–88.

————. "Odes of Absorption in the Restoration and Early Eighteenth Century." *Studies in English Literature* 47, no. 3 (Summer 2007): 659–78.

Kramnick, Jonathan. *Actions and Objects from Hobbes to Richardson.* Stanford: Stanford University Press, 2010.

Kroll, Richard. *The Material Word: Literate Culture in the Restoration and Early Eighteenth Century.* Baltimore: The Johns Hopkins University Press, 1991.

Lamb, Jonathan. *The Things Things Say.* Princeton: Princeton University Press, 2011.

Latour, Bruno. *Reassembling the Social.* Oxford: Oxford University Press, 2005.

————. *We Have Never Been Modern.* Translated by Catherine Porter. Cambridge, MA: Harvard University Press, 1993.

Laughton, John. *The Testimony of a Good Conscience.* London: John Ward, 1712.

Leibniz, Gottfried. *New Essays on Human Understanding.* Edited by Peter Remnant and Jonathan Bennett. Cambridge: Cambridge University Press, 1996.

Lewis, Jayne Elizabeth. *Air's Appearance: Literary Atmosphere in British Fiction, 1660–1794.* Chicago: University of Chicago, 2012.

Levinson, Marjorie. "What Is New Formalism?" *PMLA* 122, no. 2 (2007): 558–69.

Locke, John. *An Essay concerning Human Understanding.* Edited by Peter H. Nidditch. Clarendon Edition of the Works of John Locke. Oxford: Oxford University Press, 1975.

Longinus. *The Works of Dionysius Longinus.* Translated by Alexander Welsted. London: Sam. Briscoe, 1712.

Low, Anthony. *The Georgic Revolution.* Princeton: Princeton University Press, 1985.

Lucretius. *On the Nature of Things (De Rerum Natura).* Translated by William Ellery Leonard. Mineola, NY: Dover Publications, 2004.

Lubey, Kathleen. "Erotic Interiors in Joseph Addison's Imagination." *Eighteenth-Century Fiction* 20, no. 3 (Spring 2008): 415–44.

————. "Haywood's Amatory Aesthetic." *Eighteenth-Century Studies* 39, no. 3 (Spring 2006): 309–22.

Lukacs, Georg. *The Theory of the Novel.* Translated by Anna Bostock. Cambridge: Massachusetts Institute of Technology Press, 1971.

Lynch, Deidre. *The Economy of Character: Novels, Market Culture and the Business of Inner Meaning.* Chicago: University of Chicago Press, 1998.

MacKay, Marina. "The Wartime Rise of The Rise of the Novel," *Representations* 119, no. 1 (2012): 119–43.

Mackenzie, Henry. "The Exile." In *The Mirror* 85 (1780): 167.

————. *Letters to Elizabeth Rose of Kilravock.* Edited by Horst W. Drescher. Meunster: Verlag Aschendorff, 1967.

Mackie, Erin, ed. *The Commerce of Everyday Life: Selections from "The Tatler" and "The Spectator."* Boston and New York: Bedford/St. Martin's, 1998.

Macpherson, Sandra. *Harm's Way: Tragic Responsibility and the Novel Form.* Baltimore: The Johns Hopkins University Press, 2010.

Marshall, Ashley. "Fabricating Defoes: From Anonymous Hack to Master of Fictions." *Eighteenth-Century Life* 36, no. 2 (2012): 1–35.

Martineau, Harriet. *Biographical Sketches 1852–1875.* 4th ed. London: Macmillan and Company, 1876.

Mason, John. *An Essay on Elocution.* London: M. Cooper, 1748.

McKeon, Michael. "Introduction." In *Theory of the Novel: A Historical Approach.* Edited by Michael McKeon, xiii-xvii. Baltimore: The Johns Hopkins University Press, 2000.

———. *The Origins of the English Novel 1600–1740.* Baltimore and London: The Johns Hopkins University Press, 1987.

———. *The Secret History of Domesticity: Public, Private, and the Division of Knowledge.* Baltimore: The Johns Hopkins University Press, 2005.

Merritt, Juliette. *Beyond Spectacle: Eliza Haywood's Female Spectators.* Toronto: University of Toronto Press, 2004.

Milton, John. *Paradise Lost.* Edited by Alistair Fowler. London: Longman, 1998.

Morris, David B. *The Religious Sublime.* Lexington: University Press of Kentucky, 1972.

Nestor, Deborah J. "Virtue Rarely Rewarded: Ideological Subversion and Narrative Form in Haywood's Later Fiction." *Studies in English Literature* 34 (1994): 579–98.

Ngai, Sianne. *Ugly Feelings.* Cambridge: Harvard University Press, 2005.

Nicolson, Marjorie Hope. *Newton Demands the Muse.* Princeton: Princeton University Press, 1946.

Noggle, James. *The Skeptical Sublime: Aesthetic Ideology in Pope and the Tory Satirists.* Oxford: Oxford University Press, 2001.

Oakleaf, David. "Circulating the Name of a Whore: Eliza Haywood's Betsy Thoughtless, Betsy Careless, and the Duplicities of the Double Standard." *Women's Writing* 15, no. 1 (2008): 107–34.

Oakley, Warren L. *A Culture of Mimickry: Laurence Sterne, His Readers and the Art of Bodysnatching.* London: Modern Humanities Research Association, 2010.

Odell, Daniel W. "Young's *Night Thoughts* as an Answer to Pope's *Essay on Man.*" *Studies in English Literature* 12 (1972): 481–501.

Oldfield, Joshua. *An Essay Towards the Improvement of Reason.* London: T. Parkhurst, J. Robinson, and J. Lawrence, 1707.

Ong, Walter J. *Orality and Literacy: The Technologizing of the Word.* London and New York: Routledge, 2002.

Opie, Amelia. *The Father and Daughter, a Tale, in Prose.* 5th ed. London: Longman, Hurst, Rees, and Orme, 1806.

———. *Madeline, A Tale.* 2 vols. London: Longman, Hurst, Rees, Orme and Brown, 1822.

———. "Memoir of John Opie." in *Lectures on Painting,* by John Opie, 3–54. London: Longmen, Hurst, Rees, and Orme, 1809.

———. *Tales of the Heart.* 4 vols. London: Longman, Hurst, Rees, Orme & Browne, 1820.

Opie, Amelia to Eliza Alderson. n.d. Correspondence of Amelia Alderson Opie, 1794–1854 (bulk 1820–1840) mssOP 1–364. Huntington Library, California.

Alderson (Opie), Amelia to Mary Wollstonecraft. 28 August 1796. Abinger Collection, MS. Abinger c 41 fol. 9v. Bodleian Library, Oxford.

———. 18 December 1796. Abinger Collection, MS. Abinger c. 41 fol. 4r, 4v. Bodleian Library, Oxford.

Otway, Thomas. *Venice Preserv'd, or, A Plot Discover'd.* London: Benjamin Tooke and George Strahan, 1704.

Packham, Catherine. *Eighteenth-Century Vitalism: Bodies, Culture, Politics.* Houndsmills, Basingstoke: Palgrave MacMillan, 2012.

Paracelsus, *Sieben Defensiones* [Seven Defenses]. Translated by C. Lillian Temkin. In *Paracelsus: Four Treatises,* ed. Henry E. Sigerist, 10–41. 1941. Reprint. Baltimore and London: The Johns Hopkins University Press, 1996.

Park, Julie. "Introduction: The Drift of Fiction." *The Eighteenth-Century: Theory and Interpretation* 52, no. 3–4 (2011): 243–8.

———. *The Self and It: Novel Objects in Eighteenth-Century England.* Stanford: Stanford University Press, 2010.

Parker, Blanford. *The Triumph of Augustan Poetics: English Literary Culture from Butler to Johnson.* New York and Cambridge: Cambridge University Press, 1998.

Pattison, William. "The Court of Venus." In *The Poetical Works of Mr. William Pattison,* 130–8. London: H. Curll, 1728.

Pashler, Harold. *The Psychology of Attention.* Cambridge, MA: Massachusetts Institute of Technology Press, 1999.

Pearson, Jacqueline. *Women's Reading in Britain, 1750–1835: A Dangerous Recreation.* Cambridge: Cambridge University Press, 1999.

Pendlebury, Henry. *Invisible Realities, the Real Christian's Greatest Concernment in Several Sermons.* London: J.D, for Ann Unsworth, 1696.

Pettit, Henry. *A Bibliography of Young's Night Thoughts.* Boulder: University of Colorado Press, 1954.

Phillips, Nicholas. *The Holy Choice.* London: Benjamin Harris, 1679.

Picciotto, Joanna. *Labours of Innocence in Early Modern England.* Cambridge, MA: Harvard University Press, 2010.

Pinch, Adela. "Lost in a Book: Jane Austen's 'Persuasion.'" *Studies in Romanticism* 32 (1993): 97–117.

———. *Strange Fits of Passion: Epistemologies of Emotion, Hume to Austen.* Stanford: Stanford University Press, 1996.

Pitt, Christopher. *Vida's Art of Poetry, Translated into English Verse, By the Reverend Mr. Christopher Pitt.* London: Sam Palmer, 1725.

Pope, Alexander. *The Twickenham Edition of the Poems of Alexander Pope.* Edited by John Butt. 11 vols. London: Methuen, 1939–69.

Posner, Michael. *Cognitive Neuroscience of Attention.* New York: Guilford Press, 2004.

Price, Leah. *How to Do Things With Books in Victorian Britain.* Princeton, N.J.: Princeton University Press, 2012.

———. *The Anthology and the Rise of the Novel.* Cambridge: Cambridge University Press, 2000.

Priestley, Joseph. *The History and Present State of Electricity.* London: J. Dodsley, etc., 1767.

———. *A Course of Lectures on Oratory and Criticism.* London: J. Johnson, 1777.

Rawson, Claude. "Mock-Heroic and English Poetry." In *The Cambridge Companion to the Epic,* edited by Catherine Bates, 167–92. Cambridge: Cambridge University Press, 2010.

Raven, James. *British Fiction 1750–1770: A Chronological Check-List of Prose Fiction Printed in Britain and Ireland.* Newark: University of Delaware Press, 1987.

Reeve, Clara. *The Progress of Romance, Through Times, Countries, and Manners, with Remarks & Etc.* London: Printed for the author, 1785.

Richardson, Samuel. *Clarissa.* Facsimile reprint of 3rd edition of 1751. 7 vols. New York: AMS Press, 2000.

———. *Clarissa.* Edited by Angus Ross. Harmondsworth and New York: Penguin, 1985.

———. *The Correspondence of Samuel Richardson.* 6 vols. Edited by Anna Laetitia Barbauld. London: Richard Phillips, 1804.

———. *Letters Written to and for Particular Friends, on the Most Important Occasions.* London: C. Rivington, J. Osborn, and J. Leake, 1741.

———. *Pamela; or, Virtue Rewarded.* Oxford: Oxford University Press, 2001.

———. *Selected Letters.* Edited by John Carroll. Oxford: Clarendon Press, 1964.

Richetti, John. "Histories by Eliza Haywood and Henry Fielding." In Saxton and Bocchicchio, *Passionate Fictions of Eliza Haywood,* 240–58.

Riskin, Jessica. *Science in the Age of Sensibility: The Sentimental Empiricists of the French Enlightenment.* Chicago: University of Chicago Press, 2002.

Rivers, Isabel. "Dissenting and Methodist Books of Practical Divinity." In *Books and their Readers in Eighteenth-Century England,* edited by Isabel Rivers, 127–64. New York: St. Martin's Press, 1982.

Rogers, John. *The Matter of Revolution: Science, Poetry, and Politics in the Age of Milton.* Ithaca: Cornell University Press, 1996.

Rothman, Tony and Stephen Boughn. "Can Gravitons be Detected?" *Foundations of Physics* 36, no. 12 (December 2006): 1801–25.

Rowland, Ann Wierda. "Romantic Poetry and the Romantic Novel." In *The Cambridge Companion to British Romantic Poetry,* edited by James Chandler and Maureen N. McLane, 117–35. Cambridge: Cambridge University Press, 2008.

Rutherford, Samuel. *Joshua Redivivus.* Rotterdam?, 1664.

Sambrook, James. *English Pastoral Poetry.* Boston: Twayne, 1983.

Saxton, Kirsten T. and Rebecca Bocchicchio, eds. *The Passionate Fictions of Eliza Haywood: Essays on her Life and Work.* Lexington, KY: The University of Kentucky Press, 2000.

Scarry, Elaine. *Dreaming by the Book.* New York: Farrar, Straus and Giroux, 1999.

Schmidgen, Wolfram. *Eighteenth-Century Fiction and the Law of Property.* Cambridge: Cambridge University Press, 2002.

———. *Exquisite Mixture: The Virtues of Impurity in Early Modern England.* Philadelphia: University of Pennsylvania Press, 2012.

Schwartze, Michael et al. "Temporal regularity effects on pre-attentive and attentive processing of deviance." *Biological Psychology* 87, no.1 (April 2011): 146–51.

Scott, John. *Sermons Upon Several Occasions.* London: Walter Kettilby and Richard Wilkin, 1704.

Seidel, Michael. *Satiric Inheritance: Rabelais to Sterne.* Princeton, N.J.: Princeton University Press, 1979.

Shakespeare, William. *A Midsummer Night's Dream,* edited by Harold F. Brooks. n.p.: Methuen & Co Ltd., 1979.

Shapiro, Barbara. *Probability and Certainty in Seventeenth-Century England.* Princeton, N.J.: Princeton University Press, 1983.

Sheridan, Richard Brinsley. *The Rivals,* edited by Elizabeth Duthie. London: A.C. Black; New York: W.W. Norton, 1979.

Siskin, Clifford. "Personification and Community: Literary Change in the Mid and Late Eighteenth Century." *Eighteenth-Century Studies* 15.4 (1982): 371–401.

——. *The Work of Writing: Literature and Social Change in Britain, 1700–1830.* Baltimore and London: The Johns Hopkins University Press, 1998.

Siskin, Clifford and William Warner, eds. *This is Enlightenment.* Chicago: University of Chicago Press, 2010.

Sitter, John. "Britannia Waives the Rules: Recent Studies of English Poetry in Principle and Practice." Review of *The Poetics of Enthusiasm in Eighteenth-Century Britain,* by Shaun Irlam; *Poems of Nation, Anthems of Empire: English Verse in the Long Eighteenth Century,* by Suvir Kaul; *The Triumph of Augustan Poetics: English Literary Culture fromButler to Johnson,* by Blanford Parker. *Eighteenth-Century Studies* 35, no. 1 (2001): 131–4.

——. *The Cambridge Introduction to Eighteenth-Century Poetry.* Cambridge: Cambridge University Press, 2011.

——. *Literary Loneliness in Mid-Eighteenth-Century England.* Ithaca and London: Cornell University Press, 1982.

——. "Questions in Poetics: Why and How Poetry Matters." In *The Cambridge Companion to Eighteenth-Century Poetry,* edited by John Sitter, 133–56. Cambridge: Cambridge University Press, 2001.

Smollett, Tobias. *The Expedition of Humphry Clinker.* Edinburgh: W. Coke Bookseller, Leith, 1788.

Sophocles. *Oedipus Tyrannus.* Edited and translated by Hugh Lloyd-Jones. Loeb Classical Library. Cambridge, MA: Harvard University Press, 1997.

Spacks, Patricia Meyer. *Reading Eighteenth-Century Poetry.* Maldan, MA: Wiley-Blackwell, 2009.

Spitzer, Leo. "Milieu and Ambiance." In *Essays in Historical Semantics,* 179–303. New York: Russell and Russell, 1948.

Starr, G. Gabrielle. *Lyric Generations: Poetry and the Novel in the Long Eighteenth Century.* Baltimore and London: The Johns Hopkins University Press, 2004.

——. "Poetic Subjects and Grecian Urns: Close Reading and the Tools of Cognitive Science." *Modern Philology* 105, no. 1 (2007): 48–61.

Stephen, Leslie. *Works of Samuel Richardson.* 12 vols. London: Sotheran, 1883–4.

Sterne, Laurence. *A Sentimental Journey through France and Italy.* In *The Florida Edition of the Works of Laurence Sterne,* edited by Melvyn New and W.G. Day, 3–165. Gainesville: University Press of Florida, 2002.

——. *The Life and Opinions of Tristram Shandy,* edited by Melvyn New and Joan New. Gainsville: University Presses of Florida, 1978–84.

——. *The Life and Opinions of Tristram Shandy, Gentleman,* 9 vols. London: O. Lynch, 1771.

Stockwell, Peter. *Cognitive Poetics: An Introduction.* London & New York: Routledge, 2002.

Suarez, Michael F. "Trafficking in the Muse: Dodsley's Collection of Poems and the Question of Canon." In *Tradition in Transition: Women Writers, Marginal Texts, and the Eighteenth-Century*

Canon, edited by Alvara Ribeiro, S.J. and James G. Baskers, 297–313. Oxford: Clarendon, 1996.

Swift, Jonathan. "A City Shower." In vol. 2 of *The Works of Jonathan Swift*, 31–3. 8 vols. Dublin: Faulkner, 1741–46.

———. *A Tale of a Tub*. London: John Nutt, 1710.

———. *The Essential Writings of Jonathan Swift*. Edited by Claude Rawson and Ian Higgins. New York and London: Norton, 2010.

Syson, Lydia. *Doctor of Love: James Graham and his Celestial Bed*. Richmond: Alma Books, 2008.

[Taylor, Mrs. John, of Norwich?] "Mrs. OPIE." *Cabinet, or, monthly report of polite literature*, 1807–1808 (Jun 1807): 217–219.

Terry, Richard. *Mock-Heroic from Butler to Cowper: An English Genre and Discourse*. Aldershot: Ashgate, 2005.

Teskey, Gordon. *Allegory and Violence*. Ithaca: Cornell University Press, 1996.

Thelwall, John. *The Peripatetic*. Edited by Judith Thompson. Detroit: Wayne State University Press, 2001.

Thomas, Keith. "The Meaning of Literacy in Early Modern England." In *The Written Word: Literacy in Transition*, edited by Gerd Baumann, 97–131. Oxford: Clarendon Press, 1986.

Thompson, Helen. *Ingenuous Subjection: Compliance and Power in the Eighteenth-Century Domestic Novel*. Philadelphia: University of Pennsylvania Press, 2005.

———. "Plotting Materialism: W. Charleton's *The Ephesian Matron*, E. Haywood's *Fantomina*, and Feminine Consistency." *Eighteenth-Century Studies* 35, no. 2 (Winter 2002): 195–214.

Thomson, James. *Spring*. In Fairer and Gerrard, *Eighteenth-Century Poetry*, 212–38.

———. *The Works of Mr. Thomson.*. 2 vols. London: A. Millar, 1738.

Thrale, Hester Lynch. *Thraliana*. Edited by Katharine C. Balderston. 2 vols. Oxford: Clarendon Press, 1942.

Todorov, Tzvetan. *Introduction to Poetics*. Translated by Richard Howard. Minneapolis: University of Minnesota Press, 1981.

Traugott, John. *Tristram Shandy's World: Sterne's Philosophical Rhetoric*. Berkeley and Los Angeles: University of California Press, 1954.

Tsur, Reuven. "Rhyme and Cognitive Poetics." *Poetics Today* 17 (1996): 55–87.

Virgil, *Aeneid*. Translated by A. S. Kline, 2002. http://www.poetryintranslation.com/PITBR/Latin/VirgilAeneidX.htm

Vives, Juan Luis. *On Memory and Recall* (1538). Translated by D.J. Murray and Helen E. Ross. *Canadian Psychology* 23, no. 1 (1982): 22–31.

Voltaire. *An Essay Upon the Civil Wars of France…and Also Upon the Epick Poetry of the European Nations from Homer Down to Milton*. London: Samuel Jallasson, 1727.

———. *The Elements of Sir Isaac Newton's Philosophy. By Mr. Voltaire. Translated from the French. Revised and Corrected by John Hanna, M.A.* London: Stephen Austen, 1738.

Wahrman, Dror. *The Making of the Modern Self: Identity and Culture in Eighteenth-Century England*. New Haven, CT and London: Yale University Press, 2007.

Wall, Cynthia Sundberg. *The Prose of Things: Transformations of Description in the Eighteenth Century*. Chicago: University of Chicago Press, 2006.

Ward, Antony. *Attention: A Neuropsychological Approach.* New York: Psychology Press, 2004.

Wasserman, Earl. "The Inherent Values of Eighteenth-Century Personification." *PMLA* 65, no. 4 (1950): 435–63.

Watkins, Francis. *A Particular Account of the Electrical Experiments Hitherto made publick, with Variety of new ones, and full Instructions for performing them.* London: Printed for the Author, 1747.

Watt, Ian. "Flat-Footed and Fly-Blown: The Realities of Realism," *Eighteenth-Century Fiction* 12, no. 2–3 (2000): 147–66.

———. *The Rise of the Novel: Studies in Defoe, Richardson and Fielding* [1957]. 2nd ed. Berkeley: University of Los Angeles Press, 2001.

Watts, Isaac. *Logick: Or, the Right Use of Reason in the Enquiry after Truth.* London: John Clark and Richard Hett, et al., 1725.

———. *The Art of Reading and Writing English.* London, 1721.

Watson, William. *Experiments and Observations tending to illustrate the Nature and Properties of Electricity.* 3rd ed. London: C. Davis, 1746.

Werner, Florian. "Kindred Spirits? John Cleland's *Fanny Hill* and Laurence Sterne's *A Sentimental Journey*." *Zeitschrift für Anglistik und Amerikanistik* 48, no. 1 (2000): 17–30.

Whytt, Robert. *Physiological Essays…Observations on the Sensibility and Irritability of the Parts of Men and other Animals.* Edinburgh: Hamilton, Baltour and Neill, 1755.

Williams, Abigail. *Poetry and the Creation of a Whig Literary Culture.* Oxford: Oxford University Press, 2005.

Wolfson, Susan, ed. "Reading for Form." Special issue, *MLQ* 61, no. 1 (2000).

Womersley, David. *Cultures of Whiggism: New Essays on English Literature in the Long Eighteenth Century.* Newark: University of Delaware Press, 2005.

———. Introduction to *Augustan Critical Writings.*, xi-xliv. Edited by David Womersley. London: Penguin, 1997.

Yolton, John. *John Locke and the Way of Ideas.* Oxford: Clarendon Press, 1991.

———. *Thinking Matter: Materialism in Eighteenth-Century Britain.* Oxford: Basil Blackwell, 1983.

Young, Edward. *An Apology for Princes, or the Reverence due to Government.* London: T. Worrall, 1729.

———. *Night Thoughts.* Edited by Stephen Cornford. Cambridge: Cambridge University Press, 1989.

———. *Ocean: An Ode.* London: Tho. Worral, 1728.

———. *A Paraphrase on Part of the Book of Job.* London: Jacob Tonson, 1719.

———. *The Correspondence of Edward Young 1683–1765.* Edited by Henry Pettit. Oxford: Clarendon Press, 1971.

Youngren, William H. "Conceptualism and Neoclassic Generality" *ELH* 47, no. 4 (1980), 705–40.

Yousef, Nancy. *Isolated Cases: The Anxieties of Autonomy in Enlightenment Philosophy and Romantic Literature.* Ithaca: Cornell University Press, 2000.

Margaret Doody is the John and Barbara Glynn Family Professor of Literature at the University of Notre Dame. She is the author of many books, including *The Daring Muse: Augustan Poetry Reconsidered* (1985; reissued 2010), *The True Story of the Novel* (1996), *Tropic of Venice* (2006), and the series of "Aristotle Detective" novels and stories. Margaret is currently working on a book on Jane Austen, and a new work entitled "Love, Change, and Chaos: The Coming of the Enlightenment."

David Fairer is professor of eighteenth-century English Literature at the University of Leeds. His most recent book, *Organising Poetry: The Coleridge Circle 1790–1798* (2009), traces the development of English poetry during the 1790s, building on the concerns of his previous comprehensive study, *English Poetry of the Eighteenth Century, 1700–1789* (2003).

Sophie Gee is associate professor of English at Princeton. She is the author of the scholarly monograph *Making Waste: Leftovers and the Literary Imagination* and the historical novel *The Scandal of the Season*. She is currently working on a book about eighteenth-century faith and the rise of the novel, and completing a novel set in the eighteenth-century and the present.

Heather Keenleyside is assistant professor of English at the University of Chicago. She has published articles in *ELH* and *Critical Inquiry*, and edited the "Animals" volume of the collection, *British It-Narratives 1750–1830*. She is at work on a book manuscript tentatively entitled *Animals and Other People: Forms of Life in Eighteenth-Century Literature.*

Shelley King is professor in the Department of English at Queen's University (Kingston, Ontario). She and John B. Pierce are co-editors of *The Collected Poems of Amelia Alderson Opie* (Oxford University Press, 2009) and are currently completing *The Correspondence of Samuel Richardson's Final Years* (Volume 12 of the *Cambridge Edition of the Correspondence of Samuel Richardson*). Her next project undertakes creating a digital edition of a part of Opie's correspondence with her cousin Henry Perronet Briggs.

Christina Lupton is reader in the Department of English and Comparative Literary Studies at the University of Warwick. She has published on self-consciousness in fiction, most recently in her book *Knowing Books: the Consciousness of Mediation in Eighteenth-Century Britain* (2012). Her new project is about the times and spaces of reading in relation to the materiality of the codex book.

Kate Parker is assistant professor of English at University of Wisconsin-La Crosse. She is the author of "Communal Sexuality: Mutual Pleasure in Sade's *La Philosophie dans le boudoir*" (*Eighteenth-Century Fiction*). Her current book project explores how affective communities impact literary representations of selfhood in eighteenth-century Britain and France.

Natalie M. Phillips is assistant professor in the Department of English and co-founder of the Digital Humanities and Literary Cognition Lab at Michigan State University. Forthcoming publications include "Literary Neuroscience and History of Mind: An Interdisciplinary fMRI Study of Attention and Jane Austen" in *The Oxford Handbook of Cognitive Literary Studies* and "Literature, Neuroscience, and Digital Humanities" in *Humanities and the Digital*. Phillips's work centers on eighteenth-century literature, history of mind, and cognitive studies; her current book project, entitled *Distraction: Problems of Attention in Eighteenth-Century Literature, 1750–1820* traces the literary history of the mental state of distraction and how evolving theories of focus in the Enlightenment redefined models of cognition and narrative.

Aran Ruth is a PhD candidate at University of Michigan, Ann Arbor. "The Novel's Poem Envy: Mid-Century Fiction and the 'Thing Poem,'" co-authored with Tina Lupton, is her first publication. Her research focuses on Romantic poetry and poetics, the works of Charlotte Smith in particular.

Wolfram Schmidgen is professor of English at Washington University in St. Louis. He has just published *Exquisite Mixture: The Virtues of Impurity in Early Modern England* (2013). He is currently working on an intellectual history of literary innovation in early eighteenth-century culture.

Courtney Weiss Smith is assistant professor of English at Wesleyan University. She is the author of articles on eighteenth-century literature and culture that have appeared in *Eighteenth Century: Theory and Interpretation* and *SEL*. Her current book project is entitled "Empiricist Devotions: Scrutinizing Nature in Early Eighteenth-Century England."

Joshua Swidzinski is a doctoral candidate at Columbia University. He is currently writing his dissertation on the relationship between poetic measure and the production of knowledge in Enlightenment England.

www.ingramcontent.com/pod-product-compliance
Lightning Source LLC
Chambersburg PA
CBHW071501110726
47908CB00003B/687